Trailblazer
TODAY'S MOST POPULAR STUDY GUIDES

Last Minute Guide

MATHEMATICS

for

CBSE XII

Editors
Rajesh Kumar Thakur

UNICORN BOOKS

Publisher
UNICORN BOOKS
F-2/16, Ansari Road, Daryaganj, New Delhi-110002
E-mail: info@unicornbooks.in • Website: www.unicornbooks.in
☎ 011-23275434, 23262683

Branch : Mumbai
23-25, Zaoba Wadi Thakurdwar, Mumbai-400002
☎ 022-22010941, 022-22053387
E-mail: rapidex@bom5.vsnl.net.in

ISBN 978-81-7806-284-6

Revised Edition: 2015

Printed at : *Param Offsetters, Okhla, New Delhi-110020*

Preface

Why should one read 'Last Minute Guide'?

This series has been designed to provide a quick and clutter-free access to ALL the important concepts of each chapter. These books give the proper exposure needed by a smart student to understand and master each chapter in accordance with the syllabus laid down by the CBSE guidelines without wastage of time.

Efforts have been made to give the outline of each chapter, such as important formulae, rules and fundamentals at the beginning itself, so that the students can revise and brush up the concepts at the last minute as well.

This book is written after extensive research and designed in such a manner that the students can know well in advance the process of writing an answer in the examination.

This format further adds to the students' development by providing *step-by-step marking scheme*, which allows the students to learn more about the specific steps, which otherwise most students ignore and, in the process, lose marks on.

This book essentially simplifies the entire process required of a student after studying it in the class:

- Revision of the concepts
- Practice of each concept with examples
- Awareness of the potential trouble areas where marks are lost
- Correct way to properly answer a question

The Publisher

Contents

DESIGN OF THE CBSE QUESTION PAPER
MATHEMATICS-CLASS XII

Time : 3 Hours **Max. Marks : 100**

Weightage of marks over different dimensions of the question paper shall be as follows:

A. Weightage to different topics/content units

S.No.	Topics		Marks
1.	Relations and Functions	(22 Periods)	10
2.	Algebra	(38 Periods)	13
3.	Calculus	(68 Periods)	44
4.	Vectors & three-dimensional Geometry	(24 Periods)	17
5.	Linear Programming	(12 Periods)	06
6.	Probability	(18 Periods)	10
	Total		**100**

B. Weightage to different forms of questions

S.No.	Forms of Questions	Marks for each question	No. of Questions	Total Marks
1.	MCQ/Objective/Very Short Answer questions (VSA)	01	06	06
2.	Short Answer questions (SA)	04	13	52
3.	Long Answer questions (LA)	06	07	42
	Total	–	**26**	**100**

C. Difficulty level of questions

S.No.	Estimated difficulty level	Percentage
1.	Easy	15
2.	Average	70
3.	Difficult	15

About 20% weightage has been assigned to questions testing higher order thinking skills of learners.

CHAPTER 1

RELATIONS AND FUNCTIONS

BASIC CONCEPTS AND RESULTS

Let A and B are two non-empty sets, then a relation R is a subset of $A \times B$.

i.e. $R \subset A \times B$

Universal Relation—A relation R in a set A is called a universal relation, if each element of A is related to every element of A.

Hence $R = \{(A \times B) \subseteq (A \times A)$ is the universal relation on A.

Example—Let $A = \{1, 2, 3\}$, then

$R = \{(A \times A) = \{(1, 1), (1, 2), (1, 3), (2, 1), (2, 2), (2, 3), (3, 1) (3, 2), (3, 3)\}$ is the universal relation in A.

TYPES OF RELATIONS

(*i*) Reflexive $\rightarrow$ If $(x, x) \in R \ \forall \ x \in A$,

i.e. if $xRx \ \forall \ x \in A$.

(*ii*) Symmetric $\rightarrow$ If $(x, y) \in R \Rightarrow (y, x) \in R \ \forall \ x, y \in A$.

i.e. if $xRy \Rightarrow yRx \ \forall \ x, y \in A$.

(*iii*) Transitive $\rightarrow$ If $(x, y) \in R$, $(y, z) \in R \Rightarrow (x, z) \in R \ \forall \ x, y, z \in A$.

i.e. if xRy and $yRz \Rightarrow xRz$.

Equivalence Relation—A relation R is said to be equivalence relation if it is reflexive, symmetric and transitive.

FUNCTION (Mappings)

Let A and B are two non-empty sets, then f is a relation from A to B such that each element of A corresponds unique element of B. It is written as $f : A \rightarrow B$ and read as f is a function from A to B.

$f(x)$ is called the image of x and x is said to be the pre-image of $f(x)$.

Set A is called domain and set B is called co-domain.

And $f(A) = \{f(x) : x \in A\}$ is called the range of f.

TYPES OF FUNCTIONS

One-one (Injective) Function—

A function $f : A \rightarrow B$ is called one-one if distinct elements in A have distinct images in B.

f is one-one when $f(x_1) = f(x_2) \Rightarrow x_1 = x_2$

or $f(x_1) \neq f(x_2) \Rightarrow x_1 \neq x_2 \ \forall \ x_1, x_2 \in R$.

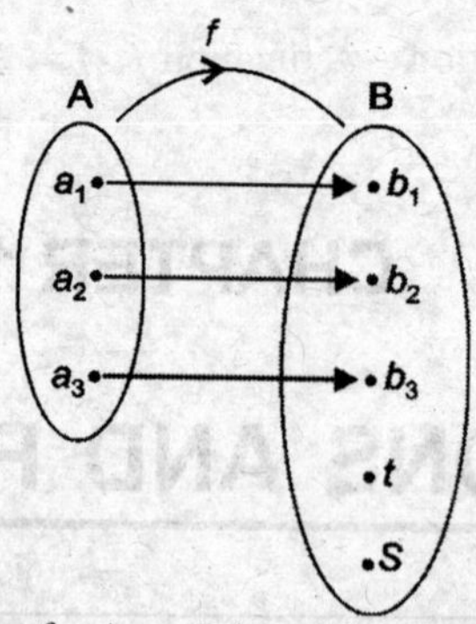

Many-one function—A function $f : A \to B$ is said to be many one function if two or more elements of A are associated with the same element of B. If $x_1 \neq x_2 \Rightarrow f(x_1) = f(x_2) \ \forall \ x_1, x_2 \in A$.

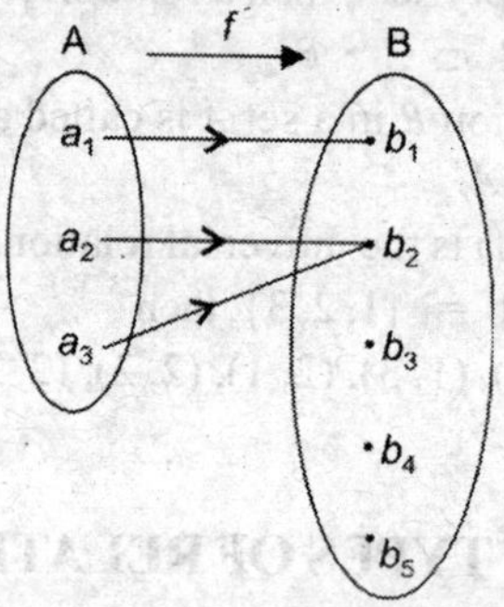

Onto or Surjective function—A function $f : A \to B$ is said to be an onto function, if every element of B is image of some element of A under the rule f i.e. $\forall \ b \in B, \ \exists$ an element $a \in A$ such that $f(a) = b$.

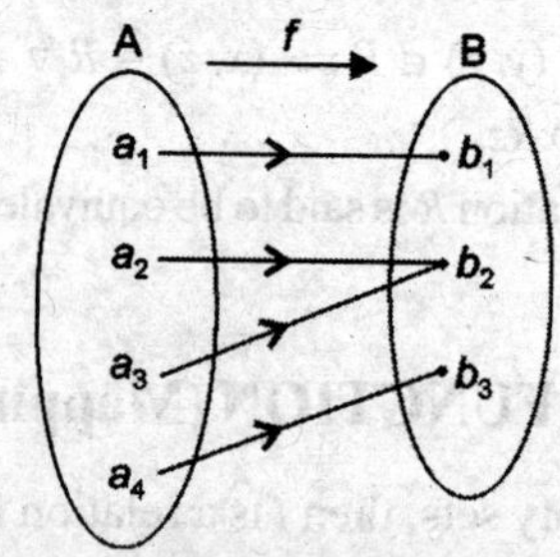

Into function—A function $f : A \to B$ is said to be an into function, if there is at least one element in B which is not an image of any element in A.

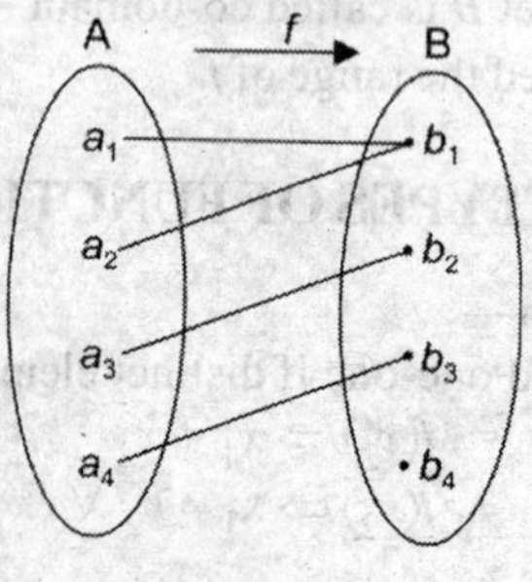

One-one onto (Bijective) function—A function $f: A \to B$ is called one-one onto function, if 'f' is one-one and onto.

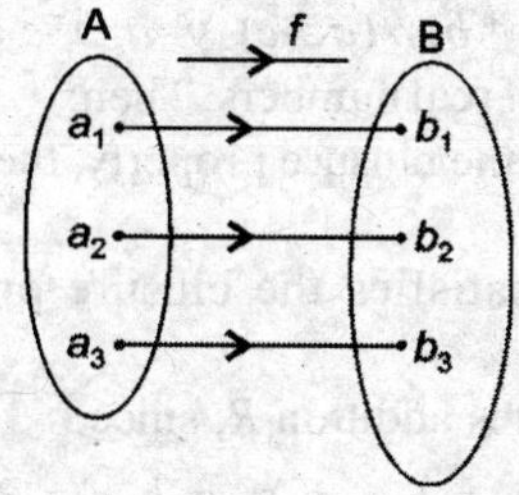

Example—Let $A = [a, b, c]$ $B = \{1, 2, 3\}$. Then:

$f_1 = \{(a, 1), (b, 2), (c, 3)\}$ is one-one and onto.

$f_2 = \{(a, 1), (b, 1), (c, 3)\}$ is many one-into.

$f_3 = \{(a, 2), (b, 3)\}$ is not a function from A to B.

COMPOSITION OF FUNCTIONS

Let $f: A \to B$ and $g: B \to C$ be two functions. Then the composition of f and g denoted by gof is the function defined by:

$$(gof): A \to C: (gof)(x) = g\{f(x)\} \ \forall \ x \in A.$$

It is clear that $\quad \text{dom}(gof) = \text{dom}(f)$

Also, gof is defined only when range $(f) \subseteq$ dom (g).

Example—If $\quad f(x) = 1 + x^2$ and

$$g(x) = \frac{1}{x-1}$$ then find $fog(x)$ and $gof(x)$.

Solution: $\quad f(x) = 1 + x^2$

$$g(x) = \frac{1}{x-1}$$

$$fog(x) = f\{g(x)\} = f\left(\frac{1}{x-1}\right)$$

$$= 1 + \left(\frac{1}{x-1}\right)^2 = 1 + \frac{1}{(x-1)^2}$$

$$gof(x) = g\{f(x)\} = g(1 + x^2) = \frac{1}{1+x^2-1} = \frac{1}{x^2}$$

BINARY OPERATION

Binary operation implies an operation involving two elements of a given set.

A binary operation * on set A is a function $* : A \times A \to A$ and is denoted by $a * b$.

Properties of Binary operation:

(*i*) Associative Law $\to$ A binary operation * on a non-empty set S is said to be associative, if

$$(a * b) * c = a * (b * c) \ \forall \ a, b, c \in S.$$

(*ii*) Commutative Law $\to$ A binary operation * on a non-empty set S is said to be commutative if

$$a * b = b * a \ \forall \ a, b \in S.$$

(*iii*) Distributive Law → Let * & *o* be two binary operations on a non-empty set *S*. We say that * is distributive over *o* if:

$$a * (boc) = (a * b) \, o \, (a * c) \; \forall \; a, b, c \in S.$$

Example—Let *R* be the set of real numbers. Then:

(*i*) addition on *R* satisfies the closure property, the association law and the Commutative Law.

(*ii*) multiplication on *R* satisfies the closure property, the associative law and the commutative law.

(*iii*) multiplication distributes addition *R*, since

$$a \, . \, (b + c) = a \, . \, b + a \, . \, c \; \forall \; a, b, c \in R.$$

SOLVED QUESTIONS

SECTION-I

1. *If $f(x) = x + 7$ and $g(x) = x - 7, x \in R$, find fog (7).*

Solution:

$$\begin{aligned} \text{fog}(7) &= f[g(7)] \\ &= f[7-7] = f[0] \\ &= 0 + 7 = 7. \end{aligned}$$

2. If *$f(x)$ is an invertible function, find the inverse of* $f(x) = \dfrac{3x-2}{5}$.

Solution:

$$y = f(x) = \frac{3x-2}{5}$$

$$\Rightarrow \quad x = \frac{5y+2}{3}$$

$$\Rightarrow \quad g(y) = f^{-1}(x) = \frac{5y+2}{3}.$$

3. *If a binary operation ⊕ be defined as* $a \oplus b = 2a - 3b$, find $8 \oplus 3$.

Solution:

$$\begin{aligned} a \oplus b &= 2a - 3b \\ 8 \oplus 3 &= 2 \times 8 - 3 \times 3 = 7. \end{aligned}$$

4. *Give an example to show that the relation R in the set of natural number defined by* $R = \{(x, y), x, y \in N, x \le y^2\}$ *is not transitive.*

Solution: *R* is not transitive as $2 \le (-3)^2$ and $(-3)^2 \le (1)^2$ but $2 \not\le (1)^2$

$\Rightarrow \quad (2, -3) \in R$ and $(-3, 1) \in R$ but $(2, 1) \notin R$.

5. *Show that relationship R on set* $A = \{1, 2, 3, 4, 5, 6\}$ *defined as*

$$R = \{(x, y) : (x, y) \in A, y = x + 1\}$$

is neither symmetric nor reflexive.

Solution: Given $A = \{1, 2, 3, 4, 5, 6\}$

and $R = \{(x, y) : x, y \in A \text{ and } y = x + 1\}$

$R = \{(1, 2), (2, 3), (3, 4), (4, 5), (5, 6)\}$

R is not reflexive, because $(1, 1) \notin R$

R is not symmetrix $(1, 2) \in R$ and but $(2, 1) \notin R$.

6. *Show that function $f : N \to N$, defined by* $f(x) = 2x$ is one-one but not onto.

Solution: The function *f* is one-one.

Let $x_1, x_2 \in N$ be such that $f(x_1) = f(x_2)$

$\Rightarrow \quad 2x_1 = 2x_2$

$\Rightarrow \quad x_1 = x_2$

Thus, f_1 is one-one.

Function is not onto.

As $1 \in N$ and there does not exist any $x \in N$, such that $f(x) = 1$. So f is not onto.

7. *Check whether the binary operation * on Q (set of rational numbers) $a * b = a^2 + b^2$ for commutativity and associativity.*

Solution: $a * b = a^2 + b^2$ for all $a, b \in Q$.

$b * a = b^2 + a^2$

$a * b = b * a = a^2 + b^2$

$\therefore$ given operation is commutative.

$$a * b = a^2 + b^2$$

Also
$$(1 * 2) * 3 = (1^2 + 2^2) * 3 = 5 * 3 = 5^2 + 3^2 = 34$$
$$1 * (2 * 3) = 1 * (2^2 + 3^2)$$
$$= 1 * 13 = 1^2 + 13^2 = 170$$

given operation is not associative.

8. *Find the number of all one-one function from set A = {1, 2, 3} to itself.*

Solution: One-one function from (1, 2, 3) is simply a permutation on 3 symbols 1, 2, 3 therefore total no of maps from {1, 2, 3} to itself is same as total number of permutation on 3 symbols 1, 2, 3 which 3! = 6.

9. *If $f : R \to R$ is given by $f(x) = (3 - x^3)^{1/3}$. Show that $fof = I_R$ where I_R is the identity map on R.*

Solution: As $f : R \to R$ fof exists and $fof : R \to R$ is given by

$$(fof)(x) = f(f(x)) = f((3 - x^3)^{1/3})$$
$$= [[3 - (3 - x^3)]]^{1/3} = x \text{ for all } x \in R.$$

SECTION-II

1. *Show that the relation R defined by (a, b) R(c, d) $\Rightarrow a + d = b + c$ on the set $N \times N$ is an Equivalence Relation.*

Solution: The given relation R is defined by $(a, b) R (c, d)$

$\Rightarrow \quad a + d = b + c$ on $N \times N$

(i) Now $(a, b) R (a, b) \Rightarrow a + b = a + b$ which is true $\forall$ $(a, b) \in N \times N$.

$\therefore$ R is reflexive

(ii) $(a, b) R (c, d) \Rightarrow a + d = b + c$

$\Rightarrow b + c = a + d$

$c + b = d + a$ [using Commutativity Law]

$\Rightarrow (c, d) R (a, b)$

$\therefore$ R is symmetric.

(iii) Let $(a, b) R(c, d)$ and $(c, d) R (e, f)$

According to question,

$\Rightarrow \quad a + d = b + c$ and $c + f = d + e$

Adding $\quad a + d + c + f = b + c + d + e$

$a + f = b + e$

$\Rightarrow \quad (a, b) \ R \ (e, f)$

R is transitive

from (i), (ii) and (iii)

R is an Equivalence Relation.

2. *Let T be set of all triangles in a plane with R as a relation in T given by* $R = [(T_1, T_2), T_1 \cong T_2)]$. *Show that R is an Equivalence Relation.*

Solution: T is set of all triangles and R is a relation T defined by $R = \{(T_1, T_2) : T_1 \cong T_2)\}$.

(*i*) Every triangle is congruent to itself defined by R is reflexive.

(*ii*) $(T_1, T_2) \in R \Rightarrow T_1 \cong T_2$
$\Rightarrow T_2 \cong T_1$
$\Rightarrow (T_2, T_1) \in R$

$\therefore$ R is symmetric.

(*iii*) $(T_1, T_2), (T_2, T_3) \in R$
$\Rightarrow T_1 \cong T_2$ and $T_2 \cong T_3$
$\Rightarrow T_1 \cong T_3$
$\Rightarrow (T_1, T_3) \in R$

$\therefore$ R is transitive.

From (*i*), (*ii*), (*iii*) R is an Equivalance relation.

3. *Let* $A = R - \{2\}$ *and* $B = R - \{1\}$ *if* $A \to B$ *is a mapping defined by*

$$f(x) = \frac{x-1}{x-2}.$$ Show that f is bijective.

Solution: *Injectivity*: Let x, y be two elements of A then $f(x) = f(y)$

$$\Rightarrow \frac{x-1}{x-2} = \frac{y-1}{y-2}$$
$$(x-1)(y-2) = (y-1)(x-2)$$
$$xy - 2x - y + 2 = xy - 2y - x + 2$$
$$x = y$$

$\therefore$ For $f(x) = f(y) \Rightarrow x = y \ \forall\ x, y \in A$

$\therefore$ f is an injective. (*i*)

Surjectivity: Let y be arbitrary element of A

$$f(x) = y \Rightarrow \frac{x-1}{x-2} = y$$
$$(x-1) = y(x-2)$$
$$x - xy = 1 - 2y$$

is a real number $\forall \quad y \neq 1$

$$x = \frac{1-2y}{1-y} \neq 2 \text{ for any } y$$

$$x = \frac{1-2y}{1-y} \quad \left[\frac{1-2y}{1-y} = 2 \text{ then } 1 = 0 \text{ False}\right]$$

Thus, every element y in B has its pre-image x in A given by $x = \dfrac{1-2y}{1-y}$.

$\therefore$ f is Surjective. (*ii*)

From (*i*) & (*ii*), f is Bijective.

4. *Consider the function* $f : R_+ \to [-5, \infty)$ *defined by* $f(x) = 9x^2 + 6x - 5$, *where* R_+ = *set of non-negative real numbers. Show that f is invertible and find its inverse.*

Solution: Function f is one-one

Consider any

$x_1, x_2 \in R_+$ such that $f(x_1) = f(x_2)$

$\Rightarrow 9x_1^2 + 6x_1 - 5 = 9x_2^2 + 6x_2 - 5$

$\Rightarrow \quad 3(x_1^2 - x_2^2) + 2(x_1 - x_2) = 0$

$\Rightarrow \quad 3(x_1 - x_2)(x_1 + x_2) + 2(x_1 - x_2) = 0$

$\Rightarrow \quad (x_1 - x_2)[3(x_1 + x_2) + 2] = 0$

$\Rightarrow \quad x_1 - x_2 = 0$

$\Rightarrow \quad (\because x_1, x_2 \in R+)$ f is one-one.

i.e. $\quad x_1 = x_2$

Range of f:

As $\quad x \in R_+ \; x \geq 0 \;\Rightarrow\; 9x^2 + 6x \geq 0$

$9x^2 + 6x - 5 \geq -5.$

$\Rightarrow \quad$ Range $= [-5, \infty]$

Function f is onto.

Hence, the given function is bijective.

To find f^{-1}.

Let $\quad f(x) = y$

$\Rightarrow \quad 9x^2 + 6x - 5 = y$

$\Rightarrow \quad (3x+1)^2 - 6 = y$

$\Rightarrow \quad (3x+1)^2 = y + 6$

$\Rightarrow \quad 3x + 1 = \sqrt{y+6}$

$\Rightarrow \quad x = \dfrac{\sqrt{y+6}-1}{3} = f^{-1}(y) \qquad \therefore \; f^{-1}(x) = \dfrac{\sqrt{x+6}-1}{3}$

5. *Let* $A = R - \left\{\frac{7}{5}\right\}, B = R - \left\{\frac{3}{5}\right\}$ *function* $f : A \to B$ *and* $g : B \to A$ *is defined by* $f(x) = \dfrac{3x+4}{5x-7}$ *and* $g(x) = \dfrac{7x+4}{5x-3}$. *Show that* $gof = I_A$ *and* $fog = I_B$ *are identity function on A and B respectively.*

Solution: As $f : A \to B$ and $g : B \to A$, gof exists and $gof : A \to A$ is given by

$$gof(x) = g[f(x)] = g\left(\frac{3x+4}{5x-7}\right)$$

$$g[f(x)] = \frac{7\left(\frac{3x+4}{5x-7}\right)+4}{5\left(\frac{3x+4}{5x-7}\right)-3} = \frac{21x+28+20x-28}{15x+20-15x+21}$$

$$= \frac{41x}{41} = x \text{ for } x \in A$$

$\Rightarrow \quad gof = I_A.$

Also $g : B \to A$ and $f : A \to B$, fog exists and $fog : B \to B$ is given by

$$fog(x) = f[g(x)]$$

$$= f\left(\frac{7x+4}{5x-3}\right) = \frac{3\left(\frac{7x+4}{5x-3}\right)+4}{5\left(\frac{7x+4}{5x-3}\right)-7}$$

$$= \frac{41x}{41} = x \text{ for all } x \in B.$$

$$\Rightarrow \quad fog = I_B.$$

6. *Let* $f\{1,3,4\} \to \{1,2,5\}$ *and* $g : \{1,2,5\} \to \{1,3\}$ *is given by* $f = \{(1,2),(3,5),(4,1)\}$

$$g = \{(1,3),(2,3),(5,1\}. \textit{ Find } gof.$$

Solution: Given

$$f = \{(1,2),(3,5),(4,1)\}$$

$$\Rightarrow \quad f(1) = 2, f(3) = 5 \quad \text{and} \quad f(4) = 1$$

Also

$$g = \{(1,3),(2,3),(5,1)\}$$

$$g(1) = 3, \quad g(2) = 3, \quad g(5) = 1.$$

We know that gof exists and is a function from $\{1, 3, 4\}$ to $\{1, 3\}$

$$(gof)(1) = gf(1) = g(2) = 3$$

$$(gof)(3) = g[f(3)] = g(5) = 1$$

$$(gof)(4) = g(1) = 3$$

$$gof = \{(1, 3), (3, 1), (4, 3)\}$$

f is bijectives, g is onto but not one-one and gof is onto but not one-one.

7. *Let* $f, g : R \to R$ *be defined as* $f(x) = |x|$ *and* $q(x) = [x]$, *where* $[x]$ *denotes greatest integer less than or equal to x. Find* $fog\left(\frac{5}{2}\right)$ *and* $gof\left(-\sqrt{2}\right)$.

Solution: $f(x) = |x|$ and $g(x) = [x]$

Clearly domain $(f) = R$ and domain $(g) = R$, therefore, each of fog and fog has domain R.

$$fog\left(\frac{5}{2}\right) = f\left\{g\left(\frac{5}{2}\right)\right\} = f\left(\left[\frac{5}{2}\right]\right) = f([2.5]) = f(2)$$

$$= f(2) = |2| = 2$$

$$gof\left(-\sqrt{2}\right) = g\left\{f\left(-\sqrt{2}\right)\right\}$$

$$= g\left(\left|-\sqrt{2}\right|\right) = g\left(\sqrt{2}\right) = 1.$$

8. *Let* $f : R \to$ *be defined as* $f(x) = 10x + 7$. *Find the function* $g : R \to R$ *such that* $gof = fog = I_R$.

Solution: We have $gof = I_R$

$$\Rightarrow \quad gof(x) = I_R(x) \text{ for all } x \in R$$

$$\Rightarrow \quad g[f(x)] = x \text{ for all } x \in R$$

$$\Rightarrow \quad g(10x + 7) = x \text{ for all } x \in R$$

$$\Rightarrow \quad g(y) = \frac{y-7}{10} \text{ for all } y \in R \text{ where } 10x + 7 = y$$

$$\Rightarrow \quad g(x) = \frac{x-7}{10} \text{ for all } x \in R$$

$g : R \to R$ defined by

$$g(x) = \frac{x-7}{10} \text{ is required function.}$$

9. *Consider* $f : R \to R$ *given by* $f(x) = 4x + 3$. *Show that f is on invertible. Find the inverse of f.*

Solution: *f is one-one*:

Let x_1 x_2 be two arbitrary elements of R, such that

$$f(x_1) = f(x_2)$$

$$\Rightarrow \quad 4x_1 + 3 = 4x_2 + 3$$

$$\Rightarrow \quad x_1 = x_2$$

for all $x_1, x_2 \in R$

f is one-one.

Let y be an arbitrary element of R.

then
$$y = f(x)$$
$$y = 4x+3$$
$$x = \frac{y-3}{4}$$

Thus, for all $y \in R$, there exists $x = \frac{y-3}{4} \in R$. Such that $f(x) = y$.

f is onto

since f is one-one and onto

$\Rightarrow f$ is invertible

Hence, there exists $g : R \to R$ such that $gof = I_R$.

$\therefore \quad (gof)(x) = x$ for all $x \in R$

$\Rightarrow \quad g[f(x)] = x$

$\Rightarrow \quad g[4x+3] = x$ where $y = f(x) = 4x + 3$

$\Rightarrow \quad g(y) = \frac{y-3}{4} = f^{-1}.$

$f^{-1} : R \to R$ is defined as $f^{-1}(x) = \frac{x-3}{4}$ for all $x \in R$.

10. *Show that relation R in the set R of real numbers, defined as*
$$R = \{(a, b) : a \le b^2\}$$
is neither reflexive nor symmetric.

Solution: We have $\quad R = \{(a, b) : a \le b^2\}$ where $a, b \in R$

R is not reflexive as $\frac{1}{2} \le \left(\frac{1}{2}\right)^2$ is not true $\Rightarrow \left(\frac{1}{2}, \frac{1}{2}\right) \ne R$

R is not symmetric as $-1 \le (2)^2$ is true $2 \not\le (-1)^2$

i.e. $\quad (-1, 2) \in R$ but $(2, -1) \notin R$

R is not transitive as $2 \le (-3)^2$ and $(-3) \le (1)^2$ but $2 \not\le (+1)^2$

$\Rightarrow \quad (2, -3) \in R$ and $(-3, 1) \in R$ but $(2, 1) \notin R$. $\quad \therefore$ R is neither reflexive nor symmetric.

11. *Let A = N × N and x be the binary operation on A defined by (a, b) * (c, d) = (a + c, b + d). Show that * is commutative and associative. Find the identity element for * on A, if any.*

Solution: Let given $A = N \times N$ and * be the binary operation on A, defined by
$$(a, b) * (c, d) = (a + c, b + d)$$

Commutativity: Let $(a, b), (c, d) \in N \times N$
$$(a, b) * (c, d) = (a + c, b + d)$$
$$= (c + a, d + b) \qquad [\because a + c = c + a, b + d = d + b \text{ commulative law for } +)]$$
$$= (c, d) * (a, b).$$

Hence, commutative law holds good.

Associativity: Let (a, b), (c, d) and $(e, f) \in N \times N$.

$[(a, b) * (c, d)] * (e, f)$
$$= [(a + c, b + d)] * (e, f)$$
$$= ((a + c) + e, \ (b + d) + f)$$

And $(a, b) * [(c, d) * (e, f)]$

$$= (a, b) * [(c + e, d + f)]$$
$$= [a + (c + e),\ b + (d + f)] \quad \{ a + (c + e) = (a + c) + e$$
$$= [(a + c) + e,\ (b + d) + f] \quad b + (d + f) = (b + d) + f$$
$$= [(a, b) * (c, d)] * (e, f) \quad \text{Associative law on } +\}$$

Hence, $(a, b) * [(c, d) * (e, f)] = [(a, b) * (c, d)] * (e, f)$

Associative law holds good.

For Identity element

Let $(e, e^1) \in N \times N$ such that

$$(a, b) * (e, e^1) = (a, b)$$
$$\Rightarrow \quad (a + e,\ b + e') = (a, b) \qquad [\because a * e = a \text{ Identity law}]$$

$\Rightarrow$ Hence, $a + e = a$ and $b + e' = b$

$\Rightarrow$ $e = 0$ and $e' = 0$

i.e. (0, 0) is the identity element

But $(0, 0) \notin N \times N$

Hence, there is no identity element.

UNSOLVED QUESTIONS

SECTION-I

1. Let $A = \{1, 2\}$, $B = \{3, 6\}$, function $f : A \to B$ be defined by $f(x) = 3x$ and function $g : A \to B$ be defined by $g : A \to B$ be defined by $g(x) = x^2 + 2$. Show that $f = g$.
2. Show that function $f : N \to N$ defined by $f(x) = 3x - 2$ is one-one.
3. Find the domain of function $f(x) = \dfrac{1}{5 - 3\sin x}$.
4. $f : R - \left\{\dfrac{4}{3}\right\} \to R$ is defined by $f(x) = \dfrac{1}{3x - y}$ find the range of f.
5. If $f(x) = |x|$ and $g(x) = [x]$ find (1) $gof\left(-\dfrac{5}{3}\right)$.
6. If $f : R \to R$ is a function defined by $f(x) = 3x + 5$, then find f^{-1}.
7. Determine whether * is commutative or associative on N defined by $a * b = 1$.
8. If binary operation '*' on I is defined by $a * b = 2a - 3b$. Find 3 * 7.
9. Show that relation R in set $A = \{1, 2, 3\}$ given by $R = \{(1, 1), (2, 2), (3, 3), (1, 2), (2, 3)\}$ is reflexive but neither symmetric nor transitive.
10. If $f : R \to R$ is given by $f(x) = (3 - x^3)^{1/3}$. Show that $fof = I_R$ where I_R is identity mapping on R.

ANSWERS

3. R {Real number}   4. $R - \{0\}$ 5. 1

6. $f^{-1} : R \to R$ *is given by* $f^{-1}(y) = \dfrac{y - 5}{3}$.

7. Both commutative and associative   8. –15

SECTION-II

1. Let $f : x \to y$ be a function. Define a relation R on X given by $R = [(a, b) : f(a) = f(b)\}$. Show that R is on equivalence relation on x.
2. Let z be set of all integers and R be a relation in Z defined by $R = \{(a, b); a - b \text{ is even}\}$. Show that R is on equivalence relation in z.
3. Let L be set of all lines in xy plane and R be a relation in L defined as $R = \{(L_1, L_2) :$ 411 $L_2\}$. Show that R is on equivalence relation.
4. Show that $f : N \to N$ given by

$$f(x) = \begin{cases} x+1 & \text{if } x \text{ is odd} \\ x-1 & \text{if } x \text{ is even} \end{cases}$$

is both one-one and onto.
5. Let $\oplus$ be binary operation on Q defined by

$$a \oplus b = \frac{ab}{4}$$

Show that $\oplus$ is commutative as well as associative. Find its identity element.
6. Let $\oplus$ be binary operation on set of natural numbers N given by

$$a \oplus b = \text{L.C.M. of } a \text{ and } b$$

Find: (*i*) $5 \oplus 7$, $20 \oplus 16$
(*ii*) Is $\oplus$ commutative
(*iii*) Is $\oplus$ associative
(*iv*) Find identity element of $\oplus$ in N.
7. Show that $f : R - \{-1\} \to R \{-1\}$ given by $f(x) = \dfrac{x}{x+1}$ is invertible. Also find f^{-1}.
8. Show that function $f : N \to Z$ defined by

$$f(x) = \begin{cases} \frac{1}{2}(n-1) & n \text{ is odd} \\ -\frac{1}{2}n & n \text{ is even} \end{cases}$$

is both one-one and onto.
9. Let $f : R - \left\{\frac{7}{5}\right\} \to R - \left\{\frac{3}{5}\right\}$ be defined by $f(x) = \dfrac{3x+4}{5x-7}$ and $g : R - \left\{\frac{3}{5}\right\} \to R - \left\{\frac{7}{5}\right\}$ be defined by $g(x) = \dfrac{7x+4}{5x-5}$. Find fog and gof.
10. Show that relation R on $N \times N$ defined by $(a, b)\, R\, (c, d) \Rightarrow a + d = b + c$ is an equivalence relation.

ANSWERS

5. Identity Element is 4.
6. (*i*) 35, 80 (*ii*) yes (*iii*) yes (*iv*) 1
7. $f^{-1}(x) = \dfrac{x}{1-x}$ $\forall\, x\ R - \{1\}$.

HOTS (TRY THESE)

1. If $f(x) = \begin{cases} x+1 & x \le 1 \\ 2x+1 & 1 < x \le 2 \end{cases}$

$g(x) = \begin{cases} x^2 & -1 \le x < 2 \\ x+2 & 2 \le x \le 3 \end{cases}$

Find *fog*.

2. Find the domain of $\log_{x-4}(x^2 - 11x + 24)$.
3. Show that $f: R \to R$, $f(x) = \frac{1}{1+|x|}$ is not bijective.
4. Let $f: R \to R$ be defined by $f(x) = \frac{e^x - e^{-x}}{2}$. Is $f(x)$ invertible ? If so, find its inverse also.

ANSWERS

1. $f[g(x)] = \begin{cases} x^2+1 & -1 \le x \le 1 \\ 2x^2+1 & 1 < x < \sqrt{2} \end{cases}$
2. Domain $(y) = (8, \infty)$
3. $f^{-1}(x) = \ln\left(x + \sqrt{1+x^2}\right)$

❑❑❑

CHAPTER 2

INVERSE TRIGONOMETRIC FUNCTIONS

BASIC CONCEPT AND FORMULAE

Inverse of a function 'f' exists if function is one-one and onto, *i.e.,* bijective.

Inverse of sine function is denoted by $\sin^{-1}$. We also write as $\sin^{-1}x$. Similarly, other inverse trigonometric functions are given by $\cos^{-1} x$, $\tan^{-1} x$, $\sec^{-1} x$, $\cot^{-1} x$ and $\text{cosec}^{-1} x$.

Note that, $\sin^{-1} x \neq \dfrac{1}{\sin x}$

$$(\sin^{-1} x)^2 \neq \sin^{-2} x,$$

and $$(\sin^{-1} x) \neq (\sin x)^{-1}.$$

Table for domain and range of Inverse Trigonometrical Functions

Functions	Domain	Range Principal Value
1. $y = \sin^{-1} x$	$[-1, 1]$	$[-\pi/2, \pi/2]$
2. $y = \cos^{-1} x$	$[-1, 1]$	$[0, \pi]$
3. $y = \tan^{-1} x$	R	$(-\pi/2, \pi/2)$
4. $y = \text{cosec}^{-1} x$	$R - (-1, 1)$	$[-\pi/2, \pi/2] - \{0\}$
5. $y = \sec^{-1} x$	$R - [-1, 1]$	$[0, \pi] - [\pi/2]$
6. $y = \cot^{-1} x$	R	$(0, \pi)$

PROPERTIES OF INVERSE TRIGONOMETRICAL FUNCTIONS

(*i*) $\sin^{-1} (\sin x) = x$; $\quad \sin (\sin^{-1} x) = x$

$\tan^{-1} (\tan x) = x$; $\quad \tan (\tan^{-1} x) = x$

$\text{cosec}^{-1} (\text{cosec } x) = x$; $\quad \text{cosec} (\text{cosec}^{-1} x) = x$

$\sec^{-1} (\sec x) = x$; $\quad \sec (\sec^{-1} x) = x$

$\cot^{-1} (\cot x) = x$; $\quad \cot (\cot^{-1} x) = x$

(*ii*) $\sin^{-1} \left(\dfrac{1}{x}\right) = \text{cosec}^{-1} x \quad \cos^{-1} \left(\dfrac{1}{x}\right) = \sec^{-1} x$

$\tan^{-1} \left(\dfrac{1}{x}\right) = \cot^{-1} x \quad \text{cosec}^{-1} \left(\dfrac{1}{x}\right) = \sin^{-1} x$

$\sec^{-1} \left(\dfrac{1}{x}\right) = \cos^{-1} x \quad \cot^{-1} \left(\dfrac{1}{x}\right) = \tan^{-1} x$

(*iii*) $\sin^{-1} x + \cos^{-1} x = \frac{\pi}{2}$

$\tan^{-1} x + \cot^{-1} x = \frac{\pi}{2}$

$\sec^{-1} x + \operatorname{cosec}^{-1} x = \frac{\pi}{2}$

(*iv*) $\sin^{-1}(-x) = -\sin^{-1} x$

$\cos^{-1}(-x) = \pi - \cos^{-1} x$

$\tan^{-1}(-x) = -\tan^{-1} x$

$\operatorname{cosec}^{-1}(-x) = -\operatorname{cosec}^{-1} x$

$\sec^{-1}(-x) = \pi - \sec^{-1} x$

$\cot^{-1}(-x) = \pi - \cot^{-1} x$

(*v*) $\tan^{-1} x + \tan^{-1} y = \tan^{-1} \frac{x+y}{1-xy}$

$\tan^{-1} x - \tan^{-1} y = \tan^{-1} \frac{x-y}{1+xy}$

(*vi*) $\sin^{-1} \frac{2x}{1+x^2} = \cos^{-1} \frac{1-x^2}{1+x^2} = \tan^{-1} \frac{2x}{1-x^2} = 2\tan^{-1} x.$

(*vii*) $\sin^{-1} x + \sin^{-1} y = \sin^{-1} \left\{x\sqrt{1-y^2} + y\sqrt{1-x^2}\right\}$

$\sin^{-1} x - \sin^{-1} y = \sin^{-1} \left\{x\sqrt{1-y^2} - y\sqrt{1-x^2}\right\}$

$\cos^{-1} x + \cos^{-1} y = \cos^{-1} \left\{xy - \sqrt{(1-x^2)(1-y^2)}\right\}$

$\cos^{-1} x - \cos^{-1} y = \cos^{-1} \left\{xy + \sqrt{(1-x^2)(1-y^2)}\right\}$

SOLVED QUESTIONS

SECTION-I

1. *Find the principal value of* $\sin^{-1}\left(-\frac{1}{2}\right)$.

Solution: Let $\sin^{-1}\left(-\frac{1}{2}\right) = x, \ -\frac{\pi}{2} \le x \le \frac{\pi}{2}$

$\Rightarrow \quad \sin x = -\frac{1}{2} \quad \Rightarrow \quad \sin x = -\sin\frac{\pi}{6}$

$\Rightarrow \quad \sin x = \sin\left(-\frac{\pi}{6}\right)$

$x = -\frac{\pi}{6} \qquad \sin^{-1}\left(-\frac{1}{2}\right) = -\frac{\pi}{6}.$

2. *Find the principal value of* $\cot^{-1}(-1)$.

Solution: $\cot^{-1}(-1) = x \qquad 0 < x < \pi$

$$\Rightarrow \quad \cot x = -1$$

$$\Rightarrow \quad \cot x = -\cot\frac{\pi}{4}$$

$$\Rightarrow \quad \cot x = \cot\left(\pi - \frac{\pi}{4}\right)$$

$$\Rightarrow \quad \cot x = \cot\frac{3\pi}{4}$$

$$x = \frac{3\pi}{4}.$$

3. *Find the value of* $\cos\left[\sin^{-1}\left(\frac{1}{7}\right) + \cos^{-1}\left(\frac{1}{7}\right)\right]$.

Solution: $\sin^{-1}\left(\frac{1}{7}\right) + \cos^{-1}\left(\frac{1}{7}\right) = \frac{\pi}{2}$

$$\cos\left[\sin^{-1}\left(\frac{1}{7}\right) + \cos^{-1}\left(\frac{1}{7}\right)\right] = \cos\left[\frac{\pi}{2}\right] = 0.$$

4. *Find the value of* $\tan^{-1}\sqrt{3} + \sec^{-1}(-2)$.

Solution: Let $\tan^{-1}\sqrt{3} = x \qquad -\frac{\pi}{2} < x < \frac{\pi}{2}$

$\Rightarrow \quad \tan x = \sqrt{3} \qquad \Rightarrow \tan x = \tan\frac{\pi}{3}$

$\Rightarrow \quad x = \frac{\pi}{3}$

Let $\quad \sec^{-1}(-2) = y \qquad 0 \le y \le \pi, y \ne \frac{\pi}{2}$

$$\Rightarrow \quad \sec y = -2$$

$$\Rightarrow \quad \sec y = -\sec\frac{\pi}{3}$$

$$\Rightarrow \quad \sec y = \sec\left(\pi - \frac{\pi}{3}\right)$$

$$y = \frac{2\pi}{3}$$

Hence, $\tan^{-1}\sqrt{3} + \sec^{-1}(-2) = \frac{\pi}{3} + \frac{2\pi}{3} = \pi.$

5. *Evaluate* $\cos^{-1}\left(\cos\frac{2\pi}{3}\right) + \sin^{-1}\left(\sin\frac{2\pi}{3}\right)$.

Solution: $\cos^{-1}\left(\cos\frac{2\pi}{3}\right) + \sin^{-1}\left(\sin\frac{2\pi}{3}\right)$

$$\cos^{-1}\left(\cos\frac{2\pi}{3}\right)+\left(\sin^{-1}\left(\pi-\frac{2\pi}{3}\right)\right)$$

$$= \frac{2\pi}{3}+\frac{\pi}{3}$$

$$= \pi.$$

6. *Show that* $\tan^{-1}\frac{1}{2}+\tan^{-1}\frac{2}{11}=\tan^{-1}\frac{3}{4}$.

Solution: $\tan^{-1} = \left(\dfrac{\frac{1}{2}+\frac{2}{11}}{1-\frac{1}{2}\times\frac{2}{11}}\right)$

$\Rightarrow$ $\tan^{-1} = \left(\dfrac{\frac{11+4}{22}}{\frac{22-2}{22}}\right) = \tan^{-1}\frac{15}{20}$

$= \tan^{-1}\frac{3}{4} = \text{R.H.S.}$

7. *Show that* $\sin^{-1}\left(2x\sqrt{1-x^2}\right)=2\sin^{-1}x.\ |x|\leq\frac{1}{\sqrt{2}}$.

Solution: Let $x = \sin y - \frac{\pi}{4}\leq y\leq-\frac{\pi}{4}$

$\sqrt{1-x^2} = \cos y$

$\sin^{-1}(2\sin y\cos y) = \sin^{-1}(\sin 2y)$

$= 2y = 2\sin^{-1}x.$

8. *Write the following function in simplest form.*

Solution: $\cot^{-1}\left(\dfrac{1}{\sqrt{x^2-1}}\right),\ x>1$

Put $x = \sec y$

$\sqrt{x^2-1} = \sqrt{\sec^2 y-1} = \tan y$

Putting the value in given expression,

$\therefore$ $\cot^{-1}\left(\dfrac{1}{\tan y}\right)$

$\Rightarrow$ $\cot^{-1}(\cot y) = y = \sec^{-1}x.$

9. *Solve for* x $\tan^{-1}\frac{1-x}{1+x}=\frac{1}{2}\tan^{-1}x\quad x>0.$

Solution: $2\tan^{-1}\frac{1-x}{1+x} = \tan^{-1}x$

$\Rightarrow$ $\tan^{-1}\dfrac{2\times\left(\frac{1-x}{1+x}\right)}{1-\left(\frac{1-x}{1+x}\right)^2} = \tan^{-1}x$

$$\Rightarrow \quad \tan^{-1}\left[\frac{2\times(1-x)(1+x)}{(1+x)^2-(1-x)^2}\right] = \tan^{-1} x$$

$$\tan^{-1}\frac{1-x^2}{2x} = \tan^{-1} x$$

$$\Rightarrow \quad \frac{1-x^2}{2x} = x$$

$$\Rightarrow \quad 1 - x^2 = 2x \times x = 2x^2$$

$$1 = 3x^2$$

Hence,
$$\boxed{x = \frac{1}{\sqrt{3}}}$$

10. *Prove that* $\tan^{-1} 1 + \tan^{-1} 2 + \tan^{-1} 3 = \pi$.

Solution:

$$\text{L.H.S.} = \tan^{-1} 1 + \tan^{-1} 2 + \tan^{-1} 3$$

$$= \frac{\pi}{4} + \left(\frac{\pi}{2} - \cot^{-1} 2\right) + \left(\frac{\pi}{2} - \cot^{-1} 3\right)$$

$$= \frac{\pi}{4} + \frac{\pi}{2} + \frac{\pi}{2} - \cot^{-1} 2 - \cot^{-1} 3$$

$$= 5\frac{\pi}{4} - \left(\tan^{-1}\frac{1}{2} + \tan^{-1}\frac{1}{3}\right) \qquad \left[\frac{\tan^{-1}\frac{1}{2}+\frac{1}{3}}{1-\frac{1}{2}\times\frac{1}{3}} = \tan^{-1}\left(\frac{5/6}{5/6}\right) = \tan^{-1} 1 = \pi/4\right]$$

$$= \frac{5\pi}{4} - \frac{\pi}{4}$$

$$= \pi.$$

SECTION-II

1. *Show that* $\sin^{-1}\frac{12}{13} + \cos^{-1}\frac{4}{5} + \tan^{-1}\frac{63}{16} = \pi$.

Solution: Let $\sin^{-1}\frac{12}{13} = x \quad \cos^{-1}\frac{4}{5} = y$

and $\tan^{-1}\frac{63}{16} = z$

$$\Rightarrow \quad \sin x = \frac{12}{13}, \quad \cos y = \frac{4}{5} \quad \text{and} \quad \tan z = \frac{63}{16}$$

$$\Rightarrow \quad \cos x = \frac{5}{13}, \quad \sin y = \frac{3}{5}$$

$$\tan x = \frac{12}{5}, \quad \tan y = \frac{3}{4}$$

Hence,
$$\tan(x+y) = \frac{\tan x + \tan y}{1 - \tan x \tan y} = \frac{\frac{12}{5}+\frac{3}{4}}{1-\frac{12}{5}\times\frac{3}{4}} = -\frac{63}{16}$$

$$\tan(x+y) = -\tan z$$

$$\tan(x+y) = \tan(\pi - z)$$

$$x + y + z = \pi$$

Since $\quad x, y, z$ are positive $x, y \neq -z$

$$\sin^{-1}\frac{12}{13}+\cos^{-1}\frac{4}{5}+\tan^{-1}\frac{63}{16}=\pi.$$

2. *Solve for* x; $\tan^{-1}\left(\frac{x-1}{x-2}\right)+\tan^{-1}\left(\frac{x+1}{x+2}\right)=\frac{\pi}{4}$; $|x|<1$.

Solution: $\tan^{-1}\left(\frac{x-1}{x-2}\right)+\tan^{-1}\left(\frac{x+1}{x+2}\right)=\frac{\pi}{4}$

[Using $(a+b)^2=a^2+b^2+2ab$
$(a+b)(a-b)=a^2-b^2$]

$$\tan^{-1}\frac{\left(\frac{x-1}{x-2}+\frac{x+1}{x+2}\right)}{1-\frac{x-1}{x-2}\times\frac{x+1}{x+2}}=\frac{\pi}{4}$$

$$\Rightarrow \quad \frac{(x-1)(x+2)+(x+1)(x-2)}{(x-2)(x+2)-(x-1)(x+1)}=\tan\frac{\pi}{4}$$

$$\Rightarrow \quad \frac{2x^2-4}{-3}=1$$

$$\Rightarrow \quad 2x^2-4=-3$$

$$\Rightarrow \quad 2x^2=1$$

$$x=\pm\frac{1}{\sqrt{2}}.$$

3. *Prove* $\cot^{-1}\left(\frac{\sqrt{1+\sin x}+\sqrt{1-\sin x}}{\sqrt{1+\sin x}-\sqrt{1-\sin x}}\right)=\frac{x}{2}.\ x\in\left(0,\frac{\pi}{2}\right)$.

Solution: $\cot^{-1}\left(\frac{\sqrt{1+\sin x}+\sqrt{1-\sin x}}{\sqrt{1+\sin x}-\sqrt{1-\sin x}}\times\frac{\sqrt{1+\sin x}+\sqrt{1-\sin x}}{\sqrt{1+\sin x}+\sqrt{1-\sin x}}\right)$

$$=\cot^{-1}\left[\frac{1+\sin x+1-\sin x+2\sqrt{1-\sin^2 x}}{1+\sin x-1+\sin x}\right]$$

$$=\cot^{-1}\left(\frac{1+\cos x}{\sin x}\right)$$

$$=\cot^{-1}\left(\frac{2\cos^2\frac{x}{2}}{2\sin\frac{x}{2}\cos\frac{x}{2}}\right) \qquad \left[1+\cos x=2\cos^2\frac{x}{2},\ \sin x=2\sin\frac{x}{2}\cdot\cos\frac{x}{2}\right]$$

$$=\cot^{-1}\left(\cot\frac{x}{2}\right)=\frac{x}{2}.$$

4. *Prove that* $\tan\left(\frac{\pi}{4}+\frac{1}{2}\cos^{-1}\frac{a}{b}\right)+\tan\left(\frac{\pi}{4}-\frac{1}{2}\cos^{-1}\frac{a}{b}\right)=\frac{2b}{a}$.

Solution: Put $\quad \cos^{-1}\frac{a}{b}=\theta$

$$a=b\cos\theta$$

$$\text{LHS} = \tan\left(\frac{\pi}{4}+\frac{\theta}{2}\right) + \tan\left(\frac{\pi}{4}-\frac{\theta}{2}\right)$$

$$= \frac{1+\tan\frac{\theta}{2}}{1-\tan\frac{\theta}{2}} + \frac{1-\tan\frac{\theta}{2}}{1+\tan\frac{\theta}{2}} \qquad \left[\text{Using } \tan(A+B) = \frac{\tan A+\tan B}{1-\tan A.\tan B}\right]$$

$$= \frac{1+\tan^2\frac{\theta}{2} + 2\tan\frac{\theta}{2} + 1+\tan^2\frac{\theta}{2} - 2\tan\frac{\theta}{2}}{1-\tan^2\frac{\theta}{2}}$$

$$= 2\left(\frac{1+\tan^2\frac{\theta}{2}}{1-\tan^2\frac{\theta}{2}}\right) \qquad \left[\text{We know, } \cos 2\theta = \frac{1-\tan^2\theta}{1+\tan^2\theta}\right]$$

$$= \frac{2}{\cos 2.\theta/2} = \frac{2}{\cos\theta}$$

$$= 2\sec\theta = 2\times\frac{b}{a}.$$

5. *Prove that* $\tan^{-1}\left[\frac{\sqrt{1+x^2}+\sqrt{1-x^2}}{\sqrt{1+x^2}-\sqrt{1-x^2}}\right] = \frac{\pi}{4}+\frac{1}{2}\cos^{-1}x^2$.

Solution: Let $x^2 = \cos\alpha \Rightarrow \cos^{-1}x^2 = \alpha$

$$\text{LHS} = \tan^{-1}\left[\frac{\sqrt{1+x^2}+\sqrt{1-x^2}}{\sqrt{1+x^2}-\sqrt{1-x^2}}\right]$$

$$= \tan^{-1}\left[\frac{\sqrt{1+\cos\alpha}+\sqrt{1-\cos\alpha}}{\sqrt{1+\cos\alpha}-\sqrt{1-\cos\alpha}}\right] \qquad \begin{bmatrix}\text{Using } 1+\cos\alpha = 2\cos^2\alpha/2 \\ 1-\cos\alpha = 2\sin^2\alpha/2\end{bmatrix}$$

$$= \tan^{-1}\left[\frac{\sqrt{2\cos^2\frac{\alpha}{2}}+\sqrt{2\sin^2\frac{\alpha}{2}}}{\sqrt{2\cos^2\frac{\alpha}{2}}-\sqrt{2\sin^{-2}\frac{\alpha}{2}}}\right]$$

$$= \tan^{-1}\left[\frac{\sqrt{2}\left(\cos\frac{\alpha}{2}+\sin\frac{\alpha}{2}\right)}{\sqrt{2}\left(\cos\frac{\alpha}{2}-\sin\frac{\alpha}{2}\right)}\right]$$

$$= \tan^{-1}\left[\frac{1+\tan\frac{\alpha}{2}}{1-\tan\frac{\alpha}{2}}\right] \qquad [\text{Dividing } N^r \text{ and } D^r \text{ by } \cos\alpha/2]$$

$$= \tan^{-1}\left[\frac{\tan\frac{\pi}{4}+\tan\frac{\alpha}{2}}{1-\tan\frac{\pi}{4}\tan\frac{\alpha}{2}}\right] \qquad \left[\tan(A+B) = \frac{\tan A+\tan B}{1-\tan A.\tan B}\right]$$

$$= \tan^{-1}\left[\tan\left(\frac{\pi}{4}+\frac{\alpha}{2}\right)\right]$$

$$= \frac{\pi}{4}+\frac{\alpha}{2} \qquad [\because \tan^{-1}(\tan\theta)=\theta]$$

$$= \frac{\pi}{4}+\frac{1}{2}\cos^{-1}x^2.$$

6. Show $\sin^{-1}\frac{3}{5} - \sin^{-1}\frac{8}{17} = \cos^{-1}\frac{84}{85}$.

Solution: Let, $\sin^{-1}\frac{3}{5} = x$ and $\sin^{-1}\frac{8}{17} = y$

$\Rightarrow \quad \sin x = \frac{3}{5}$ and $\sin y = \frac{8}{17}$

Hence, $\quad \cos x = \frac{4}{5}$ and $\cos y = \frac{15}{17}$

We know that $\quad \cos(x-y) = \cos x\cos y + \sin x\sin y = \frac{4}{5}\times\frac{15}{17}+\frac{3}{5}\times\frac{8}{17}$

$$= \frac{60}{85}+\frac{24}{85}=\frac{84}{85}$$

$\Rightarrow \quad x - y = \cos^{-1}\left(\frac{84}{85}\right)$

Hence, $\sin^{-1}\frac{3}{5} - \sin^{-1}\frac{8}{17} = \cos^{-1}\frac{84}{85}$.

7. *Find the value of* $\tan\left(\sin^{-1}\frac{3}{5}+\cot^{-1}\frac{3}{2}\right)$.

Solution: Let $\quad x = \sin^{-1}\frac{3}{5}$; $\quad y = \cot^{-1}\frac{3}{2}$

$\Rightarrow \quad \sin x = \frac{3}{5}$; $\quad \cot y = \frac{3}{2}$

$\Rightarrow \quad \tan x = \frac{4}{5}$; $\quad \tan y = \frac{2}{3}$

we know, $\quad \tan(x+y) = \frac{\tan x + \tan y}{1-\tan x\tan y}$

$$= \frac{\frac{3}{4}+\frac{2}{3}}{1-\frac{3}{4}\times\frac{2}{3}} = \frac{17}{6}$$

$\Rightarrow \quad \tan(x+y) = \frac{17}{6}$

Hence, $\quad \tan\left[\sin^{-1}\frac{3}{5}+\cot^{-1}\frac{3}{2}\right] = \frac{17}{6}$.

8. *If* $\tan^{-1}x+\tan^{-1}y+\tan^{-1}z=\pi$ *prove that* $x+y+z=xyz$.

Solution: Let, $\tan^{-1}x = A$; $\quad \tan^{-1}y = B$ and $\tan^{-1}z = C$

$\Rightarrow \quad x = \tan A$; $\quad y = \tan B$ and $z = \tan C$

$$\Rightarrow \quad \tan^{-1} x + \tan^{-1} y + \tan^{-1} z = \pi \quad \text{(given)}$$

$$\Rightarrow \quad A + B + C = \pi$$

$$\Rightarrow \quad A + B = \pi - C$$

$$\Rightarrow \quad \tan (A + B) = \tan (\pi - C)$$

$$\frac{\tan A + \tan B}{1 - \tan B . \tan B} = -\tan C$$

$$\tan A + \tan B + \tan C = \tan A \tan B \tan C$$

$$\Rightarrow \quad x + y + z = xyz.$$

9. *Solve for x;* $\sin^{-1} x + \sin^{-1} 2x = \frac{\pi}{3} \quad x > 0.$

Solution: Put $\sin^{-1} x = t$

$$\Rightarrow \quad x = \sin t$$

$$\Rightarrow \quad t + \sin^{-1} 2x = \frac{\pi}{3} \quad x > 0 \quad \text{(given)}$$

$$\Rightarrow \quad \sin^{-1} 2x = \left(\frac{\pi}{3} - t\right)$$

$$\Rightarrow \quad 2x = \sin\left(\frac{\pi}{3} - t\right)$$

$$\Rightarrow \quad 2x = \sin \frac{\pi}{3} \cos t - \cos \frac{\pi}{3} \sin t \qquad \text{[Expanding } \sin (A - B)]$$

$$2x = \frac{\sqrt{3}}{2} \cos t - \frac{1}{2} \sin t$$

$$4x = \sqrt{3}\sqrt{1 - \sin^2 t} - \sin t$$

$$5x = \sqrt{3}\sqrt{1 - x^2} \qquad [\because \sin t = x]$$

$$\Rightarrow \quad 25x^2 = 3(1 - x^2) \qquad \text{[Squaring both sides]}$$

$$\Rightarrow \quad 28x^2 = 3$$

$$\Rightarrow \quad x = \pm \frac{1}{2}\sqrt{\frac{3}{7}}.$$

10. *Find the value of* $\tan^{-1}\left[2\cos\left(2\sin^{-1}\frac{1}{2}\right)\right]$.

Solution: Let $\sin^{-1} \frac{1}{2} = x$

$$\sin x = \frac{1}{2}$$

$$\cos 2x = 1 - 2\sin^2 x \qquad [\because 1 - \cos 2x = 2\sin^2 x]$$

$$= 1 - 2 \times \frac{1}{4} = 1 - \frac{1}{2} = \frac{1}{2}$$

Hence, $\cos\left(2\sin^{-1}\frac{1}{2}\right) = \frac{1}{2}$

Putting the value in given expression $= \tan^{-1}\left[2\cos\left(2\sin^{-1}\frac{1}{2}\right)\right]$

$$\Rightarrow \quad \tan^{-1}\left(\cancel{2}\times\frac{1}{\cancel{2}}\right) = \tan^{-1} 1 = \frac{\pi}{4}.$$

11. *Find the value* $\frac{1}{2}\left[\sin^{-1}\frac{2x}{1+x^2} + \cos^{-1}\frac{1-y^2}{1+y^2}\right]$, $|x| < 1, y > 0$ *and* $y < 1$.

Solution: Put $x = \tan x$ and $y = \tan \beta$.

$$= \tan\frac{1}{2}\left[\sin^{-1}\left(\frac{2\tan\alpha}{1+\tan^2\alpha}\right)+\cos^{-1}\left(\frac{1-\tan^2\beta}{1+\tan^2\beta}\right)\right]$$

$$= \tan\frac{1}{2}\left[\sin^{-1}(\sin 2\alpha)+\cos^{-1}(\cos 2\beta)\right]$$

$$= \tan\frac{1}{2}[2\alpha + 2\beta] \qquad [\text{Since } \sin^{-1}(\sin\theta) = \theta, \cos^{-1}(\cos\theta) = \theta]$$

$$= \tan[\alpha + \beta]$$

$$= \frac{\tan\alpha + \tan\beta}{1 - \tan\alpha - \tan\beta}$$

$$= \frac{x+y}{1-xy}.$$

UNSOLVED QUESTIONS

SECTION-I

1. Find the value of $\cos^{-1}\left(\frac{1}{2}\right) + 2\sin^{-1}\left(\frac{1}{2}\right)$.
2. Prove $3\sin^{-1} x = \sin^{-1}(3x - 4x^3), x \in \left[-\frac{1}{2}, \frac{1}{2}\right]$.
3. Find the value of $\tan^{-1}\left(\tan\frac{7\pi}{6}\right)$.
4. Prove that $\tan^{-1} x + \tan^{-1}\frac{2x}{1-x^2} = \tan^{-1}\left(\frac{3x-x^3}{1-3x^2}\right) |x| < \frac{1}{\sqrt{3}}$.
5. Write the function in simplest form $\tan^{-1}\frac{x}{\sqrt{a^2-x^2}}$.
6. Find the principal value of $\cos^{-1}\left(\cos\frac{2\pi}{3}\right) + \sin^{-1}\sin\frac{2\pi}{3}$.
7. Simplify $\tan^{-1}\left\{\frac{a\cos x - b\sin x}{b\cos x + a\sin x}\right\}$, if $\frac{a}{b}\tan x > -1$.
8. Find the value of $\sec^{-2}(\tan^{-1} 2) + \text{cosec}^{-1}(\cot^{-1} 3)$.
9. Find the value of $\tan^{-1}(1) + \cos^{-1}\left(-\frac{1}{2}\right) + \sin^{-1}\left(-\frac{1}{2}\right)$.

10. Show that $\sin^{-1}\left(\frac{2x}{\sqrt{1-x^2}}\right) = 2\sin^{-1} x$.

ANSWERS

1. $2\frac{\pi}{3}$ 3. $\frac{\pi}{6}$ 5. $\sin^{-1}\frac{x}{a}$

6. π 7. $\tan^{-1}\frac{a}{b} - x$ 8. 15

9. $3\frac{\pi}{4}$

SECTION-II

1. Prove that $\tan^{-1}\sqrt{x} = \frac{1}{2}\cos^{-1}\left(\frac{1-x}{1+x}\right)$ $x \in [0, 1]$.
2. Solve for x $\tan^{-1}(x-1) + \tan^{-1} x + \tan^{-1}(x+1) = \tan^{-1} 3x$.
3. Prove $\tan\left(\frac{\pi}{4} + \frac{1}{2}\cos^{-1}\frac{a}{b}\right) + \tan\left(\frac{\pi}{4} - \frac{1}{2}\cos^{-1}\frac{a}{b}\right) = \frac{2b}{a}$.
4. If $\cos^{-1}\frac{x}{a} + \cos^{-1}\frac{y}{b} = \alpha$, prove that $\frac{x^2}{a^2} - \frac{2xy}{ab}\cos\alpha + \frac{y^2}{b^2} = \sin^2\alpha$.
5. Prove that $\tan\left\{\frac{1}{2}\sin^{-1}\left(\frac{2x}{1-x^2}\right) + \frac{1}{2}\cos^{-1}\left(\frac{1-y^2}{1+y^2}\right)\right\} = \frac{x+y}{1-xy}$.
6. Prove that $\tan^{-1}\left(\frac{1}{5}\right) + \tan^{-1}\left(\frac{1}{7}\right) + \tan^{-1}\left(\frac{1}{3}\right) + \tan^{-1}\left(\frac{1}{8}\right) = \frac{\pi}{4}$.
7. Solve the equation $\sin^{-1}\left(\frac{5}{x}\right) + \sin^{-1}\left(\frac{12}{x}\right) = \frac{\pi}{2}$.
8. Prove that $2\tan^{-1}\left(\tan\frac{\alpha}{2}\tan\frac{B}{2}\right) = \cos^{-1}\left(\frac{\cos\alpha + \cos B}{1 + \cos\alpha\cos B}\right)$.
9. Express in simplest form $\tan^{-1}\left(\frac{3a^2x - x^3}{a^3 - 3ax^2}\right)$ $-\frac{a}{\sqrt{3}} < x \le \frac{a}{\sqrt{3}}$ $a > 0$.
10. Evaluate $\tan^{-1} 1 + \tan^{-1} 2 + \tan^{-1} 3$.

ANSWERS

1. $x = 0$ or $\pm\frac{1}{2}$ 7. $x = 13$ 9. $3\tan^{-1}\frac{x}{a}$

10. π

HOTS (TRY THESE)

1. Find the angle $\sin^{-1}\sin 5$ (where 5 is in radians).

2. If $\cos^{-1} x + \cos^{-1} y + \cos^{-1} z = \pi$. Prove that $x^2 + y^2 + z^2 + 2xyz = 1$.

3. Write in simplest form $\tan^{-1}\left(\dfrac{\cos x}{1+\sin x}\right)$ where $-\dfrac{\pi}{2} \le x \le 3\dfrac{\pi}{2}$.

4. Sum to n terms of the series $\tan^{-1}\dfrac{1}{1+1+1^2} + \tan^{-1}\dfrac{1}{1+2+2^2} + \tan^{-1}\dfrac{1}{1+3+3^2} + \ldots$

5. Compute $\cot^{-1}\left\{\cot\left[\sin^{-1}\sqrt{\dfrac{2-\sqrt{3}}{4}} + \cos^{-1}\dfrac{\sqrt{3}}{2} + \cos^{-1}\dfrac{1}{\sqrt{2}}\right]\right\}$.

ANSWERS

1. $5 - 2\pi$

3. $\dfrac{\pi}{4} = \dfrac{x}{2}$

4. $\tan^{-1}\left(\dfrac{n}{n+2}\right)$

5. $\dfrac{\pi}{2}$

❑❑❑

CHAPTER 3

MATRICES

Matrix $\rightarrow$ A matrix is a rectangular array of numbers.

Row matrix $\rightarrow$ A matrix having only one row.

Ex—[1 2 5], [3 0]

Column matrix $\rightarrow$ A matrix having only one column.

Ex— $\begin{bmatrix} 1 \\ 2 \\ 3 \end{bmatrix}$

Square matrix $\rightarrow$ The matrix in which the no. of rows and no. of columns are equal.

e.g. $\begin{bmatrix} 1 & 2 \\ 4 & 5 \end{bmatrix}, \begin{bmatrix} 3 & 0 & 4 \\ 8 & 1 & 2 \\ 1 & 1 & 2 \end{bmatrix}$

Zero or Null matrix $\rightarrow$ The matrix in which each element is zero is called a zero matrix or a null matrix. It is denoted by 0.

e.g. $\begin{bmatrix} 0 & 0 \\ 0 & 0 \end{bmatrix}, \begin{bmatrix} 0 & 0 & 0 \\ 0 & 0 & 0 \end{bmatrix}$

Diagonal matrix $\rightarrow$ A square matrix in which all non-diagonal elements are zero is called a diagonal matrix.

e.g. $A = \begin{bmatrix} 6 & 0 & 0 \\ 0 & 5 & 0 \\ 0 & 0 & 2 \end{bmatrix}$

We may write it as

$A = \text{diag } [6 \quad 5 \quad 2]$

Scalar matrix $\rightarrow$ A diagonal matrix whose all the elements are same is known as a scalar matrix.

e.g. $\begin{bmatrix} 3 & 0 \\ 0 & 3 \end{bmatrix} \begin{bmatrix} 2 & 0 & 0 \\ 0 & 2 & 0 \\ 0 & 0 & 2 \end{bmatrix}$

Unit or Identity matrix $\rightarrow$ A square matrix in which all non-diagonal elements are zero and all diagonal elements are equal to 1 is called a unit matrix.

e.g. $I_2 = \begin{bmatrix} 1 & 0 \\ 0 & 1 \end{bmatrix} I_3 = \begin{bmatrix} 1 & 0 & 0 \\ 0 & 1 & 0 \\ 0 & 0 & 1 \end{bmatrix}$

Equal matrices $\rightarrow$ Two matrices are said to be equal if they are of same order and their corresponding elements are equal.

Transpose of a matrix. The matrix of order $n \times m$ obtained by interchanging the rows and columns of an $m \times n$ matrix A is called the transpose of A and is denoted by A^1 or A^T.

Addition and Subtraction of matrices $\rightarrow$ Addition/subtraction of matrices are defined only when they are of the same order.

PROPERTIES OF MATRIX ADDITION

(*i*) **Commutative** $\rightarrow A + B = B + A$, for matrices A and B.

(*ii*) **Associative** $\rightarrow A + (B + C) = (A + B) + C$, for matrices A, B and C.

(*iii*) **Additive identity** $\rightarrow$ For a given matrix A, a **zero matrix** of the same order as that of A is called its additive identity as $A + 0 = 0 + A = A$.

(*iv*) **Additive Inverse** $\rightarrow$ For a given matrix A, a matrix $(-A)$ is called its additive inverse as $A + (-A) = 0$.

(*v*) **Compliment Rule** $\rightarrow (A + B)^T = A^T + B^T$.

Symmetric matrix $\rightarrow$ A square matrix A is called symmetric matrix if

$$A^T = A \quad i.e. \quad a_{ij} = a_{ji} \ \forall \ i, j.$$

Skew symmetric $\rightarrow$ A square matrix A is called skew matrix, if

$$A^T = -A \quad i.e. \quad a_{ij} = -a_{ji} \ \forall \ i, j.$$

Inverse of a matrix using elementary operation $\rightarrow$ We can find inverse of a matrix, if it exists, by using elementary row operations or column operations but not both in the same solution.

Generally, we find the inverse using row operation (transformations).

Steps to find inverse by using transformation:

(*i*) We write $A + IA$, I is a unit matrix of same order as that of matrix A.

(*ii*) Using the sequence of elementary operations, reduce L.H.S. to I and perform similar operations in I on R.H.S.

(*iii*) We obtain $I = BA$, so, by definition, B is inverse of matrix A, *i.e.* $B = A^{-1}$.

A square matrix A can be expressed as the sum of symmetric and skew symmetric matrix as follows,

$A = \frac{A + A^T}{2} + \frac{A - A^T}{2}$, where $\frac{A + A^T}{2}$ is symmetric matrix and $\frac{A - A^T}{2}$ is a skew symmetric matrix respectively.

SOLVED QUESTIONS

SECTION-I

1. *Construct a* 2×3 *matrix, whose elements are given by* $a_{ij} = \frac{1}{2} |2i - 3j|$.

Solution: $A = \begin{bmatrix} a_{11} & a_{12} & a_{13} \\ a_{21} & a_{22} & a_{23} \end{bmatrix}$ Now $a_{ij} = \frac{1}{2}|2i - 3j|$

$$\therefore \quad a_{11} = \frac{1}{2}|2 \times 1 - 3 \times 1| = \frac{1}{2}$$

$$a_{12} = |2 \times 1 - 3 \times 2| \times \frac{1}{2} = 2$$

$$a_{13} = \frac{|2 \times 1 - 3 \times 3|}{2} = \frac{7}{2}$$

$$a_{21} = \frac{1}{2}|2 \times 2 - 3 \times 1| = \frac{1}{2}$$

$$a_{22} = \frac{1}{2}|2 \times 2 - 3 \times 2| = \frac{1}{2}|4 - 6| = 1$$

$$a_{23} = \frac{1}{2}|2 \times 2 - 3 \times 3| = \frac{5}{2}$$

$$\text{Matrix } A = \begin{bmatrix} \frac{1}{2} & 2 & \frac{7}{2} \\ \frac{1}{2} & 1 & \frac{5}{2} \end{bmatrix}.$$

2. *Find the values of x and y if* $\begin{bmatrix} 3x+y & -y \\ 2y-x & 3 \end{bmatrix} = \begin{bmatrix} 1 & 2 \\ -5 & 3 \end{bmatrix}$.

Solution: $\begin{bmatrix} 3x+y & -y \\ 2y-x & 3 \end{bmatrix} = \begin{bmatrix} 1 & 2 \\ -5 & 3 \end{bmatrix}$

$\Rightarrow \quad 3x + y = 1, \quad -y = 2 \quad$ and $\quad 2y - x = -5$

$3x - 2 = 1$

$3x = 3$

$\boxed{x = 1} \quad \boxed{y = -2}$

3. *For what value of x is the following matrix singular* $\begin{bmatrix} 5-x & x+1 \\ 2 & 4 \end{bmatrix}$?

Solution: Let $A = \begin{bmatrix} 5-x & x+1 \\ 2 & 4 \end{bmatrix}$

A is singular matrix if

$$|A| = 0$$

$$\Rightarrow \quad (5 - x) \times 4 - 2(x + 1) = 0$$

$$20 - 4x - 2x - 2 = 0$$

$$18 - 6x = 0$$

$$\boxed{x = 3}$$

4. *If* $A = \begin{bmatrix} 1 & 0 \\ -1 & 7 \end{bmatrix}$, *find K such that* $A^2 - 8A + KI = 0$.

Solution: $A^2 = A \cdot A$

$$= \begin{bmatrix} 1 & 0 \\ -1 & 7 \end{bmatrix}\begin{bmatrix} 1 & 0 \\ -1 & 7 \end{bmatrix} = \begin{bmatrix} 1\times1+0\times-1 & 0\times1+0\times7 \\ -1\times1+7\times-1 & -1\times6+7\times7 \end{bmatrix}$$

$$= \begin{bmatrix} 1 & 0 \\ -8 & 49 \end{bmatrix}$$

Now $\quad A^2 - 8A + KI = 0$

$$\Rightarrow \quad \begin{bmatrix} 1 & 0 \\ -8 & 49 \end{bmatrix} - 8\begin{bmatrix} 1 & 0 \\ -1 & 7 \end{bmatrix} + K\begin{bmatrix} 1 & 0 \\ 0 & 1 \end{bmatrix} = \begin{bmatrix} 0 & 0 \\ 0 & 0 \end{bmatrix}$$

$$\Rightarrow \quad \begin{bmatrix} 1-8+K & 0-0+0 \\ -8+8+0 & 49-56+K \end{bmatrix} = \begin{bmatrix} 0 & 0 \\ 0 & 0 \end{bmatrix}$$

$$\Rightarrow \quad -7+K=0$$

$$\boxed{K=7}$$

5. *What's the value of* $|3I_3|$, *where* I_3 *is the Identity matrix of order* 3?

Solution: I_3 is a matrix of order 3 × 3

$$I_3 = \begin{bmatrix} 1 & 0 & 0 \\ 0 & 1 & 0 \\ 0 & 0 & 1 \end{bmatrix} \qquad 3I_3 = \begin{bmatrix} 3 & 0 & 0 \\ 0 & 3 & 0 \\ 0 & 0 & 3 \end{bmatrix}$$

$$|3I_3| = 3 \times 3 \times 3\, |I_3| = 27 \times 1 = 27$$

6. *If A is a matrix of order* 3× 4 *and B is a matrix of order* 4 × 6. *What is the order of matrix* $(AB)^1$ *or* $(AB)^T$?

Solution: A is a matrix of order 3 × 4

B is a matrix of order 4 × 6

AB is a matrix of order 3 × 6

$(AB)^T$ is a matrix of order 6 × 3.

7. *If* $A' = \begin{bmatrix} -2 & 3 \\ 1 & 2 \end{bmatrix}$ *and* $B = \begin{bmatrix} -1 & 0 \\ 1 & 2 \end{bmatrix}$, *then find* $(A + 2B)'$.

Solution: $$A' = \begin{bmatrix} -2 & 3 \\ 1 & 2 \end{bmatrix}$$

$$A = \begin{bmatrix} -2 & 1 \\ 3 & 2 \end{bmatrix}$$

and $$B = \begin{bmatrix} -1 & 0 \\ 1 & 2 \end{bmatrix}$$

$$A + 2B = \begin{bmatrix} -2 & 1 \\ 3 & 2 \end{bmatrix} + 2\begin{bmatrix} -1 & 0 \\ 1 & 2 \end{bmatrix}$$

$$= \begin{bmatrix} -2+(-2) & 1 \\ 3+2\times1 & 2+x \end{bmatrix}$$

$$= \begin{bmatrix} -4 & 1 \\ 5 & 6 \end{bmatrix}$$

$$(A+2B)' = \begin{bmatrix} -4 & 5 \\ 1 & 6 \end{bmatrix}$$

8. *If* $A = \begin{bmatrix} 4 & 1 \\ 5 & 8 \end{bmatrix}$*, show that* $A + A^1$ *is symmetric matrix.*

Solution:

$$P = A + A^T$$

$$= \begin{bmatrix} 4 & 1 \\ 5 & 8 \end{bmatrix} + \begin{bmatrix} 4 & 5 \\ 1 & 8 \end{bmatrix}$$

$$= \begin{bmatrix} 8 & 6 \\ 6 & 16 \end{bmatrix}$$

$\Rightarrow$ $$P^T = \begin{bmatrix} 8 & 6 \\ 6 & 16 \end{bmatrix}$$

Now, $$P^T = P$$

$\Rightarrow$ P is symmetric.

9. *By using elementary operations, find the inverse of matrix* $A = \begin{bmatrix} 1 & 2 \\ 2 & -1 \end{bmatrix}$.

Solution:

$$A = IA$$

$$\begin{bmatrix} 1 & 2 \\ 2 & -1 \end{bmatrix} = \begin{bmatrix} 1 & 0 \\ 0 & 1 \end{bmatrix} A$$

$$\begin{bmatrix} 1 & 2 \\ 0 & -5 \end{bmatrix} = \begin{bmatrix} 1 & 0 \\ -2 & 1 \end{bmatrix} A \quad \text{applying } R_2 \to R_2 - 2R_1$$

$$\begin{bmatrix} 1 & 2 \\ 0 & 1 \end{bmatrix} = \begin{bmatrix} 1 & 0 \\ 2/5 & -1/5 \end{bmatrix} \quad \text{applying } R_2 \to -\frac{1}{5} R_2$$

$$\begin{bmatrix} 1 & 0 \\ 0 & 1 \end{bmatrix} = \begin{bmatrix} 1/5 & 2/5 \\ 2/5 & -1/5 \end{bmatrix} A \quad (\text{applying } R_1 \to R_1 - 2R_2)$$

$$A^{-1} = \begin{bmatrix} 1/5 & 2/5 \\ 2/5 & -1/5 \end{bmatrix}.$$

10. *If* $A = \begin{bmatrix} 1 & 4 \\ 3 & 7 \end{bmatrix}$ *show that* $A - A^T$ *is skew symmetric.*

Solution: Let

$$P = A - A^T$$

$$= \begin{bmatrix} 1 & 4 \\ 3 & 7 \end{bmatrix} - \begin{bmatrix} 1 & 4 \\ 3 & 7 \end{bmatrix}^T$$

$$= \begin{bmatrix} 1 & 4 \\ 3 & 7 \end{bmatrix} - \begin{bmatrix} 1 & 3 \\ 4 & 7 \end{bmatrix}$$

$$P = \begin{bmatrix} 0 & 1 \\ -1 & 0 \end{bmatrix}, \quad P^T = \begin{bmatrix} 0 & -1 \\ 1 & 0 \end{bmatrix}.$$

Now $$P = -P^T$$

$\therefore$ P is skew symmetric matrix.

SECTION-II

11. *If* $A = \begin{bmatrix} 0 & -\tan\frac{\alpha}{2} \\ \tan\frac{\alpha}{2} & 0 \end{bmatrix}$ *and I is the identity matrix of order* 2, *show that*

$$I + A = (I - A)\begin{bmatrix} \cos\alpha & -\sin\alpha \\ \sin\alpha & \cos\alpha \end{bmatrix}.$$

Solution: Let $\tan\frac{\alpha}{2} = t$, then

$$\cos\alpha = \frac{1-\tan^2\frac{\alpha}{2}}{1+\tan^2\frac{\alpha}{2}} = \frac{1-t^2}{1+t^2}$$

and
$$\sin\alpha = \frac{2\tan\frac{\alpha}{2}}{1+\tan^2\frac{\alpha}{2}} = \frac{2t}{1+t^2}$$

$$\text{L.H.S.} = I + A = \begin{bmatrix} 1 & 0 \\ 0 & 1 \end{bmatrix} + \begin{bmatrix} 0 & -t \\ t & 0 \end{bmatrix} = \begin{bmatrix} 1 & -t \\ t & 1 \end{bmatrix}$$

and
$$I - A = \begin{bmatrix} 1 & 0 \\ 0 & 1 \end{bmatrix} - \begin{bmatrix} 0 & -t \\ t & 0 \end{bmatrix} = \begin{bmatrix} 1 & t \\ -t & 1 \end{bmatrix}$$

$$\text{R.H.S.} = \begin{bmatrix} 1 & t \\ -t & 1 \end{bmatrix}\begin{bmatrix} \frac{1-t^2}{1+t^2} & \frac{-2t}{1+t^2} \\ \frac{2t}{1+t^2} & \frac{1-t^2}{1+t^2} \end{bmatrix}$$

$$= \begin{bmatrix} \frac{1-t^2}{1+t^2} + \frac{2t^2}{1+t^2} & \frac{-2t}{1+t^2} + \frac{t(1-t^2)}{1+t^2} \\ \frac{-t(1-t^2)}{1+t^2} + \frac{2t}{1+t^2} & \frac{2t^2}{1+t^2} + \frac{1-t^2}{1+t^2} \end{bmatrix} = \begin{bmatrix} 1 & -t \\ t & 1 \end{bmatrix}$$

L.H.S. = R.H.S.

12. *If* $A = \begin{bmatrix} a & b \\ 0 & 1 \end{bmatrix}$, $a \neq 1$, *prove by induction that* $A^n = \begin{bmatrix} a^n & \frac{b(a^n-1)}{a-1} \\ 0 & 1 \end{bmatrix}$ *for all positive integers n.*

Solution: We want to prove that for all positive integers n

$$A^n = \begin{bmatrix} a^n & \frac{b(a^n-1)}{a-1} \\ 0 & 1 \end{bmatrix} \qquad (i)$$

For $n = 1, A^1 = A = \begin{bmatrix} a & b \\ 0 & 1 \end{bmatrix} = \begin{bmatrix} a^1 & \dfrac{b(a^1-1)}{a-1} \\ 0 & 1 \end{bmatrix}$

$\Rightarrow$ (*i*) is true for $n = 1$.

Let us assume that (*i*) is true for a positive integer $n = m$.

i.e.
$$A^m = \begin{bmatrix} a^m & \dfrac{b(a^m-1)}{a-1} \\ 0 & 1 \end{bmatrix}$$

Now
$$A^{m+1} = AA^m = \begin{bmatrix} a & b \\ 0 & 1 \end{bmatrix} \begin{bmatrix} a^m & \dfrac{b(a^m-1)}{a-1} \\ 0 & 1 \end{bmatrix}$$

$$= \begin{bmatrix} a^{m+1}+0 & \dfrac{ab(a^m-1)}{a-1}+b \\ 0+0 & 0+1 \end{bmatrix}$$

$$= \begin{bmatrix} a^{m+1} & \dfrac{b(a^{m+1}-a+a-1)}{a-1} \\ 0 & 1 \end{bmatrix} = \begin{bmatrix} a^{m+1} & \dfrac{b(a^{m+1}-)}{a-1} \\ 0 & 1 \end{bmatrix}$$

$\Rightarrow$ (*i*) is true for $n = m + 1$.

Hence by induction, (*i*) is true for all positive integers *n*.

13. *Obtain the inverse of the following matrix using elementary operations:*

$$A = \begin{bmatrix} 3 & 0 & -1 \\ 2 & 3 & 0 \\ 0 & 4 & 1 \end{bmatrix}.$$

Solution: Write $A = IA$

$$\Rightarrow \begin{bmatrix} 3 & 0 & -1 \\ 2 & 3 & 0 \\ 0 & 4 & 1 \end{bmatrix} = \begin{bmatrix} 1 & 0 & 0 \\ 0 & 1 & 0 \\ 0 & 0 & 1 \end{bmatrix} A$$

$$\Rightarrow \begin{bmatrix} 1 & -3 & -1 \\ 2 & 3 & 0 \\ 0 & 4 & 1 \end{bmatrix} = \begin{bmatrix} 1 & -1 & 0 \\ 0 & 1 & 0 \\ 0 & 0 & 1 \end{bmatrix} A \text{ (applying } R_1 \to R_1 - R_2)$$

$$\Rightarrow \begin{bmatrix} 1 & -3 & -1 \\ 0 & 9 & 2 \\ 0 & 4 & 1 \end{bmatrix} = \begin{bmatrix} 1 & -1 & 0 \\ -2 & 3 & 0 \\ 0 & 0 & 1 \end{bmatrix} A \text{ (applying } R_2 \to R_2 - 2R_1)$$

$$\Rightarrow \begin{bmatrix} 1 & -3 & -1 \\ 0 & 1 & 0 \\ 0 & 4 & 1 \end{bmatrix} = \begin{bmatrix} 1 & -1 & 0 \\ -2 & 3 & -2 \\ 0 & 0 & 1 \end{bmatrix} A \text{ (applying } R_2 \to R_2 - 2R_3)$$

$$\Rightarrow \begin{bmatrix} 1 & 0 & 0 \\ 0 & 1 & 0 \\ 0 & 0 & 1 \end{bmatrix} = \begin{bmatrix} 3 & -4 & 3 \\ -2 & 3 & -2 \\ 8 & -12 & 9 \end{bmatrix} A \text{ (applying } R_1 \to R_1 - 3R_2 \text{ and } R_3 \to R_3 - 4R_2)$$

$$\Rightarrow \begin{bmatrix} 1 & 0 & 0 \\ 0 & 1 & 0 \\ 0 & 0 & 1 \end{bmatrix} = \begin{bmatrix} 3 & -4 & 3 \\ -2 & 3 & -2 \\ 8 & -12 & 9 \end{bmatrix} A \text{ (applying } R_1 \to R_1 + R_2)$$

Hence, $$A^{-1} = \begin{bmatrix} 3 & -4 & 3 \\ -2 & 3 & -2 \\ 8 & -12 & 9 \end{bmatrix}.$$

14. *For the matrix* $A = \begin{bmatrix} 1 & 1 & 1 \\ 1 & 2 & -3 \\ 1 & -1 & 3 \end{bmatrix}$. $A^3 - 6A^2 + 5A + 11\,I = 0$. Find A^{-1}.

Solution: $A^3 - 6A^2 + 5A + 11\,I = 0$

$A^{-1}\,(A^3 - 6A^2 + 6A^2 + 5A + 11\,I) = 0$ (Multiply throughout by A^{-1})

$A^2 - 6A + 5I + 11A^{-1} = 0$

$11\,A^{-1} = -A^2 + 6A - 5I$

$$A^2 = A \times A = \begin{bmatrix} 1 & 1 & 1 \\ 1 & 2 & -3 \\ 1 & -1 & 3 \end{bmatrix} \begin{bmatrix} 1 & 1 & 1 \\ 1 & 2 & -3 \\ 2 & -1 & 3 \end{bmatrix}$$

$$= \begin{bmatrix} 1+1+2 & 1+2-1 & 1-3+3 \\ 1+2-6 & 1+4+3 & 1-6-9 \\ 2-1+6 & 2-2-3 & 2+3+9 \end{bmatrix} = \begin{bmatrix} 4 & 2 & 1 \\ -3 & 8 & -14 \\ 7 & -3 & 14 \end{bmatrix}$$

$$11\,A^{-1} = -A^2 + 6A - 5I$$

$$11\,A^{-1} = \begin{bmatrix} 4 & 2 & 1 \\ -3 & 8 & -14 \\ 7 & -3 & 14 \end{bmatrix} + 6 \begin{bmatrix} 1 & 1 & 1 \\ 1 & 2 & -3 \\ 2 & -1 & 3 \end{bmatrix} - 5 \begin{bmatrix} 1 & 0 & 0 \\ 0 & 1 & 0 \\ 0 & 0 & 1 \end{bmatrix}$$

$$11\,A^{-1} = \begin{bmatrix} -4+6-5 & -2+6+0 & -1+6+0 \\ 3+6+0 & -8+12-5 & 14-18+0 \\ -7+12+0 & 3-6+0 & -14+18-5 \end{bmatrix}$$

$$A^{-1} = \frac{1}{11} \begin{bmatrix} -3 & 4 & 5 \\ -9 & -1 & -4 \\ 5 & -3 & -1 \end{bmatrix}.$$

15. *Using elementary transformations find the inverse of matrix*

$$\begin{bmatrix} 1 & 3 & -2 \\ -3 & 0 & -5 \\ 2 & 5 & 0 \end{bmatrix}.$$

Solution: Let $$A = \begin{bmatrix} 1 & 3 & -2 \\ -3 & 0 & -5 \\ 2 & 5 & 0 \end{bmatrix}$$

Now $$A = IA$$

$$\begin{bmatrix} 1 & 3 & -2 \\ -3 & 0 & -5 \\ 2 & 5 & 0 \end{bmatrix} = \begin{bmatrix} 1 & 0 & 0 \\ 0 & 1 & 0 \\ 0 & 0 & 1 \end{bmatrix} A$$

Operating $R_2 \to R_2 + 3R_2$, $R_3 \to R_3 - 2R_1$ we get

$$\begin{bmatrix} 1 & 3 & -2 \\ 0 & 9 & -11 \\ 9 & -1 & 4 \end{bmatrix} = \begin{bmatrix} 1 & 0 & 0 \\ 3 & 1 & 0 \\ -2 & 0 & 1 \end{bmatrix} A$$

Operating $R_1 \to R_1 + 3R_3$.

$$\begin{bmatrix} 1 & 0 & 10 \\ 0 & 9 & -11 \\ 0 & -1 & 4 \end{bmatrix} = \begin{bmatrix} -5 & 0 & 3 \\ 3 & 1 & 0 \\ -2 & 0 & 1 \end{bmatrix} A$$

Operating $R_1 \to R_1 + 3R_3$

$$\begin{bmatrix} 1 & 0 & 10 \\ 0 & 1 & 21 \\ 0 & -1 & 4 \end{bmatrix} = \begin{bmatrix} -5 & 0 & 3 \\ -13 & 1 & 8 \\ -2 & 0 & 1 \end{bmatrix} A$$

$R_3 \to R_3 + R_2$

$$\begin{bmatrix} 1 & 0 & 10 \\ 0 & 1 & 21 \\ 0 & 0 & 25 \end{bmatrix} = \begin{bmatrix} -5 & 0 & 3 \\ -13 & 1 & 8 \\ -15 & 1 & 9 \end{bmatrix} A$$

$R_3 \to \frac{1}{25} R_3$

$$\begin{bmatrix} 1 & 0 & 10 \\ 0 & 1 & 21 \\ 0 & 0 & 1 \end{bmatrix} = \begin{bmatrix} -5 & 0 & 3 \\ -13 & 1 & 8 \\ -15/25 & 1/25 & 9/25 \end{bmatrix} A$$

$R_1 \to R_1 - 10R_3$, $R_2 \to R_2 - 21R_3$ we get

$$\begin{bmatrix} 1 & 0 & 0 \\ 0 & 1 & 0 \\ 0 & 0 & 1 \end{bmatrix} = \begin{bmatrix} 1 & \frac{-10}{25} & \frac{-15}{25} \\ \frac{-10}{25} & \frac{4}{25} & \frac{11}{25} \\ \frac{-15}{25} & \frac{1}{25} & \frac{9}{25} \end{bmatrix} A$$

$$I = A^{-1} A$$

$$A^{-1} = \begin{bmatrix} 1 & \frac{-10}{25} & \frac{-15}{25} \\ \frac{-10}{25} & \frac{4}{25} & \frac{11}{25} \\ \frac{-15}{25} & \frac{1}{25} & \frac{9}{25} \end{bmatrix}.$$

QUESTIONS FOR PRACTICE

SECTION-I

1. Construct a 2 × 2 matrix whose elements are

$$a_{ij} = \frac{(i+2j)^2}{2}.$$

2. If $\begin{bmatrix} x+y & 2 \\ 5+z & xy \end{bmatrix} = \begin{bmatrix} 6 & 2 \\ 5 & 8 \end{bmatrix}$

Find x, y, z.

3. Find X and Y if

$$Y + X = \begin{bmatrix} 7 & 0 \\ 2 & 5 \end{bmatrix} \text{ and } X - Y = \begin{bmatrix} 3 & 0 \\ 0 & 3 \end{bmatrix}.$$

4. Show that $\cos\theta \begin{bmatrix} \cos\theta & \sin\theta \\ -\sin\theta & \cos\theta \end{bmatrix} + \sin\theta \begin{bmatrix} \sin\theta & -\cos\theta \\ \cos\theta & \sin\theta \end{bmatrix} = I.$

5. Let $A = \begin{bmatrix} 0 & -\tan\frac{\alpha}{2} \\ \tan\frac{\alpha}{2} & 0 \end{bmatrix}$ and T is the identity matrix of order 2 show that

$$(I+A) = (I-A)\begin{bmatrix} \cos\alpha & -\sin\alpha \\ \sin\alpha & \cos\alpha \end{bmatrix}$$

SECTION-II

1. If $A = \begin{bmatrix} \cos\theta & -\sin\theta \\ \sin\theta & \cos\theta \end{bmatrix}$ then show that

$$A^n = \begin{bmatrix} \cos n\theta & -\sin n\theta \\ \sin n\theta & \cos n\theta \end{bmatrix}, \text{ where } n \text{ is a positive number.}$$

2. Express the following matrix as sum of symmetric and skew symmetric matrix

$$\begin{bmatrix} 1 & 3 & 5 \\ -6 & 8 & 3 \\ -4 & 6 & 5 \end{bmatrix}.$$

3. Find the inverse of $A = \begin{bmatrix} 0 & 1 & 2 \\ 1 & 2 & 3 \\ 3 & 1 & 1 \end{bmatrix}$ using elementary transformations.

4. Find inverse of following matrix using elementary transformations $\begin{bmatrix} 3 & 0 & -1 \\ 2 & 3 & 0 \\ 0 & 4 & 1 \end{bmatrix}$.

5. Verify that matrix $A = \begin{bmatrix} 2 & -1 & 1 \\ -1 & 2 & -1 \\ 1 & -1 & 2 \end{bmatrix}$ satisfies.

Equation $\quad A^3 - 6A^2 + 9A - 4I = 0$

Find A^{-1} it $\quad I$ = Identity matrix of order 3×3

0 = Zero matrix of order 3×3.

ANSWERS

1. $\begin{bmatrix} \frac{9}{2} & \frac{25}{2} \\ 8 & 18 \end{bmatrix}$

2. $x = 2,\ y = 4,\ z = 0.$

3. $X = \begin{bmatrix} 5 & 0 \\ 1 & 4 \end{bmatrix}$, . $Y = \begin{bmatrix} 2 & 0 \\ 1 & 1 \end{bmatrix}$

8. $\begin{bmatrix} \frac{1}{2} & \frac{-1}{2} & \frac{+1}{2} \\ -4 & 3 & -1 \\ \frac{5}{2} & \frac{-3}{2} & \frac{1}{2} \end{bmatrix}$

9. $\begin{bmatrix} 3 & -4 & 3 \\ -2 & 3 & -2 \\ 8 & -12 & 9 \end{bmatrix}$

HOTS

1. If $A = \begin{bmatrix} 1 & 1 & 1 \\ 1 & 1 & 1 \\ 1 & 1 & 1 \end{bmatrix}$ prove that

Prove $\quad A^n = \begin{bmatrix} 3^{n-1} & 3^{n-1} & 3^{n-1} \\ 3^{n-1} & 3^{n-1} & 3^{n-1} \\ 3^{n-1} & 3^{n-1} & 3^{n-1} \end{bmatrix}, n \in N.$

2. If $A = \begin{bmatrix} 0 & 1 & 2 \\ 1 & 2 & 3 \\ 3 & a & 1 \end{bmatrix}$ and $A^{-1} = \begin{bmatrix} \frac{1}{2} & \frac{-1}{2} & \frac{1}{2} \\ -4 & 3 & c \\ \frac{5}{2} & \frac{-3}{2} & \frac{1}{2} \end{bmatrix}$. Find a and c.

3. $f(x) = \begin{bmatrix} \cos x & -\sin x & 0 \\ \sin x & \cos x & 0 \\ 0 & 0 & 1 \end{bmatrix}$. Show that $f(x) \,.\, f(y) = f(x + y)$.

4. Find the values of x, y, z if the matrix

$$A = \begin{bmatrix} 0 & 2y & z \\ x & y & -z \\ x & -y & z \end{bmatrix} \text{ Satisfy Equation.}$$

$A'A = I_3$.

ANSWERS

2. $a = 1,\ c = -1$

4. $x = \pm \dfrac{1}{\sqrt{2}},\quad y = \pm \dfrac{1}{\sqrt{6}},\quad z = \pm \dfrac{1}{\sqrt{3}}$.

❑❑❑

CHAPTER 4

DETERMINANTS

BASIC CONCEPTS AND RESULTS

Determinant of a square matrix $\rightarrow$ The determinant of a square matrix associated with every square matrix A is a number called the determinant of matrix and denoted by $|A|$.

If $$A = \begin{bmatrix} a_{11} & a_{12} \\ a_{21} & a_{22} \end{bmatrix}, \text{ then } |A| = a_{11} \times a_{22} - a_{12} \times a_{21}$$

If $$A = \begin{bmatrix} a_{11} & a_{12} & a_{13} \\ a_{21} & a_{22} & a_{23} \\ a_{31} & a_{32} & a_{33} \end{bmatrix}, \text{ then}$$

$$|A| = a_{11} \begin{vmatrix} a_{22} & a_{23} \\ a_{32} & a_{33} \end{vmatrix} - a_{12} \begin{vmatrix} a_{21} & a_{23} \\ a_{31} & a_{33} \end{vmatrix} + a_{13} \begin{vmatrix} a_{21} & a_{22} \\ a_{31} & a_{32} \end{vmatrix}$$

Singular and non-singular matrices.

A matrix is said to be singular, if it is a square matrix and $|A| = 0$. A matrix is said to be non-singular matrix, if A is a square matrix and $|A| \neq 0$.

Properties of determinants: For any square matrix, $|A|$ satisfies the following properties:—

(*i*) $|A^1| = |A|$, where A^1 = transpose of matrix A.

(*ii*) If we interchange any two rows (or columns), the sign of the determinant changes.

(*iii*) If any two rows or any two columns in a determinant are identical (or proportional), then the value of the determinant is zero.

(*iv*) Multiplying a determinant by K means multiplying the elements of only one row (or one column) by K.

(*v*) If we multiply each element of a row (or a column) of a determinant by constant K, then value of the determinant is multiplied by K.

(*vi*) If elements of a row (or a column) in a determinant can be expressed as the sum of two or more elements, then the given determinant can be expressed as the sum of two or more determinants.

(*vii*) To the elements of any row or column of a determinant if we add or subtract the multiples of corresponding elements of any other row or column, then the value of determinant remains unchanged.

AREA OF TRIANGLE

Area of a triangle with vertices (x_1, y_1) (x_2, y_2) and (x_3, y_3) is given by:

$$\Delta = \frac{1}{2} \begin{vmatrix} x_1 & y_1 & 1 \\ x_2 & y_2 & 1 \\ x_3 & y_3 & 1 \end{vmatrix}.$$

MINORS AND CO-FACTORS

(*i*) Minor of an element a_{ij} of the determinant of matrix A is the determinant obtained by deleting i^{th} row and j^{th} column, and it is denoted by M_{ij}.

(*ii*) Co-factor of an element a_{ij} is given by

$$A_{ij} = (-1)^{i+j} M_{ij}$$

(*iii*) Value of determinant of a matrix A is obtained by the sum of products of elements of a row (or a column) with corresponding co-factors. For example

$$|A| = a_{11}A_{11} + a_{12}A_{12} + a_{13}A_{13}$$

(*iv*) If elements of a row (or column) are multiplied with co-factors of elements of any other row (or column), then their sum is zero. For example

$$a_{11}A_{11} + a_{12}A_{22} + a_{13}A_{23} = 0$$

ADJOINT AND INVERSE OF A MATRIX

(*i*) The adjoint of a square matrix $A = [a_{ij}]_{n \times n}$ is defined as the transpose of the matrix $[a_{ij}]_{n \times n}$, when A_{ij} is the co-factor of the element a_{ij}. It is denoted by adj A.

If $$A = \begin{bmatrix} a_{11} & a_{12} & a_{13} \\ a_{21} & a_{22} & a_{23} \\ a_{31} & a_{32} & a_{33} \end{bmatrix}, \text{ then}$$

$$\text{adj } A = \begin{bmatrix} A_{11} & A_{12} & A_{13} \\ A_{21} & A_{22} & A_{23} \\ A_{31} & A_{32} & A_{33} \end{bmatrix}, \text{ where } A_{ij} \text{ is co-factor of } a_{ij}.$$

(*ii*) $A(\text{adj } A) = (\text{adj } A)A = |A|I$, where A is square matrix of order n.

(*iii*) If A is a square matrix of order n, then $|\text{adj } A| = |A|^{n-1}$.

(*iv*) If A and B are non-singular matrices of the same order, then AB and BA are also non-singular matrices of the same order.

(*v*) The determinant of the product of matrixes is equal to the product of their respective determinants,

i.e. $$|AB| = |A|\,|B|.$$

(*vi*) If $AB = BA = I$, where A and B are square matrices, then B is called inverse of A and is written as $B = A^{-1}$. Also $B^{-1} = (A^{-1})^{-1} = A$.

(*vii*) A square matrix A is invertible if and only if A is non-singular matrix.

(*viii*) If A is invertible matrix, then

$$A^{-1} = \frac{1}{|A|}(\text{adj } A)$$

SYSTEM OF LINEAR EQUATIONS

(*i*) Consider the equations:

$$a_1x + b_1y + c_1z = d_1$$
$$a_2x + b_2y + c_2z = d_2$$
$$a_3x + b_3y + c_3z = d_3$$

In matrix form, these equations can be written as $AX = B$, where

$$A = \begin{bmatrix} a_1 & b_1 & c_1 \\ a_2 & b_2 & c_2 \\ a_3 & b_3 & c_3 \end{bmatrix}, X = \begin{bmatrix} x \\ y \\ z \end{bmatrix} \text{ and } B = \begin{bmatrix} d_1 \\ d_2 \\ d_3 \end{bmatrix}$$

(*ii*) Unique solution of equation $AX = B$ is given by $X = A^{-1}B$, where $|A| \neq 0$.

(*iii*) A system of equations is consistent or inconsistent according as its solution exists or not.

(*iv*) For a square matrix A in matrix equation $AX = B$.

(*a*) If $|A| \neq 0$, then there exists unique solution.

(*b*) If $|A| = 0$ and (adj A)$B \neq 0$, then there exists no solution.

(*c*) If $|A| = 0$ and (adj A)$B = 0$, then system may or may not be consistent.

SOLVED QUESTIONS

SECTION-I

1. *Find the value of x* $\begin{vmatrix} x & 4 \\ 2 & 2x \end{vmatrix} = 8.$

Solution: $\begin{vmatrix} x & 4 \\ 2 & 2x \end{vmatrix} = 8.$

$$\Rightarrow \quad 2x^2 - 8 = 8$$

$$x = \pm 2.$$

2. *If A is a square matrix of order 3 such that* $|Adj\ A| = 64$ find $|A'|$

Solution: $|\text{Adj } A| = |A|^{3-1} = 64$ | [$|\text{Adj } A| = |A|^{n-1}$, A is square matrix of order n]

$$|A|^2 = 64$$

$$|A| = \pm 8$$

$$|A'| = |A| = \pm 8.$$

3. *Without expanding, evaluate the following determinants* $\begin{vmatrix} 1 & a & b+c \\ 1 & b & c+a \\ 1 & c & a+b \end{vmatrix}$.

Solution:

$$\begin{vmatrix} 1 & a & b+c \\ 1 & b & c+a \\ 1 & c & a+b \end{vmatrix} = \begin{vmatrix} 1 & a & a+b+c \\ 1 & b & a+b+c \\ 1 & c & a+b+c \end{vmatrix} \quad [\text{Operating } C_3 \to C_3 + C_2]$$

$$= (a+b+c) \begin{vmatrix} 1 & a & 1 \\ 1 & b & 1 \\ 1 & c & 1 \end{vmatrix} \quad (\because C_1 = C_3)$$

$$= (a+b+c) \times 0$$

$$= 0.$$

4. *Using the determinants find the area of triangle with vertices* (–3, 5), (3, –6) *and* (7, 2).

Solution: Area of triangle with vertical (–3, 5), (3, –6) and (7, 2)

$$= \text{Absolute value of } \frac{1}{2} \begin{vmatrix} -3 & 5 & 1 \\ 3 & -6 & 1 \\ 7 & 2 & 1 \end{vmatrix}$$

$$= \frac{1}{2}[-3(-6-2)-5(3-7)+1(6+42)]$$

$$= \frac{1}{2}[24+20+48] = 46 \text{ square units.}$$

5. *In points with vertices (p_1, q_1), (p_2, q_2), $(p_1 + q_1, p_2 + q_2)$ are collinear.*

Solution: $\begin{vmatrix} p_1 & q_1 & 1 \\ p_2 & q_2 & 1 \\ p_1+q_1 & p_2+q_2 & 1 \end{vmatrix} = 0$ [For points to be collinear]

$$\Rightarrow \quad \begin{vmatrix} p_1 & q_1 & 1 \\ p_2 & q_2 & 1 \\ 0 & 0 & -1 \end{vmatrix} = 0 \text{ (operating } R_3 \to R_3 - R_1 - R_2)$$

$$\Rightarrow \quad (-1)\begin{vmatrix} p_1 & q_1 \\ p_2 & q_2 \end{vmatrix} = 0$$

$$p_1q_2 = p_2q_1.$$

6. *If* $A = \begin{vmatrix} 3 & -2 & 3 \\ 2 & 1 & -1 \\ 4 & -3 & 2 \end{vmatrix}$, *find A (adj A) without computing adj A.*

Solution: $A(\text{adj } A) = |A| \times I$

$$|A| = \begin{vmatrix} 3 & -2 & 3 \\ 2 & 1 & -1 \\ 4 & -3 & 2 \end{vmatrix}$$

$$= 3(2-3) - (-2)(4+4) + 3(-6-4)$$

$$= -3 + 16 - 30 = -17$$

$$A(\text{adj } A) = |A| \times I$$

$$= -17\begin{vmatrix} 1 & 0 & 0 \\ 0 & 1 & 0 \\ 0 & 0 & 1 \end{vmatrix} = \begin{vmatrix} -17 & 0 & 0 \\ 0 & -17 & 0 \\ 0 & 0 & -17 \end{vmatrix}.$$

7. *Evaluate the determinant* $\begin{vmatrix} 1 & 2 & 3 \\ -1 & 3 & 0 \\ 4 & 1 & 0 \end{vmatrix}$.

Solution: Expanding the third column

$$\Delta = 3(-1-12) - 0(1-8) + 0(3+2)$$

$$= -52.$$

8. *Find the cofactor of a_{12} in the following* $\begin{vmatrix} 2 & -3 & 5 \\ 6 & 0 & 4 \\ 1 & 5 & -7 \end{vmatrix}$.

Solution: Cofactor of $a_{12} = \begin{vmatrix} 6 & 4 \\ 1 & -7 \end{vmatrix} = (-1)^{1+2}(-42-4) = (-1) \times (-46) = +46.$

9. *If* $\begin{vmatrix} x-2 & -3 \\ 3x & 2x \end{vmatrix} = 3$. *Find integral value of* x.

Solution: $\begin{vmatrix} x-2 & -3 \\ 3x & 2x \end{vmatrix} = 3$

$$(x-2)\,2x - 3x(-3) = 3$$
$$2x^2 + 5x - 3 = 0$$
$$x = \frac{1}{2} \text{ or } -3$$
$$x = -3 \quad \{x \text{ is an integer}\}.$$

10. *If a, b, c are in A.P. prove that* $\begin{vmatrix} x+1 & x+2 & x+a \\ x+2 & x+3 & x+b \\ x+3 & x+4 & x+c \end{vmatrix} = 0$.

Solution: If a, b, c are in A.P. $a + c = 2b$.

Operating $R_1 \to R_1 + R_3 - 2R_2$ we get

$$\Rightarrow \begin{vmatrix} x+1 & x+2 & x+a \\ x+2 & x+3 & x+b \\ x+3 & x+4 & x+c \end{vmatrix} = \begin{vmatrix} 0 & 0 & a+c-2b \\ x+2 & x+3 & x+b \\ x+3 & x+4 & x+c \end{vmatrix}$$

$$\Rightarrow \begin{vmatrix} 0 & 0 & 0 \\ x+2 & x+3 & x+b \\ x+3 & x+4 & x+c \end{vmatrix} = 0.$$

SECTION-II

1. *Prove that* $\begin{vmatrix} -bc & b^2+bc & c^2+bc \\ a^2+ac & -ac & c^2+ac \\ a^2+ab & b^2+ab & -ab \end{vmatrix} = (ab + bc + ca)^3$.

Solution: $\begin{vmatrix} -bc & b^2+bc & c^2+bc \\ a^2+ac & -ac & c^2+ac \\ a^2+ab & b^2+ab & -ab \end{vmatrix}$

Operating $R_1 \to aR_1$, $R_2 \to bR_2$ and $R_3 \to cR_1$

$$\Rightarrow \frac{1}{abc}\begin{vmatrix} -abc & ab^2+abc & ac^2+abc \\ a^2b+abc & -abc & bc^2+abc \\ a^2c+abc & b^2c+abc & -abc \end{vmatrix}$$

Take a, b, c out from C_1, C_2 and C_3 respectively.

$$\Rightarrow \frac{abc}{abc}\begin{vmatrix} -bc & ab+ac & ac+ab \\ ab+bc & -ac & bc+ab \\ ac+bc & bc+ac & -ab \end{vmatrix}$$

Operating $R_1 \to R_1 + R_2 + R_3$

$$\begin{vmatrix} ab+bc+ca & ab+bc+ca & ab+bc+ca \\ ab+bc & -ac & bc+ab \\ ac+bc & bc+ac & -ab \end{vmatrix}$$

$$= (ab + bc + ca) \begin{vmatrix} 1 & 1 & 1 \\ ab+bc & -ac & bc+ab \\ ac+bc & bc+ac & -ab \end{vmatrix}$$

Operating $C_1 \to C_1 - C_3$, $C_2 \to C_2 - C_3$.

$$= (ab + bc + ca) \begin{vmatrix} 0 & 0 & 1 \\ 0 & -(ab+bc+ca) & bc+ab \\ ab+bc+ca & (ab+bc+ca) & -ab \end{vmatrix}$$

$$= (ab + bc + ca)\ [0 + (ab + bc + ca)^2]$$

$$= (ab + bc + ca)^3.$$

2. *Using properties of determinants prove that* $\begin{vmatrix} 1 & 1 & 1 \\ \alpha & \beta & \gamma \\ \beta\gamma & \gamma\alpha & \alpha\beta \end{vmatrix} = (\alpha - \beta)(\beta - \gamma)(\gamma - \alpha).$

Solution: Operating $C_2 \to C_2 - C_1$ and $C_3 \to C_3 - C_1$.

$$\begin{vmatrix} 1 & 1 & 1 \\ \alpha & \beta & \gamma \\ \beta\gamma & \gamma\alpha & \alpha\beta \end{vmatrix} = \begin{vmatrix} 1 & 0 & 0 \\ \alpha & \beta-\alpha & \gamma-\alpha \\ \beta\gamma & \gamma(\alpha-\beta) & \beta(\alpha-\gamma) \end{vmatrix}$$

Take $(\alpha - \beta)$ out from C_2 and $(\gamma - \alpha)$ out from C_3

$$(\alpha - \beta)(\gamma - \alpha) \begin{vmatrix} 1 & 0 & 0 \\ \alpha & 1 & 1 \\ \beta\gamma & \gamma & -\beta \end{vmatrix}$$

$$= (\alpha - \beta)(\gamma - \alpha)\ 1 \begin{vmatrix} -1 & 1 \\ \gamma & -\beta \end{vmatrix}$$

$$= (\alpha - \beta)(\gamma - \alpha)(\beta - \gamma).$$

3. *Prove that* $\begin{vmatrix} 1 & a & a^3 \\ 1 & b & b^3 \\ 1 & c & c^3 \end{vmatrix} = (a - b)(b - c)(c - a)(a + b + c).$

Solution: Operating $R_1 \to R_1 - R_2$ and $R_2 \to R_2 - R_3$.

$$\begin{vmatrix} 0 & a-b & a^3-b^3 \\ 0 & b-c & b^3-c^3 \\ 1 & c & c^3 \end{vmatrix}$$ (Take $(a - b)$ out from R_1 and $(b - c)$ from R_2)

$$= (a-b)(b-c)\begin{vmatrix} 0 & 1 & a^2+ab+b^2 \\ 0 & 1 & b^2+bc+c^2 \\ 1 & c & c^3 \end{vmatrix}$$

$= (a-b)(b-c)\, 1[1(b^2+bc+c^2) - 1(a^2+ab+b^2]$
$= (a-b)(b-c)[c^2-a^2+bc-ab]$
$= (a-b)(b-c)[(c-a)(c+a)+b(c-a)]$
$= (a-b)(b-c)(c-a)(a+b+c).$

4. *Show that* $\begin{vmatrix} b^2+c^2 & ab & ac \\ ba & c^2+a^2 & bc \\ ca & cb & a^2+b^2 \end{vmatrix} = 4a^2b^2c^2.$

Solution: Operating $R_1 \to aR_1$, $R_2 \to bR_2$, $R_3 \to bR_3$

$$\Rightarrow \begin{vmatrix} b^2+c^2 & ab & ac \\ ba & c^2+a^2 & bc \\ ca & cb & a^2+b^2 \end{vmatrix} = \frac{1}{abc}\begin{vmatrix} a(b^2+c^2) & a^2b & a^2c \\ b^2a & b(c^2+a^2) & b^2c \\ c^2a & c^2b & c(a^2+b^2) \end{vmatrix}$$

$$= \frac{abc}{abc}\begin{vmatrix} b^2+c^2 & a^2 & a^2 \\ b^2 & c^2+a^2 & b^2 \\ c^2 & c^2 & a^2+b^2 \end{vmatrix} \quad \text{[Take } a, b, c \text{ out from } C_1, C_2, C_3 \text{ respectively.]}$$

$$= \begin{vmatrix} 0 & -2c^2 & -2b^2 \\ b^2 & c^2+a^2 & b^2 \\ c^2 & c^2 & a^2+b^2 \end{vmatrix} \quad \text{[Operating } R_1 \to R_1 - R_2 - R_3\text{]}$$

$$= -2\begin{vmatrix} 0 & c^2 & b^2 \\ b^2 & c^2+a^2 & b^2 \\ c^2 & c^2 & a^2+b^2 \end{vmatrix} \quad \text{[Operating } R_2 \to R_2 - R_1, R_3 \to R_3 - R_1\text{]}$$

$$= -2\begin{vmatrix} 0 & c^2 & b^2 \\ b^2 & a^2 & 0 \\ c^2 & 0 & a^2 \end{vmatrix}$$

$= -2[-c^2(a^2b^2) + b^2(0 - c^2a^2)$
$= 4a^2b^2c^2.$

5. $\begin{vmatrix} 1+a & 1 & 1 \\ 1 & 1+b & 1 \\ 1 & 1 & 1+c \end{vmatrix} = abc\left(1+\frac{1}{a}+\frac{1}{b}+\frac{1}{c}\right) = ab+bc+ca+abc.$

Solution: Taking a, b, c from R_1, R_2 and R_3.

$$\Rightarrow \begin{vmatrix} 1+a & 1 & 1 \\ 1 & 1+b & 1 \\ 1 & 1 & 1+c \end{vmatrix} = abc \begin{vmatrix} 1+\frac{1}{a} & \frac{1}{a} & \frac{1}{a} \\ \frac{1}{b} & 1+\frac{1}{b} & \frac{1}{b} \\ \frac{1}{c} & \frac{1}{c} & 1+\frac{1}{c} \end{vmatrix} \quad \text{[Applying } R_1 \to R_1 + R_2 + R_3.\text{]}$$

$$abc \begin{vmatrix} 1+\frac{1}{a}+\frac{1}{b}+\frac{1}{c} & 1+\frac{1}{a}+\frac{1}{b}+\frac{1}{c} & 1+\frac{1}{a}+\frac{1}{b}+\frac{1}{c} \\ \frac{1}{b} & \frac{1}{b}+1 & \frac{1}{b} \\ \frac{1}{c} & \frac{1}{c} & \frac{1}{c}+1 \end{vmatrix}$$

$$= abc \left(\frac{1}{a}+\frac{1}{b}+\frac{1}{c}\right) \begin{vmatrix} 1 & 1 & 1 \\ \frac{1}{b} & \frac{1}{b}+1 & \frac{1}{b} \\ \frac{1}{c} & \frac{1}{c} & \frac{1}{c}+1 \end{vmatrix}$$

Applying $C_2 \to C_2 - C_1$, $C_3 \to C_3 - C_1$ we get

$$\Delta = abc \left(1+\frac{1}{a}+\frac{1}{b}+\frac{1}{c}\right) \begin{vmatrix} 1 & 0 & 0 \\ \frac{1}{b} & 1 & 0 \\ \frac{1}{c} & 0 & 1 \end{vmatrix}$$

$$= abc \left(1+\frac{1}{a}+\frac{1}{b}+\frac{1}{c}\right) [1 \times (1-0)]$$

$$= abc \left(1+\frac{1}{a}+\frac{1}{b}+\frac{1}{c}\right) = abc + bc + ca + ab$$

6. *Using matrix, solve the following system of equations*:

$3x - y + z = 5$
$2x - 2y + 3z = 7$
$x + y - z = -1.$

Solution: The given system of equation can be written as $AX = B$ where

$$A = \begin{bmatrix} 3 & -1 & 1 \\ 2 & -2 & 3 \\ 1 & 1 & -1 \end{bmatrix}, X = \begin{bmatrix} x \\ y \\ z \end{bmatrix} \text{ and } B = \begin{bmatrix} 5 \\ 7 \\ -1 \end{bmatrix}$$

Now, $|A| = \begin{vmatrix} 3 & -1 & 1 \\ 2 & -2 & 3 \\ 1 & 1 & -1 \end{vmatrix} = 3(2-3) - (-1)(-2-3) + 1(2+2)$

$= -3-5+4 = -4 \neq 0$

$\Rightarrow$ A^{-1} exists and so the given system has a unique solution $X = A^{-1} B$.

Here, $A_{11} = \begin{vmatrix} -2 & 3 \\ 1 & -1 \end{vmatrix} = -1,\ A_{12} = -\begin{vmatrix} 2 & 3 \\ 1 & -1 \end{vmatrix} = 5$

$A_{13} = \begin{vmatrix} 2 & -2 \\ 1 & 1 \end{vmatrix} = 4$

$A_{21} = -\begin{vmatrix} -1 & 1 \\ 1 & -1 \end{vmatrix} = 0,\ A_{22} = \begin{vmatrix} 3 & 1 \\ 1 & -1 \end{vmatrix} = -4$

$A_{23} = -\begin{vmatrix} 3 & -1 \\ 1 & 1 \end{vmatrix} = -4,\ A_{31} = \begin{vmatrix} -1 & 1 \\ -2 & 3 \end{vmatrix} = -1$

$A_{32} = -\begin{vmatrix} 3 & 1 \\ 2 & 3 \end{vmatrix} = -7,\ A_{33} = \begin{vmatrix} 3 & -1 \\ 2 & -2 \end{vmatrix} = -4$

$$\text{adj } A = \begin{bmatrix} -1 & 5 & 4 \\ 0 & -4 & -4 \\ -1 & -7 & -4 \end{bmatrix}^t = \begin{bmatrix} -1 & 0 & -1 \\ 5 & -4 & -7 \\ 4 & -4 & -4 \end{bmatrix}$$

$$\therefore \quad A^{-1} = \frac{1}{|A|} \text{adj } A = -\frac{1}{4}\begin{bmatrix} -1 & 0 & -1 \\ 5 & -4 & -7 \\ 4 & -4 & -4 \end{bmatrix}$$

$$\therefore \quad X = A^{-1} B = -\frac{1}{4}\begin{bmatrix} -1 & 0 & -1 \\ 5 & -4 & -7 \\ 4 & -4 & -4 \end{bmatrix}\begin{bmatrix} 5 \\ 7 \\ -1 \end{bmatrix}$$

$$= -\frac{1}{4}\begin{bmatrix} -5 & +0 & +1 \\ 25 & -28 & +7 \\ 20 & -28 & +4 \end{bmatrix} = -\frac{1}{4}\begin{bmatrix} -4 \\ 4 \\ -4 \end{bmatrix} = \begin{bmatrix} -1 \\ -1 \\ 1 \end{bmatrix}$$

$$\Rightarrow \quad \begin{bmatrix} x \\ y \\ z \end{bmatrix} = \begin{bmatrix} 1 \\ -1 \\ 1 \end{bmatrix} \Rightarrow x = 1, \quad y = -1, \quad z = 1.$$

Hence the solution of the given system of equations is $x = 1, y = -1, z = 1$.

7. *Solve the following system of equations, using matrix:*

$$\frac{2}{x} + \frac{3}{y} + \frac{10}{z} = 4, \quad \frac{4}{x} - \frac{6}{y} + \frac{5}{z} = 1,$$

$$\frac{6}{x} + \frac{9}{y} - \frac{20}{z} = 2.$$

Solution: Let $\frac{1}{x} = a,\ \frac{1}{y} = b,\ \frac{1}{z} = c$, then the given system of equation becomes

$2a + 3b + 10c = 4$

$4a - 6b + 5c = 1$

$6a + 9b - 20c = 2$

This system of equations can be given as $AX = B$.

Where $A = \begin{bmatrix} 2 & 3 & 10 \\ 4 & -6 & 5 \\ 6 & 9 & -20 \end{bmatrix}, X = \begin{bmatrix} a \\ b \\ c \end{bmatrix}$ and $B = \begin{bmatrix} 4 \\ 1 \\ 2 \end{bmatrix}$

Now $|A| = \begin{vmatrix} 2 & 3 & 10 \\ 4 & -6 & 5 \\ 6 & 9 & -20 \end{vmatrix} = 2.3.5 \begin{vmatrix} 1 & 1 & 2 \\ 2 & -2 & 1 \\ 3 & 3 & -4 \end{vmatrix} = 30 \begin{vmatrix} 0 & 1 & 2 \\ 4 & -2 & 1 \\ 0 & 3 & -4 \end{vmatrix}$

$= 30\,[-4(-4-6)] = 1200$

$\Rightarrow$ A^{-1} exists and so system (i) has a unique solution.

Here $A_{11} = \begin{vmatrix} -6 & 5 \\ 9 & -20 \end{vmatrix} = 75, \quad A_{12} = \begin{vmatrix} 4 & 5 \\ 6 & -20 \end{vmatrix} = 110, \quad A_{13} = \begin{vmatrix} 4 & -6 \\ 6 & 9 \end{vmatrix} = 72$

$A_{21} = -\begin{vmatrix} 3 & 10 \\ 9 & -20 \end{vmatrix} = 150, \quad A_{22} = \begin{vmatrix} 2 & 10 \\ 6 & -20 \end{vmatrix} = -100, \quad A_{23} = -\begin{vmatrix} 2 & 3 \\ 6 & 9 \end{vmatrix} = 0$

$A_{31} = \begin{vmatrix} 3 & 10 \\ -6 & 5 \end{vmatrix} = 75, \quad A_{32} = -\begin{vmatrix} 2 & 10 \\ 4 & 5 \end{vmatrix} = 30, \quad A_{33} = \begin{vmatrix} 2 & 3 \\ 4 & -6 \end{vmatrix} = -24$

$$\text{adj } A = \begin{bmatrix} 75 & 110 & 72 \\ 150 & -100 & 0 \\ 75 & 30 & -24 \end{bmatrix}^t = \begin{bmatrix} 75 & 150 & 75 \\ 110 & -100 & 30 \\ 72 & 0 & -24 \end{bmatrix}$$

$$A^{-1} = \frac{(A)}{|A|} = \frac{1}{1200}\begin{bmatrix} 75 & 150 & 75 \\ 110 & -100 & 30 \\ 72 & 0 & -24 \end{bmatrix}\begin{bmatrix} 4 \\ 1 \\ 2 \end{bmatrix} = \frac{1}{1200}\begin{bmatrix} 600 \\ 400 \\ 240 \end{bmatrix}$$

$$\begin{bmatrix} a \\ b \\ c \end{bmatrix} = \begin{bmatrix} \frac{1}{2} \\ \frac{1}{3} \\ \frac{1}{5} \end{bmatrix}$$

$\frac{1}{x} = \frac{1}{2} \qquad \frac{1}{y} = \frac{1}{3} \qquad \frac{1}{z} = \frac{1}{5}$

$x = 2 \qquad y = 3 \qquad z = 5.$

8. $A = \begin{bmatrix} 2 & -1 & 1 \\ -1 & 2 & -1 \\ 1 & -1 & 2 \end{bmatrix}$ *and* $B = \begin{bmatrix} 3 & 1 & -1 \\ 1 & 3 & 1 \\ -1 & 1 & 3 \end{bmatrix}$. *Find AB. Use the result to solve the following system of linear equations*

$2x - y + z = -1$

$-x + 2y - z = 4$

$x - y + 2z = -3.$

Solution:

$$AB = \begin{bmatrix} 2 & -1 & 1 \\ -1 & 2 & -1 \\ 1 & -1 & 2 \end{bmatrix}\begin{bmatrix} 3 & 1 & -1 \\ 1 & 3 & 1 \\ -1 & 1 & 3 \end{bmatrix}$$

$$= 4\begin{bmatrix} 1 & 0 & 0 \\ 0 & 1 & 0 \\ 0 & 0 & 1 \end{bmatrix} = 4I$$

$$B = 4A^{-1}$$

$$\Rightarrow \qquad A^{-1} = \frac{B}{4}$$

Given system of equation

$2x - y + z = -1$

$-x + 2y - z = 4$

$x - y + 2z = -3.$

Rewriting in matrix form

$$\begin{bmatrix} x \\ y \\ z \end{bmatrix} = \begin{bmatrix} 2 & -1 & 1 \\ -1 & 2 & -1 \\ 1 & -1 & 2 \end{bmatrix}\begin{bmatrix} -1 \\ 4 \\ -3 \end{bmatrix} \Rightarrow \text{using } A^{-1} = \frac{B}{4} = \frac{1}{4}\begin{bmatrix} 3 & 1 & -1 \\ 1 & 3 & 1 \\ -1 & 1 & 3 \end{bmatrix}\begin{bmatrix} -1 \\ 4 \\ -3 \end{bmatrix}$$

$$= \frac{1}{4}\begin{bmatrix} -\not{3} & +4 & +\not{3} \\ -1 & +12 & -3 \\ 1 & +4 & -9 \end{bmatrix} = \frac{1}{4}\begin{bmatrix} 4 \\ 8 \\ -4 \end{bmatrix} = \begin{bmatrix} 1 \\ 2 \\ -1 \end{bmatrix}$$

hence, $x = 1$

$y = 2$

$z = -1$

QUESTIONS FOR PRACTICE

SECTION-I

1. Evaluate $\Delta = \begin{vmatrix} 0 & \sin\alpha & -\cos\alpha \\ -\sin\alpha & 0 & \sin B \\ \cos\alpha & -\sin B & 0 \end{vmatrix}$.

2. Using properties of determinant, show that $\begin{vmatrix} 2 & 7 & 65 \\ 3 & 8 & 75 \\ 5 & 9 & 86 \end{vmatrix} = 0$.

3. It $A = \begin{vmatrix} 1 & 2 & 3 \\ 5 & 7 & -1 \\ 3 & -1 & 5 \end{vmatrix}$. Write determinant $|3A|$.

4. For the determinant $\begin{vmatrix} 3 & -2 & 1 \\ 4 & 6 & 5 \\ 2 & -1 & 7 \end{vmatrix}$. Find minor M_{32} and cofactor A_{12}.

5. Evaluate $\begin{vmatrix} 1 & bc & a(b+c) \\ 1 & ca & b(c+a) \\ 1 & ab & c(a+b) \end{vmatrix}$.

6. Using matrix method, determine whether the following system of equation is consistent or inconsistent.

$$\begin{aligned} 3x - y - 2z &= 2 \\ 2y - z &= -1 \\ 3x - 5y &= 3. \end{aligned}$$

7. Prove that the determinant $\begin{vmatrix} x & \sin\theta & \cos\theta \\ -\sin\theta & -x & 1 \\ \cos\theta & 1 & x \end{vmatrix}$ is independent of θ.

8. If $A \begin{bmatrix} 3 & -5 \\ 4 & 2 \end{bmatrix}$, Find A (adj. A).

9. If the matrix $\begin{bmatrix} x+4 & x & x \\ x & x+4 & x \\ x & x & x+4 \end{bmatrix}$ is singular. Find x.

10. If A is a square matrix of order 3 such that $|\text{adj } A| = 64$. Find $|A|$.

SECTION-II

1. Show that $\Delta = \begin{vmatrix} (y+2)^2 & xy & zx \\ xy & (x+z) & yz \\ xz & yz & (x+y)^2 \end{vmatrix} = 2xy2\ (x+y+z)^3$.

2. Show that $\begin{vmatrix} x & x^3 & 1+px^3 \\ y & y^3 & 1+py^3 \\ z & z^3 & 1+p2^3 \end{vmatrix} = (1+pxyz)(x-y)(y-z)(z-x)$.

3. Using properties of determinants, prove that

$$\begin{vmatrix} (b+c)^2 & a^2 & a^2 \\ b^2 & (c+a)^2 & b^2 \\ c^2 & c^2 & (a+b)^2 \end{vmatrix} = 2abc\ (a+b+c)^3.$$

4. Using properties of determinant prove that

$$\begin{vmatrix} b+c & c+0 & 0+b \\ q+r & r+p & p+q \\ y+z & z+x & x+y \end{vmatrix} = 2\begin{vmatrix} a & n & c \\ p & q & r \\ x & y & z \end{vmatrix}.$$

5. Using properties of determinant prove that

$$\begin{vmatrix} a & a+b & a+b+c \\ 2a & 3a+2b & 4a+3b+2c \\ 3a & 6a+3b & 100+60+3c \end{vmatrix} = a^3.$$

6. If $A = \begin{vmatrix} 3 & -4 & 2 \\ 2 & 3 & 5 \\ 1 & 0 & 1 \end{vmatrix}$. Find A^{-1} hence solve the following system of equations.

$$3x + 4y + 2z + 1 = 0$$
$$2x + 3y + 5z - 7 = 0$$
$$x + z - 2 = 0$$

7. Use matrix method solve the system of equations

$$3x + 4y - z = 23$$
$$2x + 2y + 32 = 20$$
$$4x - y + 22 = 12.$$

8. The sum of three numbers is 6. If we multiply third number by 3 and second number to it we get 11. By adding first and third number, we get double of second number. Represent it algebraically and find the number using matrix method.

9. Solve using matrix method

$$x + y + z = 4$$
$$2x - y + z = -1$$
$$2x + y - 3z = -9.$$

10. Prove using properties of determinants

$$\begin{vmatrix} 3a & -a+b & -a+c \\ -b+a & 3b & -b+c \\ -c+a & -c+b & 3c \end{vmatrix} = 3(a+b+c)(ab+bc+ca).$$

ANSWERS

SECTION-I

1. 0

3. $|3A| = \begin{vmatrix} 3 & 6 & 9 \\ 5 & 7 & -1 \\ 3 & -1 & -5 \end{vmatrix}$

4. $M_{32} = 11, \quad A_{12} = -18$

5. 0

6. $|A| = 0$, Inconsistent

8. $\begin{bmatrix} 26 & 0 \\ 0 & 26 \end{bmatrix}$

9. $-\dfrac{4}{3}$

10. ± 8

SECTION-II

1. $A^{-1} = -\dfrac{1}{9}\begin{bmatrix} 3 & 4 & -26 \\ 3 & 1 & -11 \\ -3 & -4 & 17 \end{bmatrix}$ $x = 3 \quad y = 2 \quad z = -1$

7. $x = , y = 4, z = 2$

8. $x = 1, y = 2, z = 3$

9. $x = -1, \ y = 2, \ z = 3$

HOTS

1. If $A = \begin{bmatrix} 1 & 0 & 0 \\ 0 & 1 & 1 \\ 0 & -2 & 4 \end{bmatrix}$ and $A^{-1} = \frac{1}{6}(A^2 + cA + dI)$ then find c and d.

2. Show that $1 \begin{bmatrix} \cos\theta & -\sin\theta \\ \sin\theta & \cos\theta \end{bmatrix} = \begin{bmatrix} 1 & \tan\frac{\theta}{2} \\ -\tan\frac{\theta}{2} & 1 \end{bmatrix}^{-1}$.

3. If $w = e^{2i\pi/3}$. Find the inverse of matrix $A = \begin{bmatrix} 1 & 1 & 1 \\ 1 & w & w^2 \\ 1 & w^2 & w \end{bmatrix}$.

4. If $a \neq p,\ b \neq q,\ c \neq r$ and $\begin{vmatrix} p & b & c \\ a & q & c \\ a & b & r \end{vmatrix} = 0$ then find the value of $\frac{p}{p-a} + \frac{q}{q-b} + \frac{r}{r-c}$.

5. If $f(x) = \begin{vmatrix} 1 & x & x+1 \\ 2x & x(x-1) & (x+1)x \\ 3x(x-1) & x(x-1)(x+1) & x(x-1) \end{vmatrix}$ then find $f(100)$.

ANSWERS

1. $c = -6$ and $d = 11$

2. $\frac{1}{3}\begin{bmatrix} 1 & 1 & 1 \\ 1 & w^2 & w \\ 1 & w & w^2 \end{bmatrix}$

4. 2
5. 0

❑❑❑

CHAPTER 5

CONTINUITY AND DIFFERENTIABILITY

CONTINUITY OF A FUNCTION AT A POINT

Let f be a real function on a subset of the real numbers and let c be a point in the domain of f. Then f is continuous of c if

$$\lim_{x\to c} f(x) = f(c).$$

We can also say that 'f' is continuous at $x = c$ if

$$\lim_{x\to a^-} f(x) = \operatorname{lt}_{x\to c^+} f(x) = f(c).$$

A function is discontinuous at $x = c$, if

(*i*) $\lim_{x\to c^-} f(x)$ and $\lim_{x\to c^+} f(x)$ exist but are not equal.

(*ii*) $\lim_{x\to c^-} f(x)$ and $\lim_{x\to c^+} f(x)$ exist and are equal but not equal to $f(c)$.

(*iii*) $f(c)$ is not defined.

CONTINUITY IN AN INTERVAL

(*i*) f is said to be continuous in an open interval (a, b) if it is continuous at every point in this interval.

(*ii*) f is said to be continuous in the closed interval $[a, b]$ if

- f is continuous in (a, b)
- $\lim_{x\to a^+} f(x) = f(a)$
- $\lim_{x\to b^-} f(x) = f(b)$

CONTINUITY OF COMPOSITE FUNCTIONS

Let f and g be real valued functions such that fog is defined at a. If g is continuous at a and f is continuous at $g(a)$ then (fog) is continuous at a.

Differentiability $\rightarrow$ A function $f(x)$ and if there is a small increment h in x, let their corresponds increment $f(x + h)$ in $f(x)$ *i.e.*

$$f(x) \rightarrow f(x + h)$$

Then $\lim_{x\to 0} \dfrac{f(x+h)-f(x)}{h}$ is called the differential co-efficient of $f(x)$ w.r.t. x.

ALGEBRA OF DERIVATIVES

If *u, v* are functions of *x*, then

(i) $\dfrac{d(u \pm v)}{dx} = \dfrac{du}{dx} \pm \dfrac{dv}{dx}$

(ii) $\dfrac{d}{dx}(u.v.) = u.\dfrac{dv}{dx} + v.\dfrac{du}{dx}$

(iii) $\dfrac{d}{dx}\left(\dfrac{u}{v}\right) = \dfrac{v.\dfrac{du}{dx} - u.\dfrac{dv}{dx}}{v^2}$

Chain Rule → Chain Rule is a rule to differentiate composition of functions. Let $f = vou$. If $t = u(x)$ and both $\dfrac{dt}{dx}$ and $\dfrac{dv}{dx}$ exist, then $\dfrac{df}{dx} = \dfrac{dv}{dt}.\dfrac{dt}{dx}$.

SECOND ORDER DERIVATIVES

$\dfrac{d}{dx}.\dfrac{dy}{dx} = \dfrac{d^2y}{dx^2}$ is called the second order derivatives of *y* w.r.t. *x*. It is denoted by y'' or y_2

if $\quad y = f(x)$

$\quad y_2 = f''(x)$

Rolle's Theorem→ Let $f: [a, b] \to R$ be continuous on $[a, b]$ and differentiable on (a, b), such that $f(a) = f(b)$, where *a* and *b* are some real numbers. Then 'there exists at least one point' *c*, in (a, b) such that

$$f'(c) = 0$$

Mean-Value Theorem (Lagrange's). Let $f: [a, b] \to R$ be a continuous function on $[a, b]$ and differentiable on (a, b). Then, there exists at least one point '*c*' in (a, b) such that

$$f'(c) = \frac{f(b) - f(a)}{b - a}.$$

SOLVED QUESTIONS

SECTION-I

1. *If f is differentiable at x = a, find* $\underset{x \to a}{\text{Lt}} \dfrac{x\,f(a) - a\,f(x)}{x - a}$.

Solution: Let $x = a + h$, so that when $x \to a,\ h \to 0$

$$\Rightarrow \quad \underset{x \to a}{\text{Lt}} \frac{x\,f(a) - a\,f(x)}{x - a} = \underset{h \to 0}{\text{Lt}} \frac{(a+h)\,f(a) - af\,(a+h)}{h}$$

$$= \underset{h \to 0}{\text{Lt}} \frac{h\,f(a) - a[f(a+h) - f(a)]}{h}$$

$$= f(a) - af'(a).$$

2. *Differentiate* $2\sqrt{\cot(x^2)}$ *w.r.t.* x.

Solution: Let $y = 2\sqrt{\cot(x^2)}$ differentiating w.r.t. x. we get

$$\frac{dy}{dx} = 2\frac{d}{dx}[\{(\cot(x^2)\}^{1/2}]$$

$$= 2\frac{1}{2\sqrt{\cot x^2}} - \text{cosec}^2 x^2 . 2x \qquad \text{[Chain Rule]}$$

$$= -2x\frac{\text{cosec}^2(x^2)}{\sqrt{\cot(x^2)}}.$$

3. *If* $\sin xy + \cos xy = 1$ *and* $\tan xy \neq 1$ *prove that* $\frac{dy}{dx} = -\frac{y}{x}$.

Solution: $\sin xy + \cos xy = 1$

Differentiating both sides w.r.t. x

$$\Rightarrow \quad \cos xy\left(x\frac{dy}{dx} + y.1\right) - \sin xy.\left(x.\frac{dy}{dx} + y\right) = 0$$

$$\Rightarrow \quad (\cos xy - \sin xy)\left(x\frac{dy}{dx} + y\right) = 0$$

$$\Rightarrow \quad \frac{dy}{dx} = -\frac{y}{x} \qquad [\tan xy \neq 1, \sin xy - \cos xy \neq 0.$$

4. *Verify the mean value theorem for function* $f(x) = x^2$ in the interval [2, 4].

Solution: $f(x) = x^2$ is continuous in [2, 4] and differentiable in (2, 4) as its derivative $f'(x) = 2x$ is defined in (2, 4).

$f(2) = 4$ and $f(4) = 16$

$$\Rightarrow \text{Hence, } \frac{f(b)-f(a)}{b-a} = \frac{16-4}{4-2} = 6$$

MVT states that there is a point $c \in (2, 4)$ such that $f'(c) = 6$

But $f'(c) = 2c = 6$

$c = 3$

$c \in [2, 4]$.

5. *Differentiate* $\sin^2 x$ w.r.t. $e^{\cos x}$.

Solution: Let $y = \sin^2 x$ and $z = e^{\cos x}$ we want to find out $\frac{dy}{dz}$.

Differentiating w.r.t. x

$$\frac{dy}{dx} = 2\sin x . \cos x$$

$$\frac{dz}{dx} = e^{\cos x}(-\sin x) = -\sin x\, e^{\cos x}$$

$$\frac{dy}{dz} = \frac{2\sin x \cos x}{-\sin x\, e^{\cos x}} = \frac{-2\cos x}{e^{\cos x}}.$$

6. *If* $x^y = e^{x-y}$ *prove that* $\frac{dy}{dx} = \frac{\log x}{(1+\log x)^2}$.

Solution: We have, $x^y = e^{x-y}$

Taking logarithm of both sides

$$y \log x = (x-y)\log e \qquad [\log e = 1]$$

$$\Rightarrow \quad y \log x = x - y$$

$$y = \frac{x}{1+\log x}$$

Differentiating w.r.t. x.

$$\frac{dy}{dx} = \frac{(1+\log x).1 - x\left(\frac{1}{x}\right)}{(1+\log x)^2}$$

$$= \frac{\log x}{(1+\log x)^2}.$$

7. *Find the values of a so that the function f defined by*

$$f(x) = \begin{cases} \dfrac{1-\cos 2ax}{x^2}; & x \neq 0 \\ 8; & x = 0 \end{cases} \text{ may be continuous at } x = 0$$

Solution: $\displaystyle \operatorname*{Lt}_{x\to 0} f(x) \quad \frac{1-\cos 2ax}{x^2} = \operatorname*{Lt}_{x\to 0} \frac{2\sin^2 ax}{x^2}$

$$= 2 \operatorname*{Lt}_{x\to 0}\left(\frac{\sin ax}{ax}\,a\right)^2 = 2a^2\left(\operatorname*{Lt}_{ax\to 0}\frac{\sin ax}{ax}\right)^2$$

$$= 2a^2$$

$$\operatorname*{Lt}_{x\to 0} f(x) = f(a) \Rightarrow 2a^2 = 8$$

$$\Rightarrow \quad a^2 = 4$$

$$\Rightarrow \quad a = \pm 2.$$

8. *If* $y = \sin^{-1}\left[\dfrac{5x+12\sqrt{1-x^2}}{13}\right]$. Find $\dfrac{dy}{dx}$.

Solution: $y = \sin^{-1}\left[\dfrac{5x+12\sqrt{1-x^2}}{13}\right]$

Let $\cos\alpha = \dfrac{5}{13}$ and $x = \sin\theta$

$$\sin\alpha = \frac{12}{13}$$

$$y = \sin^{-1}[\cos\alpha \sin\theta + \sin\alpha\cos\theta]$$

$$= \sin^{-1}[\sin(\theta+\alpha)]$$

$$= \theta + \alpha$$

$$= \sin^{-1} x + \cos^{-1}\frac{5}{13}.$$

$$\frac{dy}{dx} = \frac{1}{\sqrt{1-x^2}}.$$

9. *If* $f(1) = 4 : f'(1) = 2$. *Find the value of the derivative* $\log f(e^x)$ *w.r.t.* x *at the point* $x = 0$.

Solution: $f(1) = 4, \quad f'(1) = 2$

$$\frac{d}{dx} \log f(e^x) = \frac{1}{f(e^x)} \frac{d}{dx} f(e^x)$$

$$= e^x \times \frac{f'(e^x)}{f(e^x)}$$

At $\quad \frac{d}{dx} [\log f(e^n)]_{x=0} = e^0 \times \frac{f'(1)}{f(1)} = \frac{1 \times 2}{4} = \frac{1}{2}.$

10. *Find* $\frac{dy}{dx}$ *if* $(x^2 + y^2)^2 = xy$.

Solution: $(x^2 + y^2)^2 = xy$

Differentiating w.r.t. x

$$\Rightarrow \quad 2(x^2 + y^2) \frac{d}{dx} (x^2 + y^2) = y + x \frac{dy}{dx}$$

$$\Rightarrow \quad 2(x^2 + y^2) \left(2x + 2y \frac{dy}{dx}\right) = y + x \frac{dy}{dx}$$

$$\Rightarrow \quad \frac{dy}{dx} [4y(x^2 + y^2) - x] = y - 4x(x^2 + y^2)$$

$$\Rightarrow \quad \frac{dy}{dx} = \frac{y - 4x(x^2 + y^2)}{4y(x^2 + y^2) - x}.$$

SECTION-II

1. *Discuss the continuity of the following function at* $x = 0$

$$f(x) = \begin{cases} \dfrac{x^4 + 2x^3 + x^2}{\tan^{-1} x} & x \neq 0 \\ 0 & , x = 0 \end{cases}.$$

Solution: $\quad$ L.H.L. $= f(0-0) = \lim_{x \to 0^-} \frac{x^2 (x^2 + 2x + 1)}{\tan^{-1} x}$

$$= \lim_{h \to 0} \frac{h^2 (h^2 + (-2h) + 1)}{\tan^{-1} (-h)}$$

$$= \lim_{h \to 0} -\left(\frac{h}{\tan^{-1} h}\right) \lim_{h \to 0} h (h^2 - 2h + 1) \qquad \left[\lim_{h \to 0} \frac{\tan^{-1} h}{h} = 1\right]$$

$$= 0.$$

R.H.L. $= f(0+0) = \lim_{x \to 0^+} \frac{x^2 (x+1)^2}{\tan^{-1} x}$

$$= \lim_{h \to 0} \frac{h^2 (h^2 + 2h + 1)}{\tan^{-1} h}$$

$$= \lim_{h\to 0} \frac{h}{\tan^{-1} h} \lim_{h\to 0} h(h^2+2h+1)$$

$$= 0.$$

Also $\quad f(0) = 0$

$$\text{L.H.L} = \text{R.H.L.} = f(0)$$

$f(x)$ is continuous at $x = 0$.

2. *If* $y = (\cos x)^{\log x} + (\log x)^x$ find $\dfrac{dy}{dx}$.

Solution: $\quad y = (\cos x)^{\log x} + (\log x)^x$

Let $\quad y = u + v$

So, $\quad u = (\cos x)^{\log x}$ and $\quad v = (\log x)^x$

Now $\quad \dfrac{dy}{dx} = \dfrac{du}{dx} + \dfrac{dv}{dx} \quad (1)$

$$u = (\cos x)^{\log x}$$

$$\log u = \log x . \log(\cos x).$$

[Taking log on both sides and differentiating w.r.t. x]

$$\frac{1}{u}\frac{du}{dx} = \log x \frac{-\sin x}{\cos x} + \log \cos x \frac{1}{x}$$

$$\frac{du}{dx} = u\left[-\tan x \log x + \frac{\log \cos x}{x}\right]$$

$$\frac{du}{dx} = (\cos x)^{\log x}\left[-\tan x \log x + \frac{\log \cos x}{x}\right] \quad ...(i)$$

Again, $\quad v = (\log x)^x$

$\log v = x \log(\log x)$, (Taking log on both sides)

$$\frac{1}{v}\frac{dv}{dx} = \not{x}\frac{1}{\log x}\frac{1}{\not{x}} + \log(\log x) \quad \text{[Differentiating w.r.t. } x]$$

$$\Rightarrow \quad \frac{dv}{dx} = v\left[\frac{1}{\log x} + \log(\log x)\right] \quad ...(ii)$$

Hence, using (i), $\quad \dfrac{dy}{dx} = (\cos x)^{\log x}\left[\dfrac{\log(\cos x) - x\tan x \log x}{x}\right]$

$$+ (\log x)^x\left[\frac{1 + \log x \log(\log x)}{\log x}\right]. \quad \text{[From } (i) \text{ and } (ii)]$$

3. *For what value of K is the function*

$$f(x) = \begin{cases} \dfrac{1-\cos x}{8x^2} & x \neq 0 \\ k & x = 0 \end{cases}$$

continuous at $x = 0$.

Solution: $\quad f(0) = k$

$$\lim_{x\to 0} f(x) = \lim_{x\to 0} \frac{1-\cos 4x}{8x^2}$$

$$= \lim_{x \to 0} \frac{2\sin^2 2x}{2 \times 4x^2} \qquad [1 - \cos 2\theta = 2\sin^2\theta]$$

$$= \left(\lim_{x \to 0} \frac{\sin 2x}{2x}\right)^2 \qquad \left[\underset{\theta \to 0}{\text{Lt}} \frac{\sin\theta}{\theta} = 1\right]$$

$$= 1$$

For continuity at $x = 0$

$$\lim_{x \to 0} f(x) = f(0) = k$$

$$k = 1.$$

4. *Verify Lagrange's mean value theorem for the following function*

$$f(x) = x^2 + 2x + 3 \text{ for } [4, 6].$$

Solution: (*i*) Given function $f(x) = x^2 + 2x + 3$ is an algebraic polynomial. Therefore it is continuous in [4, 6] and differentiable in (4, 6).

(*ii*) $f(4) = (4)^2 + 2 \times 4 + 3 = 27$

and $f(6) = 51$

there exists some c in (4, 6) such that

$$f'(c) = \frac{f(6) - f(4)}{6 - 4}$$

$$f'(x) = 2x + 2 \Rightarrow f'(c) = 2c + 2$$

$$2c + 2 = \frac{51 - 27}{2} = 12$$

$$c = 5 \in (4, 6)$$

Hence L.M.V.T. is verified.

5. *If* $x^m y^n = (x + y)^{m+n}$, prove that $\frac{dy}{dx} = \frac{y}{x}$.

Solution: $x^m y^n = (x + y)^{m+n}$ (given)

Taking log on both sides,

$$\log(x^m y^n) = \log(x + y)^{m+n} \qquad [\text{Using } \log m^n = n \log m]$$

$$m \log x + n \log y = (m + n) \log(x + y) \qquad [\log(m \,.\, n) = \log m + \log n]$$

Differentiating both sides w.r.t. x

$$\frac{m}{x} + \frac{n}{y}\frac{dy}{dx} = (m + n)\frac{1}{x + y} \cdot \frac{d}{dx}(x + y)$$

$$\left[\frac{n}{y} - \frac{m + n}{x + y}\right]\frac{dy}{dx} = \frac{m + n}{x + y} - \frac{m}{x}$$

$$\left[\frac{nx - my}{y(x + y)}\right] \cdot \frac{dy}{dx} = \frac{nx - my}{x(x + y)}$$

$$\frac{dy}{dx} = \frac{y}{x}.$$

6. *Find* $\frac{dy}{dx}$ *if* $y = \tan^{-1}\left[\frac{\sqrt{1 + x^2} + \sqrt{1 - x^2}}{\sqrt{1 + x^2} - \sqrt{1 - x^2}}\right]$ $0 < |x| < 1$.

Solution: $y = \tan^{-1}\left[\dfrac{\sqrt{1+x^2}+\sqrt{1-x^2}}{\sqrt{1+x^2}-\sqrt{1-x^2}}\right]$

put $x^2 = \cos\theta$ or $\theta = \cos^{-1} x^2$

$$y = \tan^{-1}\left[\frac{\sqrt{1+\cos\theta}+\sqrt{1-\cos\theta}}{\sqrt{1+\cos\theta}-\sqrt{1-\cos\theta}}\right]$$

$$y = \tan^{-1}\left[\frac{\sqrt{2\cos^2\frac{\theta}{2}}+\sqrt{2\sin^2\frac{\theta}{2}}}{\sqrt{2\cos^2\frac{\theta}{2}}-\sqrt{2\sin^2\frac{\theta}{2}}}\right]$$ [Using $1 + \cos\theta = 2\cos^2\theta/2$
$1 - \cos\theta = 2\sin^2\theta/2$]

$$= \tan^{-1}\left[\frac{\sqrt{2}\left(\cos\frac{\theta}{2}+\sin\frac{\theta}{2}\right)}{\sqrt{2}\left(\cos\frac{\theta}{2}-\sin\frac{\theta}{2}\right)}\right]$$ [Dividing N^r and D^r by $\cos\theta/2$]

$$= \tan^{-1}\left[\frac{1+\tan\frac{\theta}{2}}{1-\tan\frac{\theta}{2}}\right] = \left[\frac{\tan\frac{\pi}{4}+\tan\frac{\theta}{2}}{1-\tan\frac{\pi}{4}.\tan\frac{\theta}{2}}\right]$$

$$y = \tan^{-1}\left[\tan\left(\frac{\pi}{4}+\frac{\theta}{2}\right)\right]$$

$$y = \frac{\pi}{4}+\frac{\theta}{2} = \frac{\pi}{4}+\frac{1}{2}\cos^{-1} x^2$$

Differentiating w.r.t. x

$$\frac{dy}{dx} = \frac{-1}{2\sqrt{1-(x^2)^2}}\times 2x = \frac{-x}{\sqrt{1-x^4}}.$$

7. *If $x = a \sin pt$ and $y = b \cos pt$. Find the value of $\dfrac{d^2y}{dx^2}$ at $t = 0$.*

Solution: We have $x = a\sin pt$ and $y = b\cos pt$.

$$\frac{dx}{dt} = ap\cos pt \quad\text{and}\quad \frac{dy}{dt} = -bp\sin pt$$

$$\frac{dy}{dx} = -\frac{b}{a}\tan pt$$

Differentiating again

$$-\frac{b}{a}\sec^2 pt\times\frac{dt}{dx} = -\frac{b}{a}\sec^2 pt\times\frac{1}{ap\cos pt}$$

$$= -\frac{b}{a^2}\sec^3 pt$$

At $t = 0$ $$\left.\frac{d^2y}{dx^2}\right]_{t=0} = -\frac{b}{a^2}[\sec 0]^3$$

$$= -\frac{b}{a^2}.$$

8. *If $f(x)$ is defined, the following is continuous at $x = 0$, find the value of a, b, c.*

$$f(x) = \begin{cases} \dfrac{\sin(a+1)x + \sin x}{x} & \text{if } x<0 \\ c & \text{if } x=0 \\ \dfrac{\sqrt{x+bx^2} - \sqrt{x}}{bx^{3/2}} & \text{if } x>0 \end{cases}.$$

Solution: We have to find a, b, c if $f(x)$ is continuous at $x = 0$.

$$\text{L.H.L.} = \lim_{x\to 0^-} \frac{\sin(a+1)x + \sin x}{x}$$

$$= \lim_{x\to 0^-} \left[(a+1)\frac{\sin(a+1)x}{(a+1)x} + \frac{\sin x}{x}\right] \qquad \left[\operatorname*{Lt}_{\theta\to 0} \frac{\sin\theta}{\theta} = 1\right]$$

$$= a + 1 + 1 = a + 2$$

$$\text{R.H.L.} = \lim_{x\to 0^+} \left[\frac{\sqrt{x+bx^2} - \sqrt{x}}{bx^{3/2}}\right]$$

$$= \lim_{x\to 0^+} \frac{\left(\sqrt{x+bx^2} - \sqrt{x}\right)\left(\sqrt{x+bx^2} + \sqrt{x}\right)}{bx^{3/2}\left(\sqrt{x+bx^2} + \sqrt{x}\right)}$$

$$= \lim_{x\to 0^+} \frac{x+bx^2 - x}{bx^{3/2}\left(\sqrt{x+bx^2} + \sqrt{x}\right)}$$

$$= \frac{1}{2}$$

and $\quad f(0) = c$

$$\text{L.H.L.} = \text{R.H.L.} = f(0)$$

$$c = \frac{1}{2}$$

$$a + 2 = \frac{1}{2}$$

$$a = -\frac{3}{2}$$

b can take any value except 0.

9. *For a positive constant a find $\dfrac{dy}{dx}$ where $y = a^{t + 1/t}$ and $x = \left(t + \dfrac{1}{t}\right)^a$.*

Solution: y and x are defined for all real $t \neq 0$

For $\quad y = a^{t + 1/t}$

$$\Rightarrow \quad \frac{dy}{dt} = a^{t + 1/t}\left(1 - \frac{1}{t^2}\right)\log a$$

For $x = \left(t + \frac{1}{t}\right)^a$

$$\frac{dx}{dt} = a\left[t + \frac{1}{t}\right]^{a-1} \frac{d}{dt}\left(t + \frac{1}{t}\right)$$

$$= a\left[t + \frac{1}{t}\right]^{a-1}\left[1 - \frac{1}{t^2}\right]$$

$\frac{dx}{dt} \neq 0$ only if $t \neq \pm 1$

$$\frac{dy}{dx} = \frac{dy/dt}{dx/dt} = \frac{a^{t+1/t}\left(1 - \frac{1}{t^2}\right)\log a}{a\left[t + \frac{1}{t}\right]^{a-1}\left[1 - \frac{1}{t^2}\right]}$$

$$= \frac{a^{t+1/t}\log a}{a\left[t + \frac{1}{t}\right]^{a-1}}.$$

10. *Discuss the continuity of the function at $x = 0$,*

$$f(x) = \begin{cases} \dfrac{\sin 3x}{\tan 2x} & \text{if} \quad x<0 \\ \dfrac{3}{2} & \text{if} \quad x=0\,. \\ \dfrac{\log(1+3x)}{e^{2x}-1} & \text{if} \quad x>0 \end{cases}$$

Solution: L.H.L. at $x = 0$

$$= \lim_{x\to 0^-} f(x) = \lim_{x\to 0^-} \frac{\sin 3x}{\tan 2x}$$

$$= \underset{x\to 0^-}{\text{Lt}} \left[\left(\frac{\sin 3x}{3x}\right)\frac{3x}{2x}\left(\frac{2x}{\tan 2x/2x}\right)\right]$$

$$= \left[\text{Using } \underset{\theta+0}{\text{Lt}} \frac{\sin\theta}{\theta} = 1,\ \underset{\theta+0}{\text{Lt}} \frac{\tan\theta}{\theta} = 1\right]$$

$$= \frac{3}{2}$$

R.H.L. at $x = 0$

$$= \lim_{x\to 0^+} f(x)$$

$$= \lim_{x\to 0^+} \log\frac{(1+3x)}{e^{2x}-1}$$

$$= \frac{3}{2} \lim_{x\to 0^+} \log \frac{1+3x}{3x} \lim_{x\to 0^+} \frac{1}{e^{2x} - \frac{1}{2x}}$$

$$= \frac{3}{2}.1.1 \qquad \left[\therefore \lim_{t\to 0} \log \frac{(1+t)}{t} = 1;\ \lim_{t\to 0} \frac{e^t - 1}{t} = 1\right]$$

$$f(0) = \frac{3}{2}$$

$$\lim_{x\to 0^-} f(x) = \lim_{x\to 0^+} f(x) = f(0)$$

Hence $f(x)$ is continuous at $x = 0$.

11. *Find the value of a and b such that the function defined by*

$$f(x) = \begin{cases} 5 & : \text{of } x \le 2 \\ ax+b & : \text{of } 2<x<10 \\ 21 & : \text{of } x \ge 10 \end{cases}$$

is a continuous function.

Solution. The given function is continuous at $x = 2$ and $x = 5$

i.e. $\qquad \underset{h+0}{\text{Lt}} f(2+h) = \underset{h+0}{\text{Lt}} f(2-h) = f(2)$

and $\qquad \underset{h+0}{\text{Lt}} f(5+h) = \underset{h+0}{\text{Lt}} f(5-h) = f(5)$

For the continuity at $x = 2$

Now, $\qquad \text{RHL} = \underset{h+0}{\text{Lt}} f(2+h) = \underset{h+0}{\text{Lt}} a(2+h) + b = 2a + b.$

$\qquad \text{LHL} = \underset{h+0}{\text{Lt}} f(2-h) = 5$

Hence, $\qquad 2a + b = 5 \qquad$ ...(*i*)

For the continuity at $x = 5$

$\qquad \text{RHL} = \underset{h+0}{\text{Lt}} f(10+h) = 21$

$\qquad \text{LHL} = \underset{h+0}{\text{Lt}} f(10-h) = \underset{h+0}{\text{Lt}} a(10-h) + b = 10a + b$

Hence, $\qquad 10a + b = 21 \qquad$ ...(*ii*)

From (*i*) and (*ii*), we get

$$\begin{aligned} 2a + b &= 5 \\ 10a + b &= 21 \\ \hline +8a &= +16 \end{aligned}$$

$\Rightarrow \qquad a = 2$

Putting $a = 2$ in equation (*i*)

$$2a + b = 5$$

$\Rightarrow \qquad 2 \times 2 + b = 5$

$\Rightarrow \qquad b = 1$

Hence $\qquad \left.\begin{aligned} a &= 2 \\ b &= 1 \end{aligned}\right\}$

SECTION-I

1. If $x\sqrt{1+y} + y\sqrt{1+x} = 0, -1 < x < 1$ then show that $\dfrac{dy}{dx} = \dfrac{-1}{(1+x)^2}$.
2. If $\cos y = x\cos(a+y)$ where $\cos a = \pm 1$ prove that

$$\frac{dy}{dx} = \frac{\cos^2(a+y)}{\sin a}.$$

3. Differentiate $\sin^4(\cos(x^2))$ w.r.t. x.
4. Find left hand and right hand derivatives of

$$f(x) = \begin{cases} x-3, & x<2 \\ 2x-5, & x\geq 2 \end{cases} \text{ at } x = 2.$$

Hence show that f is not derivable at $x = 2$.

5. Differentiate $\tan^{-1}\left(\dfrac{\sqrt{1+\sin x}}{\sqrt{1-\sin x}}\right)$ w.r.t. x.
6. If $x^{2/3} + y^{2/3} = a^{2/3}$, find $\dfrac{dy}{dx}$.
7. If $\sin xy + \cos xy = 1$ and $\tan xy \neq 1$ prove that $\dfrac{dy}{dx} = -\dfrac{y}{x}$.
8. Differentiate $\log\left(x+\sqrt{x^2+a^2}\right)$ w.r.t. x.
9. For $y = (\sin x)^{\sin^{-1}x}$. Find $\dfrac{dy}{dx}$.
10. Find $\dfrac{dy}{dx}$ when $x = a\dfrac{(1+t^2)}{1-t^2}$, $y = \dfrac{2t}{1-t^2}$.

ANSWERS

3. $-2x\sin x^2\cos(\cos x^2)$ 5. $\dfrac{1}{2}$ 6. $-\sqrt[3]{\dfrac{y}{x}}$

8. $\dfrac{1}{\sqrt{x^2-a^2}}$ 9. $(\sin x)^{\sin^{-1}x}\left[\sin^{-1}x.\cot x + \dfrac{\log(\sin x)}{\sqrt{1-x^2}}\right]$ 10. $\dfrac{2t}{1+t^2}$

SECTION-II

1. If $y = \tan^{-1}\left[\dfrac{\sqrt{a}-\sqrt{x}}{1+\sqrt{ax}}\right]$, find $\dfrac{dy}{dx}$.
2. If $(\sin x)^y = (\cos x)^{\sin y}$, find $\dfrac{dy}{dx}$.
3. If $x = \sin t$ and $y = \sin pt$ then prove that $(1-x^2)\,y_2 - x\,y_1 + p^2\,y = 0$.
4. Use long range mean value theorem to determine a point on the curve $y = \sqrt{x-2}$ defined on [2, 3]. Where the tangent is parallel to the chord joining the end points of the chord on the curve.

5. Find all the points of discontinuity of the function f defined by

$$f(x) = \begin{cases} x+2 & \text{if } x<1 \\ 0 & \text{if } x=1 \\ x-2 & \text{if } x>1 \end{cases}.$$

6. If $\cos y = x \cos (a + y)$ where $\cos a \neq \pm 1$ prove that

mean value theorem $\frac{dy}{dx} = \frac{\cos^2 (a+y)}{\sin a}$.

7. Determine if f defined by $f(x) = \begin{cases} x^2 \sin \frac{1}{x} & \text{if } x \neq 0 \\ 0 & \text{if } x=0 \end{cases}$ is a continuous function.

8. Differentiate $(x \cos x)^x + (x \sin x)^{1/x}$.

9. $x^y + y^x = a^b$ find $\frac{dy}{dx}$.

10. Given that $f(x) = \begin{cases} \frac{1-\cos 4x}{x^2} & \text{if } x<0 \\ a & \text{if } x=0 \\ \frac{\sqrt{x}}{\sqrt{16--}+\sqrt{x}-4} \end{cases}$ is continuous at $x = 0$. Find a.

ANSWERS

1. $\frac{-1}{2\sqrt{x}(1+x)}$

2. $\frac{\cos y \cot x + \sin y \tan x}{\cos y \log (\cos x) + \sin y \log (\sin x)}$

4. $\left(\frac{9}{4}, \frac{1}{2}\right)$

5. $x = 1$

8. $\frac{(x\cos x)^x [1 - x\tan x + \log (x \cos x)] + (x \sin x)^{1/x} [x \cos x + 1 - \log (x \sin x)]}{x^2}$

9. $-\left[\frac{yx^{y-1} + y^x \log y}{x^y \log x + xy^{x-1}}\right]$

10. $a = 8$.

HOTS

1. Let $f(x) = \frac{(x^3 - 6x^2 + 11x - 6)}{x^3 - 6x^2 + 11x - 6}$. Find the set of points 'a' where $\lim_{x \to a} f(x)$ does not exist.

2. Evaluate $\lim_{x \to 0} \frac{(1+x)^{1/x} + e(x-1)}{x}$.

3. Evaluate $\lim_{x \to 0} \frac{ae^x - b}{x} = 2$. Find a and b.

4. If $\lim_{x \to 0} (1 + a \sin x) \cos ax = 3$. Then find a.

ANSWERS

1. $\{1, 2, 3\}$
2. $\dfrac{e}{2}$
3. $a = 2$ and $b = 2$
4. in 3

❑❑❑

CHAPTER 6

APPLICATIONS OF DERIVATIVES

1. RATE OF CHANGE OF QUANTITIES

Let $y = f(x)$, be a relation between two variables, x and y. Then dy/dx represents the rate of change of y w.r.t. x and its value at $x = a$ is denoted by $\left[\frac{dy}{dx}\right]_{x=a}$.

If $x = f(t)$, $y = g(t)$ then we have $\frac{dy}{dx} = \frac{\frac{dy}{dt}}{\frac{dx}{dt}} = \frac{dy}{dt} \cdot \frac{dt}{dx}$.

Some useful results:

- Area of square $= a^2$, where a is the side.
  and perimeter $= 4a$.
- Area of rectangle $= a.b$
  and Perimeter $= 2\,(a + b)$, (where a and b are length & breath).
- Area of trapezium $= \frac{1}{2}$ (sum of parallel sides) × perpendicular distance between them.
- Area of circle $= \pi r^2$, circumference of a circle $= 2\pi r$, where r is the radius.
- Volume of sphere $= \frac{4}{3}\pi r^3$, surface area $= 4\pi r^2$, $r =$ radius.
- Surface area of right circular cylinder $= 2\pi rh + 2\pi r^2$, curved surface area $= 2\pi rh$.
  Volume $= \pi r^2 h$, where $r =$ radius and $h =$ height.
- Volume of right circular cone $= \frac{1}{3}\pi r^2 h$. Curved surface area $= \pi rl$, where $l =$ slaint height.
  Surface area $= \pi rl + \pi r^2$.
- Volume of a cube $= a^3$.
  Surface area $= 6a^2$, where $a =$ side.
- Area of an equilateral triangle $= \frac{\sqrt{3}}{4}$ (side)^2, Perimeter = 3a.

2. TANGENTS AND NORMALS

- Equation of tangent to the curve $y = f(x)$ at the point (x_1, y_1) is given by

$$y - y_1 = \left.\frac{dy}{dx}\right]_{(x_1, y_1)} (x - x_1)$$

- Equation of Normal to the curve, $y = f(x)$ at the pt. (x_1, y_1) is given by:

$$y - y_1 = \left.\frac{-dx}{dy}\right]_{(x_1, y_1)} (x - x_1)$$

- When tangent is parallel to x-axis: $\frac{dy}{dx} = 0$.

- When tangent is parallel to y-axis: $\frac{dx}{dy} = 0$.
- Tangents at a curve will be parallel
  if $m_1 = m_2$
  and perpendicular (orthogonal)
  if $m_1 \times m_2 = -1$

APPROXIMATION

Since $f'(x) = \lim_{\Delta x \to 0} \frac{f(x+\Delta x) - f(x)}{\Delta x}$, we can say that $f'(x)$ is approximately equal to $\frac{f(x+\Delta x) - f(x)}{\Delta x}$

$\Rightarrow$ Approximate value of $f(x+\Delta x)$ is

$$= f(x) + \Delta x . f'(x)$$

$$\Rightarrow \quad f(x+\Delta x) = f(x) + \Delta x . f'(x).$$

INCREASING AND DECREASING FUNCTIONS

Increasing Function$\rightarrow$A function $f(x)$ defined on $]a, b[$ is said to be increasing if

$x_1 < x_2 \Rightarrow f(x_1) \le f(x_2)$ for all $x_1, x_2 \in]a, b[$.

$x_1 > x_2 \Rightarrow f(x_1) \ge f(x) \ge f(x_2)$ for all $x_1, x_2 \in]a, b[$.

Strictly increasing Function$\rightarrow$A function $f(x)$ is defined on $]a, b[$ is called strictly increasing if

$x_1 < x_2 \Rightarrow f(x_1) < f(x_2)$ for all $x_1, x_2 \in]a, b[$

or $x_1 > x_2 \Rightarrow f(x_1) > f(x_2)$ for all $x_1, x_2 \in]a, b[$

Alternatively$\rightarrow f(x)$ is increasing in $]a, b[$ if $f'(x) > 0$ for $a < x < b$.

Decreasing Function$\rightarrow$A function $f(x)$ is defined on $]a, b[$ is called decreasing if

$x_1 < x_2 \Rightarrow f(x_1) \ge f(x_2)$ for all $x_1, x_2 \in]a, b[$

or $x_1 > x_2 \Rightarrow f(x_1) \le f(x_2)$ for all $x_1, x_2 \in]a, b[$

Strictly decreasing Function$\rightarrow$A function $f(x)$ defined on $]a, b[$ is said to be strictly decreasing if

$x_1 < x_2 \Rightarrow f(x_1) > f(x_2)$ for all $x_1, x_2 \in]a, b[$

or $x_1 > x_2 \Rightarrow f(x_1) < f(x_2)$ for all $x_1, x_2 \in]a, b[$

Alternatively$\rightarrow f(x)$ is decreasing in $]a, b[$ if $f'(x) < 0$ for $a < x < b$.

If $(x-a)(x-b) > 0$ and $a > b$

$\Rightarrow$ $x > a$ or $x < b$

$\Rightarrow$ $x \in (a, \infty)$ or $(-\infty, b)$

$\Rightarrow$ $x \in (-\infty, b) \cup (b, \infty)$

If $(x-a)(x-b) < 0$

$\Rightarrow$ $a < x < b$ if $a < b$.

MAXIMA AND MINIMA

First Derivative Test. In order to find the extremum values of a given function $f(x)$ by using the first derivative test, we proceed according to the following steps.

(*a*) Find $f'(x)$

(*b*) Solve $f'(x) = 0$. Let its roots be *a, b, c,* etc. Then these are the candidates for maxima or minima.

(*c*) We test the function at each one of these values. Let us take $x = c$.

(*d*) Determine the sign of $f'(x)$ for values of x slightly less than c and for values of x slightly greater than c.

Conclusion→(*i*) If $f'(x)$ changes sign from +ve to –ve as x increases through $x = c$ as a point of maximum.

(*ii*) If $f'(x)$ changes sign from negative to positive as x increases through c then $x = c$ is a point of minimum.

(*iii*) If $f'(x)$ does not change sign as x increases through c, we say that x is neither a point of maximum nor a point of minimum. In this case, $x = c$ is called a point of inflection.

SECOND ORDER DERIVATIVE TEST

Working rule for finding Extremum values.

(1) Find $f'(x)$.

(2) Solve $f'(x) = 0$

Each value of x so obtained is a candidate for maximum or minimum. Let $x = c$ be one of its points.

(3) Find $f''(x)$ and put $x = c$ to find $f''(c)$.

Now, if $f''(c) < 0$ then $x = c$ is a point of local maximum.

if if $f''(c) > 0$ then $x = c$ is a point of local minimum.

if if $f''(c) = 0$ then use the first derivative test. (point of inflexion)

SOLVED QUESTIONS

SECTION-II

1. *The volume of cube is increasing at the rate of* 7 cm^3/sec. *How fast is the surface area increasing when the length of an edge is* 12 cm.

Solution: Let x be length of an edge of cube at time t.

So its surface areas $S = 6x^2$ ...(*i*)

Volume $V = x^3$ ...(*ii*)

Differentiating (*ii*) w.r.t. t we get

$$\frac{dv}{dt} = 3x^2 \frac{dx}{dt}$$

$$\frac{dv}{dt} = 7 \text{ cm}^3/\text{sec} = 3x^2 \frac{dx}{dt}$$

$$\frac{dx}{dt} = \frac{7}{3x^2}$$

Differentiate (*i*) w.r.t. t

$$\frac{ds}{dt} = 12x\frac{dx}{dt} = 12x \times \frac{7}{3x^2}$$

$$= 28x$$

When $x = 12$, $$\left.\frac{ds}{dt}\right]_{x=12} = \frac{28}{12} = \frac{7}{3}$$

Surface area is increasing at the rate of $\frac{7}{3}$ cm^2/sec. when length of edge = 12 cm.

2. *A water tank has the shape of inverted right circular cone with its axis vertical and vertex lower most. Its semivertical angle is* $\tan^{-1}(0.5)$. *Water is poured into it at a constant rate of* 5 *cubic per minute. Find the rate at which the level of water is rising at the instant. When the depth of water in tank is* 10 m.

Solution: At any time t, water forms a right circular cone of semivertical angle $\tan^{-1}(0.5)$. Let r metres be the radius of this cone and h metres be its height.

$$\alpha = \tan^{-1} 0.5$$

$$\tan\alpha = 0.5 = \frac{1}{2}$$

$$\tan\alpha = \frac{r}{h} = \frac{1}{2}$$

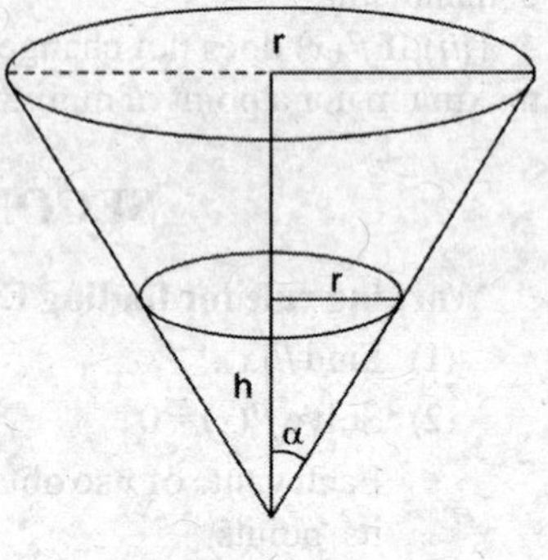

Fig. 6.1

Volume of cone $\quad V = \frac{1}{3}\pi r^2 h$

$\Rightarrow \quad r = \frac{h}{2}$

Volume of cone at any time t.

$$V = \frac{1}{3}\pi\left(\frac{h}{12}\right)^2 \times h = \frac{\pi}{12}h^3.$$

Diff. w.r.t., we get $\quad \frac{dV}{dt} = \frac{\pi}{12} 3h^2 \frac{dh}{dt}$

$$= \frac{\pi}{4}h^2\frac{dh}{dt}.$$

But $\quad \frac{dV}{dt} = 5 \text{ m}^3/\text{min}$

$\therefore \quad 5 = \frac{\pi}{4}h^2\frac{dh}{dt} \Rightarrow \frac{dh}{dt} = \frac{20}{\pi h^2}$

$h = 10$ m $\quad \frac{dh}{dt} = \frac{20}{\pi\times 10^2} = \frac{1}{5\pi}.$

Water level is rising at the rate $\frac{1}{5\pi}$ m/min.

3. *Prove that the curves* $x = y^2$ *and* $xy = k$ *intersect at right angles if* $8k^2 = 1$.

Solution: Equation of given curves are

$$x = y^2 \qquad ...(i)$$

and $\quad xy = k \qquad ...(ii)$

From (*i*) and (*ii*), we get

$$y^3 = k \text{ or } y = k^{1/3}$$

$$x = (k^{1/3})^2$$

$$x = k^{2/3}.$$

$\therefore$ Point of intersection is $(k^{2/3}, k^{1/3})$.

Differentiating (*i*) and (*ii*) we get

$\Rightarrow \quad \frac{dx}{dy} = 2y$ or $\frac{dy}{dx} = \frac{1}{2y} = \frac{1}{2}k^{-1/3}.$

and $\Rightarrow \quad x\frac{dy}{dx} + y.1 = 0$ or $\frac{dy}{dx} = \frac{-y}{x} = -k^{1/3}.$

If (i) and (ii) intersect at right angles

$$\left(\frac{1}{2}k^{-1/3}\right)(-k^{1/3}) = -1 \qquad \text{[Two lines intersect at 90°, if } m_1m_2 = -1]$$

$$\frac{1}{2}k^{-2/3} = 1 \qquad \text{where } m = \text{slope}$$

$$2k^{2/3} = 1$$

$$8k^2 = 1.$$

4. *Find the intervals in which function*

$$f(x) = 2x^3 - 9x^2 + 12x + 15 \textit{ is}$$

(i) increasing $\quad$ (ii) decreasing

Solution: $f(x) = 2x^3 - 9x^2 + 12x + 15$

Differentiating w.r.t. x

$$f'(x) = 6x^2 - 18x + 12$$
$$= 6(x^2 - 3x + 2)$$
$$= 6(x-1)(x-2)$$

(i) For increasing function

$\Rightarrow$ $f'(x) > 0$

$\Rightarrow$ $6(x-1)(x-2) > 0$

$x > 2$ and $x < 1$

$f(x)$ is increasing function for $(-\infty, 1) \cup (2, \infty)$

(ii) For decreasing function

$\Rightarrow$ $f'(x) < 0$

$\Rightarrow$ $6(x-1)(x-2) < 0$

$1 < x < 2$

$f(x)$ is decreasing function in interval $(1, 2)$.

5. *At what points on the curve $x^2 + y^2 - 2x - 4y + 1 = 0$, the tangents are parallel to y-axis.*

Solution: Let $P(x_1, y_1)$ be required point.

Given curve is $x^2 + y^2 - 2x - 4y + 1 = 0$ ...(i)

Diff. (i) w.r.t. x, we get

$$2x + 2y\frac{dy}{dx} - 2 - 4\frac{dy}{dx} = 0$$

$$\frac{dy}{dx} = \frac{1-x}{y-2} \quad \Rightarrow \quad \frac{dx}{dy} = \frac{y-2}{1-x}$$

$$\Rightarrow \quad \left(\frac{dy}{dx}\right)_P = \frac{y_1-2}{1-x_1}$$

Since tangent at P is parallel to y-axis

$$\left(\frac{dy}{dx}\right)_P = 0 \quad \Rightarrow \quad \frac{y_1-2}{1-x_1} = 0$$

$$y_1 = 2$$

As P lies on the curve

$$x_1^2 + y_1^2 - 2x_1 - 4y_1 + 1 = 0$$

$\Rightarrow$ $x_1^2 + 2^2 - 2x_1 - 4.2 + 1 = 0$

$\Rightarrow$ $x_1^2 - 2x_1 - 3 = 0$

$\Rightarrow$ $x_1 = 3, -1.$

Required points are $(3, 2)$ and $(-1, 2)$.

6. *Find maximum and minimum values of function*

$$f(x) = \sin x + \frac{1}{2}\cos 2x \text{ in } 0 \le x \le \frac{\pi}{2}.$$

Solution: $$f(x) = \sin x + \frac{1}{2}\cos 2x \qquad ...(i)$$

Given function is differentiable for all x in $\left[0, \frac{\pi}{2}\right]$.

Diff. (i) w.r.t. x

$$f'(x) = \cos x + \frac{1}{2}(-\sin 2x)\,2$$
$$= \cos x - \sin 2x$$
$$f'(x) = 0$$

$\Rightarrow$ $\cos x - 2\sin x\cos x = 0$

$\Rightarrow$ $\cos x\,(1 - 2\sin x) = 0$

$\Rightarrow$ $\cos x = 0$ or $\sin x = \frac{1}{2}$

$\Rightarrow$ $x = \frac{\pi}{2}$ or $x = \frac{\pi}{6}$

But $x = \frac{\pi}{2}$ is an end point and $\frac{\pi}{6}$ lies in $\left[0, \frac{\pi}{2}\right]$, therefore $\frac{\pi}{6}$ is the only critical point.

Further $$f\left(\frac{\pi}{2}\right) = \sin\frac{\pi}{2} + \frac{1}{2}\cos\pi\ \frac{1}{2} = \frac{1}{2}$$

$\Rightarrow$ $$f\left(\frac{\pi}{6}\right) = \sin\frac{\pi}{6} + \frac{1}{2}\cos\frac{\pi}{3} = \frac{1}{2} + \frac{1}{2}\times\frac{1}{2} = \frac{3}{4}.$$

$\Rightarrow$ $$f(0) = \sin 0 + \frac{1}{2}\cos 0 = \frac{1}{2}$$

Maximum value is $\frac{3}{4}$ and minimum value is $\frac{1}{2}$

Point of maxima is $\frac{\pi}{6}$

Point of minima are $0, \frac{\pi}{2}$.

7. *A ladder* 10 m *long is placed against a wall. The ladder is pulled slowly from the bottom along the ground and away from the wall at the rate of* 15 m/minute. *Find the rate at which height of the wall is decreasing when the bottom of the ladder is* 6 m *away from the wall.*

Solution: Let AB be the ladder placed against the wall, such that $AO = x$ metres and $BO = y$ metres.

Then $$OA^2 + OB^2 = AB^2 = 10^2 \text{ (Pythagoras Theorem).}$$
$$x^2 + y^2 = (10)^2 \qquad ...(i)$$
$$\frac{dx}{dt} = 1.5 \text{ m/min}$$

Diff. (i) w.r.t. t

$$2x\frac{dx}{dt} + 2y\frac{dy}{dt} = 0$$

$$x\frac{dx}{dt}+y\frac{dy}{dt}=0 \quad ...(ii)$$

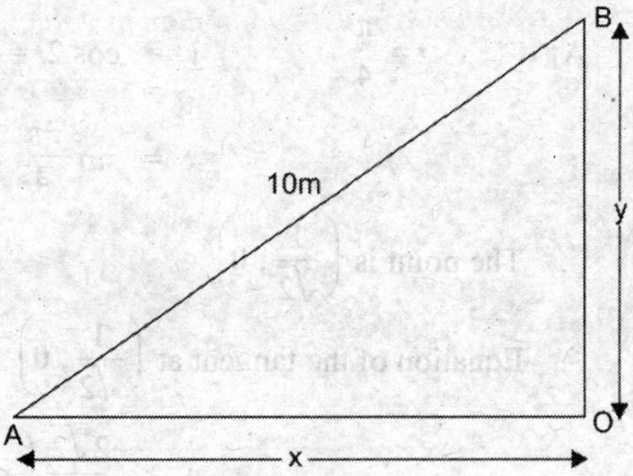

Fig. 6.2

We are given $x = 6$ m

$\therefore$ From (*i*)

$$(6)^2 + y^2 = 100$$
$$y^2 = 64$$
$$y = 8 \text{ m}$$

Substituting $x = 6$ and $y = 8$ and we get

$$6 \times 15 + 8\frac{dy}{dt} = 0$$
$$\frac{dy}{dt} = -\frac{9}{8}$$

Hence the height of wall is decreasing at the rate $\frac{9}{8}$ m/min.

8. *Find the approximate value of* $\sqrt{0.037}$.

Solution: Let $\quad y = \sqrt{x} \quad ...(i)$

Diff. (*i*) w.r.t. x, we get

$$\Rightarrow \quad \frac{dy}{dx} = \frac{1}{2\sqrt{x}}$$

Let $\quad x = 0.04$ and $x + \delta x = 0.037$

So that $\quad \delta x = -0.003.$

For $x = 0.04$, $\quad y = \sqrt{0.04} = 0.2$

$$\delta y = \frac{dy}{dx}\delta x = \frac{1}{2\sqrt{x}}\delta x = \frac{1}{2\sqrt{0.04}} \times (-0.03)$$
$$= -\frac{3}{400} = -0.0075.$$

Now $\quad y + \delta y = \sqrt{x+\delta x}$

$$0.2 - 0.0075 = \sqrt{0.037}$$
$$\sqrt{0.037} = 0.1925 \text{ approximately.}$$

9. *Find the equation of tangent to the curve* $y = \cos 2t$, $x = \sin 3t$ *at* $t = \frac{\pi}{4}$.

Solution: Given equations of curve are

$$y = \cos 2t \quad \text{and} \quad x = \sin 3t$$
$$\frac{dy}{dt} = -2\sin 2t \quad \text{and} \quad \frac{dx}{dt} = 3\cos 3t$$
$$\frac{dy}{dx} = \frac{dy}{dt} \div \frac{dx}{dt} = -\frac{2}{3}\frac{\sin 2t}{\cos 3t}$$
$$\left.\frac{dy}{dx}\right]_{t=\pi/4} = \frac{-2\sin\frac{\pi}{2}}{3\cos 3\frac{\pi}{4}} = \frac{2\sqrt{2}}{3}$$

At $\quad t = \frac{\pi}{4} \quad y = \cos 2t = \cos \frac{\pi}{2} = 0$

$$x = \sin \frac{3\pi}{4} = \frac{1}{\sqrt{2}}$$

$\therefore$ The point is $\left(\frac{1}{\sqrt{2}}, 0\right)$

$\therefore$ Equation of the tangent at $\left(\frac{1}{\sqrt{2}}, 0\right)$ is

$$y - 0 = \frac{2\sqrt{2}}{3}\left(x - \frac{1}{\sqrt{2}}\right)$$

$$2\sqrt{2}x - 3y - 2 = 0$$

10. *Find the equation of tangent lines to the curve $y = 4x^3 - 3x + 5$, which are perpendicular to the line*

$$9y + x + 3 = 0.$$

Solution: Given curve is $y = 4x^3 - 3x + 5$ ...(*i*)
which is perpendicular to $9y + x + 3 = 0$ ...(*ii*)

Slope of this line $= \frac{-\text{co.eff. of } x}{\text{co.eff. of } y} = -\frac{1}{9}$.

Slope of tangent $= \frac{dy}{dx} = 12x^2 - 3$ [Differentating (*i*) w.r.t. *x*]

Tangent is perpendicular to line [Two lines are perpendicular if $m_1 \times m_2 = -1$]

$$(12x^2 - 3) \times -\frac{1}{9} = -1$$

$\Rightarrow \quad 12x^2 = 12$

$\Rightarrow \quad x^2 = 1$

$x = +1, -1.$

Putting $\quad x = 1$ in (*i*) we get

$y = 4 \times (1)^3 = 3 \times (1) + 5 = 6$

Put $\quad x = -1$

$y = 4(-1)^3 - 3(-1) + 5$

$= 4$

Required points are (1, 6) and (–1, 4)
Slope of curve = 9
Equation of tangent at (1, 6) is

$$y - 6 = 9(x - 1)$$

$$9x - y - 3 = 0$$

Equation of tangent at (–1, 4) is

$$y - 4 = 9[x - (-1)]$$

$$9x - y + 13 = 0$$

Hence, equations of required tangent lines are

$$9x - y - 3 = 0 \quad \text{and} \quad 9x - y + 13 = 0.$$

SECTION-III

1. *Find the volume of the largest cone that can be inscribed in a sphere of radius a* cm.
Solution: Let $\quad OA = x$ and radius AB of cone $= y$

$$\text{Height of Cone} = AC = AO + OC = a + x$$

In rt. $\angle d$ ΔOAB

$$x^2 + y^2 = a^2$$
$$y^2 = a^2 - x^2$$

$$\text{Volume of cone.} = \frac{1}{3}\pi y^2 (a + x)$$

$$V = \frac{1}{3}\pi (a^2 - x^2)(a + x)$$

$$\frac{dV}{dx} = \frac{\pi}{3}[(a^2 - x^2)1 + (a + x)(-2x)]$$

$$= \frac{\pi}{3}[(a + x)(a - 3x)]$$

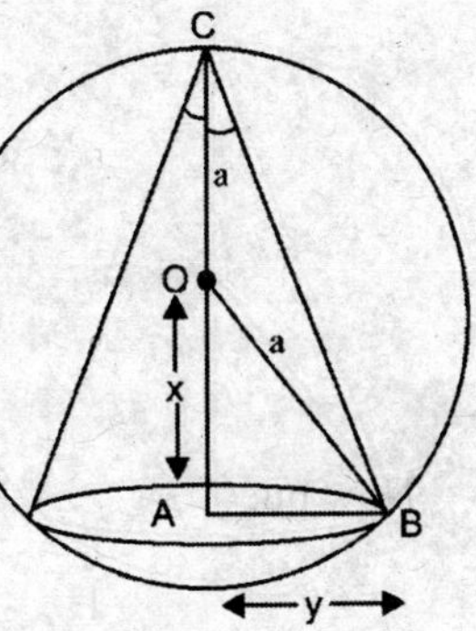

Fig. 6.3

Put

$$\frac{dV}{dx} = 0$$

$$\frac{\pi}{3}[(a + x)(0 - 3x)] = 0$$

$\Rightarrow$ for $a - 3x = 0$ $\quad x = \frac{a}{3}$

and $$\frac{d^2V}{dx^2} = \frac{\pi}{3}[(a + x)(-3) + (a - 3x)\,1]$$

$$\left.\frac{d^2V}{dx^2}\right]_{x+a/3} = \frac{-4a\pi}{3} < 0 \text{ at } x = \frac{a}{3}$$

Hence, Volume is maximum at $x = \frac{a}{3}$

Therefore, $$V = \frac{1}{3}\pi\left(a^2 - \frac{a^2}{9}\right)\left(a + \frac{a}{3}\right)$$

Maximum volume $= \dfrac{32\pi a^3}{81}$ cu units.

2. *An open box with square base is to be made out of a given quantity of sheet area a^2. Show that maximum volume of box is $\frac{a^3}{6\sqrt{3}}$.*

Solution: Let x unit be side of a square box and h = height.

Surface area of open box $= x^2 + 4xh = a^2$

$$h = \frac{a^2 - x^2}{4x}$$

$$V = \text{Volume of box}$$
$$V = x \times x \times h$$

$$= x \times x \times \frac{a^2 - x^2}{4x} = \frac{a^2x - x^3}{4}$$

$$\frac{dV}{dx} = \frac{1}{4}(a^2 - 3x^2) \text{ and } \frac{d^2V}{dx^2} = \frac{1}{4}(0 - 3 \times 2x)$$

$$\frac{d^2V}{dx^2} = -\frac{3}{2}x$$

Now put $\frac{dV}{dx} = 0$

$$\frac{1}{4}(a^2 - 3x^2) = 0$$

$$x = \frac{a}{\sqrt{3}}$$

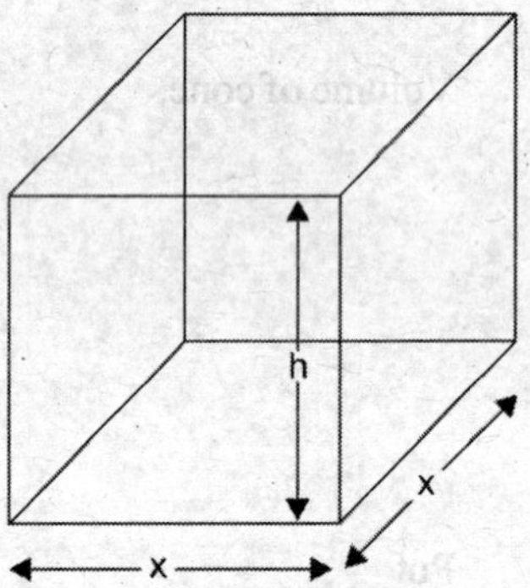

Fig. 6.4

Also $\left(\frac{d^2V}{dx^2}\right)_{x=\frac{a}{\sqrt{3}}} = \frac{-3}{2}\frac{a}{\sqrt{3}} < 0$

$\Rightarrow$ V is maximum when $x = \frac{a}{\sqrt{3}}$

Maximum volume of the box $= \frac{1}{4}x(a^2 - x^2)$

$$= \frac{1}{4}\frac{a}{\sqrt{3}}\left(a^2 - \frac{a^2}{3}\right) = \frac{a^3}{6\sqrt{3}} \text{ cubic units.}$$

3. *A helicopter is flying along the curve $y = x^2 + 2$. A soldier is placed at the point (3, 2). Find the nearest distance between the soldier and the helicopter.*

Solution: Let $P(x, y)$ be the position of the helicopter and soldier a placed at A (3, 2).

For each value of x, the helicopters position is at the point $p(x, x^2 + 2)$ $[y = x^2 + 2]$ therefore the distance b/w helicopter at the point $P(x, x^2 + 2)$ and solider placed at point $A(3, 2)$ is

$$PA = \sqrt{(x-3)^2 + (x^2 + 2 - 2)^2}$$

$$PA = \sqrt{(x-3)^2 + x^4}$$

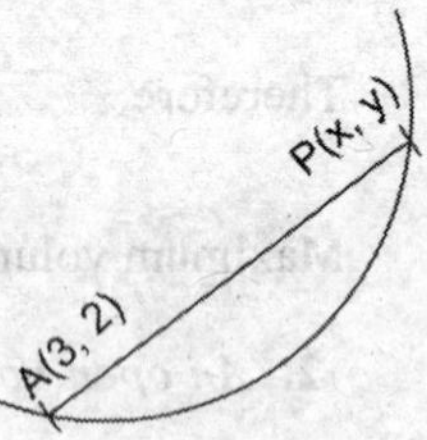

$\Rightarrow$ $PA^2 = (x - 3)^2 + x^4$

Let $f(x) = (x - 3)^2 + x^4$

$f'(x) = 2(x - 3) + 4x^3$

$\Rightarrow$ $f'(x) = 2(x - 3) + 4x^3$

$\Rightarrow$ $f'(x) = 2[x - 3 + 2x^3]$

First order condition for maxima

$f'(x) = 0$

$\Rightarrow$ $2(x - 1)(2x^2 + 2x + 3) = 0$

$\Rightarrow$ $x - 1 = 0$ or $(2x^2 + 2x + 3) = 0$

$(2x^2 + 2x + 3)$ gives imaginary values of x

$\therefore$ $x = 1$

Second condition for minimum requires

$f''(x) > 0$

$f''(x) = 12x^2 + 2$

$$\Rightarrow \qquad f''(x)|_{x=1} = 12(1)^2 + 2 = 14 > 0$$

Thus, f is minimum when $x = 1$

$\Rightarrow$ PA^2 is minimum when $x = 1$

Substituting $x = 1$ in $PA^2 = (1-3)^2 + (1)^2$

$= 4 + 1 = 5$

PA is minimum when helicopter is at point

$P(1, 1^2 + 2)$

$P(1, 3)$ on the curve

Nearest distance is given by $PA = \sqrt{5}$.

4. *A square tank of capacity 250 cubic metre has to be dug out. The cost of the land is Rs. 50 per square metre. The cost of digging increases with depth and for the whole tank it is Rs. 400 × h^2 where h metres is the depth of the tank. What should be the dimension of the tank so that cost is minimum?*

Solution: Let the side of the square tank be x metres. It is given that depth of tank is h metres.

$$\text{Volume} = x^2h \text{ cubic metre}$$

$$x^2h = 250$$

$$x^2 = \frac{250}{h}$$

Cost of land of x^2 sq. metre = Rs. $50x^2$

Cost of digging the tank of height h metres = Rs. $400 \times h^2$.

$$\text{Total cost} = 50x^2 + 400\,h^2$$

$$C = 50 \times \frac{250}{h} + 400\,h^2$$

$$C = \frac{12500}{h} + 400\,h^2$$

For maximum or minimum we have

$$\frac{dC}{dh} = 0$$

$$-\frac{12500}{h^2} + 800h = 0$$

$$h^3 = \frac{12500}{800}$$

$$h = \frac{5}{2}\text{ m}$$

Second order condition

$$\frac{d^2C}{dh^2} > 0$$

$$\frac{d^2C}{dh^2} = \frac{25000}{h^3} + 800$$

$$\left|\frac{d^2C}{dh^2}\right|_{h=5/2} = \frac{25000}{\left(\frac{5}{2}\right)^3} + 800$$

$$= \frac{25000}{125} \times 8 + 800$$

$$= 1600 + 800 = 2400 > 0$$

C is minimum when $h = \frac{5}{2}$ metres

Substituting $h = \frac{5}{2}$

$$x^2 = \frac{250}{\frac{5}{2}} = 100 = 10^2$$

$$\boxed{x = 10\,\text{m}}$$

Hence, for minimum cost the tank must have square base of side 10 m and depth $\frac{5}{2}$ m.

5. *Find the maximum and minimum values of* $(x-3)^5 (x+1)^4$.

Solution: Let $f(x) = (x-3)^5 (x+1)^4$

$f(x)$ is a polynomial function and is differentiable for all $x \in R$.

Diff. w.r.t. x we get

$$f'(x) = (x-3)^5\, 4(x+1)^3 . 1 + (x+1)^4\, 5\,(x-3)^4 .$$

$$= (x-3)^4 (x+1)^3 [4(x-3) + 5(x+1)]$$

$$= (x-3)^4 (x+1)^3 (9x-7)$$

For turning points

$$f'(x) = 0 \Rightarrow (x-3)^4 (x+1)^3 (9x-7) = 0$$

$$\Rightarrow \quad x = 3, \ -1, \ \frac{7}{9}$$

Therefore, the points where extremum may occur are

$$x = 3, -1, \frac{7}{9}$$

At $x = 3$

When $x < 3$ slightly

$$f'(x) = (+ve)\,(+ve)\,(+ve) = (+ve)$$

$f'(x)$ does not change sign as we move from slightly < 3 to slightly > 3.

$\Rightarrow$ f has neither maximum or minima $x = 3$ is a point of inflexion.

At $x = -1$

When $x < -1$ Slightly $f'(x) = (+ve)\,(-ve)\,(-ve) = (+ve)$

$x > -1$ Slightly $f'(x) = (+ve)\,(+ve)\,(-ve) = -ve$

f has local maximum value at $x = -1$.

$$f(-1) = (-1-3)^5 (-1+1)^4 = 0$$

At $x = \frac{7}{9}$

When $x < \frac{7}{9}$ Slightly

then $f'(x) = (+ve)\,(+ve)\,(-ve) = (-ve)$

When $x > \frac{7}{9}$ Slightly

$$f'(x) = (+ve)(+ve)(+ve) = +ve$$

$\Rightarrow$ f has local minimum value at $x = \frac{7}{9}$

$$f\left(\frac{7}{9}\right) = \left(\frac{7}{9}-3\right)^5\left(\frac{7}{9}+1\right)^5$$

$$= \frac{-5^5\,4^{13}}{3^{18}}$$

Maximum value = 0

Minimum value = $\frac{-5^5\,4^{13}}{3^{18}}$.

6. *A window has the shape of a rectangle surmounted by an equilateral triangle. If the perimeter of the window is* 12 m. *Find the dimensions of rectangle so that it may produce the largest area of window.*

Solution: Let length and breadth of rectangle be x and y metres respectively.

Perimeter of window = $4x + 2y = 12$ m

$\Rightarrow$ $y = 6 - 2x$

Area of window

= Area of rectangle + Area of equilateral triangle

$$= xy + \frac{\sqrt{3}}{4}x^2$$

$$= x(6-2x) + \frac{\sqrt{3}}{4}x^2$$

$$= 6x - 2x^2 + \frac{\sqrt{3}}{4}x^2$$

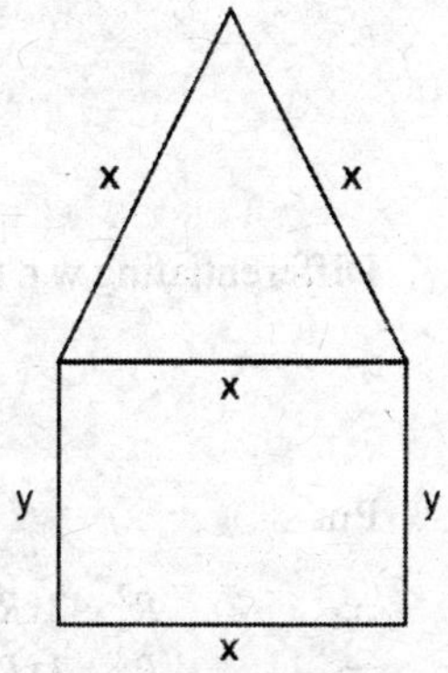

Fig. 6.5

Differentiating w.r.t. x we get

$$\frac{dA}{dx} = 6 - 4x + \frac{\sqrt{3}\,x}{2} \quad \text{and} \quad \frac{d^2A}{dx^2} = -4 + \frac{\sqrt{3}}{2}.$$

Now $\frac{dA}{dx} = 0$

$$6 - 4x + \frac{\sqrt{3}}{2}x = 0 \Rightarrow x = \frac{12}{8-\sqrt{3}}$$

$$x = \frac{12}{8-\sqrt{3}} \times \frac{8+\sqrt{3}}{8+\sqrt{3}} = \frac{12}{55}\left(8+\sqrt{3}\right)$$

$$x = \frac{12}{55}\left(8+\sqrt{3}\right)$$

$$\frac{d^2A}{dx^2} = -4 + \frac{\sqrt{3}}{2} < 0$$

A is maximum when $x = \frac{12}{55}\left(8+\sqrt{3}\right)$

$$y = 6-2x$$

$$6-2.\frac{12}{55}\left(8+\sqrt{3}\right)$$

Length of rectangle $= \dfrac{330-192-24\sqrt{3}}{55} = \dfrac{138-24\sqrt{3}}{55}$

7. *Prove that the volume of the largest cone that can be inscribed in a sphere of radius R is 8/27 of the volume of sphere.*

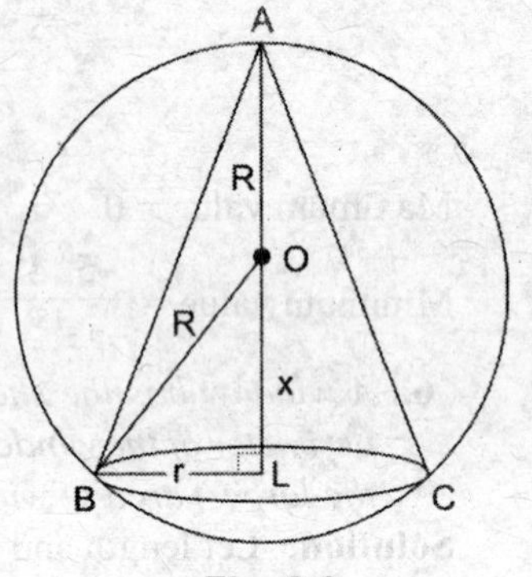

Fig. 6.6

Solution: In the given figure, O is the centre of sphere of radius R.

$OA = OB =$ Radius of sphere $= R$

$BL = LC =$ radius of cone $= r$.

Let $OL = x$

Height of cone $= R + x = h$.

$$V = \text{Volume of cone} = \frac{1}{3}\pi r^2 h$$

$$V = \frac{1}{3}\pi(R^2 - x^2)(R + x) \qquad [\text{In } \Delta OBL\ R^2 = x^2 + r^2]$$

$$V = \frac{1}{3}\pi[R^3 + R^2x - Rx^2 - x^3] \qquad \ldots(i)$$

Differentiating w.r. to x

$$\frac{dV}{dx} = \frac{1}{3}\pi[R^2 - 2xR - 3x^2] \qquad \ldots(ii)$$

Put $\dfrac{dV}{dx} = 0$

$\Rightarrow$ $R^2 - 2xR - 3x^2 = 0$

$\Rightarrow$ $R^2 - 3xR + xR - 3x^2 = 0$

$\Rightarrow$ $R(R-3x) + x(R-3x) = 0$

$\Rightarrow$ $(R+x)(R-3x) = 0$

$\Rightarrow$ Either $R + x = 0$ or $R - 3x = 0$

$R = -x$ (not possible) $R = 3x \Rightarrow x = \dfrac{R}{3}$

Differentiating (*ii*) w.r. to x

$$\frac{d^2V}{dx^2} = \frac{1}{3}\pi[-2R - 6x]$$

$$= -\frac{2}{3}\pi[R + 3x] < 0$$

since $\dfrac{d^2V}{dx^2} < 0$ at $x = \dfrac{R}{3}$. Hence volume is maximum.

Now, $$V = \frac{1}{3}\pi(R^2 - x^2)(R + x) \qquad [\text{From } (i)]$$

$$= \frac{1}{3}\pi\left[R^2 - \frac{R^2}{9}\right]\left[R + \frac{R}{3}\right] \qquad \left(\text{put } x = \frac{R}{3}\right)$$

$$= \frac{1}{3}\pi \times \frac{8}{9}R^2 \times \frac{4}{3}R$$

$$= \frac{8}{27}\left(\frac{4}{3}\pi R^3\right)$$

$$= \frac{8}{27} \times \text{volume of sphere.}$$

8. *Show that the semi-vertical angle of the cone of the maximum volume and of given slant height is* $\tan^{-1}\sqrt{2}$.

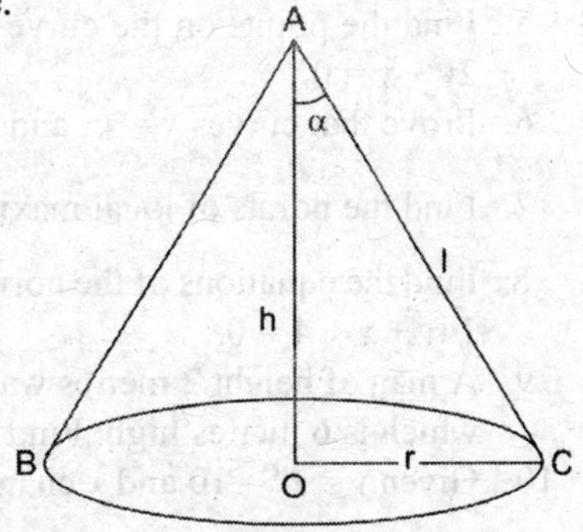

Fig. 6.7

Solution: In the figure, $\angle OAC = \alpha$ semivertical angle

$$OC = r = \text{radius of cone.}$$

$$OA = h = \text{height of cone.}$$

$$l^2 = r^2 + h^2$$

$$V = \frac{1}{3}\pi r^2 h$$

$$= \frac{1}{3}\pi(l^2 - h^2)\,.\,h$$

$$= \frac{1}{3}\pi(l^2 h - h^3) \quad \text{...}(i)$$

Differentiating (*i*) w.r.t. *h*

$$\frac{dV}{dh} = \frac{1}{3}\pi\,(l^2 - 3h^2) \quad \text{...}(ii)$$

Put $\frac{dV}{dh} = 0$

$$l^2 - 3h^2 = 0$$

$$\Rightarrow \quad l^2 = 3h^2$$

$$\Rightarrow \quad r^2 + h^2 = 3h^2$$

$$\Rightarrow \quad r^2 = 2h^2$$

$$\Rightarrow \quad r = \sqrt{2}h$$

In ΔAOC $\quad \tan\alpha = \frac{r}{h} = \frac{\sqrt{2}h}{h} = \sqrt{2}$

$$\Rightarrow \quad \alpha = \tan^{-1}\sqrt{2}$$

Differentiating Equation (*ii*) w.r.t. *x*

$$\frac{d^2V}{dh^2} = \frac{1}{3}\pi(-6h) = -2\pi h < 0$$

Hence, volume is maximum at $\alpha = \tan^{-1}\sqrt{2}$.

UNSOLVED QUESTIONS

SECTION-II

1. Find the intervals in which the function
$$f(x) = 2x^3 - 9x^2 + 12x + 30 \text{ is } (i) \text{ increasing } (ii) \text{ decreasing.}$$
2. Find the equation of tangent and normal to the curve
$$y = x^4 - 6x^3 + 13x^2 - 10x + 5 \text{ at } (1, 3).$$
3. The length *x* of a rectangle is decreasing at the rate of 5 cm/metre and width *y* is increasing at the rate of 4 cm/minute.

When $x = 8$ cm and $y = 6$ cm. Find the rate of change of
(*a*) the perimeter (*b*) area of rectangle.

4. Using differentiables, Evaluate $\sqrt{49.5}$.
5. Find the points on the curve $4x^2 + 9y^2$, where the tangents are perpendicular to the line $2y + x = 0$.
6. Prove that curves $x = y^2$ and $xy = K$ intersect at right angles if $8K^2 = 1$.
7. Find the points of local maxima and minima of $f(x) = \sin 2x - x, -\frac{\pi}{2} < x < \frac{\pi}{2}$.
8. Find the equations of the normals to the curve $y = x^3 + 2x + 6$ which are parallel to the line $14y + x + 4 = 0$.
9. A man of height 2 metres walks at a uniform speed of 5 km/hour away from a lamp post which is 6 metres high. Find the rate at which length of his shadow increases.
10. Given $y = x^4 - 10$ and x changes from 2 to 1.99. What is approximate change in y.

ANSWERS

1. (*i*) $\{x . x > 2\} \cup \{x : x < 1\}$ (*ii*) $\{x : 1 < x < 2\}$
2. Tangent : $y = 2x + 1$; Normal $x + 2y - 7 = 0$
3. (*a*) – 2 cm/minute (*b*) 2 sq. cm/minute
4. 7.04 5. $\left(\frac{3}{2\sqrt{10}}, \frac{-1}{3\sqrt{10}}\right), \left(\frac{-3}{2\sqrt{10}}, \frac{1}{3\sqrt{10}}\right)$
7. Local minima $x = -\frac{\pi}{6}$, Local maxima $x = +\frac{\pi}{6}$
8. $x + 14y - 254 = 0$ and $x + 14y + 86 = 0$ 9. $\frac{5}{2}$ km/hr. 10. y change from 6 to 5.68.

SECTION-III

1. Find the volume of largest right circular cylinder that can be increased in a sphere of radius r.
2. Find a point of the $y = (x - 3)^2$ where the tangent is parallel to the chord joining the points (3, 0) and (4, 1).
3. A square piece of tin of side 24 cm is to be made into a box without top by cutting a square from each corner and folding up the flops to form a box.
What should be the side of a square to be cut off so that volume is maximum? Also find maximum volume.
4. Show that maximum volume of cylinder which can be increased in a cone of height h and semivertical angle α is $\frac{4}{27}\pi h^3 \tan^2 \alpha$.
5. Find the coordinates of a point on the parabola $y = x^2 + 7x + 2$ which is closest to the straight line $y = 3x - 3$.

ANSWERS

1. $\frac{4\pi r^3}{3\sqrt{3}}$ 2. $\left(\frac{7}{2}, \frac{1}{4}\right)$ 3. 4 cm; 1024 cu cm 4. (–2, –8)

HOTS

1. Find the approximate value of tan 46° if it being given that $1° = 0.01745$ radian.
2. $y = a \log |x| + bx^2 + x$ has its extreme values at $x = -1$ and $x = 2$ find a and b.
3. Show that curves $x^3 - 3xy^2 = a$ and $3x^2y - y^3 = b$ cut each other orthogonally where a and b are constants.
4. Find the shortest distance of point $(0, c)$ from the parabola $y = x^2$ where $½ < c \le 5$.
5. Taking the functions $f(x) = (x - 3) \log x$ prove that there is at least one value of x in (1, 3) which satisfies.

$$x \log x = 3 - x.$$

ANSWERS

1. 1.03490 2. $a = 2,\ b = -\dfrac{1}{2}$ 4. $\dfrac{\sqrt{4c-1}}{2}$

❑❑❑

CHAPTER 7

INTEGRATION

The process of finding the function when the derivative of the function is given is called "integration".

It is called indefinite integral because it is not unique. Actually, there exist infinitely many integrals of each function, which can be obtained by choosing c arbitrary constant from the set of real numbers.

List of some standard Integrals

(*i*) $\int x^n .dx: \frac{x^{n+1}}{n+1} + c$

(*ii*) $\int \frac{1}{x} . dx = \log |x| + c$

(*iii*) $\int 1.dx = x + c$

(*iv*) $\int \sin x.dx = -\cos x + c$

(*v*) $\int \cos x \, dx = \sin x + c$

(*vi*) $\int \sec^2 x \, dx = \tan x + c$

(*vii*) $\int \text{cosec}^2 x \, dx = -\cot x + c$

(*viii*) $\int \sec x.\tan x \, dx = \sec x + c$

(*ix*) $\int \text{cosec}\, x.\cot x \, dx = -\text{cosec}\, x + c$

(*x*) $\int e^x \, dx = e^x + \text{c}$

(*xi*) $\int a^x \, dx = \frac{a^x}{\log a} + c$

(*xii*) $\int \frac{1}{\sqrt{1-x^2}} \, dx = \sin^{-1} x + c$

(*xiii*) $\int \frac{1}{1+x^2} \, dx = \tan^{-1} x + c$

(*xiv*) $\int \frac{1}{x\sqrt{x^2-1}} \, dx = \sec^{-1} x + c$

Method of integration:

(*i*) Integration by substitution

(*ii*) Integration by parts

(*iii*) Integration By partial fractions

(*iv*) Integration of substitution

More standard results:

- $\int \tan x \, dx = -\log |\cos x| + c = \log |\sec x| + c$
- $\int \cot x \, dx = \log |\sin x| + c$
- $\int \sec x \, dx = \log |\sec x + \tan x| + c = \log \left|\tan\left(\frac{\pi}{4}+\frac{x}{2}\right)\right| + c$

- $\int \operatorname{cosec} x\, dx = \log|\operatorname{cosec} x - \cot x| + c = \log\left|\tan\frac{x}{2}\right| + c$
- **Integration by parts**— Let u & v be two functions of x, then

$$\int u.v\, dx = u\int v\, dx - \int\left\{\frac{du}{dx}.\int v\, dx\right\}dx$$

SPECIAL INTEGRALS

- $\int \frac{dx}{a^2+x^2} = \frac{1}{a}\tan^{-1}\frac{x}{a} + c$
- $\int \frac{dx}{x^2-a^2} = \frac{1}{2a}\log\left|\frac{x-a}{x+a}\right| + c$
- $\int \frac{dx}{a^2-x^2} = \frac{1}{2a}\log\left|\frac{a+x}{a-x}\right| + c$
- $\int \frac{1}{\sqrt{a^2+x^2}}dx = \log\left|x+\sqrt{a^2+x^2}\right| + c$
- $\int \frac{1}{\sqrt{x^2-a^2}}dx = \log\left|x+\sqrt{x^2-a^2}\right| + c$
- $\int \frac{1}{\sqrt{a^2-x^2}} = \sin^{-1}\frac{x}{a} + c$
- $\int \sqrt{a^2-x^2}\, dx = \frac{x}{2}\sqrt{a^2-x^2} + \frac{a^2}{2}\sin^{-1}\frac{x}{a} + c$
- $\int \sqrt{x^2-a^2}\, dx = \frac{x}{2}\sqrt{x^2-a^2} - \frac{a^2}{2}\log\left|x\sqrt{x^2-a^2}\right| + c$
- $\int \sqrt{a^2+x^2}\, dx = \frac{x}{2}\sqrt{a^2+x^2} + \frac{a^2}{2}\log\left|x+\sqrt{a^2+x^2}\right| + c$

PARTIAL FRACTIONS

Rational Function Partial Fraction

$$\frac{px+q}{(x-a)(x-b)} = \frac{A}{x-a} + \frac{B}{x-b}$$

$$\frac{px+q}{(x-a)^2(x-b)} = \frac{A}{x-a} + \frac{B}{(x-a)^2} + \frac{C}{x-b}$$

$$\frac{px+q}{(x-a)^2(x-b)} = \frac{A}{(x-a)} + \frac{B}{(x-a)^2} + \frac{C}{(x-a)^3} + \frac{D}{x-b}$$

$$\frac{px+q}{(x-a)(x^2+b)} = \frac{A}{x-a} + \frac{Bx+c}{x^2+b}$$

DEFINITE INTEGRALS

If $F(x)$ be the integral of $f(x)$ over this interval $[a, b]$, *i.e.* $\int f(x)\,dx = F(x)$

Then $\int_a^b f(x)\,dx = [F(x)]_a^b = F(b) - F(a)$

where 'a' is called the lower limit & 'b' is called the upper limit of integration.

INTEGRATION AS THE LIMIT OF A SUM

If $f(x)$ be a continuous real-valued function, defined in the closed interval $[a, b]$, then

$$\int_a^b f(x)\,dx = \lim_{n\to 0} h[f(a) + f(a+b) + f(a+2h) + ... + f\{a + (n-1)h\}]$$

Some useful results for Direct Applications

(*i*) $1 + 2 + 3 + 4 + ... + (n-1) = \frac{n(n-1)}{2}$

(*ii*) $1^2 + 2^2 + 3^2 + 4^2 + ... + (n-1)^2 = \frac{n(n-1)(2n-1)}{6}$

(*iii*) $1^3 + 2^3 + 3^3 + 4^3 + ... + (n-1)^3 = \left[\frac{n(n-1)}{2}\right]^2$

(*iv*) $a + ar + ar^2 + ... + ar^{n-1} = \frac{a(r^n-1)}{r-1}$ if $r > 1 = \frac{a(1-r^n)}{1-r}$ if $r < 1$

(*v*) $\sin a + \sin(a+h) + \sin(a+2h) + ... + \sin\{a + (n+1)\} = \frac{\sin\left\{a + \frac{n-1}{2}h\right\}\sin\left(\frac{nh}{2}\right)}{\sin\left(\frac{h}{2}\right)}$

(*vi*) $\cos a + \cos(a+h) + \cos(a+2h) + ... + \cos\{a + (n-1)h\}$

$$= \frac{\cos\left\{a + \frac{n-1}{2}h\right\}.\sin\left(\frac{nb}{2}\right)}{\sin\left(\frac{b}{2}\right)}$$

(*vii*) $\operatorname*{Lt}_{x\to 0} \frac{e^x - 1}{x} = 1$

PROPERTIES OF DEFINITE INTEGRALS

(*i*) $\int_a^b f(x)\,dx = \int_a^b f(t)\,dt$

(*ii*) $\int_a^b f(x)\,dx = -\int_b^a f(x)\,dx$

(*iii*) $\int_a^b f(x)\,dx = \int_a^b f(x)\,dx + \int_b^c f(x)\,dx$ (where $a < c < b$)

(*iv*) $\int^a f(x)dx = \int^a f(a-x)\,dx$

(v) $\int_a^b f(x)\,dx = \int_a^b f(a+b-x)\,dx$

(vi) $\int_{-a}^{a} f(x)\,dx = \begin{cases} 0, \text{ when } f(x) \text{ is an odd funcion} \\ 2\int_0^a f(x)\,dx, \text{ when } f(x) \text{ is an even function} \end{cases}$

(vii) $\int_0^{2a} f(x)\,dx = \begin{cases} 0, \text{ if } f(2a-x) = -f(x) \\ 2\int_0^a f(x)\,dx, \text{ if } f(2a-x) = f(x) \end{cases}$

SOLVED QUESTIONS

SECTION-I

1. *Write the value of* $\int_{-1}^{1} x^{17}\cos^4 x\,dx$.

Solution: Here, $f(-x) = (-x)^{17}\cos^4(-x)$
$= -x^{17}\cos^4 x = -f(x)$

$\Rightarrow$ $f(x)$ is odd function

Thus $\int_{-1}^{1} x^{17}\cos^4 x\,dx = 0$, because $f(-x) = -f(x)$. [odd function]

2. Evaluate : $\int \sin^3 x\cos^2 x\,dx$.

Solution: $\int \sin^3 x\cos^2 x\,dx = \int \sin^2 x\cos^2 x(\sin x)\,dx$

$= \int (1-\cos^2 x)\cos^2 x(\sin x)\,dx$

put $t = \cos x$ so that $dt = -\sin x\,dx$.

Therefore, $\int \sin^2 x\cos^2 x(\sin x)\,dx = -\int (1-t^2)t^2\,dt$

$= -\int (t^2 - t^4)\,dt = -\left(\frac{t^3}{3} - \frac{t^5}{5}\right) + c$

$= -\frac{1}{3}\cos^3 x + \frac{1}{5}\cos^5 x + c.$

3. *Evaluate*: $\int \frac{dx}{\sqrt{2x-x^2}}$.

Solution: $\int \frac{dx}{\sqrt{2x-x^2}} = \int \frac{dx}{\sqrt{1-(x-1)^2}}$

put $x - 1 = t$. Then $dx = dt$

Therefore, $\int \frac{dx}{\sqrt{2x-x^2}} = \int \frac{dt}{\sqrt{1-t^2}}$

$$= \sin^{-1} t + C$$
$$= \sin^{-1}(x-1) + C.$$

4. *Find* $\int x e^x \, dx.$

Solution: Take first function as x and second function as e^x. The integral of second function is e^x.

Therefore, $\int x e^x \, dx = x e^x - \int 1.e^x \, dx$

$$= xe^x - e^x + c.$$

5. *Evolute* : $\int_0^1 \frac{\tan^{-1} x}{1+x^2} dx.$

Solution: Let $t = \tan^{-1} x$, then $dt = \frac{1}{1+x^2} dx.$

The new limits are, when $x = 0$, $t = 0$ and when $x = 1$, $t = \frac{\pi}{4}$.

Thus, as x varies from 0 to 1, t varies from 0 to $\frac{\pi}{4}$.

Therefore $\int_0^1 \frac{\tan^{-1} x}{1+x^2} dx = \int_0^{\pi/4} t \, dt$

$$= \left[\frac{t^2}{2}\right]_0^{\frac{\pi}{4}} = \frac{1}{2}\left[\frac{\pi^2}{16} - 0\right]$$

$$= \frac{\pi^2}{32}.$$

6. *Find* $\int \cos 6x \sqrt{1+\sin 6x} \, dx.$

Solution: Put $t = 1 + \sin 6x$, so that $dt = 6 \cos 6x \, dx$.

Therefore $\int \cos 6x \sqrt{1+\sin 6x} = \frac{1}{6} \int t^{1/2} \, dt$

$$= \frac{1}{6} \times \frac{2}{3} (t)^{3/2} + C$$

$$= \frac{1}{9} (1+\sin 6x)^{3/2} + C.$$

7. *Evaluate:* $\int \sqrt{25-36x^2} \, dx.$

Solution: $\int \sqrt{25-36x^2} \, dx = 6 \int \sqrt{\left(\frac{5}{6}\right)^2 - x^2} \, dx$

$$= 6\left[\frac{x\sqrt{(5/6)^2 - x^2}}{2} + \frac{(5/6)^2}{2} \sin^{-1}\left(\frac{x}{5/6}\right)\right] + C$$

$$= \frac{x\sqrt{25-36x^2}}{2} + \frac{25}{12}\sin^{-1}\left(\frac{6x}{5}\right) + c.$$

8. *Find* $\int e^x\left(\tan^{-1}x + \frac{1}{1+x^2}\right)dx.$

Solution: $\int e^x\left(\tan^{-1}x + \frac{1}{1+x^2}\right)dx = \int \tan^{-1}x\, e^x\, dx + \int \frac{1}{1+x^2}e^x\, dx$

$$= \tan^{-1}x\, e^x - \int \frac{1}{1+x^2}e^x\, dx + \int \frac{1}{1+x^2}e^x\, dx + C$$

$$= e^x \tan^{-1}x + C.$$

9. *Evaluate the following definite integral:* $\int_3^5 \frac{dt}{1+3t}.$

Solution: $\int_3^5 \frac{dt}{1+3t} = \left[\frac{\log|1+3t|}{3}\right]_3^5 = \frac{1}{3}(\log 16 - \log 10)$

$$= \frac{1}{3}\log\frac{16}{10} = \frac{1}{3}\log\frac{8}{5}.$$

10. *Evaluate* : $\int \frac{1-\tan x}{1+\tan x}dx.$

Solution: $\int \frac{1-\tan x}{1+\tan x}dx = \int \frac{\cos x - \sin x}{\cos x + \sin x}$

put $t = \cos x + \sin x,\ dt = (-\sin x + \cos x)\,dx$

$$\int \frac{dt}{t} = \log|t|$$

$$= \log|\cos x + \sin x| + C.$$

UNSOLVED QUESTIONS

SECTION-I

1. $\int_0^1 \frac{dx}{1+x^2}$

2. Evaluate $\int_{-3}^{3}|x+1|\,dx$

3. Evaluate $\int_0^{\pi}\frac{x}{1+\sin x}dx$

4. Prove that $\int_0^{2a} f(x)\,dx = \int_0^{2a} f(2a-x)\,dx$

5. $\int \frac{x^2}{1+x^3}dx$

6. $\int \frac{x+\cos 6x}{3x^2+\sin 6x}dx$

7. $\int (x^2+1)^2\,dx$

8. $\int \frac{5}{\sqrt{x+3}-\sqrt{x-2}}dx$

9. $\int \frac{\sin\sqrt{x}}{\sqrt{x}}dx$

10. $\int 7^x . e^x\,dx$

ANSWERS

1. $\frac{\pi}{4}$ 2. 10 3. π

5. $\frac{1}{3}\log|1+x^3|+C$ 6. $\frac{1}{6}\log|3x^2+\sin 6x|+C$ 7. $\frac{x^5}{5}+\frac{2x^3}{3}+x+C$

8. $\frac{2}{3}(x+3)^{3/2}+\frac{2}{3}(x-2)^{3/2}+C$ 9. $-2\cos\sqrt{x}+C$ 10. $\frac{(7e)^x}{\log(7e)}+C$

SOLVED QUESTIONS

SECTION-II

1. $\int(\sin^4 2x)\,dx.$

Solution: $\int(\sin^2 2x)^2\,dx = \int(\sin^2 2x)^2\,dx$

$\Rightarrow$ $\int\left(\frac{1-\cos 4x}{2}\right)^2 dx = \frac{1}{4}\int(1-2\cos 4x+\cos^2 4x)\,dx$ [Using $2\sin^2 x = 1-\cos 2x$]

$= \frac{1}{4}\int\left(1-2\cos 4x+\frac{1+\cos 8x}{2}\right)dx$ [using $1+\cos 2x = 2\cos^2 x$]

$= \frac{1}{4\times 2}\int(3-4\cos 4x+\cos 8x)\,dx$

$= \frac{1}{4\times 2}\left[3x-\not{4}\,\frac{\sin 4x}{\not{4}}+\frac{\sin 8x}{8}\right]+c$

$= \frac{1}{8\times 8}\,[24x-8\sin 4x+\sin 8x]+c$

$= \frac{1}{64}\,[24x-8\sin 4x+\sin 8x]+c$

2. $\int\frac{\sin 2x}{a^2\sin^2 x+b^2\cos^2 x}\,dx.$

Solution: Put $a^2\sin^2 x + b^2\cos^2 x = t$

Differentiating w.r.t. x.

$\Rightarrow$ $[a^2\times 2\sin x\cos x+b^2\,2\cos x\,(-\sin x)]\,dx = dt$

$\Rightarrow$ $(a^2-b^2)\sin 2x\,.\,dx = dt$ [$\sin 2x = 2\sin x\cos x$]

$\Rightarrow$ $\sin 2x\,.\,dx = \frac{dt}{a^2-b^2}$

$\therefore$ $\int\frac{\sin 2x}{a^2\sin^2 x+b^2\cos^2 x}\,dx = \frac{1}{a^2-b^2}\int\frac{1}{t}\,dt$

$= \frac{1}{a^2-b^2}+\log|t|+c$

$$= \frac{1}{a^2 - b^2} + \log |a^2 \sin^2 x + b^2 \cos^2 x| + c.$$

Above formula fails when $a = \pm b$. If $a = \pm b$

$$\int \frac{\sin 2x}{a^2 \sin^2 x + b^2 \cos^2 x} dx = \int \frac{\sin 2x}{a^2 (\sin^2 x + \cos^2 x)} dx$$

$$= \frac{1}{a^2} \int \sin 2x \, dx = \frac{1}{a^2} \left(-\frac{\cos 2x}{2} \right) + c$$

$$= - \frac{1}{2a^2} \cos 2x + c.$$

3. $\displaystyle\int \frac{2x+1}{2x^2 + 4x - 3} dx.$

Solution: Let $\quad 2x + 1 = A \dfrac{d}{dx} (2x^2 + 4x - 3) + B$

$$= A(4x + 4) + B$$

Equating the coefficients of x and constant on both sides, we get

$\Rightarrow \quad 4A = 2$ and $4A + B = 1 \Rightarrow A = \dfrac{1}{2}$ and $B = -1$

$$\therefore \quad \int \frac{2x+1}{2x^2 + 4x - 3} dx = \int \frac{\frac{1}{2}(4x+4) - 1}{2x^2 + 4x - 3} dx$$

$$= \frac{1}{2} \int \frac{4x+4}{2x^2 + 4x - 3} dx - \int \frac{dx}{2x^2 + 4x - 3} = \frac{1}{2} I_1 - I_2.$$

Where $\quad I_1 = \displaystyle\int \frac{(4x+4)\, dx}{2x^2 + 4x - 3}$. Put $2x^2 + 4x - 3 = t \Rightarrow (4x + 4)\, dx = dt.$

$\Rightarrow \quad (4x + 4)\, dx = dt$ on differentiating

$$= \int \frac{dt}{t} = \log |t| + c_1$$

$$= \log |2x^2 + 4x - 3| + c$$

and $\quad I_2 = \displaystyle\int \frac{dx}{2x^2 + 4x - 3} = \frac{1}{2} \int \frac{dx}{x^2 + 2x - \frac{3}{2}}$

$$= \frac{1}{2} \int \frac{dx}{(x+1)^2 - \frac{3}{2} - 1} = \frac{1}{2} \int \frac{dx}{(x+1)^2 - \left(\sqrt{\frac{5}{2}}\right)^2}$$

Put $\quad x + 1 = u \Rightarrow dx = du$

$$= \frac{1}{2} \int \frac{du}{u^2 - \left(\sqrt{\frac{5}{2}}\right)^2} = \frac{1}{2} \cdot \frac{1}{2\sqrt{\frac{5}{2}}} \log \left| \frac{u - \sqrt{\frac{5}{2}}}{u + \sqrt{\frac{5}{2}}} \right| + c_2$$

$$= \frac{1}{2\sqrt{10}} \log \left| \frac{\sqrt{2}(x+1)-\sqrt{5}}{\sqrt{2}(x+1)+\sqrt{5}} \right| + c_2$$

$$\therefore \quad \int \frac{2x+1}{2x^2+4x-3}\, dx = \frac{1}{2} \log |2x^2+4x-3| - \frac{1}{2\sqrt{10}} \log \left| \frac{\sqrt{2}(x+1)-\sqrt{5}}{\sqrt{2}(x+1)+\sqrt{5}} \right| + c.$$

4. *Evaluate* $\displaystyle\int \frac{2\sin x+3\cos x}{3\sin x+4\cos x}\, dx.$

Solution: Let $2 \sin x + 3 \cos x = l(3 \sin x + 4 \cos x) + m \,.\, \frac{d}{dx} (3 \sin x - 4 \cos x)$

Equating the coefficients of $\sin x$ and $\cos x$ on both sides we get $2 = 3l - 4m$ and $3 = 4l + 3m$
Solving these, we get

$$l = \frac{18}{25} \text{ and } m = \frac{1}{25}$$

$$\therefore \quad \int \frac{2\sin x+3\cos x}{3\sin x+4\cos x} = \int \frac{l(3\sin x+4\cos x)+m(3\cos x-4\sin x)}{3\sin x+4\cos x}$$

$$= l \int 1\, dx + m \int \frac{3\cos x - 4\sin x}{3\sin x+4\cos x}\, dx$$

Put $\quad 3 \sin x + 4 \cos x = t \;\Rightarrow\; (3 \cos x - 4 \sin x)\, dx = dt.$

$$= lx + m \log |3 \sin x + 4 \cos x| + c$$

$$= \frac{18x}{25} + \frac{1}{25} \log |3 \sin x + 4 \cos x| + c.$$

5. *Evaluate* $\displaystyle\int x \tan^{-1} x\, dx.$

Solution: $\displaystyle\int x \tan^{-1} x\, dx = \tan^{-1} x \,.\, \frac{x^2}{2} - \int \frac{1}{1+x^2} \cdot \frac{x^2}{2}\, dx$

[Integration by parts, taking $\tan^{-1} x$ as the first function]

$$= \frac{1}{2} x^2 . \tan^{-1} x - \frac{1}{2} \int \frac{x^2}{1+x^2}\, dx$$

$$= \frac{1}{2} x^2 . \tan^{-1} x - \frac{1}{2} \int \left(1 - \frac{1}{1+x^2}\right) dx$$

$$= \frac{1}{2} x^2 . \tan^{-1} x - \frac{1}{2} (x - \tan^{-1} x) + c$$

$$= \frac{1}{2} [(x^2 + 1) \tan^{-1} x - x] + c.$$

6. *Evaluate* $\displaystyle\int e^{\tan^{-1} x} \left(\frac{1+x+x^2}{1+x^2}\right) dx.$

Solution: Put $\tan^{-1} x = t \;\Rightarrow\; x = \tan t$

$\Rightarrow \qquad dx = \sec^2 t\, dt$

$$\Rightarrow \quad \int e^{\tan^{-1} x} \left(\frac{1+x+x^2}{1+x^2}\right) dx = \int e^t \frac{(1+\tan t+\tan^2 t)\sec^2 t\, dt}{1+\tan^2 t}$$

$$= \int e^t \frac{(\sec^2 t + \tan t)}{\cancel{\sec^2 t}} \cancel{\sec^2 t}\, dt$$

$$= \int e^t \sec^2 t\, dt + \int e^t \tan t\, dt$$

(Integrate first integral by parts, taking e^t as the first function)

$$= e^t \tan t - \int e^t \tan t\, dt + \int e^t \tan t\, dt + c$$

$$= e^t \tan t + c = x e^{\tan^{-1} x} + c.$$

7. *Evaluate the following definite interval* $\int_0^{\pi} \frac{dx}{5+4\cos x}$.

Solution: Put $\tan \frac{x}{2} = t \Rightarrow \sec^2 \frac{x}{2} \cdot \frac{1}{2}\, dx = dt$

$$dx = \frac{2\,dt}{\sec^2 \frac{x}{2}} = \frac{2\,dt}{1+\tan^2 \frac{x}{2}} = \frac{2}{1+t^2}\, dt.$$

When $x = 0, t = 0$

When $x \to \pi, t \to \infty$

$$\cos x = \frac{1-t^2}{1+t^2}$$

$$\int_0^{\pi} \frac{dx}{5+4\cos x} = \int_0^{\infty} \frac{\frac{2}{1+t^2}\, dt}{5+4.\frac{(1-t^2)}{1+t^2}}$$

$$= 2\int_0^{\infty} \frac{dt}{9+t^2} = 2 . \frac{1}{3}\left[\tan^{-1}\frac{t}{3}\right]_0^{\infty} = \frac{2}{3}\left[\frac{\pi}{2} - 0\right] \qquad \left[\int \frac{dx}{a^2+x^2} = \frac{1}{a}\tan^{-1}\frac{x}{a}\right]$$

$$= \frac{\pi}{3}.$$

8. $\int_0^{\pi/2} \sin 2x \log(\tan x)\, dx.$

Solution: Let $I = \int_0^{\pi/2} \sin 2x \log(\tan x)\, dx$

Then by using property

$$\int_0^a f(x)\, dx = \int_0^a f(a-x)\, dx$$

$$I = \int_0^{\pi/2} \sin\left[2\left(\frac{\pi}{2} - x\right)\right] \log\left[\tan\left(\frac{\pi}{2} - x\right)\right] dx$$

$$= \int_0^{\pi/2} \sin(\pi - 2x) \log(\cot x)\, dx$$

$$= \int_0^{\pi/2} \sin 2x \log((\tan x)^{-1})\, dx$$

$$= \int_0^{\pi/2} \sin 2x(-1) \log \tan x$$

$$= -\int_0^{\pi/2} \sin 2x \log(\tan x)\, dx$$

$\Rightarrow \quad I = -I$

$\Rightarrow \quad 2I = 0$

$\Rightarrow \quad I = 0.$

9. *Evaluate the following integral* $\int_0^{\pi} \frac{x \sin x}{1+\cos^2 x} dx.$

Solution: Let
$$I = \int_0^{\pi} \frac{x \sin x}{1+\cos^2 x} dx \qquad ...(1)$$

By using property $\int_0^a f(x)\,dx = \int_0^a f(a-x)\,dx$

$$I = \int_0^{\pi} \frac{(\pi - x)\sin(\pi - x)\,dx}{1+\cos^2(\pi - x)} = \int_0^{\pi} \frac{(\pi - x)\sin x\,dx}{1+\cos^2 x} \qquad ...(2)$$

Adding (1) and (2)

$$2I = \int_0^{\pi} \frac{(x+\pi-x)\sin x}{1+\cos^2 x} dx$$

$$= \pi \int_0^{\pi} \frac{\sin x}{1+\cos^2 x} dx$$

Put $\cos x = t \Rightarrow -\sin x\,dx = dt \Rightarrow \sin x\,dx = -dt$

When $x = 0,\ t = 1$ and when $x = \pi,\ t = \cos \pi = -1$

$$2I = \pi \int_1^{-1} \frac{dt}{1+t^2} = -\pi\left[\tan^{-1} t\right]_1^{-1} = -\pi[\tan^{-1}(-1) - \tan^{-1}(1)]$$

$$= -\pi\left[-\frac{\pi}{4} - \frac{\pi}{4}\right] = \frac{\pi^2}{2}$$

$$I = \frac{\pi^2}{4}.$$

10. *If f and g are continuous on* $[0, a]$ *satisfying* $f(a-x) = f(x)$ *and* $g(x) + g(a-x) = 2$, *show that*

$$\int_0^a f(x)g(x)\,dx = \int_0^a f(x)\,dx.$$

Solution: Let
$$I = \int_0^a f(x)g(x)\,dx$$

then
$$I = \int_0^a f(a-x)g(a-x)\,dx \qquad \left[\int_0^a f(x)\,dx = \int_0^a f(a-x)\,dx\right]$$

But $\quad f(a-x) = f(x)$ and $g(x) + g(a-x) = 2$

$\Rightarrow \quad g(a-x) = 2 - g(x)$

$$I = \int_0^a f(x)[2 - g(x)]\,dx$$

$$= 2\int_0^a f(x)\,dx - \int_0^a f(x)g(x)\,dx$$

$\Rightarrow$
$$I = 2\int_0^a f(x)dx - I$$

$$\Rightarrow \qquad 2I = \int_0^a f(x)dx$$

$$\Rightarrow \qquad I = \int_0^a f(x)dx.$$

SECTION-III

1. *Evaluate* $\int_0^\pi \frac{x\tan x}{\sec x+\tan x}\,dx.$

Solution: Let

$$I = \int_0^\pi \frac{x\tan x}{\sec x+\tan x}\,dx$$

$$= \int_0^\pi \frac{x\sin x}{1+\sin x}dx = \int_0^\pi \frac{(\pi-x)\sin(\pi-x)}{1+\sin(\pi-x)}\,dx \qquad ...(i)$$

[Using $\int_0^a f(x)dx = \int_0^a f(a-x)dx$]

$$I = \int_0^\pi \frac{(\pi-x)\sin x}{1+\sin x}\,dx \qquad ...(ii)$$

Adding (*i*) and (*ii*), we get

$$2I = \pi\int_0^\pi \frac{\sin x}{1+\sin x}\,dx$$

$$= \pi\int_0^\pi \left(1-\frac{1}{1+\sin x}\right)dx$$

$$= \pi\int_0^\pi 1\,dx - \pi\int_0^\pi \frac{1-\sin x}{\cos^2 x}\,dx$$

$$= \pi(x)_0^\pi - \pi\int_0^\pi (\sec^2 x - \sec x\tan x)\,dx$$

$$= \pi\,.\,\pi - \pi\,(\tan x - \sec x)_0^\pi$$

$$= \pi^2 - \pi\,(1+1)$$

$$2I = \pi(\pi-2)$$

$$I = \frac{\pi}{2}\,(\pi-2).$$

2. *Evaluate* $\int \frac{1}{\sin^4 x+\cos^4 x}\,dx.$

Solution:

$$I = \int \frac{dx}{\sin^4 x+\cos^4 x} = \int \frac{\sec^4 x}{\tan^4 x+1}\,dx$$

[Dividing N^r and D^r by $\cos^4 x$]

$$= \int \frac{\sec^2 x(1+\tan^2 x)}{(\tan^4 x+1)}\,dx$$

Put $\tan x = t$ then $\sec^2 x\,dx = dt$

$$I = \int \frac{1+t^2}{1+t^4}\,dt$$

$$= \int \frac{1+\frac{1}{t^2}}{t^2+\frac{1}{t^2}}\,dt \qquad \text{[Taking } t^2 \text{ common from } N^r \text{ and } D^r]$$

$$= \int \frac{1+\frac{1}{t^2}}{t^2+\frac{1}{t^2}-2+2}\,dt$$

$$= \int \frac{\left(1+\frac{1}{t^2}\right)}{\left(t-\frac{1}{t}\right)^2+2}\,dt$$

Let $\quad t-\frac{1}{t} = z,\;$ then $\left(1+\frac{1}{t^2}\right) dt = dz$

$$I = \int \frac{dz}{z^2+\left(\sqrt{2}\right)^2}$$

$$= \frac{1}{\sqrt{2}}\tan^{-1}\left(\frac{z}{\sqrt{2}}\right)+c \qquad \left[\int \frac{dx}{a^2+x^2} = \frac{1}{a}\tan^{-1}\frac{x}{a}\right]$$

$$= \frac{1}{\sqrt{2}}\tan^{-1}\left[\frac{t-1/t}{\sqrt{2}}\right]+c$$

$$= \frac{1}{\sqrt{2}}\tan^{-1}\left(\frac{t^2-1}{\sqrt{2}\,t}\right)+c$$

$$= \frac{1}{\sqrt{2}}\tan^{-1}\left[\frac{\tan^2 x-1}{\sqrt{2}\tan x}\right]+c.$$

3. *Evaluate* $\int_0^4 (x+e^{2x})\,dx$ *as a limit of sums.*

Solution: Compare $\int_0^4 (x+e^{2x})\,dx$ with $\int_0^b f(x)\,dx$

Here

$$f(x) = x+e^{2x},\; a=0 \;\text{ and }\; b=4$$
$$f(a) = f(0)=0+e^0=1$$
$$f(a+h) = h+e^{2h}$$
$$f(a+2h) = 2h+e^{4h}$$
$$\equiv \equiv \equiv \equiv$$
$$f(a+n-1h) = (n-1)\,h+e^{2(n-1)\,h}$$

$$\therefore \int_0^4 (x+e^{2x})\,dx = \lim_{h\to 0} h[f(a)+f(a+h)+\ldots.+f(a+(h-1)\,h)]$$

$$= \lim_{h\to 0} h[1+h+e^{2h}+2h+e^{4h}+\ldots+(n-1)h+e^{2(n-1)\,h}]$$

$$= \underset{h\to 0}{\text{Lt}}\ h[(1+2+3+\ldots n-1 \text{ terms})$$
$$+ h(1 + e^{2h} + e^{4h} + \ldots + e^{2(n-1)}h)]$$

Where $nh = b - a = 4 - 0 = 4$

$$= \underset{h\to 0}{\text{Lt}}\ h\left[\frac{n(n-1)}{2}h + \frac{(e^{2h})^n - 1}{e^{2h} - 1}\right] \quad \text{where } nh = 4$$

$$= \underset{h\to 0}{\text{Lt}}\left[\frac{nh(nh-h)}{2} + \frac{e^{2nh}-1}{\dfrac{e^{2h}-1}{2h}2}\right]$$

$$= \frac{4(4-0)}{2} + \frac{e^8 - 1}{12} \qquad \left[\underset{h+0}{\text{Lt}}\ \frac{e^h - 1}{h} = 1\right]$$

$$= 8 + \frac{e^8-1}{2} = \frac{1}{2}\ (15 + e^8).$$

4. *Evaluate* $\int_0^1 \cot^{-1}(1+x+x^2)\,dx.$

Solution: We have

$$\int_0^1 .\cot^{-1}(1-x+x^2) = \int_0^1 \tan^{-1}\left[\frac{1}{1-x+x^2}\right]dx$$

$$= \int_0^1 \tan^{-1}\left[\frac{1}{1-x(1-x)}\right]dx$$

$$= \int_0^1 \tan^{-1}\left[\frac{x+1-x}{1-x(1-x)}\right]dx$$

$$= \int_0^1 [\tan^{-1} x + \tan^{-1}(1-x)]\,dx$$

$$\left[\text{Using } \tan^{-1} A + \tan^{-1} B = \tan^{-1}\frac{A+B}{1-AB}\right]$$

$$= \int_0^1 \tan^{-1} x\,dx + \int_0^1 \tan^{-1}(1-x)\,dx$$

$$= \int_0^1 \tan^{-1} x\,dx + \int_0^1 \tan^{-1}[1-(1-x)]\,dx$$

$$\left[\int_0^a f(x)\,dx = \int_0^a f(a-x)\,dx\right]$$

$$= \int_0^1 \tan^{-1} x\,dx + \int_0^1 \tan^{-1} x\,dx$$

$$= 2\int_0^1 1.\tan^{-1} x\,dx$$

Integrating by parts by taking 1 as 2nd function and $\tan^{-1} x$ as the first function

$$= 2\left\{\left[\tan^{-1} x . x\right]_0^1 - \int_0^1 \frac{1}{1+x^2} x\, dx\right\}$$

$$= 2\left[(1 \tan^{-1} 1 - 0 \tan^{-1} 0) - \frac{1}{2}\int_0^1 \frac{2x}{1+x^2} dx\right].$$

$$= 2 \times \left[\frac{\pi}{4} - \frac{1}{2}\left\{\log|1+x^2|\right\}_0^1\right]$$

$$= 2\left[\frac{\pi}{4} - \frac{1}{2}\{\log 2 - \log 1\}\right]$$

$$= \frac{\pi}{2} - \log 2.$$

5. *By using the properties of definite integrals.*

Evaluate: $\int_0^{\pi/4} \log(1+\tan x)\, dx.$

Solution: Let $I = \int_0^{\pi/4} \log(1+\tan x)\, dx$

$$= \int_0^{\pi/4} \log\left[1+\tan\left(\frac{\pi}{4}-x\right)\right] dx \quad \left[\text{Using } \int_0^a f(x)\,dx = \int_0^a f(a-x)\,dx\right]$$

$$= \int_0^{\pi/4} \log\left[1+\frac{1-\tan x}{1+\tan x}\right] dx \quad \left[\text{Using } \tan(A-B) = \frac{\tan A - \tan B}{1+\tan A . \tan B}\right]$$

$$= \int_0^{\pi/4} \log\left[\frac{2}{1+\tan x}\right] dx$$

$$= \int_0^{\pi/4} [\log 2 - \log(1+\tan x)]\, dx$$

$$= \int_0^{\pi/4} \log 2\, dx - \int_0^{\pi/4} \log(1+\tan x)\, dx$$

$\Rightarrow \quad I = \log 2\, [x]_0^{\pi/4} - I$

$\Rightarrow \quad 2I = \frac{\pi}{4} \log 2$

$\Rightarrow \quad I = \frac{\pi}{8} \log 2.$

6. *Evaluate the following integral* $\int_1^4 f(x)\, dx$, *where* $f(x) = |x-1| + |x-2| + |x-3|$.

Solution: When $1 \le x \le 2$, $f(x) = (x-1) - (x-2) - (x-3) = -x + 4$

$2 \le x \le 3$, $f(x) = (x-1) + (x-2) - (x-3) = x$

$3 \le x \le 4$, $f(x) = x - 1 + x - 2 + x - 3 = 3x - 6$

$$\therefore \quad \int_1^4 f(x)\,dx = \int_1^2 f(x)\,dx + \int_2^3 f(x)\,dx + \int_3^4 f(x)\,dx$$

$$= \int_1^2 (-x+4)\,dx + \int_2^3 x\,dx + \int_3^4 (3x-6)\,dx$$

$$= \left[-\frac{x^2}{2} + 4x\right]_1^2 + \left[\frac{x^2}{2}\right]_2^3 + \left[\frac{3x^2}{2} - 6x\right]_3^4$$

$$= (-2+8) - \left(-\frac{1}{2}+4\right) + \frac{1}{2}(9-4) + (24-24) - \left(\frac{27}{2}-18\right)$$

$$= 6 - \frac{7}{2} + \frac{5}{2} + \frac{9}{2} = \frac{19}{2}.$$

7. *Evaluate* $\int \frac{dx}{x^3+1}$.

Solution:
$$\frac{1}{x^3+1} = \frac{1}{(x+1)(x^2-x+1)} = \frac{A}{x+1} + \frac{Bx+c}{x^2-x+1}$$

$$\Rightarrow \quad 1 = A(x^2-x+1) + (Bx+c)(x+1)$$

$$1 = (A+B)x^2 + (-A+B+C)x + A + C$$

Equating coefficients of x^2, x and constant terms we get

$$A + B = 0, \quad -A + B + C = 0 \text{ and } A + C = 1$$

Solving these equations

$$A = \frac{1}{3},\ B = -\frac{1}{3},\ C = \frac{2}{3}$$

$$\therefore \quad \frac{1}{x^3+1} = \frac{1}{3(x-1)} - \frac{x-2}{3(x^2-x+1)}$$

$$\Rightarrow \quad \int \frac{1}{x^3+1}\,dx = \frac{1}{3}\int \frac{dx}{x+1} - \frac{1}{3}\int \frac{x-2}{x^2-x+1}\,dx$$

$$= \frac{1}{3}\log|x+1| - \frac{1}{3}I_1 + c$$

Where
$$I_1 = \int \frac{x-2}{x^2-x+1}\,dx$$

Let
$$x - 2 = A\frac{d}{dx}(x^2-x+1) + B$$

$$= A(2x-1) + B$$

Equating the coefficients of x and constant form, we get

$$A = \frac{1}{2},\ B = -\frac{3}{2}$$

Hence,
$$I_1 = \int \frac{2x-1}{x^2-x+1}\,dx - \frac{3}{2}\int \frac{dx}{x^2-x+1}$$

$$= \frac{1}{2}I_2 - \frac{3}{2}I_3$$

Where $$I_2 = \int \frac{2x-1}{x^2-x+1}\,dx$$

Put $x^2 - x + 1 = t \Rightarrow (2x-1)\,dx = dt$

$$\int \frac{dt}{t} = \log|t| = \log|x^2 - x + 1|$$

and $$I_3 = \int \frac{dx}{x^2-x+1} = \int \frac{dx}{\left(x-\frac{1}{2}\right)^2 + \left(\frac{\sqrt{3}}{2}\right)^2}$$

$$= \frac{2}{\sqrt{3}}\tan^{-1}\left[\frac{2(x-1/2)}{\sqrt{3}}\right]$$

$$\int \frac{dx}{x^3+1} = \frac{1}{3}\log|x+1| - \frac{1}{6}\log|x^2-x+1| + \frac{1}{\sqrt{3}}\tan^{-1}\left(\frac{2x-1}{\sqrt{3}}\right) + C$$

8. *Evaluate* $\int \frac{2+\sin x}{1+\cos x} e^{x/2}\,dx.$

Solution: $$I = \int \frac{2+\sin x}{1+\cos x} e^{x/2}\,dx$$

$$= \int \frac{2+2\sin\frac{x}{2}\cos\frac{x}{2}}{2\cos^2\frac{x}{2}} e^{x/2}\,dx$$

$$= \int \frac{1+\sin\frac{x}{2}\cos\frac{x}{2}}{\cos^2\frac{x}{2}} e^{x/2}\,dx$$

$$\left[\text{Using } \sin x = 2\sin\frac{x}{2}\cos\frac{x}{2}\ \ 1+\cos x = 2\cos^2\frac{x}{2}\right]$$

$$= \int\left(\sec^2\frac{x}{2} + \tan\frac{x}{2}\right) e^{x/2}\,dx$$

$$= \int \sec^2\frac{x}{2} e^{x/2}\,dx + \int \tan\frac{x}{2} e^{x/2}\,dx$$

$$= \int e^{x/2}\sec^2\frac{x}{2}\,dx + \tan\frac{x}{2} \times \frac{e^{x/2}}{1/2}$$

$$- \int \sec^2\frac{x}{2} \times \frac{1}{2} \times \frac{e^{x/2}}{1/2}\,dx + c$$

$$= \int e^{x/2}\sec^2\frac{x}{2} + 2\tan\frac{x}{2} \times e^{x/2} - \int e^{x/2}\sec^2\frac{x}{2}\,dx + c$$

$$I = 2e^{x/2}\tan\frac{x}{2} + C.$$

9. $\int\left[\sqrt{\cot x}+\sqrt{\tan x}\right]dx.$

Solution: We have $\quad I = \int\left[\sqrt{\cot x}+\sqrt{\tan x}\right]dx. \qquad \left(\sqrt{\tan x}+\dfrac{1}{\sqrt{\tan x}}\right)dx$

$$= \int\sqrt{\tan x}\,(1+\cot x)\,dx$$

Put $\quad \tan x = t^2$ so $\sec^2 x\,dx = 2t\,dt$

$$dx = \frac{2t\,dt}{1+t^4}$$

Then
$$I = \int t\left(1+\frac{1}{t^2}\right)\frac{2t}{(1+t^4)}\,dt$$

$$= 2\int\frac{(t^2+1)}{t^4+1}\,dt$$

$$= 2\int\frac{\left(1+\frac{1}{t^2}\right)dt}{t^2+\frac{1}{t^2}} \qquad \text{[Dividing } N^r, D^r \text{ by } t^2]$$

$$= 2\int\frac{\left(1+\frac{1}{t^2}\right)dt}{\left(t-\frac{1}{t}\right)^2+2} \qquad [\text{Using } a^2+b^2=(a-b)^2+2ab]$$

Put $\quad t-1/t = y$ so that $\left(1+\dfrac{1}{t^2}\right)dt = dy$

Then
$$I = 2\int\frac{dy}{y^2+\left(\sqrt{2}\right)^2} = \sqrt{2}\tan^{-1}\frac{y}{\sqrt{2}}+c \qquad \left[\text{Using } \int\frac{dx}{x^2+a^2}=\frac{1}{a}\tan^{-1}\frac{x}{a}\right]$$

$$= \sqrt{2}\tan^{-1}\frac{\left(t-\frac{1}{t}\right)}{\sqrt{2}}+c$$

$$= \sqrt{2}\tan^{-1}\left(\frac{t^2-1}{\sqrt{2}\,t}\right)+c$$

$$= \sqrt{2}\tan^{-1}\left(\frac{\tan x-1}{\sqrt{2\tan x}}\right)+c$$

10. *Evaluate* $\displaystyle\int_0^{\pi}\frac{x\,dx}{a^2\cos^2 x+b^2\sin^2 x}.$

Solution: Let
$$I = \int_0^{\pi}\frac{x\,dx}{a^2\cos^2 x+b^2\sin^2 x}$$

$$= \int_0^{\pi} \frac{(\pi - x)\,dx}{a^2 \cos^2(\pi - x) + b^2 \sin^2(\pi - x)}$$

$$\left[\text{Using } \int_0^a f(x)\,dx = \int_0^a f(a-x)\,dx\right]$$

$$= \pi \int_0^{\pi} \frac{dx}{a^2 \cos^2 x + b^2 \sin^2 x} - \int_0^{\pi} \frac{x\,dx}{a^2 \cos^2 x + b^2 \sin^2 x}$$

$$= \int_0^{\pi} \frac{dx}{a^2 \cos^2 x + b^2 \sin^2 x} - I$$

$$2I = \pi \int_0^{\pi} \frac{dx}{a^2 \cos^2 x + b^2 \sin^2 x}$$

$$I = \frac{\pi}{2} \int_0^{\pi} \frac{dx}{a^2 \cos^2 x + b^2 \sin^2 x}$$

$$\Rightarrow \quad 2\,\frac{\pi}{2} \int_0^{\pi/2} \frac{dx}{a^2 \cos^2 x + b^2 \sin^2 x} = \pi \int_0^{\pi/2} \frac{\sec^2 x\,dx}{a^2 + b^2 \tan^2 x}$$

(Dividing N^r/D^r by $\cos^2 x$)

Put $b \tan x = t$, so that $b \sec^2 x\,dx = dt$.

Also When $x = 0$, $t = 0$

When $x = \frac{\pi}{2}$, $t \to \infty$

Therefore $I = \frac{\pi}{b} \int_0^{\infty} \frac{dt}{a^2 + t^2} = \frac{\pi}{b} \cdot \frac{1}{a} \left[\tan^{-1} \frac{t}{a}\right]_0^{\infty}$

$$= \frac{\pi}{ab}\left[\frac{\pi}{2} - 0\right] = \frac{\pi^2}{2ab}.$$

UNSOLVED QUESTIONS

SECTION-I

1. Evaluate $\int \left[\log(\log x) + \frac{1}{(\log x)^2}\right] dx.$
2. Evaluate $\int \frac{x+3}{\sqrt{5 - 4x - x^2}}\,dx.$
3. Evaluate $\int_0^2 x\sqrt{2-x}\,dx.$
4. Evaluate $\int \frac{dx}{\sin x - \sin 2x}.$
5. $\int \frac{x^2}{(x^2+1)(x^2+4)}\,dx.$ Solve
6. $\int \frac{x^2}{x^4 + x^2 + 1}\,dx.$ Evaluate

7. $\int x^2 \sin^{-1} x \, dx$. Evaluate

8. $\int_{-1}^{2} |x^3 - x| \, dx$. Evaluate

9. By using the properties of definite integrals evaluate the integral

$$\int_0^{\pi/2} \frac{\sin^{3/2} x \, dx}{\sin^{3/2} x + \cos^{3/2} x}.$$

10. Evaluate $\int e^{ax} \cos(bx + c)$.

ANSWERS

1. $x \log(\log x) - \dfrac{x}{\log x} + c$

2. $-\sqrt{5-4x-x^2} + \sin^{-1}\left(\dfrac{x+2}{3}\right) + c$

3. $\dfrac{16\sqrt{2}}{5}$

4. $-\dfrac{1}{2} \log|1 - \cos x| - \dfrac{1}{6} \log|1 + \cos x| + \dfrac{2}{3} \log|1 - \cos 2x| + c$

5. $-\dfrac{1}{3} \tan^{-1} x + \dfrac{2}{3} \tan^{-1}\left(\dfrac{x}{2}\right) + c$

6. $\dfrac{1}{4} \log\left|\dfrac{x^2 - x + 1}{x^2 + x + 1}\right| + \dfrac{1}{2\sqrt{3}} \tan^{-1}\left(\dfrac{x^2 - 1}{x\sqrt{3}}\right) + c$

7. $\dfrac{1}{3} x^3 \sin^{-1} x + \dfrac{1}{3}\sqrt{1-x^2} - \dfrac{1}{9}(1 - x^2)^{3/2} + c$

8. $\dfrac{11}{4}$

9. $\dfrac{\pi}{4}$

10. $\dfrac{e^{ax}}{a^2 + b^2}[a \cos(bx + c) + b \sin(bx + x)] + c_1$

SECTION-III

1. Evaluate : $\int_0^{\pi/2} \dfrac{\sin 2x}{\sin^4 + \cos^2 x} dx$

2. $\int_{-1}^{3/2} |x \sin \pi x| \, dx$

3. Evaluate : $\int_0^1 (3x^2 + 2x + 1) \, dx$ as a limit of sum.

4. Evaluate the following as limit of sum $\int_0^2 (e^{3x} + 1) dx$.

5. Evaluate : $\int_{-a}^{a} \sqrt{\dfrac{a-x}{a+x}} dx$.

6. Evaluate : $\int x + 1\sqrt{1 - x - x^2} \, dx$.

7. Evaluate : $\int_0^{\pi/2} \dfrac{dx}{5 + 4\sin x}$.

8. Evaluate : $\int_0^{\pi} \frac{x \tan x}{\sec x + \tan x}\, dx$.

9. Evaluate : $\int_0^{\pi} \log(1+\cos x)\, dx$.

10. $\int_0^{4} [|x-1| + |x-2| + |x-3|]\, dx$.

ANSWERS

1. $\frac{\pi}{2}$ 2. $\frac{3}{\pi} + \frac{1}{\pi^2}$ 3. 3

4. $\frac{1}{3}(e^6 + 5)$ 5. $a\pi$

6. $-\frac{1}{3}(1-x-x^2)^{3/2} + \frac{2x+1}{8}\sqrt{1-x+x^2} + \frac{5}{16}\sin^{-1}\left(\frac{2x+1}{\sqrt{5}}\right) + c$

7. $\frac{2}{3}\tan^{-1}\frac{1}{3}$ 8. $\frac{\pi}{2}(\pi-2)$ 9. $-\pi \log 2$ 10. $\frac{19}{2}$

HOTS (TRY THESE)

1. Evaluate : $\int \frac{dx}{x^4(x^3+2)^3}$

2. Evaluate : $\int \sqrt{\frac{1-\sqrt{x}}{1+\sqrt{x}}}\, dx$

3. Evaluate : $\int_0^{\pi} \frac{x\, dx}{1+\cos^2 x}$

4. $\int_{-\sqrt{2}}^{\sqrt{2}} \frac{dx}{(1+e^x)(1+x^2)}$

ANSWERS

1. $-\frac{1}{48}\left[t - 3\ln|t| - \frac{3}{t} - \frac{1}{2t^2}\right] + c$ where $t = 1 + \frac{2}{x^3}$

2. $\cos^{-1}\sqrt{x} - 2\sqrt{1-x} + \sqrt{1-x}\sqrt{x}$

3. $\frac{\pi^2}{2\sqrt{2}}$

4. $\frac{\pi}{3}$

❑❑❑

CHAPTER 8

APPLICATION OF INTEGRALS

1. **Area of a curve between two ordinates:** Let $y = f(x)$ be a continuous and finite function in $[a, b]$.

Case (I). When the curve $y = f(x)$ lies above the x-axis.

The area bounded by the curve $y = f(x)$, the x-axis and the ordinates $x = a$ and $x = b$ is given by

$$\text{area} = \int_a^b y\,dx$$

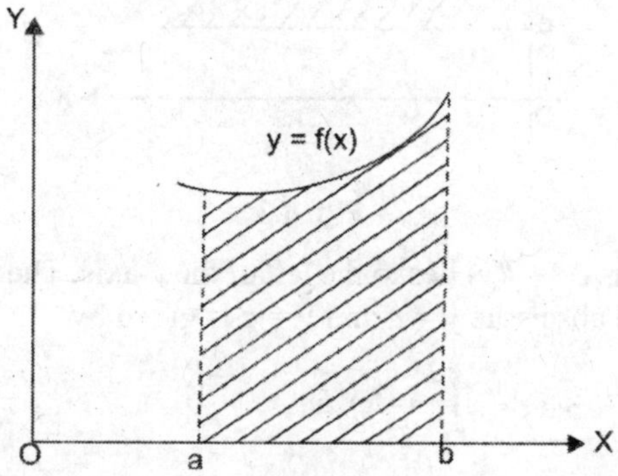

Fig. 8.1

Case (II). When the curve $y = f(x)$ lies below the x-axis.

The area between the curve $y = f(x)$ the x-axis, and the ordinates $x = a$ and $x = b$ is given by

$$\text{area} = \int_a^b (-y)\,dx$$

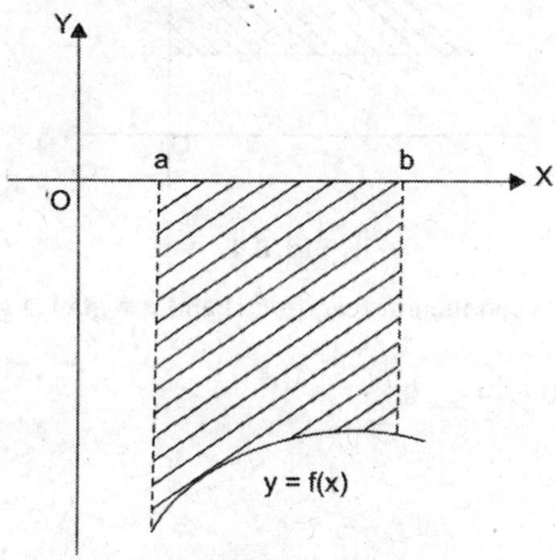

Fig. 8.2

2. **Area of a curve between two abscissae.**

Case (I). When the curve $I = f(y)$ lies to the right of the y-axis. The area bounded by the curve $x = f(y)$, the h-axis and the abscissae $y = c$ and $y = d$ is given by

$$\text{area} = \int_c^a x\,dy$$

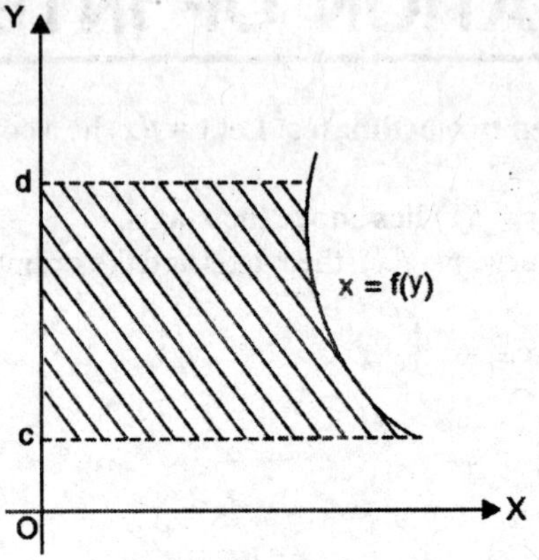

Fig. 8.3

Case (II). When the curve $x = f(y)$ lies to the left of the y-axis. The area bounded by the curve $x = f(y)$, the y-axis and the abscissae $y = c$ and $y = d$ is given by

$$\text{area} = \int_c^d (-x)\,dy$$

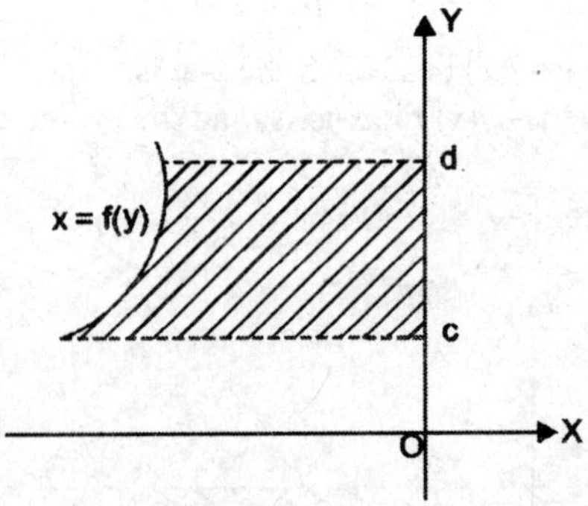

Fig. 8.4

3. The area bounded between the curves $y = f(x)$ and $y = g(x)$ is given by

$$\int_a^b [f(x) - g(x)]\,dx$$

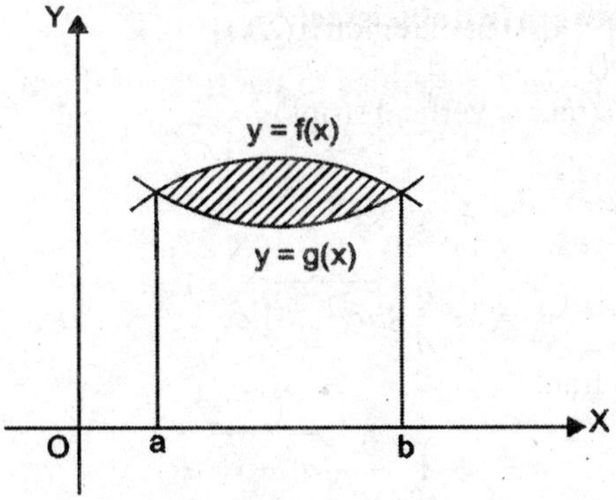

Fig. 8.5

HOW TO TRACE THE CURVE

- First check the symmetricity.
  If power of x is even the curve is symmetric about y-axis or vice versa.
- Put $x = 0$ or $y = 0$ to find the point the curve passes through.
- Area $= \int_a^b y dx$ or $\int_a^b x\, dy$.
- If there are two curves, put the value of one into other to find the point of intersection besides following the above rules.

$$\text{Area} = \int_a^b [f(x) - g(x)] dy$$

SOLVED QUESTIONS

SECTION-III

1. *Find the area enclosed by the Ellipse* $\frac{x^2}{a^2} + \frac{y^2}{b^2} = 1.$

The given equation of ellipse is symmetrical about x-axis and y-axis.
Solution: Area enclosed by ellipse = Area of region $AB\,A'B'A$

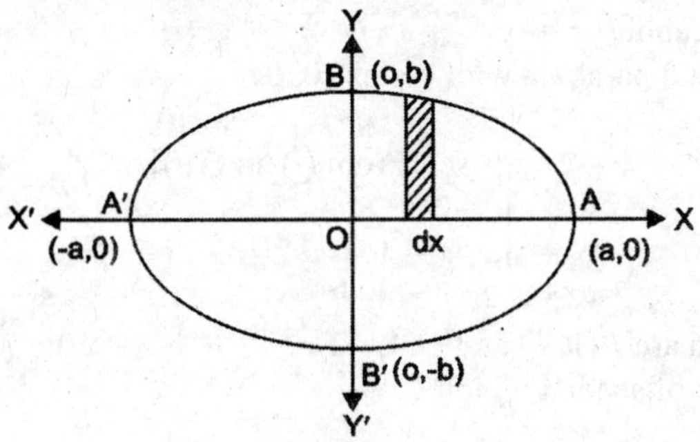

Fig. 8.1

Area of region $AB\,A'B'A = 4$[Area of region $AOBA$]

$$= 4 \int_0^a y\,dx \quad \text{(taking vertical strips)}$$

Now $\quad \dfrac{x^2}{a^2} + \dfrac{y^2}{b^2} = 1$ gives

$$y = \pm \frac{b}{a}\sqrt{a^2 - x^2}$$

But y is +ve in first quadrant

$$\text{Area} = 4 \int_0^a \frac{b}{a}\sqrt{a^2 - x^2}\,dx$$

$$= \frac{4b}{a} \int_0^a \sqrt{a^2 - x^2}\,dx$$

$$= \frac{4b}{a}\left[\frac{x}{2}\sqrt{a^2 - x^2} + \frac{a^2}{2}\sin^{-1}\frac{x}{a}\right]_0^a$$

$$= \frac{4b}{a}\left[\left(\frac{a}{2}\times 0 + \frac{a^2}{2}\sin^{-1}1\right) - 0\right]$$

$$= \frac{\cancel{4}b}{\cancel{a}} \times \frac{a^{\cancel{2}}}{\cancel{2}} \times \frac{\pi}{\cancel{2}} = \pi ab$$

ALTERNATIVELY: Considering horizontal strips

$$\text{Area} = 4 \int_0^b x\,dy$$

$$= \frac{4a}{b} \int_0^b \sqrt{b^2 - y^2}\,dy$$

$$= \frac{4a}{b}\left[\frac{y}{2}\sqrt{b^2 - y^2} + \frac{b^2}{2}\sin^{-1}\frac{y}{b}\right]_0^a$$

$$= \frac{\cancel{4}a}{\cancel{b}}\,\frac{b^{\cancel{2}}}{\cancel{2}}\,\frac{\pi}{\cancel{2}} = \pi ab.$$

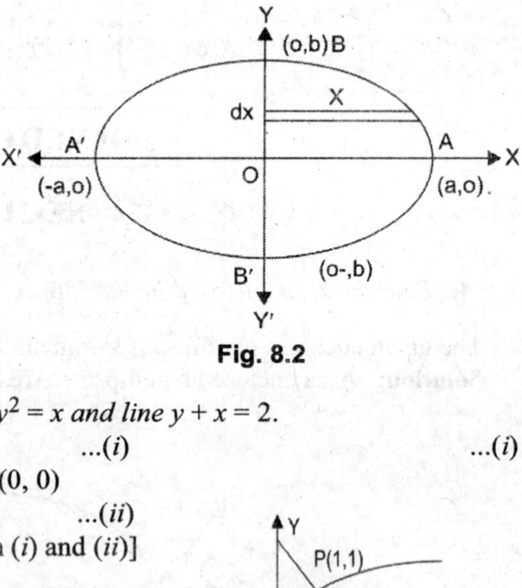

Fig. 8.2

2. *Find the area enclosed by the parabola $y^2 = x$ and line $y + x = 2$.*

Solution: Given parabola $y^2 = x$ ...(*i*) ...(*i*)

It represents right hand parabola with vertex (0, 0)

Given line is $y + x = 2$ ...(*ii*)

$y^2 = 2 - y \Rightarrow \quad y^2 + y - 2 = 0$ [From (*i*) and (*ii*)]

$$y = 1, -2$$

When $\quad y = 1, \; x = 1$

$$y = -2, \; x = 4$$

Points of intersection are $P(1, 1)$ and $Q(4, -2)$.

Required area = area of shaded region

$$= \int_2^4 [(2 - y) - y^2]\,dy$$

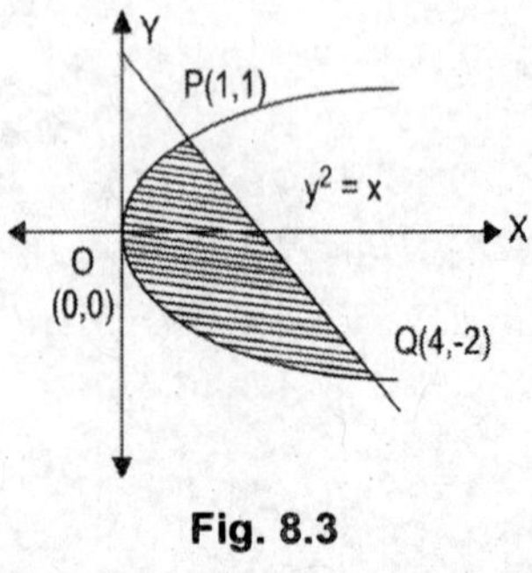

Fig. 8.3

$$= \left[2y - \frac{y^2}{2} - \frac{y^3}{3}\right]_{-2}^{1} = 2 - \frac{1}{2} - \frac{1}{3} + 6 - \frac{8}{3} = \frac{9}{2} \text{ sq. units.}$$

3. *Find the area of region* $\{(x, y) : 0 \le y \le x^2 + 1,\ 0 \le y \le x + 1,\ 0 \le x \le 2\}$.

Solution: Let us first sketch the region whose area is to be found out

$$A_1 = \{(x, y)\quad 0 \le y \quad \le x^2 + 1\}$$
$$A_2 = \{(x, y)\quad 0 \le y \quad \le x + 1\}$$
$$A_3 = \{(x, y)\quad 0 \le x \quad \le 2\}$$

The points of intersection of $y = x^2 + 1$ and $y = x + 1$ are points $P(0, 1)$ and $Q(1, 2)$.

From the figure the required region is *OP QRTSO* whose area

= Area of region *OTPQO* + *AREA* of region *TSRQT*

$$= \int_0^1 x^2 + 1\, dx + \int_1^2 x + 1\, dx = \left[\left(\frac{x^3}{3} + x\right)\right]_0^1 + \left[\left(\frac{x^2}{2} + x\right)\right]_1^2$$

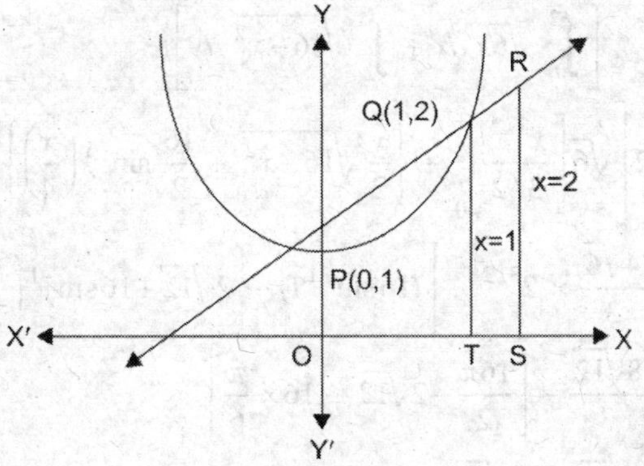

Fig. 8.4

$$= \left[\left(\frac{1}{3} + 1\right) = 0\right] + \left[(2 + 2) - \left(\frac{1}{2} + 1\right)\right] = \frac{23}{6}.$$

4. *Find the area of that part of circle* $x^2 + y^2 = 16$ *which is exterior to the parabola* $y^2 = 6x$.

Solution:

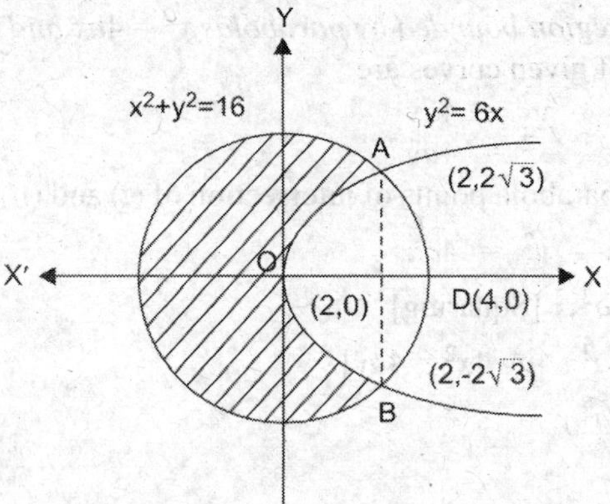

Fig. 8.5

$x^2 + y^2 = 16 = (4)^2$ represents a circle with centre (0, 0) and Radius = 4 where as $y^2 = 6x$ represents a parabola, passing through centre and is symmetric to *x-axis*.

Given curve are $\quad y^2 = 6x \quad$ ...(*i*)

and $\quad x^2 + y^2 = 16 \quad$ ...(*ii*)

From (*i*) and (*ii*)

$$x^2 + 6x = 16$$
$$x^2 + 6x - 16 = 0$$
$$x = -8,\ x = 2$$

$x = -8$ not possible

$$x = 2$$
$$y^2 = 12$$
$$y = \pm 2\sqrt{3}$$

Points of intersection are $A\left(2, 2\sqrt{3}\right)$ and $B\left(2, -2\sqrt{3}\right)$.

Area of Shaded region = Area of circle – Area *ADBOA*

$$= \pi(4)^2 - 2\left[\int_0^2 \sqrt{6x}\,dx + \int_2^4 \sqrt{16-x^2}\,dx\right]$$

$$= 16\pi - 2\left[\sqrt{6}\left[\frac{x^{3/2}}{3/2}\right]_0^2 + \left\{\frac{x}{2}\sqrt{16-x^2} + \frac{16}{2}\sin^{-1}\left(\frac{x}{4}\right)\right\}_2^4\right]$$

$$= 16\pi - \frac{4\sqrt{6}}{3} \times 2^{3/2} - \left[(16\sin^{-1}1) - \left\{2\sqrt{12} + 16\sin^{-1}\left(\frac{1}{2}\right)\right\}\right]$$

$$= 16\pi - \frac{8\sqrt{12}}{3} - \left[\frac{16\pi}{2} - 2\sqrt{12} - 16 \times \frac{\pi}{6}\right]$$

$$= 16\pi - \frac{8\sqrt{12}}{3} - \frac{8\sqrt{12}}{3} - 8\pi + 2\sqrt{12} + \frac{8\pi}{3}$$

$$= \frac{32\pi - 2\sqrt{12}}{3}$$

$$= \frac{32\pi - 4\sqrt{3}}{3} \text{ sq. units}$$

5. *Find the area of region bounded by parabolas $y^2 = 4ax$ and $x^2 = 4ay$.*

Solution: Equation of given curves are

$$y^2 = 4ax \quad \text{...}(i)$$
$$x^2 = 4ay \quad \text{...}(ii)$$

(*i*) and (*ii*) represents parabola points of intersection of (*i*) and (*ii*) are *O*(0, 0) and *A*(4*a*, 4*a*)

Point of intersection:— $y^2 = 4ax$

$$y^4 = 16a^2x^2 \text{ [Squaring]}$$
$$= 16a^2 \cdot 4ay \quad [x^2 = 4ay]$$
$$y^4 = 64a^3 y$$
$$y(y^3 - 64a^3) = 0$$
$$y = 0$$
$$y = 4a$$

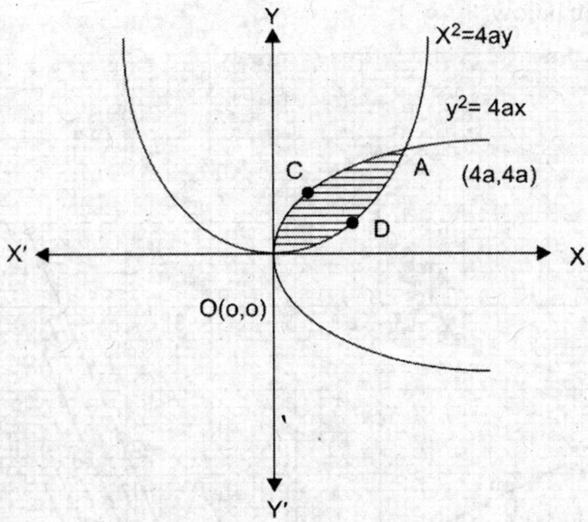

Fig. 8.6

For $y = 0 \Rightarrow x = 0$

$y = 4a \Rightarrow x = 4a.$

Required Area = Area of shaded region

= Area of region *OCADO* – Area of region *ODABO*

$$= \int_0^{4a} \sqrt{4ax}\, dx - \int_0^{4a} \frac{x^2}{4a} dx$$

$$= \left[2\sqrt{a}\,\frac{2}{3}x^{3/2}\right]_0^{4a} - \frac{1}{4a}\left[\frac{x^3}{3}\right]_0^{4a}$$

$$= \frac{4\sqrt{a}}{3}(4a)^{3/2} - \frac{1}{4a}\frac{1}{3}(4a)^3$$

$$= \frac{32a^2}{3} - \frac{16a^2}{3} = \frac{16a^2}{3} \text{ sq. units.}$$

6. *Sketch the graph of*

$$f(x) = \begin{cases} |x-2|+2, & x \le 2 \\ x^2\ 2, & x > 2 \end{cases}$$

Evaluate $\int_0^4 f(x)$. *What does value of this integral represent on the graph?*

Solution:

$$f(x) = \begin{cases} |x-2|+2, & x \le 2 \\ x^2\ 2, & x > 2 \end{cases}$$

$$f(x) = \begin{cases} |x-2|+2 = 2 & \text{for } x = 2 \\ 4-x & \text{for } x < 2 \\ x^2-2 & \text{for } x > 2 \end{cases}$$

Graph of $f(x)$ is given below:

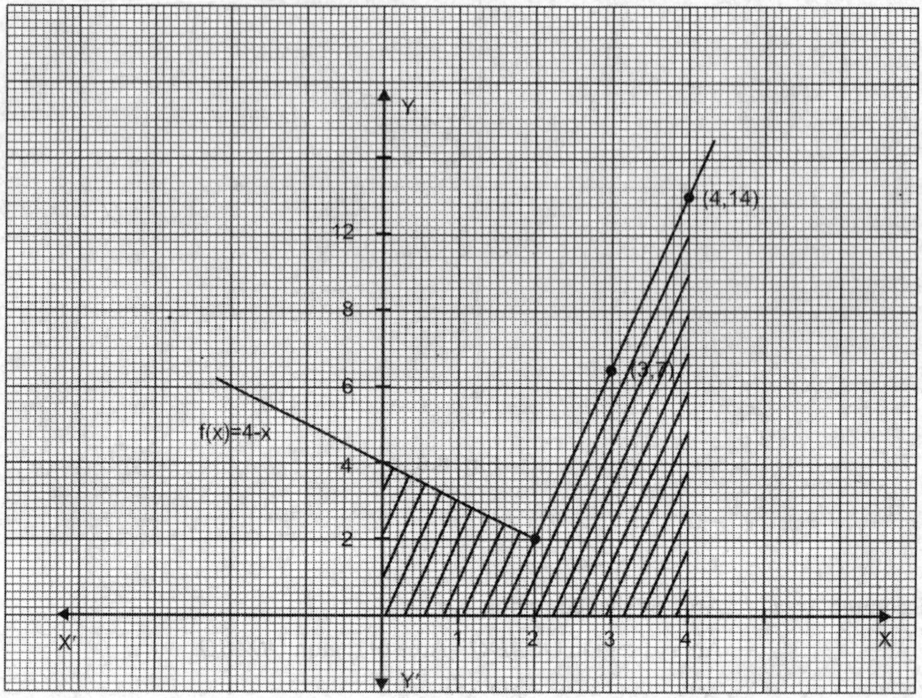

Fig. 8.7

$$\int_0^4 f(x)\,dx = \int_0^2 f(x)\,dx + \int_2^4 f(x)\,dx$$

$$\int_0^4 f(x)\,dx = \int_0^2 \{|x-2|+2\}\,dx + \int_2^4 (x^2-2)\,dx$$

$$= \int_0^2 (-x+4)\,dx + \int_2^4 (x^2-2)\,dx$$

$$= \int_0^2 (4-x)\,dx + \left[\frac{x^3}{3} - 2x\right]_2^4$$

$$= \left[4x - \frac{x^2}{2}\right]_0^2 + \left[\frac{4^3}{3} - 2(4) - \left(\frac{2^3}{3} - 2\times 2\right)\right]$$

$$= \left[4\times 2 - \frac{2^2}{2}\right] + \left[\frac{56-12}{3}\right]$$

$$= 6 + \frac{44}{3} = \frac{62}{3}.$$

7. *Find the area of smaller region bounded by ellipse* $\frac{x^2}{9} + \frac{y^2}{4} = 1$ *and the straight line* $\frac{x}{3} + \frac{y}{2} = 1.$

Solution: We have two curves

$$\frac{x^2}{9} + \frac{y^2}{4} = 1 \qquad ...(1)$$

$$\frac{x}{3} + \frac{y}{2} = 1 \qquad ...(2)$$

Euqation (1) represents an ellipse in the form of $\frac{x^2}{a^2} + \frac{y^2}{b^2} = 1$

Here $a = 3,\ b = 2$

Equation (2) represents the euqation of line in intercept form, with x intercept = 3, y intercept = 2.

Solving (1) and (2)

$$\frac{x^2}{9} + \left(1 - \frac{x}{3}\right)^2 = 1$$

$\Rightarrow$ Either $\frac{x}{3} = 0$ or $\frac{x}{3} - 1 = 0$

$\Rightarrow$ Either $x = 0$ or $x = 3$

Then $y = 2$ then $y = 0$

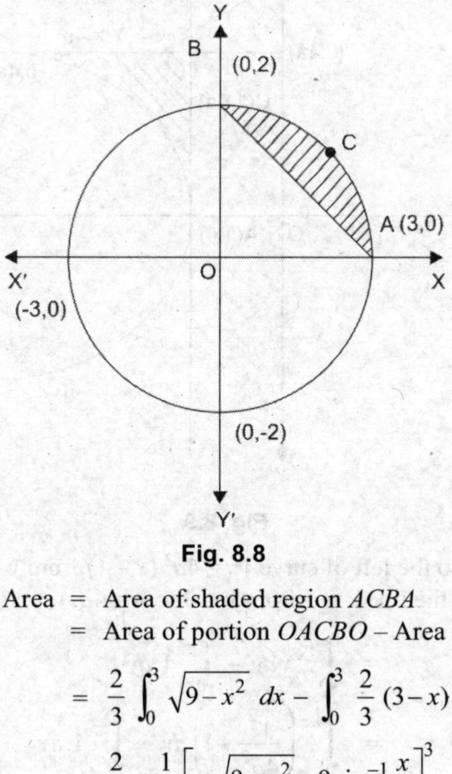

Fig. 8.8

Required Area = Area of shaded region $ACBA$

= Area of portion $OACBO$ – Area of portion $AOBO$

$$= \frac{2}{3}\int_0^3 \sqrt{9-x^2}\,dx - \int_0^3 \frac{2}{3}(3-x)\,dx$$

$$= \frac{2}{3} \times \frac{1}{2}\left[x\sqrt{9-x^2} + 9\sin^{-1}\frac{x}{3}\right]_0^3 - \frac{2}{3}\left[3x - \frac{x^2}{2}\right]_0^3$$

$$= \frac{9}{3}\left[\left\{3(0) + 9\sin^{-1}\left(\frac{3}{3}\right)\right\} - \left\{0 + 9\sin^{-1}\left(\frac{0}{3}\right)\right\}\right]$$

$$- \frac{2}{3}\left[\left(\frac{9-9}{2} - (0-0)\right)\right.$$

$$= \frac{1}{3} \times 9 \times \frac{\pi}{2} - \frac{2}{3} \times \frac{9}{2}$$

$$= \frac{3}{2}(\pi - 2) \text{ square units.}$$

8. *Find the area bounded by the curve $y^2 = 4a^2(x-1)$ and the lines $x = 1$ and $y = 4a$.*

Solution: Given curves and lines are

$$y^2 = 4a^2(x-1) \quad ...(1)$$

$$x = 1 \quad ...(2)$$

$$y = 4a \quad ...(3)$$

Solving (1) and (2)

$$y^2 = 4a(1-1) \Rightarrow y^2 = 0 \Rightarrow y = 0$$

Solving (1) and (3)

$$(4a)^2 = 4a^2(x-1)$$

$$x = 5$$

points of intersection of (1), (2) and (3) are $A(1, 0)$, $C(1, 4a)$ and $B(5, 40)$.

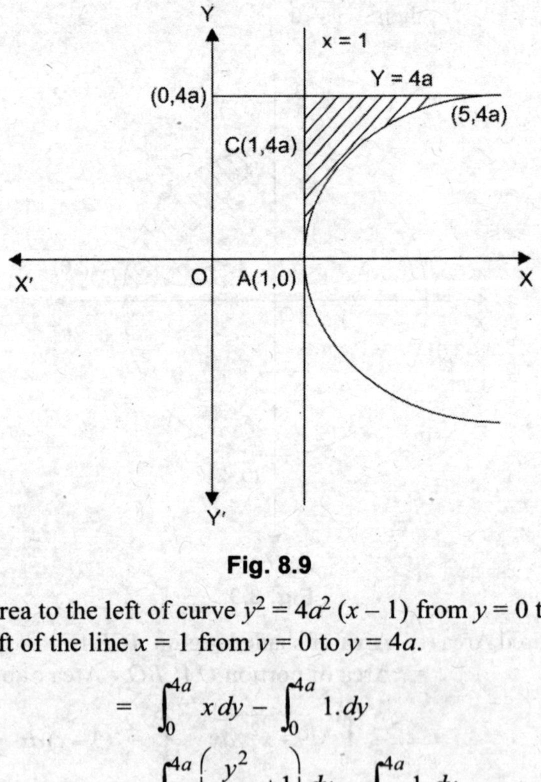

Fig. 8.9

Required Area = Area to the left of curve $y^2 = 4a^2(x-1)$ from $y = 0$ to $y = 4a$ – Area to the left of the line $x = 1$ from $y = 0$ to $y = 4a$.

$$= \int_0^{4a} x\,dy - \int_0^{4a} 1.dy$$

$$= \int_0^{4a} \left(\frac{y^2}{4a^2} + 1\right) dy - \int_0^{4a} 1.dy$$

$$= \int_0^{4a} \frac{y^2}{4a^2}\,dy$$

$$= \frac{1}{4a^2}\left[\frac{y^3}{3}\right]_0^{4a}$$

$$= \frac{1}{12a^2} \times 64a^3 = \frac{16a}{3} \text{ sq. unit.}$$

9. *Using the method of integration, find the area of the region bounded by lines* $2x + y = 4$, $3x - 2y = 6$ *and* $x - 3y + 5 = 0$.

Solution: The given lines are

$$2x + y = 4 \quad ...(i)$$
$$3x - 2y = 6 \quad ...(ii)$$
$$x - 3y = -5 \quad ...(iii)$$

Multiplying (*iii*) by (*ii*) and subtracting from (*i*)

We get, $x = 1$ and $y = 2$

Put $y = 2$ in (*i*) $\Rightarrow$

$$2x + 2 = 4$$
$$\Rightarrow \quad x = 1$$

$$2x - 6y = -10$$
$$2x + y = 4$$
$$- \quad - \quad -$$
$$+7y = +14 \Rightarrow y = 2$$

Hence line (*i*) and (*iii*) intersect at (1, 2)

Again, Multiply (*iii*) by 3 and subtracting it from (*ii*)

$$3x - 9y = -15$$
$$3x - 2y = 6$$
$$- \quad + \quad -$$
$$+7y = +21$$
$$y = 3$$

Put $y = 3$ in (*ii*) we get,

$$3x - 2 \times 3 = 6$$
$$\Rightarrow \quad x = 4$$

Lines (*ii*) and (*iii*) intersecting at (4, 3)

Now, multiply equation (*i*) by (*ii*) and add it to (*ii*)

$$4x + 2y = 8$$
$$3x - 2y = 6$$
$$7x = 14$$
$$x = 2$$

Put $x = 2$ in equation (*ii*)

$$4 + y = 4 \Rightarrow y = 0$$

Hence, lines (*i*) and (*ii*) intersect at (2, 0).

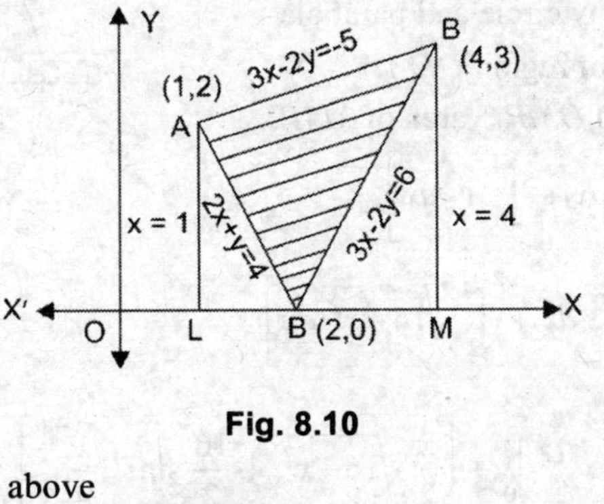

Fig. 8.10

Plot the graph as shown above

$$\text{ar}(\Delta ABC) = \text{ar}(ALMB) - \text{ar}(ALC) - \text{ar}(BCM)$$

$$= \int_1^4 y_1\, dx - \int_1^2 y_2\, dx - \int_2^4 y_3\, dx$$

$$= \int_1^4 \frac{x+5}{3} dx - \int_1^2 (4-2x)\, dx - \int_2^4 \frac{3x-6}{2}$$

$$= \frac{1}{3}\left[\frac{x^2}{2} + 5x\right]_1^4 - \left[4x - x^2\right]_1^2 - \frac{1}{2}\left[\frac{3x^2}{2} - 6x\right]_2^4$$

$$= \frac{1}{3}\left(\left[\frac{16}{2} + 20\right] - \left[\frac{1}{2} + 5\right]\right) - [(8-4)-(4-1)]$$

$$- \frac{1}{2}\left[\left(\frac{3\times 16}{2} - 24\right) - \left(\frac{3\times 4}{2} - 12\right)\right]$$

$$= \frac{7}{2} \text{ sq. unit.}$$

10. *Find the area enclosed between circle $x^2 + y^2 = 16$, exterior to parabola $y^2 = 6x$.*

Solution: The given curves are

$$x^2 + y^2 = 16 \quad ...(1)$$

$$y^2 = 6x \quad ...(2)$$

Putting $y^2 = 6x$ in (1)

$$x^2 + 6x = 16$$

$$x^2 + 6x - 16 = 0$$

$\Rightarrow$ $$(x+8)(x-2) = 0$$

$\Rightarrow$ $$x = -812$$

$$x \neq -8 \quad \text{and} \quad x = 2$$

From (2) $$y^2 = 6x = 6 \times 2 = 12$$

$\Rightarrow$ $$y = \pm 2\sqrt{3}$$

Area of whole circle $$= 4\int_0^4 \sqrt{16-x^2}\, dx$$

$$= 4\left[\frac{x}{2}\sqrt{16-x^2} + \frac{16}{2}\sin^{-1}\frac{x}{4}\right]_0^4$$

$$= 16\pi \text{ sq. units}$$

Circle and Parabola intersect at $P(2, 2\sqrt{3})$ and $Q(2, -2\sqrt{3})$

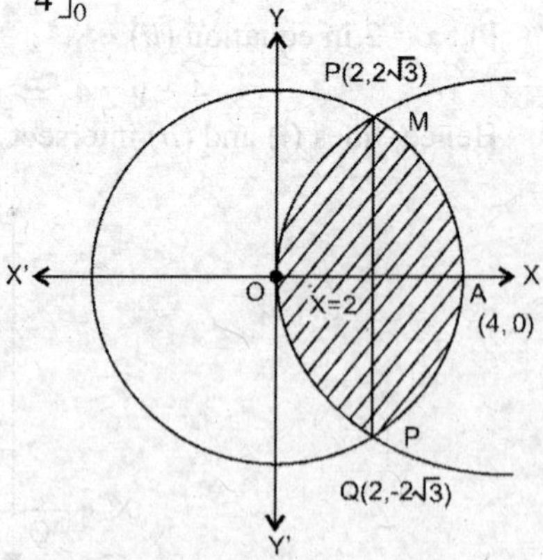

Fig. 8.10

Smaller area enclosed by circle and parabola

$= 2 \times$ Area of region $OMAP$

$= 2$ [Area of OMP + area of MAP]

$$= 2\left[\int_0^2 y_1\, dx + \int_2^4 y_2\, dx\right]$$

$$= 2\left[\int_0^2 \sqrt{6x}\, dx + \int_2^4 \sqrt{16-x^2}\, dx\right]$$

$$= 2\left[\sqrt{6}\frac{2}{3}\left[x^{3/2}\right]_0^2 + \left[\frac{x}{2}\sqrt{16-x^2} + \frac{16}{2}\sin^{-1}\frac{x}{4}\right]_2^4\right]$$

$$= \left(\frac{16\sqrt{3}}{3} - 4\sqrt{3}\right) + \frac{16}{3}\pi$$

$$= \frac{4\sqrt{3}}{3} + \frac{16}{3}\pi$$

Common area exterior to the parabola $y^2 = 6x$

$$= 16\pi - \left(\frac{4\sqrt{3}}{3} + \frac{16}{3}\pi\right)$$

$$= \frac{4}{3}\left(8\pi - \sqrt{3}\right).$$

UNSOLVED QUESTIONS

1. Find the area of region enclosed by the parabola $x^2 = y$, the line $y = x + 2$ and the x-axis.
2. Find the area of circle $4x^2 + 4y^2 = 9$, which is interior to parabola $x^2 = 4y$.
3. Find the area of region $\{(x, y) : y^2 \le 4x, \quad 4x^2 + 4y^2 \le 9\}$.
4. Find the area of circle $x^2 + y^2 = 16$. Which is exterior to parabola $y^2 = 6x$.
5. Draw the graph of curve $y = \sqrt{9 - x^2}$ find the area bounded by the curve and coordinate axes.
6. Find the area of region $\{(x, y) : x^2 + y^2 \le 1, \quad x \le y\}$.
7. Find the area of smaller region bounded by ellipse $\frac{x^2}{a^2} + \frac{y^2}{b^2} = 1$ and straight line $\frac{x}{a} + \frac{y}{b} = 1$.
8. Find the area of region enclosed between circles

   $x^2 + y^2 = 1$ and $(x - 1)^2 + y^2 = 1$.
9. Using integration find the region bounded by the following curves

   $y = |x + 1| + 1, \quad x = -2, \quad x = 3, \quad y = 0.$
10. Using integration, compute area bounded by lines $x + 2y = 2$, $y = x = 1$ and $2x + y = 7$.

ANSWERS

1. $\frac{9}{2}$
2. $\frac{\sqrt{2}}{6} + \frac{9}{4}\sin^{-1}\frac{2\sqrt{2}}{3}$
3. $\left[\frac{\sqrt{2}}{6} + \frac{9\pi}{8} - \frac{9}{4}\sin^{-1}\left(\frac{1}{3}\right)\right]$ sq. units
4. $\left(\frac{32\pi}{3} - \frac{4}{\sqrt{3}}\right)$ sq. units
5. $\frac{9\pi}{4}$ sq. units
6. $\left(\frac{\pi}{4} - \frac{1}{2}\right)$ sq. units
7. $\frac{1}{2}\left(\frac{\pi}{2} - 1\right)$ sq. units
8. $\left(\frac{2\pi}{3} - \frac{\sqrt{3}}{2}\right)$ sq. units
9. 13.5 sq. units
10. 6 sq. units

❑❑❑

CHAPTER 9

DIFFERENTIAL EQUATIONS

Definition→An equation involving the independent variable x, dependent variable y and the differential co-efficienls $\frac{dy}{dx}, \frac{d^2y}{dx^2}$ ....., is called a differential equation.

For example; $\frac{d^2y}{dx^2} - 6y = 5x^2$ is a differential equation.

Order and degree of a differential equation→The order of a differential equation is the order of the highest derivative of the unknown function occurring in the differential equation.

For example, $\frac{d^2y}{dx^2} + 6y = x$ is a differential equation of 2nd order because the order of the highest derivative occurring in it is 2.

The degree of a differential equation is the degree of the highest derivative occurring in the equation when the differential co-efficients are free from radicals and fractions.

Example: $5x^2 \frac{d^2y}{dx^2} + x \cdot \frac{dy}{dx} + 15y = 0$ is a differential equation of order 2 and degree 1.

Solution of a differential equation→A function of the form $y = f(x) + c$ which satisfies a given differential equation is called its solution.

General solution of a differential equation→Suppose a differential equation of order n is being, given. If its solution contains n arbitrary constants then it is called a general solution.

Particular solution of a differential equation→Giving particular values to arbitrary constants in the general solution of a differential equation, we get its particular solution.

SOLUTION OF DIFFERENTIAL EQUATIONS

Solving differential equations with variables separable→If the given differential equation can be expressed in the form $f(x)dx = g(y)dy$, then $\int f(x)\,dx = \int g(y) . dy + c$ is the solution of such differential equation.

Homogeneous differential equaiton→An equation of the form $\frac{dy}{dx} = \frac{f(x,y)}{g(x,y)}$, where both $f(x, y)$ and $g(x, y)$ are homogeneous function of degree n, is called a homogeneous differential equation.

Example→ $\frac{dy}{dx} = \frac{x^2 - y^2}{xy}$ is a homogeneous differential equation.

Method of solving a homogenous differential equation: Let $\frac{dy}{dx} = \frac{f(x,y)}{g(x,y)}$ be a homogeneous differential equation.

Putting $\quad y = vx$

$$\Rightarrow \quad \frac{dy}{dx} = v + x \cdot \frac{dv}{dx}$$

$$\therefore \quad v + x \cdot \frac{dv}{dx} = F(v)$$

$$\Rightarrow \quad \frac{dv}{F(v) - v} = \frac{dx}{x}$$

$$\Rightarrow \quad \int \frac{dv}{F(v) - v} = \int \frac{dx}{x}$$

$$\Rightarrow \quad \int \frac{dv}{F(v) - v} = \text{Log}\,|x| + c$$

Now, replace v by $\frac{y}{x}$ to obtain the required solution.

Linear differential equations. The most general form of linear differential equations is $\frac{dy}{dx} + Py = Q$, where P and Q are the functions of x.

The other common form of linear differential equations is $\frac{dy}{dx} + Px = a$, where P is a constant and Q is a constant or a function of y.

Solution of $\frac{dy}{dx} + Py = Q$.

First, we find $e^{\int Pdx}$, which is known as Integrating Factor (I.F.)

Now, $\quad \frac{dy}{dx} + Py = Q$

$$\Rightarrow \quad e^{\int Pdx} \frac{dy}{dx} + P \cdot y\, e^{\int Pdx} = Q \cdot e^{\int Pdx}$$

$$\Rightarrow \quad e^{\int Pdx}\, dy + P \cdot y\, e^{\int Pdx}\, dx = Q \cdot e^{\int Pdx}$$

$$\Rightarrow \quad d\left(y . e^{\int Pdx}\right) = Q . e^{\int Pdx}\, dx$$

$$\Rightarrow \quad y \cdot e^{\int Pdx} = \int Q . e^{\int Pdx}\, dx + c$$

which is the required solution.

Working rules for solving $\frac{dy}{dx} + Py = Q$

(*i*) Find I.F. = $e^{\int Pdx}$

(*ii*) The solution is given by $y \times I.F. = \int (Q \times I.F.)\, dx + c$

SOLVED QUESTIONS

SECTION-I

1. *Verify that* $y = A \cos x - B \sin x$ *is a solution of differential equation* $\frac{d^2y}{dx^2} + y = 0$.

Solution: $y = A \cos x - B \sin x$

Differentiating w.r.t. x, we get

$$\frac{dy}{dx} = -A \sin x - B \cos x$$

$$\Rightarrow \quad \frac{d^2y}{dx^2} = -A \cos x + B \sin x$$

$$= -(A \cos x - B \sin x) = -y$$

$$\Rightarrow \quad \frac{d^2y}{dx^2} + y = 0.$$

2. *Form a differential equation not containing arbitrary constants and satisfied by the equation* $y^2 = a(b - x^2)$, *a, b are arbitrary constants.*

Solution: $y^2 = a(b - x^2)$

Differentiating w.r.t. x ...(1)

$$2y \frac{dy}{dx} = a(0 - 2x)$$

$$y \frac{dy}{dx} = -ax \qquad ...(2)$$

Differentiating (2) w.r.t. x

$$y \frac{d^2y}{dx^2} + \frac{dy}{dx}\frac{dy}{dx} = -a \,.\, 1 = +\frac{1}{x}\, y \frac{dy}{dx}$$

$$\Rightarrow \quad xy \frac{d^2y}{dx^2} + x\left(\frac{dy}{dx}\right)^2 - y\frac{dy}{dx} = 0$$ is the required differential equation.

3. *Solve the following differential equation* $\frac{dy}{dx} = e^{x+y} + x^2 e^y$.

Solution: Given $\frac{dy}{dx} = e^{x+y} + x^2 e^y$

$$\Rightarrow \quad \frac{dy}{dx} = e^x \,.\, e^y + x^2 e^y$$

$$\Rightarrow \quad dy = e^y (e^x + x^2)\, dx$$

$$\Rightarrow \quad \frac{d_y}{e^y} = (e^x + x^2)\, dx$$

Integrating both sides

$$\frac{e^{-y}}{-1} = e^x + \frac{x^3}{3} + c$$

$$e^x + e^{-y} + \frac{x^3}{3} + c =$$ where c is on arbitrary constant.

4. *Solve the following differential equation* $x\dfrac{dy}{dx} - y - 2x^3 = 0.$

Solution: $x\dfrac{dy}{dx} - y - 2x^3 = 0 \quad \Rightarrow \quad \dfrac{dy}{dx} - \dfrac{1}{x}\, y = 2x^2$

Comparing it with standard form

$$\frac{dy}{dx} + Py = Q \quad \text{we get}$$

$$P = -\frac{1}{x}, \quad Q = 2x^2 \quad \text{so it is a linear differential equation in } y$$

$$I.F. = e^{\int P dx} = e^{\int -\frac{1}{x} dx} = e^{-\log x} = \frac{1}{x}$$

Therefore
$$y \cdot \frac{1}{x} = \int 2x^2 \cdot \frac{1}{x}\, dx + c$$

$$\Rightarrow \frac{y}{x} = 2\int x\, dx + c$$

$$y = x^3 + cx, \ c \text{ is an arbitrary constant.}$$

5. *Solve differential equation* $(1 + x^2)\dfrac{dy}{dx} + y = \tan^{-1} x.$

Solution:
$$\frac{dy}{dx} + \frac{y}{1+x^2} = \frac{\tan^{-1} x}{1+x^2}$$

is a linear differential equation in y, where $P = \dfrac{1}{1+x^2}$ and $Q = \dfrac{\tan^{-1} x}{1+x^2}$

$$I.F. = e^{\int \frac{1}{1+x^2} dx} = e^{\tan^{-1} x}$$

Therefore Solution (1) is

$$y\, e^{\tan^{-1} x} = \int e^{\tan^{-1} x} \frac{\tan^{-1} x}{1+x^2}\, dx + c \qquad \left(\text{put } \tan^{-1} x = t \Rightarrow \frac{1}{1+x^2}\, dx = dt\right)$$

$$= \int e^t . t\, dt + c$$

$$= t\, e^t - \int 1.e^t\, dt + c$$

$$y e^{\tan^{-1} x} = t\, e^t - e^t + c$$

$$= (t - 1)\, e^t + c$$

$$= (\tan^{-1} x - 1)\, e^{\tan^{-1} x} + c$$

$$y = (\tan^{-1} x - 1) + c\, e^{-\tan^{-1} x}, \ c \text{ is arbitrary constant.}$$

6. *Solve* $\dfrac{dy}{dx} = y \sin 2x$*, given that* $y(0) = 1.$

Solution:
$$\frac{dy}{dx} = y \sin 2x$$

$$\Rightarrow \qquad \frac{1}{y}\, dy = \sin 2x\, dx$$

Integrating both sides, we get

$$\log |y| = -\frac{1}{2}\cos 2x + c$$

$$|y| = e^{-1/2 \cos 2x + c}$$

$$\Rightarrow \qquad y = \pm\, e^{-1/2\cos 2x} . e^{c} = A e^{-1/2 \cos 2x}$$

Given that $y(0) = 1$ i.e. When $x = 0,\ y = 1$

$$\Rightarrow \qquad 1 = Ae^{-1/2} \quad \Rightarrow \quad A = e^{1/2}$$

$$y = e^{1/2}\, e^{-1/2 \cos 2x} = e^{1/2\,(1 - \cos 2x)}$$

$$y = e^{\sin^2 x} \text{ is particular solution.}$$

7. $\dfrac{dy}{dx} = \dfrac{1-\cos x}{1+\cos x}$ *solve differential equation.*

Solution: $$\frac{dy}{dx} = \frac{1-\cos x}{1+\cos x} = \frac{\not 2 \sin^2 \frac{x}{2}}{\not 2 \cos^2 \frac{x}{2}} = \tan^2\frac{x}{2} = \sec^2\frac{x}{2} - 1$$

$$\frac{dy}{dx} = \left(\sec^2\frac{x}{2} - 1\right)$$

$$dy = \left(\sec^2\frac{x}{2} - 1\right) dx$$

Integrating both sides we get

$$y = \frac{\tan\frac{x}{2}}{\frac{1}{2}} - x + c$$

Hence solution is $y = 2\tan\dfrac{x}{2} - x + c.$

Where c is an arbitrary constant.

8. *Solve the following differential equation* $(x^2 + 1)\dfrac{dy}{dx} + 2xy = \sqrt{x^2 + 4}.$

Solution: $$(x^2 + 1)\frac{dy}{dx} + 2xy = \sqrt{x^2+4}$$

$$\frac{dy}{dx} + \frac{2xy}{x^2+1} = \frac{\sqrt{x^2+4}}{x^2+1}$$

This is linear differential equation

$$I.F. = e^{\int \frac{2x}{1+x^2} dx} = e^{\log(x^2+1)} = x^2 + 1$$

$$y . (x^2 + 1) = \int \frac{\sqrt{x^2+4}}{x^2+1} \times (x^2 + 1)\, dx$$

$$y.(x^2+1) = \int \sqrt{x^2+4}\,dx$$

$$y.(x^2+1) = \frac{1}{2}x\sqrt{x^2+4} + 2\log\left(x+\sqrt{x^2+4}\right)+c.$$

9. *Solve the differential equation $y(1+e^x)\,dy = (y+1)\,e^x\,dx$.*

Solution:

$$y(1+e^x)\,dy = (y+1)\,e^x\,dx$$

$$\frac{y}{y+1}dy = \frac{e^x}{e^x+1}dx$$

$$\int\left(1-\frac{1}{y+1}\right)dy = \int\frac{e^x}{e^x+1}dx$$

$$y - \log|y+1| = \log|e^x+1| + \log c$$

$$y = \log|y+1| + \log|e^x+1| + \log c$$

$$e^y = c\,(1+e^x)\,(y+1)$$

$$\frac{e^y}{y+1} = c(1+e^x).$$

10. *Form the differential equation of a family of circles which pass through origin and have centre on x-axis.*

Solution: Let the equation of family of circles be

$$x^2+y^2+2gx+2fy+c=0$$

Since circle passes through origin (0, 0)

$$0+0+2g.0+2f.(0)+c=0$$

$$c=0$$

Since centres $(-g\,.\,f)$ be on x axis i.e. $y=0$

$$-f=0 \Rightarrow f=0$$

Equation of family is

$$x^2+y^2+2gx=0 \quad ...(ii)$$

Differentiating w.r.t. x

$$2x+2y\frac{dy}{dx}+2g=0 \Rightarrow g=-\left(x+y\frac{dy}{dx}\right)$$

Substituting this value of g in (ii)

$$x^2+y^2-2\left(x+y\frac{dy}{dx}\right)x=0$$

$2xy\dfrac{dy}{dx} = y^2-x^2$ is the required differential equation.

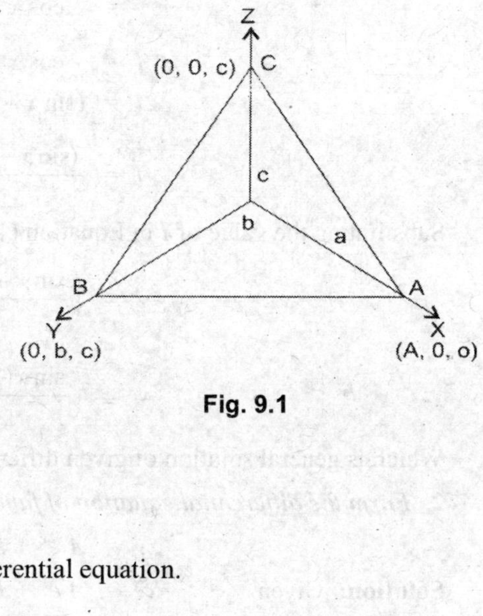

Fig. 9.1

SECTION-II

1. *Find the general solution of the differential equation*

$$\frac{dy}{dx} - y = \cos x$$

Solution: Given differential equation is of the form

$\dfrac{dy}{dx} + Py = Q$, where $P = -1$ and $Q = \cos x$

Therefore $\quad \text{I.F.} = e^{\int -1\,dx}$

$$= e^{-x}$$

Multiplying both sides of equation by I.F., we get

$$e^{-x}\frac{dy}{dx} - e^{-x}y = e^{-x}\cos x$$

$$\frac{dy}{dx}(y\,e^{-x}) = e^{-x}\cos x$$

Integrating both sides w.r.t. x, we get

$$ye^{-x} = \int e^{-x}\cos x\,dx + C$$

$$I = \int e^{-x}\cos x\,dx$$

$$= \cos x\left(\frac{e^{-x}}{-1}\right) - \int(-\sin x)(-e^{-x})\,dx$$

$$= -\cos x\,e^{-x} - \int \sin x\,e^{-x}\,dx$$

$$= -\cos x\,e^{-x} - \left[\sin x(-e^{-x}) - \int \cos x\left(-e^{-x}\right)dx\right]$$

$$I = -\cos x\,e^{-x} + \sin x\,e^{-x} - I$$

$$2I = (\sin x - \cos x)\,e^{-x}$$

$$I = \frac{(\sin x - \cos x)e^{-x}}{2}$$

Substituting the value of I in Equation (1) we get

$$y.e^{-x} = \left(\frac{\sin x - \cos x}{2}\right)e^{-x} + C$$

$$y = \left(\frac{\sin x - \cos x}{2}\right) + C\,e^{x}$$

Which is general solution of given differential equation.

2. *Form the differential equation of family of curves*

$$xy = A\,e^{x} + B\,e^{-x} + x^2.$$

Solution: Given $\quad xy = A\,e^{x} + B\,e^{-x} + x^2$

Differentiating w.r.t. x

$$x\frac{dy}{dx} + y\,.\,1 = A\,e^{x} + B\,e^{-x}(-1) + 2x$$

Differentiating again w.r.t. x

$$\frac{d^2y}{dx^2} + \frac{dy}{dx}.1 + \frac{dy}{dx} = A\,e^{x} - B\,e^{-x}(-1) + 2$$

$$\Rightarrow \qquad x\frac{d^2y}{dx^2} + 2\frac{dy}{dx} = A e^{x} + B e^{-x} + 2$$

$$\Rightarrow \qquad x\frac{d^2y}{dx^2} + 2\frac{dy}{dx} = (xy - x^2) + 2$$

Which is the required differential equation.

3. *Solve the following differential equation*

$$x\frac{dy}{dx} + y = x\log x.$$

Solution: Give $\quad x\frac{dy}{dx} + y = x\log x$

$$\frac{dy}{dx} + \frac{1}{x}y = \log x$$

This is a linear differential equation in y, when $P = \frac{1}{x}$ and $Q = \log x$.

$$IF = e^{\int \frac{1}{x}dx} = e^{\log x} = x$$

$\therefore$ Solution of the above equation is

$$Y.x = \int \log x . x\, dx + C$$

$$= \log x\frac{x^2}{2} - \int \frac{1}{x}\frac{x^2}{x}dx + C$$

$$= \frac{x^2}{2}\log x - \frac{1}{2}\frac{x^2}{2} + C$$

$$= \frac{x^2}{2}\log x - \frac{1}{2}\int x\,dx + C$$

$$= \frac{x^2}{2}\log x - \frac{x^2}{4} + C$$

$$= \frac{x^2}{2}\log x - \frac{1}{2}\frac{x^2}{2} + C$$

$$= \frac{x^2}{2}\log x - \frac{x^2}{4} + C$$

4. *Form the differential equation representing the parabolas having vertex at origin and oxine along positive direction of x-axis.*

Solution: Equation of family of parabolas having vertex at origin and axis along positive direction of x-axis of form

$$y^2 = 4ax \qquad ...(i)$$

a is a positive arbitrary real number.

Differentiating w.r.t. x_1 we get

$$2y\frac{dy}{dx} = 4a = . \frac{4y^2}{4x} = \frac{y^2}{x}$$

$$2xy\frac{dy}{dx} - y^2 = 0,$$

which is the required differential equation.

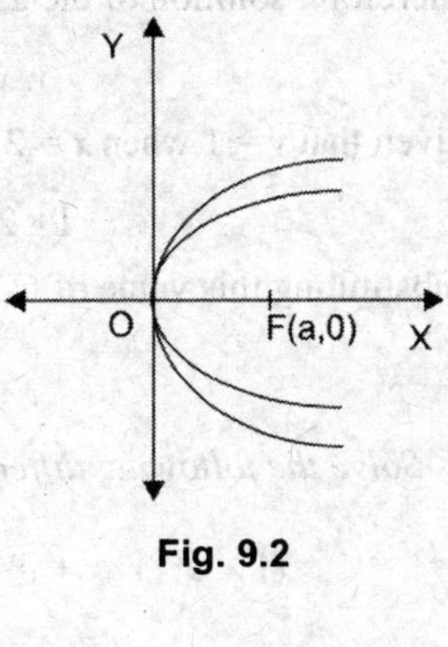

Fig. 9.2

5. *Solve for the following differential equation*:

$$(3xy + y^2)\,dx + (x^2 + xy)\,dy = 0.$$

Solution: Given $(3xy + y^2)dx + (x^2 + xy)dy = 0$

$$\Rightarrow \quad \frac{dy}{dx} = -\frac{3xy + y^2}{x^2 + xy}$$

This is a homogenous equation of order 3.

Put $\quad y = vx \;\Rightarrow\; \dfrac{dy}{dx} = v + x\dfrac{dy}{dx}$ ...(*i*)

$\therefore$ (*i*) becomes

$$v + x\frac{dv}{dx} = -\frac{(3vx^2 + v^2x^2)}{x^2 + vx^2} = -\frac{-3v + v^2}{1 + v}$$

$$\Rightarrow \quad x\frac{dv}{dx} = -\frac{(3v + v^2)}{1 + v} - v = -\frac{(2v^2 + 4v)}{1 = v}$$

$$\Rightarrow \quad \frac{(1 + v)\,dv}{(2v^2 + 4v)} = -\frac{dx}{x} \Rightarrow \frac{2 + 2v}{4(2v + v^2)\_}dv = -\frac{dx}{x}$$

$$\Rightarrow \quad \frac{2 + 2v}{2v + v^2}dv = -\frac{4}{x}dx$$

Integrating both sides

$$\log|2v + v^2| = -4\log|x| + c$$

$$\Rightarrow \quad \log|(2v + v^2)x^4| = c \;\Rightarrow\; |(2v + v^2)x^4| = e^c$$

$$\Rightarrow \quad (2v + v^2)x^4 = \pm e^c = A \text{ (say)}$$

$$\Rightarrow \quad \left(\frac{2y}{x} + \frac{y^2}{x^2}\right)x^4 = A$$

$$\Rightarrow \quad (2x + y)\,yx^2 = A, \text{ arbitrary constant.}$$

6. *Solve* : $x\dfrac{dy}{dx} + y = x^3$, *given that* $y = 1$ *when* $x = 2$.

Solution: Given $\dfrac{dy}{dx} + y = x^3 \;\Rightarrow\; \dfrac{dy}{dx} + \dfrac{1}{x}y = x^2$

It is a linear differential equation in y; where $P = \dfrac{1}{x}$ and $Q = x^2$

$$\text{I.F.} = e^{\int \frac{1}{x}dx} = e^{\log x} = x$$

Therefore, solution of the given equation is

$$y.x = \int x^2.x\,dx + c = \frac{x^4}{4} + c$$

Given that $y = 1$ when $x = 2$

$$\Rightarrow \quad 1 \times 2 = \frac{1}{4} \times 16 + c \Rightarrow c = -2.$$

Substituting this value of C in (*i*), the particular solution of the given equation is

$$yx = \frac{x^4}{y} - 2 \quad \text{or} \quad y = \frac{1}{4}x^3 - \frac{2}{x}.$$

7. *Solve the following differential equation*

$$(1 + e^{x/y})\,dx + e^{x/y}\left(1 - \frac{x}{y}\right)dy = 0.$$

Solution: Given $(1 + e^{x/y})\, dx + e^{x/y}\left(1-\dfrac{x}{y}\right) dy = 0$

$$\Rightarrow \quad \frac{dx}{dy} = -\frac{e^{x/y}\left(1-\dfrac{x}{y}\right)}{1+e^{x/y}} \qquad ...(i)$$

Since (i) is a form $\dfrac{dx}{dy} = g\left(\dfrac{x}{y}\right)$, it is a homogeneous differential equation.

Put $\quad \dfrac{x}{y} = v$ *i.e.* $x = vy \Rightarrow \dfrac{dx}{dy} = v + y\dfrac{dv}{dy}$

Substituting the values of x and $\dfrac{dx}{dy}$ in (i), we get

$$v + y\frac{dv}{dy} = -e^v \frac{(1-v)}{1+e^v} \Rightarrow y\frac{dv}{dy} = -e^v \frac{(1-v)}{1+e^v} - v$$

$$\Rightarrow \quad -\frac{dy}{y} = \frac{1+e^v}{v+e^v}\, dv$$

On Integration

$$\log|v + e^v| = -\log|y| + C$$

$$\Rightarrow \quad \log|y\,(v+e^v)| = C$$

$$\Rightarrow \quad |y\,(v+e^v)| = e^c$$

$$\Rightarrow \quad y\left(\frac{x}{y} + e^{x/y}\right) = \pm e^c = A$$

$$\Rightarrow \quad |y\,(v+e^{x/y})| = A, \text{ Arbitrary constant.}$$

8. *Show that $y = (a + bx)\, e^{2x}$ is a solution of the differential equation*

$$y_2 - 4y_1 + 4y = 0.$$

Solution: Given $\quad y = (a + bx)\, e^{2x} \qquad ...(i)$

Differentiating (i) w.r.t. x we get

$$y_1 = (a + bx)\, e^{2x} . 2 + e^{2x} (0 + 0.1)$$

$$= 2y + be^{2x}$$

Differentating again w.r.t. x, we get

$$y_2 = 2y_1 + be^{2x}\, 2$$

$$\Rightarrow \quad y_2 = 2y_1 + 2(y_1 - 2y)$$

$$\Rightarrow \quad y_2 - 4y_1 + 4y = 0$$

Hence $Y = (a + bx)\, e^{2x}$ is a solution of above differential equation.

9. *Find the general solution of the differential equation*

$$\frac{dy}{dx} = \frac{1+y^2}{1+x^2}.$$

Solution:

$$\frac{dy}{dx} = \frac{1+y^2}{1+x^2}$$

$$\frac{dy}{1+y^2} = \frac{dx}{1+x^2} \qquad ...(i)$$

Integrating both sides of equation (i), we get

$$\int \frac{dy}{1+y^2} = \int \frac{dx}{1+y^2}$$

$$\tan^{-1} y = \tan^{-1} x + c$$

Which is the general solution of the equation.

10. *Solve the following differential equation* $(x^2 + 1)\frac{dy}{dx} + 2xy = \sqrt{x^2+4}$.

Solution: The given differential equation is

$$(x^2 + 1)\frac{dy}{dx} + 2xy = \sqrt{x^2+4}$$

or
$$\frac{dy}{dx} + \frac{2x}{1+x^2}y = \frac{\sqrt{x^2+4}}{x^2+1}$$

This is a linear differential equation.

Here $\qquad I.F. = e^{\int \frac{2x}{1+x^2}dx} = e^{\log(x^2+1)} = x^2 + 1$

$\therefore$ Solution is

$$\Rightarrow \quad y.(x^2+1) = \int \frac{\sqrt{x^2+4}}{x^2+1} \times (x^2+1)\,dx$$

$$\Rightarrow \quad y.(x^2+1) = \int \sqrt{x^2+4}\,dx$$

$$\Rightarrow \quad y.(x^2+1) = \frac{1}{2}x\sqrt{x^2+4} + 2\log\left(x+\sqrt{x^2+4}\right)+C.$$

SECTION-III

1. *Form the differential equation of the family of ellipses having their foci on x-axis and centre at the origin.*

Solution: As the foci of the family of ellipse lie on x-axis and centres are at the origin, equation of the family is

$$\frac{x^2}{a^2} + \frac{y^2}{b^2} = 1 \quad \text{where } a, b \text{ are arbitrary constants}$$

Differentiating w.r.t. x

$$\frac{1}{a^2}2x + \frac{1}{b^2}2y\,y_1 = 0 \Rightarrow \frac{yy_1}{b^2} = \frac{-x}{a^2}$$

$$\Rightarrow \quad \frac{yy_1}{x} = \frac{-b^2}{a^2}$$

Differentiating again w.r.t. x we get

$$\frac{x(yy_2 + y_1.y_2) - yy_1}{x^2} = 0$$

$\Rightarrow \quad x(yy_2 + y_1^2) = yy_1$ is the required differential equation.

2. *Solve the differential equation* $(1-x^2)\dfrac{dy}{dx} - xy = x^2$, given that $y = 2$ when $x = 0$.

Solution: $(1-x^2)\dfrac{dy}{dx} - xy = x^2$ ...(1)

$\Rightarrow \quad \dfrac{dy}{dx} - \dfrac{x}{1-x^2}\,y = \dfrac{x^2}{1-x^2}$ (1) it is a linear differentiable equation in y.

[Dividing throughout by $1 - x^2$].

In the form of $\dfrac{dy}{dx} + Py = Q$.

Here

$$P = \frac{x}{1+x^2},\ Q = \frac{x^2}{1-x^2}$$

$$I.F. = e^{\int -\frac{x}{1-x^2}dx} = e^{\frac{1}{2}\int -\frac{2x}{1-x^2}dx}$$

$$= e^{1/2\log(1-x^2)} \qquad \text{(assuming } |x| < 1)$$

$$= \sqrt{1-x^2}\,.$$

Solution of the given equation (Multiplying (1) by I.F. and integrating both sides)

$$y.\sqrt{1-x^2} = \int \frac{x^2}{1-x^2}\sqrt{1-x^2}\,dx + c$$

$$= \int -\frac{(1-x^2)+1}{\sqrt{1-x^2}}\,dx$$

$$= -\int \sqrt{1-x^2}\,dx + \int \frac{1}{\sqrt{1-x^2}}\,dx + c$$

$$= -\left[\frac{x\sqrt{1-x^2}}{2} + \frac{1}{2}\sin^{-1}x\right] + \sin^{-1}x + c$$

$$= -x\,\frac{\sqrt{1-x^2}}{2} + \frac{1}{2}\sin^{-1}x + c \qquad ...(i)$$

Given that $y = 2$ when $x = 0$

$\Rightarrow \quad 2\sqrt{1-0} = 0 + c \Rightarrow c = 2$

From (i)

$$y\sqrt{1-x^2} = -\frac{x\sqrt{1-x^2}}{2} + \frac{1}{2}\sin^{-1}x + 2.$$

3. *Solve the following differential equation* $x^2\dfrac{dy}{dx} = y^2 + 2xy$. *Given that* $y = 1$, *when* $x = 1$.

Solution:

$$x^2\frac{dy}{dx} = y^2 + 2xy$$

$$\frac{dy}{dx} = \frac{y^2}{x^2} + \frac{2y}{x}$$

This is a homogeneous differential equation in $f(y/x)$

Let $$\frac{y}{x} = v \quad \text{or} \quad y = vx$$

$$\frac{dy}{dx} = v + x\frac{dv}{dx}$$

Substituting in (*i*) we get

$$v + x\frac{dv}{dx} = v^2 + 2v$$

$$x\frac{dv}{dx} = v^2 + v = v(v+1)$$

$$\frac{dv}{v(v+1)} = \frac{dx}{x}$$

$$\int\left(\frac{1}{v} - \frac{1}{v+1}\right)dv = \log x + \log c = \log cx$$

$$\log\frac{v}{v+1} = \log cx$$

$$cx = \frac{v}{v+1} = \frac{\frac{y}{x}}{\frac{y}{x}+1}$$

$$cx = \frac{y}{x+y} \qquad \text{...(ii)}$$

When $x = 1,\ y = 1$ $$c = \frac{1}{2}$$

From (*ii*)

$$\therefore \quad \frac{1}{2}x = \frac{y}{x+y}$$

$$x^2 + xy - 2y = 0$$

$$y = \frac{x^2}{2-x} \text{ is required solution.}$$

4. *Form the differential equation representing the parabola having vertex at the origin and axis along positive direction of x-axis.*

Solution: The equation of the parabola with vertex at origin and axis along +ve direction of *x*-axis is

$$y^2 = 4ax \qquad \text{...(i)}$$

$$2y\frac{dy}{dx} = 4a \qquad \text{...(ii)}$$

Substituting for 4a from (*ii*) in (*i*) we get

$$y^2 = \left(2y\frac{dy}{dx}\right)x$$

$$y - 2x\frac{dy}{dx} = 0$$

is the required differential equation of the given family of parabolas.

5. *Solve the following differential equation* $(3xy + y^2)\,dx + (x^2 + xy)dy = 0$.

Solution: $(3xy + y^2)dx + (x^2 + xy)\,dy = 0$

$$\frac{dy}{dx} = -\frac{3xy+y^2}{x^2+xy} = -\frac{\frac{3y}{x}+\left(\frac{y}{x}\right)^2}{1+\frac{y}{x}} \qquad ...(i)$$

It is a homogeneous differentiable equation, let $\frac{y}{x} = v$ or $y = vx$.

From (*i*)
$$v + x\frac{dv}{dx} = -\frac{(3v+v^2)}{1+v}$$

$$x\frac{dv}{dx} = -\frac{(3v+v^2)}{1+v} - v$$

$$= -\frac{[3v+v^2+v+v^2]}{1+v}$$

$$= -\frac{[4v+2v^2]}{1+v}$$

$$\frac{1+v}{2v+v^2}dv = -2\frac{dx}{x}$$

$$\frac{1}{2}\int\frac{2+2v}{2v+v^2}dv = -2\int\frac{dx}{x}$$

$$\frac{1}{2}\log|2v+v^2| = -2\log|x| + \log c$$

$$\frac{1}{2}\log\left|\frac{2y}{x}+\frac{y^2}{x^2}\right| = -2\log|x| + \log c$$

$$2\log|x| + \frac{1}{2}\log\left|\frac{y^2+2xy}{x^2}\right| = \log C$$

$$4\log|x| + \log\left|\frac{y^2+2xy}{x^2}\right| = 2\log C = \log K$$

$$\log\left|\frac{y^2+2xy}{x^2}\times x^4\right| = \log K$$

$$x^2(y^2+2xy) = K$$

Which is the required solution.

6. *Verify that function* $y = c_1 e^{ax}\cos bx + c_2 e^{ax}\sin bx$ *where* c_1, c_2 *are arbitrary constants is a solution of the differential equation*

$$\frac{d^2y}{dx^2} - 2a\frac{dy}{dx} + (a^2+b^2)y = 0.$$

Solution:
$$y = e^{ax}[c_1\cos bx + c_2\sin bx]$$

Differentiating w.r.t. x

$$\frac{dy}{dx} = e^{ax}[-bc_1 \sin bx + bc_2 \cos bx] + [c_1 \cos bx + c_2 \sin bx]\, e^{ax}\, a.$$

Differentiating again w.r.t. x

$$\begin{aligned}\frac{d^2y}{dx^2} &= e^{ax}[(bc_2 + ac_1)(-b \sin bx) + (ac_2 - bc_1)\, b \cos bx] \\ &\quad + [(bc_2 + ac_1) \cos bx + (ac_2 - bc_1) \sin bx] e^{ax}\, a. \\ &= e^{ax}[(a^2 c_2 - 2abc_1 - b^2c_2) \sin bx + (a^2c_1 - 2ab\, c_2 - b^2c_1) \cos bx]\end{aligned}$$

Substituting the value of $\frac{d^2y}{dx^2}$ and $\frac{dy}{dx}$ and y in the given differential equation

$$\begin{aligned}\text{L.H.S.} &= e^{ax}[(a^2 c_2 - 2abc_1 - b^2c_2) \sin bx + (a^2 c_1 + 2\, abc_2 - b^2c_1) \cos bx] \\ &\quad - 2a\, e^{ax}[(bc_2 + ac_1) \cos bx + (ac_2 - bc_1) \sin bx] \\ &\quad + (a^2 + b^2)\, e^{ax}[c_1 \cos bx + c_2 \sin bx] \\ &= e^{ax}[(a^2c_2 - 2abc_1 - b^2c_2 - 2a^2c_2 + 2abc_1 + a^2c_2 + b^2 c_2) \sin bx \\ &\quad + (a^2 c_1 + 2abc_2 - b^2c_1 - 2abc_2 - 2a^2c_1 + a^2c_1 + b^2c_1) \cos bx] \\ &= e^{ax}[ox \sin bx + ox \cos bx] \\ &= e^{ax} \times 0 = 0 = \text{R.H.S.}\end{aligned}$$

Hence, the given function is a solution of above differential function.

7. *In a bank, principal increases continuously at the rate of 5% per year. In how many years, Rs. 1000 double itself.*

Solution: Let P be the principle at any time t, then according to given condition

$$\frac{dP}{dt} = 5\% \times P = \frac{P}{20}$$

$$\frac{dP}{P} = \frac{dt}{20}$$

Integrating both sides

$$\Rightarrow \quad \log P = \frac{t}{20} + \log c$$

$$\Rightarrow \quad \log P - \log c = \frac{t}{20}$$

$$\log \frac{P}{c} = \frac{t}{20}$$

$$P = c\, e^{t/20}$$

$P = 1000$ When $t = 0$

$$1000 = c\, e^0$$

$$P = 1000\, e^{t/20}$$

When $\quad P = 2000$

$$2000 = 1000\, e^{t/20}$$

$$20 \log_e 2 = t$$

Hence, Rs. 1000 is doubled in $20 \log_e 2$ years.

8. *If $(x - a)^2 + (y + b)^2 = c^2$ for some $c > a$ prove that*

$$\frac{\left[1+\left(\frac{dy}{dx}\right)^2\right]^{3/2}}{\frac{d^2y}{dx^2}}$$

is a constant independent of a and b.

Solution: $(x-a)^2 + (y-b)^2 = c^2$ ...(1)

Differentiating w.r.t. x

$$2(x-a) + 2(y-b)\frac{dy}{dx} = 0$$

$$\Rightarrow \qquad (x-a) + (y-b)\frac{dy}{dx} = 0 \qquad ...(2)$$

Differentiating again w.r.t. x, we get

$$1 + (y-b)\frac{d^2y}{dx^2} + \frac{dy}{dx}\cdot\frac{dy}{dx} = 0$$

$$(y-b)\frac{d^2y}{dx^2} = -\left[1+\left(\frac{dy}{dx}\right)^2\right]$$

Substituting this value of $y-b$ in (2), we get

$$(x-a) + \left\{\frac{-\left[1+\left(\frac{dy}{dx}\right)^2\right]}{\frac{d^2y}{dx}}\right\}\frac{dy}{dx} = 0$$

$$x - a = \frac{\left[1+\left(\frac{dy}{dx}\right)^2\right]}{\frac{d^2y}{dx^2}}\frac{dy}{dx}.$$

Substituting value of $(x-a)$ and $(y-b)$ in (1)

$$\left[\frac{1+\left(\frac{dy}{dx}\right)^2}{\frac{d^2y}{dx^2}}\frac{dy}{dx}\right]^2 + \frac{\left[1+\left(\frac{dy}{dx}\right)^2\right]^2}{\left[\frac{d^2y}{dx}\right]^2} = c^2$$

$$\Rightarrow \qquad \frac{\left[1+\left(\frac{dy}{dx}\right)^2\right]^2}{\left(\frac{d^2y}{dx^2}\right)^2}\left[\left(\frac{dy}{dx}\right)^2 + 1\right] = c^2$$

$$\Rightarrow \qquad \frac{\left[\left(\frac{dy}{dx}\right)^2 + 1\right]^3}{\left(\frac{d^2y}{dx^2}\right)^2} = c^2$$

Taking positive square root of both sides

$$\frac{\left[1+\left(\frac{dy}{dx}\right)^2\right]^{3/2}}{\frac{d^2y}{dx^2}} = c \text{ is constant independent of } a \text{ and } b.$$

9. *Solve the differential equation* $y + x\sin\left(\frac{y}{x}\right) = x\frac{dy}{dx}$.

Solution:

$$y + x\sin\frac{y}{x} = x\frac{dy}{dx}$$

$$\frac{dy}{dx} = \frac{y}{x} + \sin\frac{y}{x}$$

It is a homogeneous differential equation.

Put $y = vx$

$$\Rightarrow \quad \frac{dy}{dx} = v + x\frac{dv}{dx}$$

$$v + x\frac{dv}{dx} = v + \sin v$$

$$\Rightarrow \quad x\frac{dv}{dx} = \sin v$$

$$\operatorname{cosec} v\, dv = \frac{dx}{x}$$

Integrating both sides

$$\int \operatorname{cosec} v\, dv = \int \frac{dx}{x}$$

$$\log|\operatorname{cosec} v - \cot v| = \log|x| + c$$

$$\log|\operatorname{cosec} v - \cot v| = \log|cx|$$

$$\sec\left(\frac{y}{x}\right) - \cot\left(\frac{y}{x}\right) = cx.$$

10. *Solve the differential equation* $\cos x\frac{dy}{dx} + y = \sin x$ *given that* $y = 2$ *when* $x = 0$.

Solution:

$$\cos x\frac{dy}{dx} + y = \sin x$$

$$\frac{dy}{dx} + y \,.\, \sec x = \tan x, \text{ it is a linear deferential equation in } y.$$

$$I.F. = e^{\int \sec x\, dx = e^{\log(\sec x + \tan x)}} = \sec x + \tan x$$

Solution of the given equation is

$$y(\sec x + \tan x) = \int \tan x(\sec x + \tan x) + c$$

$$= \int \sec x \tan x\, dx + \int \tan^2 x\, dx + c$$

$$= \sec x + \int (\sec^2 x - 1)\, dx + c$$

$$= \sec x + \tan x - x + c$$

Given that $y = 2$ when $x = 0$

$\Rightarrow \quad 2(1+0) = 1 + 0 - 0 + c \Rightarrow c = 1$

Substituting the value of c

$$y(\sec x + \tan x) = \sec x + \tan x - x + 1.$$

11. Solve the differential equation

$$(\tan^{-1} y - x)\, dy = (1 + y^2)dx \qquad \text{(6 marks)}$$

The given differential equation can be written as

$$\frac{dx}{dy} + \frac{x}{1+y^2} = \frac{\tan^{-1} y}{1+y^2}$$

which is in the form of linear differential equation $\frac{dx}{dy} + Px = Q.$

$$\text{when} \quad P = \frac{1}{1+y^2} \quad \text{and } Q = \frac{\tan^{-1} y}{1+y^2}$$

$$\text{I.F.} = e^{\int \frac{1}{1+y^2} dy} = e^{\tan^{-1} y}$$

Hence, the solution is

$$x \,.\, e^{\tan^{-1} y} = \int e^{\tan^{-1} y} . \frac{\tan^{-1} y}{1+y^2}\, dy + c$$

Put $\quad \tan^{-1} = t$

$$\Rightarrow \quad \frac{1}{1+y^2}\, dy = dt$$

$$\Rightarrow \quad \int e^t . t\, dt = (t-1)\, e^t + c$$

$$= e^{\tan^{-1}} y\, (\tan^{-1} y - 1)$$

Hence, $\quad x = (\tan^{-1} y - 1) + \left(e^{\tan^{-1}} y\right)$

UNSOLVED QUESTIONS

SECTION-I

1. Solve the initial value problem $Y^1 + 2y = e^{-2x} \sin x, y(0) = 0.$
2. Solve the differential equation

$$(1 + x^2)\, \frac{dy}{dx} + y = \tan^{-1} x.$$

3. Form the differential equation of the family of curves represent by equation $y = c(x - c)^2$.
4. Solve the differential equation

$$\left[x \sin^2\left(\frac{y}{x}\right) - y\right] dx + x\, dy = 0,$$

$y = \frac{\pi}{4}$ when $x = 1$.

5. Form the differential equation of family of circles touching the y-axis at origin.
6. Verify that $y = e^{-3x}$ is solution of the differential equation

$$\frac{d^2y}{dx^2} + \frac{dy}{dx} - 6y = 0.$$

7. Show that $y = Ax + \frac{B}{x}$ is a solution of the differential equation

$$x^2 \frac{d^2y}{dx^2} + x \frac{dy}{dx} - y = 0.$$

8. Solve the following differential equation : $(1 + y + x^2 y)\, dx + (x + x^3)\, dy = 0$, Where $y = 0$, when $x = 1$.

ANSWERS

1. $y\, e^{2x} = 1 - \cos x$
2. $y = (\tan^{-1} x - 1)\, c\, e^{\tan^{-1} x}$
3. $\left(\frac{dy}{dx}\right)^3 = 4y\left(x \frac{dy}{dx} - 2y\right)$
4. $\cot\left(\frac{y}{x}\right) = \log |ex|$
5. $2xy \frac{dy}{dx} + x^2 = y^2$
8. $xy + \tan^{-1} x = \frac{\pi}{4}$

SECTION-III

1. Solve the differential equation $(1+ y^2)\, dx = (\tan^{-1} y - x)\, dy$.
2. Solve the differential equation

$$x\, e^{y/x} - y \sin \frac{y}{x} + x \frac{dy}{dx} \sin \frac{y}{x} = 0$$

given that $y = 0$ when $x = 1$, *i.e.* $y(1) = 0$.

3. Solve the differential equation $\frac{dy}{dx} - 2y = \cos 3x$.
4. Verify that the function $y = c_1 e^{ax} \cos bx + c_2\, e^{ax} \sin bx$ where c_1 and c_2 are arbitrary constants is a solution of differential equation

$$\frac{d^2y}{dx^2} - 2a \frac{dy}{dx} + (a^2 + b^2)y = 0.$$

5. Form the differential equation representing the family of ellipses having foci on x-axis and centre at origin.
6. Solve the differential equation

$$(x\, dy - y\, dx)\, y \sin\left(\frac{y}{x}\right) = (y\, dx + x\, dy)\, x \cos\left(\frac{y}{x}\right).$$

7. Form the differential equation of family of parabolas having their vertices at origin and axes along the positive direction of x-axis.
8. Solve the differential equation

$$\frac{dy}{dx} = \sin (x + y) + \cos (x + y).$$

ANSWERS

1. $xe^{\tan^{-1}y} = e^{\tan^{-1}y}(\tan^{-1}y - 1) + c$ 2. $e^{-y/x}\left(\sin\frac{y}{x} + \cos\frac{y}{x}\right) = 1 + \log x^2\ (x \neq 0)$

3. $y = \frac{(3\sin 3x - 2\cos 3x)}{13} + Ce^{2x}$ 5. $xy = \frac{d^2y}{dx^2} + x\left(\frac{dy}{dx}\right)^2 - y\frac{dy}{dx}$

6. $xy\cos\left(\frac{y}{x}\right) = A$, A is arbitrary constant 7. $2xy\frac{dy}{dx} - y^2 = 0$

8. $x = \log\left|1 + \tan\left(\frac{x+y}{2}\right)\right| + C$ c is arbitrary constant.

HOTS QUESTIONS

1. Solve $\frac{d^3y}{dx^3} - 8\frac{d^2y}{dx^2} = 0$ satisfying $y(0) = \frac{1}{8}$ $y_1(0) = 0$ and $y_2(0) = 1$.
2. Solve the differential equation $\frac{dy}{dx} = x^3y^3 - xy$.
3. Find the order and degree of differential equation of all parabolas whose axes are parallel to the x-axes and having a latus rectum a.

ANSWERS

1. $y = \frac{1}{8}\left(\frac{e^{8x}}{8} - x + \frac{7}{8}\right)$ 2. $(1 + x^2 + ce^{x^2})\,y^2 = 1$ 3. $a\left(\frac{d^2y}{dx^2}\right) + 2\left(\frac{dy}{dx}\right)^3 = 0$

❑❑❑

CHAPTER 10

VECTOR ALGEBRA

BASIC CONCEPTS

Scalars→A quantity that has magnitude only is known as a scalar.

Example→Mass, length, time, speed, etc.

Vectors→A quantity that has magnitude as well as direction is called a vector.

Example→Force, velocity, momentum, etc.

A directed line segment with initial point A and the terminal point B, is the vector denoted by $\overrightarrow{AB}$.

Fig. 10.1

The magnitude of $\overrightarrow{AB}$ is denoted by $|\overrightarrow{AB}|$.

SOME IMPORTANT FORMULAE

- If $\vec{a}$ and $\vec{b}$ are the position vector of two points A and B. then

$$\overrightarrow{AB} = \vec{b} - \vec{a}.$$

- If $\vec{a} = a_1\hat{i} + b_1\hat{j} + c_1\hat{k}$, then

$$|\vec{a}| = \sqrt{a_1^2 + b_1^2 + c_1^2}.$$

- If $\vec{a}$ is any vector, then unit vector in direction $\vec{a}$

i.e. $$\hat{a} = \frac{\vec{a}}{|\vec{a}|}.$$

- Section Formulae→(*i*) Internal division: Let A and B be two points with position vectors $\vec{a}$ and $\vec{b}$ respectively and let P be a point dividing AB internally in the ratio $m : n$. Let $\overrightarrow{OP} = \vec{r}$, then

$$\vec{r} = \frac{m\vec{b} + n\vec{a}}{m+n}$$

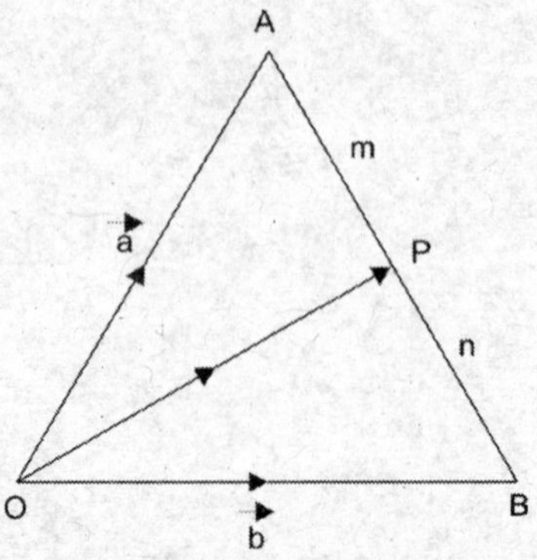

Fig. 10.2

(*ii*) External division→Let A and B are two points with position vectors $\vec{a}$ and $\vec{b}$ respectively and let P be a point dividing AB externally in the ratio $m:n$.

Let $\overline{OP} = \vec{r}$, then

$$\vec{r} = \frac{m\vec{b} - n\vec{a}}{m-n}.$$

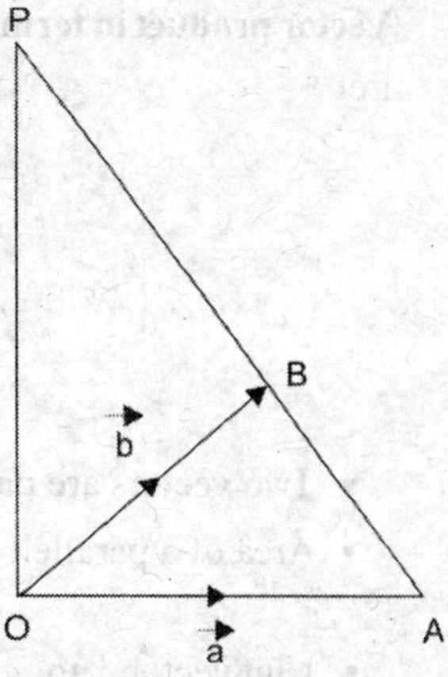

Fig. 10.3

- Dot porduct (Scalar product) of two vectors $\vec{a}$ and $\vec{b}$ is given by $\vec{a} \cdot \vec{b} = |\vec{a}||\vec{b}|\cos\theta$, where θ is the angle between $\vec{a}$ and $\vec{b}$.
- $\vec{a} \cdot \vec{b} = \vec{b} \cdot \vec{a}$ (Commutative Law).
- $\vec{a}\,(m\vec{b}) = (m\vec{a}) \cdot \vec{b} = m(\vec{a} \cdot \vec{b})$ m is scalar.
- Distributive Law→

  $\vec{a} \cdot (\vec{b} + \vec{c}) = \vec{a} \cdot \vec{b} + \vec{a} \cdot \vec{c}$

  $\vec{a} \cdot \vec{b} = 0 \Rightarrow \vec{a} + \vec{b}$ or $\vec{a} = 0$ or $\vec{b} = 0$
- $\vec{a} = a_1\hat{i} + a_2\hat{j} + a_3\hat{k}$ & $\vec{b} = b_1\hat{i} + b_2\hat{j} + b_3\hat{k}$, then $\vec{a} \cdot \vec{b} = a_1b_1 + a_2b_2 + a_3b_3$.
- Projection of $\vec{a}$ on $\vec{b} = \dfrac{\vec{a}.\vec{b}}{|\vec{b}|}$ and projection of $\vec{b}$ on $\vec{a} = \dfrac{\vec{a}.\vec{b}}{|\vec{a}|}$.
- $\hat{i}.\hat{i} = \hat{j}.\hat{j} = \hat{k}.\hat{k} = 1$ and $\hat{i}.\hat{j} = \hat{j}.\hat{k} = \hat{k}.\hat{i} = 0$
- If θ be the angle between $\vec{a} = a_1\hat{i} + a_2\hat{j} + a_3\hat{k}$ and $\vec{b} = b_1\hat{i} + b_2\hat{j} + b_3\hat{k}$ is given by

$$\cos\theta = \frac{\vec{a}.\vec{b}}{|\vec{a}||\vec{b}|} = \frac{a_1b_1 + a_2b_2 + a_3b_3}{\sqrt{a_1^2 + a_2^2 + a_3^2}\,\sqrt{b_1^2 + b_2^2 + b_3^2}}$$

- Cross product of two vectors $\vec{a}$ and $\vec{b}$ is given by $\vec{a} \times \vec{b} = |\vec{a}||\vec{b}|\sin\theta\,\hat{n}$, where θ is the angle between $\vec{a}$ and $\vec{b}$ and $\vec{n}$ is a unit vector perpendicular to the plane $\vec{a}$ and $\vec{b}$.
- $\vec{a} \times \vec{b} = -\vec{b} \times \vec{a}$
- For mutually perpendicular unit vector $\hat{i}, \hat{j}, \hat{k}$, we have

$$\hat{i} \times \hat{i} = \hat{j} \times \hat{j} = \hat{k} \times \hat{k} = 0$$

$$\hat{i} \times \hat{j} = \hat{k} = -\hat{j} \times \hat{i},\ \hat{j} \times \hat{k} = \hat{i} = -\hat{k} \times \hat{j}$$

and $$\hat{k} \times \hat{i} = \hat{j} = -\hat{i} \times \hat{k}$$

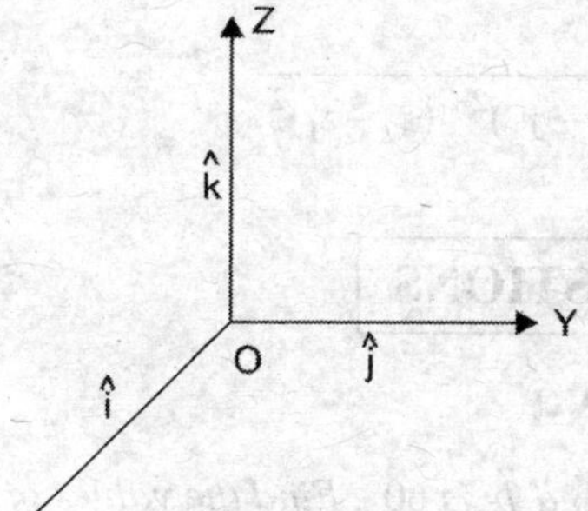

Fig. 10.4

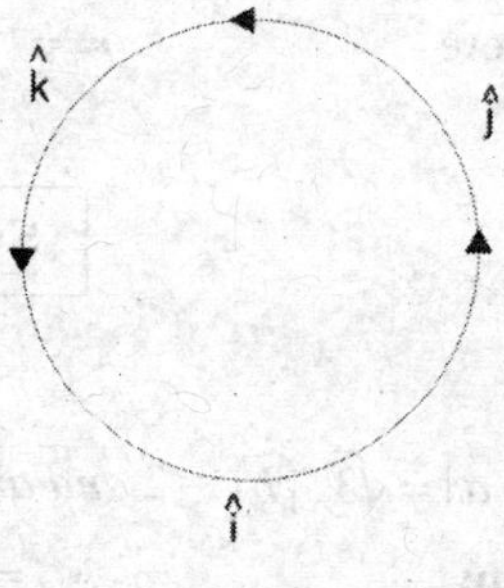

Fig. 10.5

Vector product in terms of components.

Let $\vec{a} = a_1\hat{i} + a_2\hat{j} + a_3\hat{k}$ and

$\vec{b} = b_1\hat{i} + b_2\hat{j} + b_3\hat{k}$, then

$$\vec{a} \times \vec{b} = \begin{vmatrix} \hat{i} & \hat{j} & \hat{k} \\ a_1 & a_2 & a_3 \\ b_1 & b_2 & b_3 \end{vmatrix}$$

- Two vectors are parallel if $\vec{a} \times \vec{b} = 0$.
- Area of a parallelogram whose sides are $\vec{a}$ and $\vec{b}$ is $|\vec{a} \times \vec{b}|$.
- Unit vector $\perp$ to $\vec{a}\,.\,\vec{b}$ is $\dfrac{\vec{a}\times\vec{b}}{|\vec{a}\times\vec{b}|}$.
- Area of parallelogram where diagonals are $\vec{a}$ and $\vec{b}$ is $\dfrac{1}{2}|\vec{a} \times \vec{b}|$.
- Area of triangle whose sides are represented by $\vec{a}$ and $\vec{b}$ is given by

  $\dfrac{1}{2}|\vec{a} \times \vec{b}|$.
- **Lagrange's Identity**

$$|a \times b|^2 = \begin{vmatrix} \vec{a}.\vec{a} & \vec{a}.\vec{b} \\ \vec{a}.\vec{b} & \vec{b}.\vec{b} \end{vmatrix}$$

- Direction Ratios and Direction Cosines of a vector.

  Consider a vector $\vec{r} = a\hat{i} + b\hat{j} + c\hat{k}$.

  Then the numbers *a, b, c* are called the direction ratios of $\vec{r}$.

  Direction cosines of $\vec{r}$ are given by

$$\frac{a}{\sqrt{a^2+b^2+c^2}} \cdot \frac{b}{\sqrt{a^2+b^2+c^2}} \text{ and } \frac{c}{\sqrt{a^2+b^2+c^2}}$$

- If $A(x_1, y_1, z_1)$ and $B(x_2, y_2, z_2)$ be two points in the space, then direction ratios of $\overrightarrow{AB}$ are $x_2 - x_1, y_2 - y_1, z_2 - z_1$ and direction cosines of $\overrightarrow{AB}$ are

$$\frac{x_2-x_1}{r}, \frac{y_2-y_1}{r}, \frac{z_2-z_1}{r}$$

where $r = \sqrt{(x_2-x_1)^2+(y_2-y_1)^{2+}(z_2-z_1)^2}$

SOLVED QUESTIONS

SECTION-I

1. *If* $|\vec{a}| = \sqrt{3}, |\vec{b}| = 2$ *and angle between* $\vec{a}$ *and* $\vec{b}$ *is* $60°$. *Find the values of* $\vec{a}\,.\,\vec{b}$.

Solution: $\vec{a}\,.\,\vec{b} = |\vec{a}|\,|\vec{b}|\cos\theta$

$$= \sqrt{3} \times 2 \times \cos 60°$$

$$= \sqrt{3} \times \not{2} \times \frac{1}{\not{2}} = \sqrt{3}.$$

2. *If* $\vec{a} = \hat{i}+2\hat{j}-\hat{k}$ *and* $\vec{b} = 3\hat{i}+2\hat{j}-5\hat{k}$. *Find a unit vector in direction* $\vec{a}-\vec{b}$.

Solution:

$$\vec{a}-\vec{b} = (\hat{i}+2\hat{j}-\hat{k}) - (3\hat{i}+\hat{j}-5\hat{k})$$

$$= -2\hat{i}+\hat{j}+4\hat{k}$$

Unit vector along $\vec{a}-\vec{b} = \dfrac{\vec{a}-\vec{b}}{|\vec{a}-\vec{b}|}$

$$= \frac{-2\hat{i}+\hat{j}+4\hat{k}}{\sqrt{4+1+16}}$$

$$= \frac{1}{\sqrt{21}}(-2\hat{i}+\hat{j}+4\hat{k}).$$

3. *Find the angle between the vectors* $\vec{a} = \hat{i} - \hat{j} + \hat{k}$ *and* $\vec{b} = \hat{i} + \hat{j} - \hat{k}$.

Solution:

$$\cos\theta = \frac{\vec{a}.\vec{b}}{|\vec{a}||\vec{b}|}$$

$$= \frac{1-1-1}{\sqrt{1+1+1}\sqrt{1+1+1}} = -\frac{1}{3}$$

$$\cos\theta = -\frac{1}{3}$$

$$\theta = \cos^{-1}\left(-\frac{1}{3}\right).$$

4. *Find* $|\vec{a} \times \vec{b}|$ *if* $\vec{a} = \hat{i} - 7\hat{j} + 7\hat{k}$ *and* $\vec{b} = 3\hat{i} - 2\hat{j} + 2\hat{k}$.

Solution:

$$\vec{a} \times \vec{b} = \begin{vmatrix} \hat{i} & \hat{j} & \hat{k} \\ 1 & -7 & 7 \\ 3 & -2 & 2 \end{vmatrix}$$

$$= \hat{i}(-14+14) - \hat{j}(2-21) + \hat{k}(-2+21)$$

$$= 0\hat{i} + 19\hat{j} + 19\hat{k}$$

$$|\vec{a} \times \vec{b}| = \sqrt{0^2+19^2+19^2}$$

$$= 19\sqrt{2}.$$

5. *Write the value of* $\hat{i}.(\hat{j} \times \hat{k}) + \hat{j}.(\hat{k} \times \hat{i}) + \hat{k}.(\hat{j} \times \hat{i})$.

Solution: $\hat{i}.(\hat{j}\times\hat{k}) + \hat{j}(\hat{k}\times\hat{i}) + \hat{k}(\hat{j}\times\hat{i})$

$= \hat{i}\,\hat{i} + \hat{j}\,\hat{j} + \hat{k}.(-\hat{k})$

$= 1 + 1 - 1$

$= 1.$

6. *Find the angle made by vector* $\hat{i} - 4\hat{j} + 8\hat{k}$ *with z-axis.*

Solution: Direction cosines of given vector are

$$\frac{1}{\sqrt{1+16+64}}, \frac{-4}{\sqrt{1+16+64}}, \frac{8}{\sqrt{81}} \text{ i.e. } \frac{1}{9}, \frac{-4}{9}, \frac{8}{9}$$

Direction cosines of z-axis are 0, 0, 1.

$$\text{Angle} \quad \theta = \cos^{-1}\left(\frac{1}{9} \times 0 + -\frac{4}{9} \times 0 + 1 \times \frac{8}{9}\right)$$

$$\theta = \cos^{-1}\left(\frac{8}{9}\right).$$

7. *$|\vec{a}| = \sqrt{2}b$, $|\vec{b}| = 7$ and $|\vec{a} \times \vec{b}| = 35$. Find $\vec{a} . \vec{b}$.*

Solution: By lagrange identity we have

$$(\vec{a} \times \vec{b})^2 = |\vec{a}|^2 |\vec{b}|^2 - (\vec{a} . \vec{b})^2$$

$$35^2 = \left(\sqrt{2}\, b\right)^2 7^2 - (\vec{a} . \vec{b})^2$$

$$(\vec{a} . \vec{b})^2 = 49$$

$$\vec{a} . \vec{b} = \pm 7.$$

8. *Find the value of λ so that two vectors $2\hat{i} + 3\hat{j} - \hat{k}$ and $-4\hat{i} - 6\hat{j} + 2\hat{k}$ are parallel.*

Solution: $\vec{a}$ and $\vec{b}$ are parallel to each other

$$\frac{a_1}{b_1} = \frac{a_2}{b_2} = \frac{a_3}{b_3}$$

$$\frac{2}{-4} = \frac{3}{-6} = \frac{-1}{\lambda} \Rightarrow \lambda = 2.$$

9. *If $|\vec{a}| = 2$, $|\vec{b}| = 3$ and $\vec{a} . \vec{b} = 4$. Find $|\vec{a} - \vec{b}|$.*

Solution:

$$|\vec{a} - \vec{b}|^2 = (\vec{a} - \vec{b}) . (\vec{a} - \vec{b})$$

$$= |\vec{a}|^2 - 2\vec{a} . \vec{b} + |\vec{b}|^2$$

$$= 2^2 - 2 \times 4 + 3^2$$

$$= 5$$

$$|\vec{a} - \vec{b}| = \sqrt{5}.$$

10. *If $\vec{a}$ is a unit vector and $(2\vec{a} + \vec{b})(2\vec{a} - \vec{b}) = 2$. Find $|\vec{b}|$.*

Solution:

$$|\vec{a}| = 1$$

$$(2\vec{a} + \vec{b}) = (2\vec{a} - \vec{b}) = 4|\vec{a}|^2 - |\vec{b}|^2$$

$$2 = 4 - |\vec{b}|^2$$

$$|\vec{b}| = \sqrt{2}.$$

SECTION-II

1. *If $i + \hat{j} + \hat{k}$, $2\hat{i} + 5\hat{j}$, $3\hat{i} + 2\hat{j} - 3\hat{k}$ and $\hat{i} - 6\hat{j} - \hat{k}$ are the position vectors of the points A, B, C, D. Find the angle between $\overrightarrow{AB}$ and $\overrightarrow{CD}$. Deduce that $\overrightarrow{AB}$ and $\overrightarrow{CD}$ are collinear..*

Solution:

$$\overrightarrow{AB} = P.V. \text{ of } B - P.V. \text{ of } A$$

$$= (2\hat{i} + 5\hat{j}) - (\hat{i} + \hat{j} + \hat{k})$$

$$= \hat{i} + 4\hat{j} - \hat{k}.$$

Similarly, $\overrightarrow{CD} = -2\hat{i} - 8\hat{j} + 2\hat{k}$

$$|\overrightarrow{AB}| = \sqrt{1+16+1} = \sqrt{18}$$

$$|\overrightarrow{CD}| = \sqrt{4+64+4} = \sqrt{72}$$

Let θ be the angle between $\overrightarrow{AB}$ and $\overrightarrow{CD}$. Then

$$\cos\theta = \frac{\overrightarrow{AB}.\overrightarrow{CD}}{|\overrightarrow{AB}||\overrightarrow{CD}|} = -\frac{\cancel{36}}{\cancel{36}} = -1$$

$$\theta = \pi$$

∴ $\overrightarrow{AB}$ and $\overrightarrow{CD}$ are collinear.

2. *If vectors $\vec{a}$, $\vec{b}$ and $\vec{c}$ are such that $\vec{a}+\vec{b}+\vec{c} = \vec{0}$ and $|\vec{a}| = 3, |\vec{b}| = 5$ and $|\vec{c}| = 7$. Find the angle between $\vec{a}$ and $\vec{b}$.*

Solution: $\vec{a}+\vec{b}+\vec{c} = \vec{0}$

$$\vec{a}+\vec{b} = -\vec{c}$$

$$\Rightarrow \quad |\vec{a}+\vec{b}|^2 = |\vec{c}|^2$$

$$\vec{a}^2 + \vec{b}^2 + 2\vec{a}.\vec{b} = \vec{c}^2$$

$$\Rightarrow \quad |\vec{a}|^2 + |\vec{b}|^2 + 2|\vec{a}||\vec{b}|\cos\theta = |\vec{c}|^2$$

$$\Rightarrow \quad 9 + 25 + 30\cos\theta = 49$$

$$\cos\theta = \frac{1}{2}$$

$$\boxed{\theta = \frac{\pi}{3}}$$

3. *If $\vec{a} = \vec{b}+\vec{c}+\vec{a}$ and $\vec{b} = \hat{j}+\hat{k}$. Find the vector $\vec{c}$ such that $\vec{a} \times \vec{c} = \vec{b}$* and *$\vec{a}.\vec{c} = 3$.*

Let $\vec{c} = (x\hat{i} + y\hat{j} + z\hat{k})$.

Solution: $\vec{a} \times \vec{c} = (\hat{i}+\hat{j}+\hat{k}) \times (x\hat{i} + y\hat{j} + z\hat{k}) = \vec{b}$

Let $\vec{c} = x\hat{i} + y\hat{j} + z\hat{k}$

$$\vec{a} \times \vec{c} = \begin{vmatrix} \hat{i} & \hat{j} & \hat{k} \\ 1 & 1 & 1 \\ x & y & z \end{vmatrix} = \vec{b}$$

$$\Rightarrow \quad (z-y)\hat{i} - (z-x)\hat{j} + \hat{k}(y-x) = \vec{b} = \hat{j}+\hat{k}$$

$$\Rightarrow \quad o\hat{i} + \hat{j} - \hat{k}$$

$y = z \qquad z = x-1$ and $y = x-1$ ...(*i*)

$$\vec{a}.\vec{c} = 3$$

Again,

$$(\hat{i}+\hat{j}+\hat{k}).(x\hat{i}+y\hat{j}+z\hat{k}) = 3$$

$x+y+z = 3$ ...(*ii*)

From (*i*) and (*ii*)

$$x + 2(x-1) = 3$$

$$3x = 5$$

$$x = \frac{5}{3}$$

$$z = \frac{5}{3} - 1 = \frac{2}{3} = y$$

$$\vec{c} = \frac{5}{3}\hat{i} + \frac{2}{3}\hat{j} + \frac{2}{3}\hat{k}.$$

4. *If $\vec{a} = 2\hat{i} + 2\hat{j} + 3\hat{k}$, $\vec{b} = -\hat{i} + 2\hat{j} + \hat{k}$, $\vec{c} = 3\hat{i} + \hat{j}$ are such that vector $\vec{a} + \lambda\vec{b}$ is perpendicular to $\vec{c}$. Find the value of λ.*

Solution: $\vec{a} + \lambda\vec{b} = (2 - \lambda)\hat{i} + (2 + 2\lambda)\hat{j} + (3 + \lambda)\hat{k}$

$$\vec{c} = 3\hat{i} + \hat{j}$$

$(\vec{a} + \lambda\vec{b}) \cdot \vec{c} = 0$ $\quad$ [$(\vec{a} + \lambda\vec{b})$ is perpendicular to $\vec{c}$]

$\Rightarrow \quad (2 - \lambda) \times 3 + (2 + 2\lambda) = 0$

$\Rightarrow \quad 6 - 3\lambda + 2 + 2\lambda = 0$

$$\boxed{\lambda = 8}$$

5. *Find the unit vector perpendicular to plane ABC where position vectors of point A, B, C are $2\hat{i} - \hat{j} + \hat{k}$, $\hat{i} + \hat{j} + 2\hat{k}$ and $2\hat{i} + 3\hat{k}$ respectively.*

Solution: $\overrightarrow{AB} = \hat{i} + \hat{j} + 2\hat{k} - (2\hat{i} - \hat{j} + \hat{k})$

$$= -\hat{i} + 2\hat{j} + \hat{k}$$

Similarly, $\overrightarrow{BC} = \hat{i} + \hat{j} + \hat{k}$

$$\overrightarrow{AB} \times \overrightarrow{BC} = \begin{vmatrix} \hat{i} & \hat{j} & \hat{k} \\ -1 & 2 & 1 \\ 1 & -1 & 1 \end{vmatrix}$$

$$= \hat{i}(2 + 1) - \hat{j}(-1 - 1) + \hat{k}(1 - 2)$$

$$= 3\hat{i} + \hat{j} - \hat{k}$$

$$|\overrightarrow{AB} \times \overrightarrow{BC}| = \sqrt{9 + 4 + 1} = \sqrt{14}$$

Unit vector perpendicular to plane *ABC*.

$$= \pm\left(\frac{3}{\sqrt{14}}\hat{i} + \frac{2}{\sqrt{14}}\hat{j} - \frac{1}{\sqrt{14}}\hat{k}\right).$$

6. *If $\vec{a}$ and $\vec{b}$ are unit vector and θ is angle between then prove that*

$$\cos\left(\frac{\theta}{2}\right) = \frac{1}{2}|\vec{a} + \vec{b}|.$$

Solution: $\vec{a}$ and $\vec{b}$ are unit vectors

$$|\vec{a}| = 1 \quad |\vec{b}| = 1$$

$$|\vec{a} + \vec{b}|^2 = |\vec{a}|^2 + 2\vec{a}\cdot\vec{b} + |\vec{b}|^2$$

$= |\vec{a}|^2 + 2|\vec{a}||\vec{b}|\cos\theta + |\vec{b}|^2$ (using $\vec{a}\cdot\vec{b} = |\vec{a}||\vec{b}|\cos\theta$)

$$= 1 + 2\cos\theta + 1$$

$$= 2+2\cos\theta = 2(1+\cos\theta) = x$$

$$|\vec{a}+\vec{b}|^2 = 2\times 2\cos^2\frac{\theta}{2}$$

$$|\vec{a}+\vec{b}| = 2\cos\frac{\theta}{2}$$

$$\frac{1}{2}|\vec{a}+\vec{b}| = \cos\frac{\theta}{2}.$$

7. *$\vec{a}, \vec{b}, \vec{c}$ are 3 non-zero vectors such that $\vec{a}\times\vec{b}=\vec{c}$ and $\vec{b}\times\vec{c}=\vec{a}$ prove that $\vec{a}, \vec{b}, \vec{c}$ are mutually perpendicular and $|\vec{b}|=1$ and $|\vec{a}|=|\vec{c}|$.*

Solution: $\vec{a}\times\vec{b} = \vec{c}$ and $\vec{b}\times\vec{c} = \vec{a}$

$\Rightarrow$ $\vec{c}\perp\vec{a},\ \vec{c}\perp\vec{b}$ and $\vec{b}\perp\vec{c},\ \vec{b}\perp\vec{c}$

$\Rightarrow$ $\vec{a}\perp\vec{b},\ \vec{b}\perp\vec{c}$ and $\vec{c}\perp\vec{a}$

Now, $\vec{a}, \vec{b}, \vec{c}$ are mutually at right angles to each other

$$|\vec{a}\times\vec{b}| = |\vec{c}|$$

$\Rightarrow$ $|\vec{a}|\,|\vec{b}|\sin\frac{\pi}{2} = |\vec{c}|$ $\quad\left(\sin\frac{\pi}{2}=1\right)$

$\Rightarrow$ $|\vec{a}|\,|\vec{b}| = |\vec{c}|$

Similarly $|\vec{b}|\,|\vec{c}| = |\vec{a}|$

$\Rightarrow$ $|\vec{b}|\,|\vec{c}|\,|\vec{b}| = |\vec{c}|$

$\Rightarrow$ $|\vec{b}| = 1$

$\Rightarrow$ $|\vec{a}|\,|\vec{b}| = |\vec{c}|$

$\Rightarrow$ $|\vec{a}| = |\vec{c}|.$

8. *If $\vec{a}, \vec{b}, \vec{c}$ are respectively the position vectors of vertices A, B, C of ΔABC, prove that area of triangle ABC is given by*

$$\Delta = \frac{1}{2}|\vec{a}\times\vec{b} + \vec{b}\times\vec{c} + \vec{c}\times\vec{a}|.$$

Solution:

$$\overrightarrow{AB} = \vec{b}-\vec{a}$$

$$\overrightarrow{BC} = \vec{c}-\vec{b}$$

$$\overrightarrow{CA} = \vec{a}-\vec{c}.$$

Area of $\Delta ABC = \frac{1}{2}|\overrightarrow{AB}\times\overrightarrow{BC}|$

$$= \frac{1}{2}|(\vec{b}-\vec{a})\times(\vec{c}-\vec{b})|$$

$$= \frac{1}{2}|\vec{b}\times\vec{c} - \vec{b}\times\vec{b} - \vec{a}\times\vec{c} + \vec{a}\times\vec{b}|$$

$$= \frac{1}{2}|\vec{a}\times\vec{b} + \vec{b}\times\vec{c} + \vec{c}\times\vec{a}|.$$

9. *Prove that points A, B, C with position vectors $\vec{a}, \vec{b}$ and $\vec{c}$ are collinear if and only if $(\vec{b}\times\vec{c})+(\vec{c}\times\vec{a})+(\vec{a}\times\vec{b})=0.$*

Solution: $\vec{A}, \vec{B}, \vec{C}$ are collinear

$\Rightarrow$ $\overrightarrow{AB}$ and $\overrightarrow{BC}$ are collinear

$\Rightarrow$ $(\vec{b}-\vec{a})$ and $(\vec{c}-\vec{b})$ are collinear

$\Rightarrow$ $(\vec{b}-\vec{a}) \times (\vec{c}-\vec{b}) = \vec{0}$

$\Rightarrow$ $(\vec{b}\times\vec{c}) - (\vec{a}\times\vec{c}) - (\vec{b}\times\vec{b}) + \vec{a}\times\vec{b} = \vec{0}$

$\Rightarrow$ $(\vec{b}\times\vec{c}) + (\vec{c}\times\vec{a}) + \vec{a}\times\vec{b} = \vec{0}$.

10. *Let $\vec{a}, \vec{b}, \vec{c}$ be three vectors such that $|\vec{a}| = 3$, $|\vec{b}| = 4$ and $|\vec{c}| = 5$ and each one of them being perpendicular to the sum of other two. Find $|\vec{a}+\vec{b}+\vec{c}|$.*

Solution: $|\vec{a}| = 3,\ |\vec{b}| = 4$ and $|\vec{c}| = 5$

$\vec{a}(\vec{b}+\vec{c}) = 0,\ \vec{b}.(\vec{c}+\vec{a}) = 0,\ \vec{c}.(\vec{a}+\vec{b}) = 0$

$$\begin{aligned}|\vec{a}+\vec{b}+\vec{c}|^2 &= (\vec{a}+\vec{b}+\vec{c})(\vec{a}+\vec{b}+\vec{c})\\ &= \vec{a}.\vec{a} + \vec{a}.(\vec{b}+\vec{c}) + \vec{b}.\vec{b} + \vec{b}(\vec{c}+\vec{a}) + \vec{c}(\vec{a}+\vec{b}) + \vec{c}.\vec{c}\\ &= |\vec{a}|^2 + |\vec{b}|^2 + |\vec{c}|^2\\ &= 9 + 16 + 25\\ &= 50\\ |\vec{a}+\vec{b}+\vec{c}| &= 5\sqrt{2}.\end{aligned}$$

11. *The Scalar Product of the vector $\hat{i}+\hat{j}+\hat{k}$ with a unit vector along the sum of vectors $2\hat{i}+4\hat{j}-5\hat{k}$ and $\lambda\hat{i}+2\hat{j}+3\hat{k}$ is equal to one. Find λ.* (4 marks)

Solution: Let $\vec{a} = \hat{i}+\hat{j}+\hat{k}$

$\vec{b} = 2\hat{i}+4\hat{j}-5\hat{k}$

and $\vec{c} = \lambda\hat{i}+2\hat{j}+3\hat{k}$.

Sum of $\vec{b}$ and $\vec{c} = \vec{b}+\vec{c} = (2+\lambda)\hat{i}+6\hat{j}-2\hat{k}$

unit vector along $\vec{b}+\vec{c} = \dfrac{\vec{b}+\vec{c}}{|\vec{b}+\vec{c}|} = \dfrac{(2+\lambda)\hat{i}+6\hat{j}-2\hat{k}}{\sqrt{(2+\lambda)^2+36+4}}$

Now $\vec{a}\,.\,\dfrac{(\vec{b}+\vec{c})}{|\vec{b}+\vec{c}|} = \dfrac{(2+\lambda)+6-2}{\sqrt{4+\lambda^2+4\lambda+40}} = \dfrac{\lambda+6}{\sqrt{\lambda^2+4\lambda+44}}$

According to question

$$\frac{\vec{a}.(\vec{b}+\vec{c})}{|\vec{b}+\vec{c}|} = 1$$

$$\Rightarrow \quad \frac{\lambda+6}{\sqrt{\lambda^2+4\lambda+44}} = 1$$

Squaring both sides

$$\lambda^2 + 12\lambda + 36 = \lambda^2 + 4\lambda + 44$$

$\Rightarrow$ $8\lambda = 8$

$\Rightarrow$ $\lambda = 1$

UNSOLVED QUESTIONS

SECTION-I

1. Simplify $\vec{a} \times (\vec{b} + \vec{c}) + \vec{b} \times (\vec{c} + \vec{a}) + \vec{c} \times (\vec{a} + \vec{b})$.
2. Find the angle between $\hat{i} - 2\hat{j} + 3\hat{k}$ and $3\hat{i} - 2\hat{j} + \hat{k}$.
3. If $\vec{a} = 5\hat{i} - 3\hat{j}$ and $\vec{b} = 3\hat{i} + 5\hat{k}$. Find unit vector in direction of $2\vec{a} - 3\vec{b}$.
4. Find the position vector of the point which divides the join of points $2\vec{a} - 3\vec{b}$ and $3\vec{a} - 2\vec{b}$ externally in the ratio 2 : 3.
5. If $|\vec{a}| = 2$, $|\vec{b}| = 5$ and $\vec{a} \cdot \vec{b} = 2$. Find $|\vec{a} - \vec{b}|.\vec{c}$
6. If $\vec{a}$ and $\vec{b}$ are two vectors such that $|\vec{a} \cdot \vec{b}| = |\vec{a} \times \vec{b}|$. Find the angle between $\vec{a}$ and $\vec{b}$.
7. Find $\vec{a} \cdot \vec{b}$ it $|\vec{a}| = \sqrt{10}$
   $|\vec{b}| = 7$ and $|\vec{a} \times \vec{b}| = 21$.
8. Find a vector in the direction of vector $3\hat{i} - \hat{j} + 4\hat{k}$ which has magnitude 6 units.
9. If $|\vec{a}| = 2$, $|\vec{b}| = 7$ and $\vec{a} \times \vec{b} = 3\hat{i} + 2\hat{j} + 6\hat{k}$. Find the angle between $\vec{a}$ and $\vec{b}$.
10. For any 3 vectors $\vec{a}$, $\vec{b}$, $\vec{c}$ write the value of $\vec{a} \times (\vec{b} + \vec{c}) + \vec{b} \times (\vec{c} + \vec{a}) + \vec{c} \times (\vec{a} + \vec{b})$.

ANSWERS

1. $\vec{0}$ 2. $\cos^{-1}\dfrac{5}{7}$ 3. $\dfrac{1}{\sqrt{262}}\hat{i} - \dfrac{6}{\sqrt{262}}\hat{j} - \dfrac{15}{\sqrt{262}}\hat{k}$

4. $-5\vec{b}$ 5. 5˙. 6. $\dfrac{\pi}{4}$

7. 7 8. $\dfrac{1}{\sqrt{26}}(18\hat{i} - 6\hat{j} + 24\hat{k})$ 9. $\dfrac{\pi}{6}$ 10. 0

SECTION-II

1. If $\vec{a}$ and $\vec{b}$ are unit vectors and θ is angle between them, then show that
$$\sin\frac{\theta}{2} = \frac{1}{2}|\vec{a} - \vec{b}|.$$
2. Show that points $A(-2\hat{i} + 3\hat{j} + 5\hat{k})$, $B(\hat{i} + 2\hat{j} + 3\hat{k})$ and $(7\hat{i} - \hat{k})$ are collinear.
3. Dot product of a vector with $3\hat{i} - 5\hat{k}$, $2\hat{i} + 7\hat{j}$ and $\hat{i} + \hat{j} + \hat{k}$ are respectively –1, 6 and 5. Find the vector.
4. Find the projection of vector $(\hat{i} + 3\hat{j} + 7\hat{k})$ on the vector $7\hat{i} - \hat{j} + 8\hat{k}$.
5. Decompose the vector $6\hat{i} - 3\hat{j} - 6\hat{k}$ onto vectors which are parallel and perpendicular to the vector
   $\hat{i} + \hat{j} + \hat{k}$.
6. If $\vec{d_1}$ and $\vec{d_2}$ are diagonals of parallelogram with sides $\vec{a}$ and $\vec{b}$, find the area of parallelogram in terms of diagonal $\vec{d_1}$ and $\vec{d_2}$. Find area when $\vec{d_1} = \hat{i} + 2\hat{j} + 3\hat{k}$ and $\vec{d_2} = 3\hat{i} - 2\hat{j} + \hat{k}$.

7. Three vectors $\vec{a}$, $\vec{b}$ and $\vec{c}$ satisfy the condition $\vec{a}+\vec{b}+\vec{c}=0$. Evaluate

$$\mu = \vec{a}.\vec{b}+\vec{b}.\vec{c}+\vec{c}.\vec{a} \text{ if } |\vec{a}|=1, |\vec{b}|=4 \text{ and } |\vec{c}|=2.$$

8. $\vec{a}=\hat{i}+\hat{j}+\hat{k}$, $\vec{b}=2\hat{i}-\hat{j}+3\hat{k}$ and $\vec{c}=\hat{i}-2\hat{j}+\hat{k}$. Find unit vector parallel to vector $2\vec{a}-\vec{b}+3\vec{c}$.

9. Let $\vec{a}$, $\vec{b}$, $\vec{c}$ be three non-zero vectors such that any two of them are non-collinear. If $\vec{a}+2\vec{b}$ is collinear with $\vec{c}$ and $\vec{b}+2\vec{c}$ is collinear with $\vec{a}$ prove that $\vec{a}+2\vec{b}+6\vec{c}=\vec{a}$.

10. $\vec{a}=\hat{i}+\hat{j}+\hat{k}$ and $\vec{b}=\hat{j}-\hat{k}$. Find a vector $\vec{c}$ such that $\vec{a}\times\vec{c}=\vec{b}$ and $\vec{a}.\vec{c}=3$.

ANSWERS

3. $3\hat{i}+2\hat{k}$ 5. $-\hat{i}-\hat{j}-\hat{k}, 7\hat{i}-2\hat{j}-5\hat{k}$ 6. $4\sqrt{3}$ sq. units

7. $\mu=-\dfrac{21}{2}$ 8. $\dfrac{3}{\sqrt{22}}\hat{i}-\dfrac{3}{\sqrt{22}}\hat{j}+\dfrac{2}{\sqrt{22}}\hat{k}$ 10. $\vec{c}=\dfrac{1}{3}(5\hat{i}+2\hat{j}+2\hat{k})$

HOTS

1. $\vec{a}$ and $\vec{b}$ are unit vectors and θ is angle between them. Find unit vector along the angular bisector of $\vec{a}$ and $\vec{b}$.

2. If $\vec{a}=2\hat{i}+\hat{k}$; $\vec{b}=\hat{i}+\hat{j}+\hat{k}$ and $\vec{c}=4\hat{i}-3\hat{j}+7\hat{k}$. Determine a vector $\vec{x}$ such that, $\vec{x}\times\vec{b}=\vec{c}\times\vec{b}$ and $\vec{x}.\vec{a}=\vec{0}$.

3. Prove by vector methods that the altitude of triangles is concurrent.

4. Let $\vec{a}=2\hat{i}+\hat{j}-2\hat{k}$, $\vec{b}=\hat{i}+\hat{j}$. If $\vec{c}$ is a vector such that $\vec{a}.\vec{c}=|\vec{c}|, |\vec{c}-\vec{a}|=2\sqrt{2}$ and the angle between $(\vec{a}\times\vec{b})$ and $\vec{c}$ is 30°. Find the value of $|(\vec{a}\times\vec{b})\times\vec{c}|$.

ANSWERS

1. $\dfrac{\vec{a}+\vec{b}}{2\cos\dfrac{\theta}{2}}$ 2. $\vec{x}=-\vec{i}-8\vec{j}+2\vec{k}$ 4. $\dfrac{3}{2}$

❑❑❑

CHAPTER 11

3-D GEOMETRY

STRAIGHT LINE IN A SPACE

Vector equation of a straight line passing through a fixed point with position vector $\vec{a}$ and parallel to a given vector $\vec{b}$ is

$$\vec{r} = \vec{a} + \lambda \vec{b}, \text{ where } \vec{r} = x\hat{i} + y\hat{j} + z\hat{k}$$

Cartesian equation of the straight line passing through a fixed point (x_1, y_1, z_1) having the direction ratios a, b, c is given by

$$\frac{x - x_1}{a} = \frac{y - y_1}{b} = \frac{z - z_1}{c}$$

The Cartesian equations of a line through $A(x_1, y_1, z_1)$ and $B(x_2, y_2, z_2)$ are

$$\frac{x - x_1}{x_2 - x_1} = \frac{y - y_1}{y_2 - y_1} = \frac{z - z_1}{z_2 - z_1}$$

Vector equation of a straight line passing through two given points with position vector $\vec{a}$ and $\vec{b}$ is

$$\vec{r} = \vec{a} + \lambda(\vec{b} - \vec{a}), \text{ where } \lambda \text{ is parameter.}$$

Angle between two straight lines whose vectors equations are

$$\vec{r} = \vec{a}_1 + \lambda \vec{b}_1 \text{ and } \vec{r} = \vec{a}_2 + \lambda \vec{b}_2$$

Then $$\cos\theta = \frac{\vec{b}_1 . \vec{b}_2}{|\vec{b}_1||\vec{b}_2|}$$

- If $\vec{b}_1 . \vec{b}_2 = 0$ then $\vec{b}_1 \perp \vec{b}_2$
- If $\vec{b}_1 = \lambda \vec{b}_2$ then $\vec{b}_1 \| \vec{b}_2$

SHORTEST DISTANCE BETWEEN TWO SKEW LINES

- The shortest distance between two skew lines $\vec{r} = \vec{a}_1 + \lambda \vec{b}_1$ and $\vec{r} = \vec{a}_2 + \mu \vec{b}_2$ is given by

$$d = \left| \frac{(\vec{b}_1 \times \vec{b}_2).(\vec{a}_2 - \vec{a}_1)}{(\vec{b}_1 \times \vec{b}_2)} \right|$$

- Distance between parallel lines.

  Let $\vec{r} = \vec{a}_1 + \lambda \vec{b}_1$ and $\vec{r} = \vec{a}_2 + \lambda \vec{b}_2$ are two $\|$ lines, then

$$d = \left| \frac{\vec{b} \times (\vec{a}_2 - \vec{a}_1)}{|\vec{b}|} \right|$$

Shortest distance between two skew lines in the Cartesian Form. The shortest distance between the skew lines

$$\frac{x-x_1}{a_1} = \frac{y-y_1}{b_1} = \frac{z-z_1}{c_1}$$

and $$\frac{x-x_2}{a_2} = \frac{y-y_2}{b_2} = \frac{z-z_2}{c_2}$$ is given by

$$D = \frac{\begin{vmatrix} x_2-x_1 & y_2-y_1 & z_2-z_1 \\ a_1 & b_1 & c_1 \\ a_2 & b_2 & c_2 \end{vmatrix}}{\sqrt{(a_1b_2-a_2b_1)^2+(b_1c_2-b_2c_1)^2+(c_1a_2-c_2a_1)^2}}$$

THE PLANE

General equation of a Plane in the Cartesian Form. Every equation $a_x + b_y + c_z = d$ of the first degree in *x, y, z* always represents a plane and *a, b, c* are the direction ratios of the normal to this plane.

- The equation of a plane passing through a point $P(x_1, y_1, z_1)$ is

  $$a(x-x_1) + b(y-y_1) + c(z-z_1) = 0$$

  where *a, b, c* are constants.
- **Equation of a plane in the intercept form**

  $$\frac{x}{a} + \frac{y}{b} + \frac{z}{c} = 1$$

- Where plane makes intercepts of lengths *a, b, c* with the *x*-axis, *y*-axis and *z*-axis respectively.
- **Equation of a plane in the Normal form.** $\vec{r} \cdot \hat{n} = p$, where $\hat{n}$ is a unit vector normal to the plane and *p* is the length of the ⊥ from the origin.

Reduction of the General Form of the Equation of a Plane to the Normal Form. Let the general equation of the plane is $ax + by + cz \neq d = 0$

Then $ax + by + cz + d = 0$

$\Rightarrow$ $-ax - by - cz = d$

$$\Rightarrow \quad \frac{-a}{\sqrt{a^2+b^2+c^2}}x + \frac{-b}{\sqrt{a^2+b^2+c^2}}y + \frac{-c}{\sqrt{a^2+b^2+c^2}}z = \frac{d}{\sqrt{a^2+b^2+c^2}}$$

[on dividing throughout by $\sqrt{(-a)^2+(-b)^2+(-c)^2}$]

$\Rightarrow$ $lx + my + nz = p$

where $$l = \frac{-a}{\sqrt{a^2+b^2+c^2}}, \; m = \frac{-b}{\sqrt{a^2+b^2+c^2}}$$

$$n = \frac{-c}{\sqrt{a^2+b^2+c^2}} \text{ and } p = \frac{d}{\sqrt{a^2+b^2+c^2}}$$

Here *l, m, n* are the *d.c.'s* of the normal to the plane and *p* is the length of the perpendicular from the origin to the plane.

Equation of a plane through the intersection of two lines

(*i*) **Vector Form→**The equation of a plane through the intersection of two planes $\vec{r}\,.\,\vec{n}_1 = d_1$ and $\vec{r}\,.\,\vec{n}_2 = d_2$ is given by

$$\vec{r}\,.(\vec{n}_1 + \lambda\,\vec{n}_2) = d_1 + \lambda d_2.$$

(*ii*) **Cartesian Form→**The equation of a plane through the intersection of two planes $a_1x + b_1y + c_1z + d_1 = 0$ and $a_2x + b_2y + c_2z + d_2 = 0$ is given by $(a_1x + b_1y + c_1z + d_1) + \lambda(a_2x + b_2y + c_2z + d_2) = 0$.

Equation of a plane passing through a given point and ⊥ to a given vector.

Vector Form→The vector equation of a plane passing through a point A with position vector $\vec{a}$ and ⊥ to a given vector $\vec{n}$ is $(\vec{r} - \vec{a}).\vec{n} = 0$

Cartesian Form

$$a_1(x - x_1) + b_1(y - y_1) + c_1(z - z_1) = 0$$

Where point be (x_1, y_1, z_1) and a_1, b_1, c_1 are direction ratios.

Equation of a plane passing through three given points.

Vector Form→If $\vec{a}\,.\,\vec{b}\,.\,\vec{c}$ be three non-collinear pts., then

$$(\vec{r} - \vec{a}).[(\vec{b} - \vec{a}) \times (\vec{c} - \vec{a}) = 0$$

Cartesian Form→Three non-collinear pts. $A(x_1, y_1, z_1)$, $B(x_2, y_2, z_2)$ and $C(x_3, y_3, z_3)$ is given by

$$\begin{vmatrix} x - x_1 & y - y_1 & z - z_1 \\ x - x_2 & y - y_2 & z - z_2 \\ x - x_3 & y - y_3 & z - z_3 \end{vmatrix} = 0$$

Angle between two planes. The acute angle θ between $\vec{r}\,.\,\vec{n}_1 = d_1$ and $\vec{r}\,.\,\vec{n}_2 = d_2$ is given by

$$\cos\theta = \frac{|\vec{n}_1\,.\,\vec{n}_2|}{|\vec{n}_1|\,|\vec{n}_2|}$$

Cartesian Form→If θ be the angles between two planes $a_1x + b_1y + c_1z + d_1 = 0$ and $a_2x + b_2y + c_2z + d_2 = 0$, then

$$\cos\theta = \frac{|a_1a_2 + b_1b_2 + c_1c_2|}{\sqrt{a_1^2 + b_1^2 + c_1^2}\,.\sqrt{a_2^2 + b_2^2 + c_2^2}}$$

Length of Perpendicular from a Point to a Plane.

Vector Form→The length p of the perpendicular drawn from a point with position vector $\vec{a}$ to the plane $\vec{r}\,.\,\vec{n} = d$ is given by

$$p = \frac{|\vec{a}\,.\vec{n} - d|}{|\vec{n}|}$$

Cartesian Form→The length p of the perpendicular from a point $A(x_1, y_1, z_1)$ to the plane $a_x + b_y + c_z + d = 0$ is given by

$$p = \left|\frac{ax_1 + by_1 + cz_1 + d}{\sqrt{a^2 + b^2 + c^2}}\right|$$

Two planes $\vec{r} = \vec{a}_1 + \lambda \vec{b}_1$ and $\vec{r} = \vec{a}_2 + \mu \vec{b}_2$ are coplanar if

$$(\vec{a}_2 - \vec{a}_1).(\vec{b}_1 \times \vec{b}_2) = 0$$

Two planes $a_1x + b_1y + c_1z + d_1 = 0$ and $a_2x + b_2y + c_2z + d_2 = 0$ are coplanar

$$\begin{vmatrix} x_2 - x_1 & y_2 - y_1 & z_2 - z_1 \\ a_1 & b_1 & c_1 \\ a_2 & b_2 & c_2 \end{vmatrix} = 0$$

SOLVED QUESTIONS

SECTION-I

1. *If a line makes an angle α, β, γ with the coordinate axes, prove that* $\sin^2 \alpha + \sin^2 \beta + \sin^2 \gamma = 2$.

Solution: Let l, m, n be direction cosines of the given line

$l = \cos \alpha, \quad m = \cos \beta, \quad n = \cos \gamma$

Now $\quad l^2 + m^2 + n^2 = 1$

$\Rightarrow \quad \cos^2 \alpha + \cos^2 \beta + \cos^2 \gamma = 1$

$\Rightarrow \quad 1 - \sin^2 \alpha + 1 - \sin^2 \beta + 1 - \sin^2 \gamma = 1$

$\sin^2 \alpha + \sin^2 \beta + \sin^2 \gamma = 2.$

2. *If line has direction ratios* 2, – 1, – 2, *determine its direction* cosines.

Solution: Direction cosines

$$\frac{2}{\sqrt{2^2 + (-1)^2 + (-2)^2}}, \frac{-1}{\sqrt{2^2 + (-1)^2 + (-2)^2}}, \frac{-2}{\sqrt{2^2 + (-1)^2 + (-2)^2}}$$

$$\Rightarrow \quad \frac{2}{3}, \frac{-1}{3}, \frac{-2}{3}.$$

3. *Find the angle between pair of lines given by*

$$\vec{r} = 3\hat{i} + 2\hat{j} - 4\hat{k} + \lambda(\hat{i} + 2\hat{j} + 2\hat{k})$$

and

$$\vec{r} = 5\hat{i} - 2\hat{j} + \mu(3\hat{i} + 2\hat{j} + 6\hat{k}).$$

Solution: $\vec{b}_1 = \hat{i} + 2\hat{j} + 2\hat{k} \quad \vec{b}_2 = 3\hat{i} + 2\hat{j} + 6\hat{k}$

Angle θ between two lines

$$\Rightarrow \quad \cos\theta = \left|\frac{\vec{b}_1 . \vec{b}_2}{|\vec{b}_1||\vec{b}_2|}\right| = \left|\frac{3+4+12}{3 \times 7}\right| = \frac{19}{21}$$

$$\Rightarrow \quad \theta = \cos^{-1}\left(\frac{19}{21}\right).$$

4. *Find the cartesian equation of plane whose vector equation is* $\vec{r} . (5\hat{i} + 7\hat{j} - 11\hat{k}) = 14$.

Solution: Since $\vec{r}$ is a position vector any point $P(x, y, z)$ on the given plane

$$\vec{r} = x\hat{i} + y\hat{j} + z\hat{k}$$

$$(x\hat{i} + y\hat{j} + z\hat{k})(5\hat{i} + 7\hat{j} - 11\hat{k}) = 14$$

$5x + 7y - 11z = 14$ is cartesian equation of plane.

5. *Find the angle between planes whose vector quantities are*

$$\vec{r}\,(2\hat{i}+2\hat{j}-3\hat{k})=5 \text{ and } \vec{r}\,(3\hat{i}-3\hat{j}+5\hat{k})=3.$$

Solution: $\vec{h_1}=2\hat{i}+2\hat{j}-3\hat{k}$ $\qquad \vec{h_2}=3\hat{i}-3\hat{j}+5\hat{k}$

Angle θ between planes

$$\cos\theta = \left|\frac{\vec{h_1}.\vec{h_2}}{|\vec{h_1}||\vec{h_2}|}\right| = \left|\frac{(2)(3)+(2)(-3)+(-3)5}{\sqrt{4+4+9}\,\sqrt{9+9+25}}\right| = \frac{15}{\sqrt{731}}$$

$$\theta = \cos^{-1}\left(\frac{15}{\sqrt{731}}\right).$$

6. *If a plane has intercepts a, b, c on the coordinate axes and is at a distance of p units from the origin prove that*

$$\frac{1}{a^2}+\frac{1}{b^2}+\frac{1}{c^2} = \frac{1}{P^2}.$$

Solution: Equation of plane which has intercepts *a, b, c* on the coordinate axes.

$$\frac{x}{a}+\frac{y}{b}+\frac{z}{c} = 1$$

Since the perpendicular distance from point 0 (0, 0, 0) to the plane (*i*) is *P* we have

$$P = \frac{|0+0+0-1|}{\sqrt{\frac{1}{a^2}+\frac{1}{b^2}+\frac{1}{c^2}}}$$

$$\Rightarrow \quad \frac{1}{a^2}+\frac{1}{b^2}+\frac{1}{c^2} = \frac{1}{P^2}.$$

7. *Find the equation of the plane which cuts off intercepts* 3, –4, *and* 6 *from the axes. Reduce it to normal form and hence find the length of perpendicular from origin to the plane.*

Solution: Equation of plane

$$\frac{x}{3}+\frac{y}{-4}+\frac{z}{6} = 1$$

$$4x-3y+2z = 12$$

Dividing both sides by $\sqrt{16+9+4}=\sqrt{29}$

$$\frac{4}{\sqrt{29}}x-\frac{3}{\sqrt{29}}y+\frac{2z}{\sqrt{29}} = \frac{12}{\sqrt{29}}$$

Equation of plane in the normal form

$$lx+my+nz = p$$

Length of perpendicular from origin to the plane

$$= \frac{12}{\sqrt{29}}.$$

8. *If the line drawn from the point* (–10, 5, 4) *meets plane at right angles at the point* (4, –1, 2), *find the equation of plane.*

Solution: Let *B*(–10, 5, 4) and *A*(4, –1, 2)

Direction ratios of line *AB* are

$$<-10-4,\ 5+1,\ 4-2> \text{ i.e. } <7, -3, -1>$$

Required plane passes through A and is perpendicular to line AB i.e. having the line AB with direction ratios $< 7, -3, -1>$ as normal therefore the equation of the plane is

$$7(x-4) + (-3)[y-(-1)] + (-1)(z-2) = 0$$

$$7x - 3y - z - 29 = 0$$

$$7x - 3y - z = +29.$$

SECTION-II

1. *Find the equation of line passing through the point $P(4, 6, 2)$ and point of intersection of the line $\frac{x-1}{3} = \frac{y}{2} = \frac{z+1}{7}$ and the plane $x + y - z = 8$.*

Solution: Let Q be the point of intersection of the line $\frac{x-1}{3} = \frac{y}{2} = \frac{z+1}{7}$ and the plane $x + y - z = 8$

Any point on the line

$$\frac{x-1}{3} = \frac{y}{2} = \frac{z+1}{7} = r \text{ (say) is}$$

$(3r+1,\ 2r,\ 7r-1)$

If it is point Q, then it lies in the plane

$$x + y - z = 8$$

$$3r + 1 + 2r - (7r-1) = 8$$

$$-2r = 6$$

$$r = -3$$

$\therefore$ Point Q is $[-9+1,\ 2 \times -3,\ 7(-3)-1]$

$[-8, -6, -22]$

Given point P is $(4, 6, 2)$.

$\therefore$ Equation of the line PQ is

$$\frac{x-4}{4+8} = \frac{y-6}{6+6} = \frac{z-2}{2+22}$$

$$\frac{x-4}{12} = \frac{y-6}{12} = \frac{z-2}{24}$$

$$\frac{x-4}{1} = \frac{y-6}{1} = \frac{z-2}{2}.$$

2. *Find the length and foot of perpendicular drawn from the point $(2, -1, 5)$ to the line $\frac{x-11}{10} = \frac{y+2}{-4} = \frac{z+8}{-11}$.*

Solution: Equation of line are

$$\frac{x-11}{10} = \frac{y+2}{-4} = \frac{z+8}{-11} = r \text{ (say)} \quad ...(1)$$

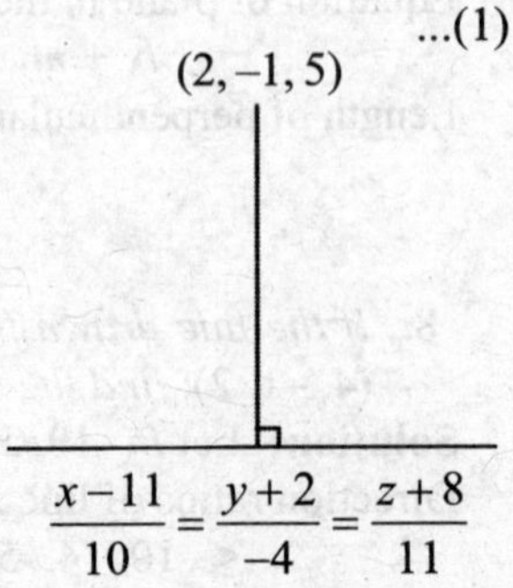

Any point P on this line is $(10r+11, -4r-2, -11r-8)$

Given point Q is $(2, -1, 5)$

Direction ratios of the line segment PQ are

$10r + 11 - 2,\ -4r - 2 + 1,\ -11r - 8 - 5$

$(10r+9, -4r-1, -11r-13)$

PQ is perpendicular to the line (1)

$$10(10r+9) - 4(4r-1) - 11(-11r-13) = 0$$

$$\Rightarrow \quad 237r + 237 = 0$$

$$\Rightarrow \quad r = -1$$

$\therefore$ Point P is $(-10+11, 4-2, 11-8)$ or $(1, 2, 3)$

$\therefore$ Foot P of perpendicular is $(1, 2, 3)$.

Distance PQ i.e. length of perpendicular segment from Q to the line

$$= \sqrt{(2-1)^2+(-1-2)^2+(5-3)^2}$$

$$= \sqrt{1+9+4} \text{ or } \sqrt{14} \text{ units.}$$

3. *A variable plane which remains at a constant distance of 9 units from the origin cuts the coordinate axes at the points A, B and C. Show that locus of the controid of* ΔABC *is*

$$\frac{1}{x^2}+\frac{1}{y^2}+\frac{1}{z^2}=\frac{1}{9}.$$

Solution: Let the equation of the plane through the points A, B and C be

$$\frac{x}{a}+\frac{y}{b}+\frac{z}{c} = 1$$

distance from the origin

$$\Rightarrow \quad \frac{1}{\sqrt{\frac{1}{a^2}+\frac{1}{b^2}+\frac{1}{c^2}}} = 9$$

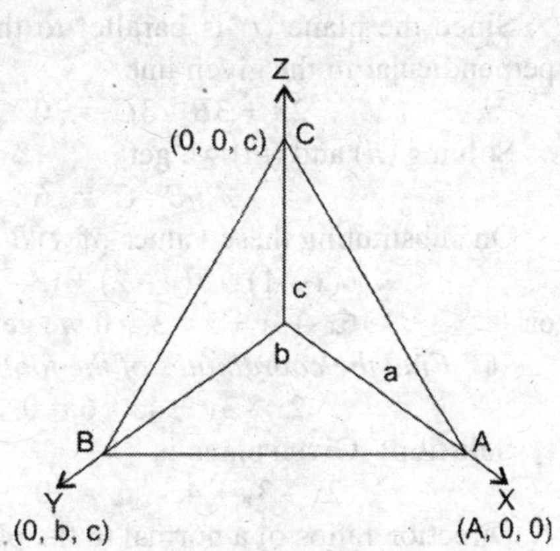

Fig. 11.1

Now centroid of ΔABC is $\left(\frac{a}{3}, \frac{b}{3}, \frac{c}{3}\right)$.

Let it denoted by (x, y, z).

$\therefore$ Equation of the locus of centroid

$$\Rightarrow \quad \left(\frac{1}{3x}\right)^2+\left(\frac{1}{3y}\right)^2+\left(\frac{1}{3z}\right)^2=\frac{1}{81}$$

$$\Rightarrow \quad \frac{1}{x^2}+\frac{1}{y^2}+\frac{1}{z^2}=\frac{1}{9}.$$

4. *Find the equation of the plane passing through intersection of planes* $2x + 3y - z + 1 = 0$ *and* $x + y - 2z + 3 = 0$ *and perpendicular to the plane* $3x - y - 2z - 4 = 0$.

Solution: Equation of any plane passing through intersection of planes

$2x + 3y - z + 1 = 0$ and $x + y - 2z + 3 = 0$ is

$\Rightarrow \quad (2x + 3y - z + 1) + \lambda (x + y - 2z + 3) = 0$

$\Rightarrow \quad (2 + \lambda)x + (3 + \lambda)y + (-1 - 2\lambda)z + (1 + 3\lambda) = 0 \qquad ...(i)$

Now (i) is perpendicular to the plane

$3x - y - 2z - 4 = 0$

$\Rightarrow \quad (2 + \lambda)3 + (3 + \lambda)(-1) + (-1 - 2\lambda)(-2) = 0 \qquad [a_1a_2 + b_1b_2 + c_1c_2 = 0]$

$\Rightarrow \quad \lambda = -\frac{5}{6}.$

Substituting this value of λ in (i) we get

$$\left(2-\frac{5}{6}\right)x+\left(3-\frac{5}{6}\right)y+\left(-1+\frac{5}{3}\right)z+\left(1-\frac{5}{2}\right)=0$$

$7x + 13y + 4z - 9 = 0$ which is the equation of the required plane.

5. *Find the equation of plane passing through the points* (1, 2, 3), (0, –1, 0) *and parallel to line* $\frac{x-1}{2} = \frac{y+2}{3} = \frac{z}{-3}$.

Solution: Equation of any plane passing through (1, 2, 3)

$$A(x-1) + B(y-2) + C(z-3) = 0 \qquad ...(i)$$

(*i*) passes through (0, –1, 0)

$$-A - 3B - 3C = 0$$
$$A + 3B + 3C = 0.$$

Direction ratio of a normal to the plane (*i*) are < *1, 3, 3* >.

Direction ratio of given line

$$\frac{x-1}{2} = \frac{y+2}{3} = \frac{z}{-3} \text{ are } <2, 3, -3>. \qquad ...(ii)$$

Since the plane (*i*) is parallel to the given line, therefore, every normal to plane (*i*) is perpendicular to the given line

$$\therefore \quad 2A + 3B - 3C = 0 \qquad ...(iii)$$

Solving (*ii*) and (*iii*) we get

$$A : B : C = 6 : -3 : 1$$

On substituting these values of *A, B* and *C* in (*i*) we get

$$6(x-1) - 3(y-2) + (z-3) = 0$$

or $\quad 6x - 3y + z - 3 = 0$ we get the required equation.

6. *Find the coordinates of the foot of perpendicular drawn from the origin to the plane* $2x - 3y + 4z - 6 = 0$.

Solution: Given plane is

$$2x - 3y + 4z - 6 = 0 \qquad ...(i)$$

Direction ratios of a normal to the plane (*i*) are < 2, – 3, 4 >.

Therefore, the equation of line through origin *O*(0, 0, 0) and perpendicular to the plane (*i*) are

$$\frac{x-0}{2} = \frac{y-0}{-3} = \frac{z-0}{4} \qquad ...(i)$$

Any point on the line (*ii*) is *N*(2λ, – 3λ, 4λ), where λ is on arbitrary real number.

If it lies on the plane (*i*) then

$$2.2\lambda - 3(-3\lambda) + 4.4\lambda - 6 = 0$$

$$\Rightarrow \quad 29\lambda = 6$$

$$\Rightarrow \quad \lambda = \frac{6}{29}$$

$\therefore$ Foot of perpendicular from origin to the given plane is

$$\left(\frac{12}{29}, \frac{-18}{29}, \frac{24}{29}\right).$$

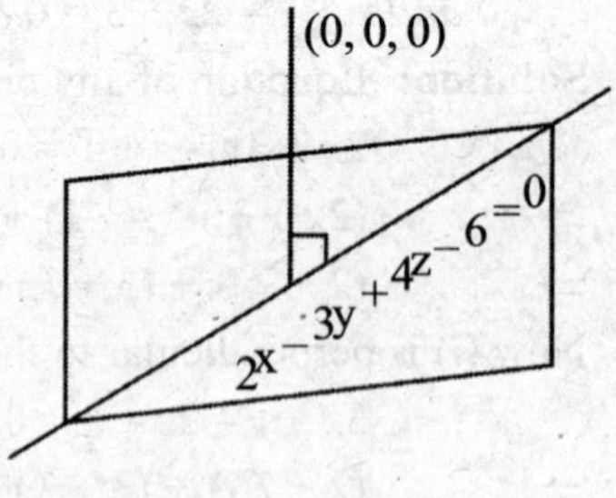

7. *Find the shortest distance between the lines*

$$\vec{r} = (1+2\lambda)\,\hat{i} + (2+3\lambda)\,\hat{j} + (3+4\lambda)\,\hat{k}$$

and $\quad \vec{r} = (2+3\mu)\,\hat{i} + 4(1+\mu)\,\hat{j} + 5(1+\mu)\,\hat{k}$.

Solution: Equation of the lines are

$$\vec{r} = \hat{i} + 2\hat{j} + 3\hat{k} + \lambda(2\hat{i} + 3\hat{j} + 4\hat{k})$$

and $\quad \vec{r} = 2\hat{i} + 4\hat{j} + 5\hat{k} + \mu(3\hat{i} + 4\hat{j} + 5\hat{k})$

$\therefore \quad \vec{a_1} = \hat{i} + 2\hat{j} + 3\hat{k}, \quad \vec{b_1} = 2\hat{i} + 3\hat{j} + 4\hat{k}$

$$\overrightarrow{a_2} = 2\hat{i}+4\hat{j}+5\hat{k}, \quad \overrightarrow{b_2} = 3\hat{i}+4\hat{j}+5\hat{k}$$

$$\overrightarrow{a_2}-\overrightarrow{a_1} = 2\hat{i}+4\hat{j}+5\hat{k}-(\hat{i}+2\hat{j}+3\hat{k})$$

$$= \hat{i}+2\hat{j}+2\hat{k}$$

$$\overrightarrow{b_1}\times\overrightarrow{b_2} = \begin{vmatrix} \hat{i} & \hat{j} & \hat{k} \\ 2 & 3 & 4 \\ 3 & 4 & 5 \end{vmatrix}$$

$$= -\hat{i}+2\hat{j}-\hat{k}$$

$$|\overrightarrow{b_1}\times\overrightarrow{b_2}| = \sqrt{1+4+1} = \sqrt{6}$$

$$\text{S.D.} = \frac{|(\overrightarrow{a_2}-\overrightarrow{a_1})\,(\overrightarrow{b_1}\times\overrightarrow{b_2})|}{|\overrightarrow{b_1}\times\overrightarrow{b_2}|}$$

$$= \frac{(\hat{i}+2\hat{j}+2\hat{k})\,.\,(-\hat{i}+2\hat{j}-\hat{k})}{\sqrt{6}}$$

$$= \frac{1}{\sqrt{6}} \text{ units.}$$

8. *Find the coordinates of the foot of the perpendicular drawn from point $A(1, 8, 4)$ to the line joining the points $B(0, -1, 3)$ and $C(2, -3, -1)$.*

Solution: Let N be the foot of perpendicular drawn from A to line BC and let L divide segment BC in ratio $L : 1$, then coordinates of the point N are

$$\left[\frac{2\lambda}{\lambda+1}, \frac{-3\lambda-1}{\lambda+1}, \frac{-\lambda+3}{\lambda+1}\right]$$

$\therefore$ Direction ratios of line AN are

$$< \frac{2\lambda}{\lambda+1}-1, \quad \frac{-3\lambda-1}{\lambda+1}-8, \quad \frac{-\lambda+3}{\lambda+1}-4 >$$

i.e. $$< \frac{\lambda-1}{\lambda+1}, \frac{-11\lambda-9}{\lambda+1}, \frac{-5\lambda-1}{\lambda+1} > \textit{i.e.}$$

i.e. $< \lambda-1, \quad -11\lambda-9, \quad -5\lambda-1 >$

Direction ratios of the line BC are

$< 2-0, -3+1, -1-3 >$

i.e. $< 2, -2, -4 >$ i.e. $< 1, -1, -2 >$

Since the line AN is perpendicular to line BC we have

$$(\lambda-1)1 + (-11\lambda-9)(-1) + (-5\lambda-1)(-2) = 0$$

$$\Rightarrow \quad 22\lambda + 10 = 0$$

$$\Rightarrow \quad \lambda = -\frac{5}{11}$$

$\therefore$ Coordinates of point N are

$$\Rightarrow \left(\frac{-\frac{10}{11}}{-\frac{5}{11}+1}, \frac{\frac{15}{11}-1}{-\frac{5}{11}+1}, \frac{\frac{5}{11}+3}{-\frac{5}{11}+1}\right) = \left(-\frac{5}{3}, \frac{2}{3}, \frac{19}{3}\right).$$

SECTION-III

1. *Find the equation of the plane mid parallel to the planes* $2x - 3y + 6z + 21 = 0$ *and* $2x - 3y + 6z - 14 = 0$.

Solution: Given planes are

$$2x - 3y + 6z + 21 = 0 \quad \ldots(i)$$

and $$2x - 3y + 6z - 14 = 0 \quad \ldots(ii)$$

First we note that given planes are parallel equation of any plane parallel to these planes is

$$2x - 3y + 6z + k = 0$$

To find a point on plane (*iii*), on putting $x = 0$, $y = 0$ we get $z = -\frac{K}{6}$, so the point, $P\left(0, 0, -\frac{K}{6}\right)$ lies on plane (*iii*).

Since the plane (*iii*) is mid parallel to planes (*i*) and (*ii*), the perpendicular distance of P from plane (*i*) = the perpendicular distance from plane (*ii*)

$$\Rightarrow \quad \frac{\left|2.0-3.0+6\left(-\frac{K}{6}\right)+21\right|}{\sqrt{2^2+(-3)^2+6^2}} = \frac{\left|2.0-3.0+6\left(-\frac{K}{6}\right)-14\right|}{\sqrt{2^2+(-3)^2+6^2}}$$

$$|-K+21| = |-K-14|$$

$$\Rightarrow \quad |-K+21| = \pm(-K-14)$$

$$\Rightarrow \quad \text{Either } -K+21 = K+14 \text{ or } -K+21 = -K-14$$

$$\Rightarrow \quad \text{Either } K = \frac{7}{2} \quad \text{or} \quad 2K = -14$$

On putting $K = \frac{7}{2}$ in (*iii*) equation of the required plane is

$$2x - 3y + 6z + \frac{7}{2} = 0 \quad i.e. \quad 4x - 6y + 12z + 7 = 0.$$

2. *Find the equation of the plane passing through the point* $(2, -1, 5)$ *and perpendicular to each of the planes* $\vec{r}\,.\,(\hat{i} + 2\hat{j} - \hat{k}) = 1$ *and* $\vec{r}\,.\,(3\hat{i} - 4\hat{j} + \hat{k}) = 5$.

Solution: Since the plane passes through the point $(2, -1, 5)$

$$\therefore \quad \vec{a} = 2\hat{i} - \hat{j} + 5\hat{k}$$

Since the plane is perpendicular to the given planes, its normal $\vec{r}$ is perpendicular to the normal $\overrightarrow{n_1}$ and $\overrightarrow{n_2}$ of the given planes

$$\vec{r}\,.\,(\hat{i} + 2\hat{j} - \hat{k}) \text{ and } \vec{r}\,.\,(3\hat{i} - 4\hat{j} + \hat{k}) = 5$$

$$\Rightarrow \quad \overrightarrow{n_1} = \hat{i} + 2\hat{j} - \hat{k} \text{ and } \overrightarrow{n_2} = 3\hat{i} - 4\hat{j} + \hat{k}$$

$$\therefore \quad \vec{n} = \overrightarrow{n_1} \times \overrightarrow{n_2} \qquad (\because \vec{n} \perp \overrightarrow{n_1} \text{ and } \vec{n} \perp \overrightarrow{n_2})$$

$$\Rightarrow \quad \vec{n} = \begin{vmatrix} \hat{i} & \hat{j} & \hat{k} \\ 1 & 2 & -1 \\ 3 & -4 & 1 \end{vmatrix} = -2\hat{i} - 4\hat{j} - 10\hat{k}$$

We know that the equation of a plane passing through a point whose position vector is $\vec{a}$ and is perpendicular to $\vec{n}$ is

$$(\vec{r} - \vec{a})\,.\,\vec{n} = 0 \quad i.e. \quad \Rightarrow \vec{r}\,.\,\vec{n} = \vec{a} - n$$

$\Rightarrow \qquad \vec{r}\,.(-2\hat{i} - 4\hat{j} - 10\hat{k}) = (2\hat{i} - \hat{j} + 5\hat{k}).(-2\hat{i} - 4\hat{j} - 10\hat{k})$

$$= -4 + 4 - 50 = -50$$

Hence the equation of the plane is

$$\vec{r}\,.(-2\hat{i} - 4\hat{j} - 10\hat{k}) = -50$$

$$\Rightarrow \qquad \vec{r}\,.(\hat{i} + 2\hat{j} + 5\hat{k}) = 25$$

3. *Find the cartesian as well as the vector equation of the planes passing through intersection of plane $\vec{r}\,(2\hat{i} + 6\hat{j} + 12) = 0$ and $\vec{r}\,(3\hat{i} - \hat{j} + 4\hat{k}) = 0$, which are at unit distance from the origin.*

Solution: Equation of given planes are

$$\vec{r}\,.\,\vec{n_1} = q_1 \quad \text{and} \quad \vec{r}\,.\,\vec{n_2} = q_2$$

Where $\vec{n_1} = 2\hat{i} + 6\hat{j}$, $\vec{n_2} = 3\hat{i} - \hat{j} + 4\hat{k}$, $q_1 = -12$ and $q_2 = 0$.

The vector equation of any plane through the intersection of the given plane is

$$\vec{r}\,.(\vec{n_1} + \lambda\vec{n_2}) = q_1 + \lambda q_2, \textit{ i.e.,}$$

$$\vec{r}\,.[(2 + 6\hat{j}) + \lambda(3\hat{k} - \hat{i} + 4\hat{k})] = -12 + \lambda(0)$$

$$\Rightarrow \qquad \vec{r}\,.[(2 + 3\lambda)\hat{i} + (6 - \lambda)\hat{j} + 4\lambda\hat{k}] + 12 = 0$$

It is given that a plane (*i*) is at unit distance from origin i.e. (0, 0, 0)

∴ Length of perpendicular from the origin (0, 0, 0) to the plane (1) = 1 unit distance

$$\Rightarrow \qquad \left[\frac{(0\hat{i} - 0\hat{j} + 0\hat{k}).[(2+3\lambda)\hat{i} + (6-\lambda)\hat{j} + 4\lambda\hat{k}] + 12}{\sqrt{(2+3\lambda)^2 + (6-\lambda)^2 + (4\lambda)^2}}\right] = 1$$

$$\left[\frac{12}{\sqrt{4 + 9\lambda^2 + 12\lambda + 36 + \lambda^2 - 12\lambda + 16\lambda^2}}\right] = 1$$

$$\frac{144}{40 + 26\lambda^2} = 1$$

$$26\lambda^2 + 40 = 144$$

$$\lambda^2 = 4$$

$$\lambda = \pm 2$$

For $\lambda = 2$, the vector equation of the plane is

$$\vec{r}\,.[(2 + 6)\hat{i} + (6 - 2)\hat{j} + 8\hat{k})] + 12 = 0$$

i.e. $\qquad \vec{r}\,.(2\hat{i} + \hat{j} + 2\hat{k}) + 3 = 0$

and cartesian equation of the plane is

$$(x\hat{i} + y\hat{j} + z\hat{k}).(2\hat{i} + \hat{j} + 2\hat{k}) = 0$$

i.e. $\qquad 2x + y + 2z + 3 = 0$

For $\lambda = -2$, the vector equation of the plane is

$$\vec{r}\,.|(2 - 6)\hat{i} + (6 + 2)\hat{j} - 8\hat{k}| + 12 = 0$$

$$\vec{r}\,.(-4\hat{i} + 8\hat{j} - 8\hat{k}) + 12 = 0$$

i.e., $\qquad \vec{r}\,.(\hat{i} - 2\hat{j} + 2\hat{k}) - 3 = 0$

and the cartesian equation of the plane is

$$(x\hat{i} + y\hat{j} + z\hat{k}).(\hat{i} - 2\hat{j} + 2\hat{k}) - 3 = 0$$

i.e., $\quad x-2y+2z-3=0$

4. *Find the distance of the point* (–1, –5, –10) *from the point of intersection of line*

$$\vec{r} = 2\hat{i} - \hat{j} + 2\hat{k} + \lambda(3\hat{i} + 4\hat{j} + 2\hat{k}) \text{ and the plane } \vec{r}\,.\,(\hat{i} - \hat{j} + \hat{k}) = 5.$$

Solution: Equation of the given line is

$$\vec{r} = 2\hat{i} - \hat{j} + 2\hat{k} + \lambda(3\hat{i} + 4\hat{j} + 2\hat{k})$$

$$\Rightarrow \quad \vec{r} = (2+3\lambda)\hat{i} + (-1+4\lambda)\hat{j} + (2+2\lambda)\hat{k} \quad \text{...(1)}$$

The equation of the given plane is

$$\vec{r}\,.\,(\hat{i} - \hat{j} + \hat{k}) = 5 \quad \text{...(2)}$$

Since the point of intersection of the line and plane lies on the plane as well as on the line, therefore, from (1)

$$\vec{r} = (2+3\lambda)\hat{i} + (-1+4\lambda)\hat{j} + (2+2\lambda)\hat{k}$$

lines on plane (2)

$$[(2+3\lambda)\hat{i} + (-1+4\lambda)\hat{j} + (2+2\lambda)\hat{k}]\,.\,(\hat{i} - \hat{j} + \hat{k}) = 5$$

$$\Rightarrow \quad (2+3\lambda) + (-1+4\lambda)(-1) + (2+2\lambda)\,1 = 5$$

$$(2 + 3\lambda + 1 - 4\lambda + 2 + 2\lambda = 5$$

$$\lambda = 0$$

Position vector of point of intersection $= 2\hat{i} - \hat{j} + 2\hat{k}$.

Distance of the point (–1, –5, –10) from $2\hat{i} - \hat{j} + 2\hat{k}$

$$= 2\hat{i} - \hat{j} + 2\hat{k} - (-1\hat{i} - 5\hat{j} - 10\hat{k})$$

$$= 2\hat{i} - \hat{j} + 2\hat{k} + \hat{i} + 5\hat{j} + 10\hat{k}$$

$$= 3\hat{i} + 4\hat{j} + 12\hat{k}$$

$$\text{Distance} = \sqrt{(3)^2 + (4)^2 + (12)^2}$$

$$= \sqrt{25+144}$$

$$= 13 \text{ units.}$$

5. *From the point P*(1, 2, 4), *a perpendicular segment is drawn on the plane* $2x + y - 2z + 3 = 0$. *Find its equation and its length. Also find the coordinates of the foot of perpendicular.*

Solution: Equation of the perpendicular drawn from the point $P(1, 2, 4)$ to the plane $2x - y - 2z + 3 = 0$ is

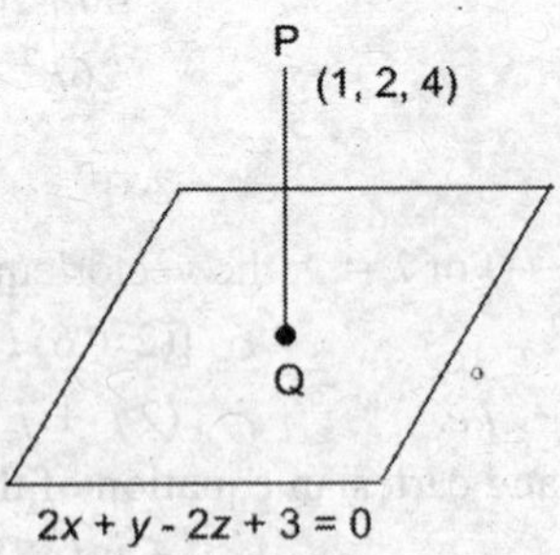

Fig. 11.2

$$\frac{x-1}{2} = \frac{y-2}{1} = \frac{z-4}{-2} = r$$

Any point Q on perpendicular is

$$(2r+1,\ r+2,\ -2r+4).$$

Let it be the foot of the perpendicular from point P to the plane

$\therefore$ It lies in the plane $2x + y - 2z + 3 = 0$

$$\therefore \quad 2(2r+1) + (r+2) - 2(-2r+4) + 3 = 0$$

$$9r = 1$$

$$r = \frac{1}{9}$$

$\therefore$ Foot of perpendicular or Q is $\left(\frac{2}{9} + 1, \frac{1}{9} + 2, -\frac{2}{9} + 4\right)$

$$= \left(\frac{11}{9}, \frac{19}{9}, \frac{34}{9}\right)$$

Also length of perpendicular segment *PQ*

$$PQ = \sqrt{\left(\frac{11}{9}-1\right)^2 + \left(\frac{19}{9}-2\right)^2 + \left(\frac{34}{9}-4\right)^2}$$

$$= \sqrt{\frac{4}{81}+\frac{1}{81}+\frac{4}{81}} \text{ units}$$

$$= \sqrt{\frac{1}{9}} \text{ units}$$

$$= \frac{1}{3} \text{ units.}$$

6. *A line makes angle α, β, γ and δ with diagonals of a cube. Prove that*

$$\cos^2\alpha + \cos^2\beta + \cos^2\gamma + \cos^2\delta = \frac{4}{3}$$

Solution:

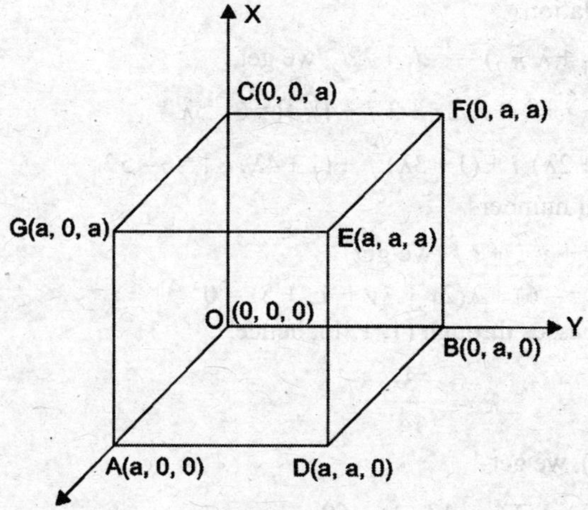

Fig. 11.3

Let *OADBFEGC* be the cube with each side *a*, having 4 diagonals *OE, AF, BG* and *CD*.

d.c. of diagonal $\qquad OE = \frac{a-0}{\sqrt{a^2+a^2+a^2}}, \frac{a-0}{\sqrt{a^2+a^2+a^2}}, \frac{a-0}{\sqrt{a^2+a^2+a^2}}$

$$= \frac{1}{\sqrt{3}}, \frac{1}{\sqrt{3}}, \frac{1}{\sqrt{3}}$$

d.c. of $AF = --\frac{1}{\sqrt{3}}, \frac{1}{\sqrt{3}}, \frac{1}{\sqrt{3}}$

$$\text{d.c. of } BG = \frac{1}{\sqrt{3}}, -\frac{1}{\sqrt{3}}, \frac{1}{\sqrt{3}}$$

$$\text{d.c. of } CD = \frac{1}{\sqrt{3}}, \frac{1}{\sqrt{3}}, -\frac{1}{\sqrt{3}}$$

Let L, m, n be the d.c. of the given line which makes $\alpha, \beta, \gamma, \delta$ with *OE, AF, BC, CD* respectively.

$$\cos\alpha = \frac{l+m+n}{\sqrt{3}} \quad \cos\beta = \left(-\frac{l+m+n}{\sqrt{3}}\right)$$

$$\cos\gamma = \frac{l-m+n}{\sqrt{3}} \quad \cos\delta = \frac{l+m-n}{\sqrt{3}}$$

Hence, $\quad \cos^2\alpha + \cos^2\beta + \cos^2\gamma + \cos^2\delta$

$$= \frac{(1+m+n)^2 + (-l+m+n)^2 + (l-m+n)^2 + (l+m-n)^2}{3}$$

$$= \frac{4}{3} \text{ (using } l^2 + m^2 + n^2 = 1, lm + mn + ln = 0)$$

7. *Find the vector equation of the plane passing through the interseclion of the plane* $\vec{r}.(\hat{i}+\hat{j}+\hat{k}) = 6$ *and* $\vec{r}.(2\hat{i}+3\hat{j}+4\hat{k}) = -5$ *and the point* (1, 1, 1).

Solution. Here $\quad \vec{n}_1 = \hat{i}+\hat{j}+\hat{k}$ and $\vec{n}_2 = 2\hat{i}+3\hat{j}+4\hat{k}$

$d_1 = 6$ and $d_2 = -5$

Hence, using the relation

$$\vec{r}.(\vec{n}_1 + \lambda\vec{n}_2) = d_1 + \lambda d_2, \text{ we get,}$$

$$\vec{r}.[\hat{i}+\hat{j}+\hat{k} + \lambda(2\hat{i}+3\hat{j}+4\hat{k})] = 6 - 5\lambda \quad \text{...(1)}$$

$$\Rightarrow \quad \vec{r}.[(1+2\lambda)\hat{i} + (1+3\lambda)\hat{j} + (1+4\lambda)\hat{k}] = 6 - 5\lambda$$

where λ is same real numbers.

Taking $\quad \vec{r} = x\hat{i} + y\hat{j} + z\hat{k}$ we get

$$(x + y + z - 6) + \lambda(2x + 3y + 4z + 5) = 0 \quad \text{...(2)}$$

Since equation (2) passes through (1, 1, 1), hence,

$$\lambda = \frac{3}{14}$$

Put λ in equation (1), we get

$$\vec{r}.\left(\frac{10}{7}\hat{i} + \frac{23}{14}\hat{j} + \frac{13}{7}\hat{k}\right) = \frac{69}{14}$$

$$\Rightarrow \quad \vec{r} = (20\hat{i} + 23\hat{j} + 26\hat{k}) = 69$$

which is the required vector equation of plane.

UNSOLVED QUESTIONS

SECTION-III

1. Find the shortest distance and vector equation of line of shortest distance between the following pair of lines

$$\vec{r} = (3+2\lambda)\hat{i} - (15-7\lambda)\hat{j} + (9+5\lambda)\hat{k}$$

$$\vec{r} = (2\mu - 1)\hat{i} + (1+\mu)\hat{j} + (9 - 3\mu)\hat{k}.$$

2. Find the equation of the plane passing through the point (1, 1, –1) and perpendicular to the planes

$$\vec{r} \cdot (\hat{i} + 2\hat{j} + 3\hat{k}) = 7$$

and $$\vec{r} \cdot (2\hat{i} - 3\hat{j} + 4\hat{k}) = 0.$$

3. Find the equation of the plane midparallel to the planes

$$2x - 3y + 6z + 21 = 0 \quad \text{and} \quad 2x - 3y + 6z - 14 = 0.$$

4. Find the coordinates of the point where the line through the points (1, –1, 2) and (3, 2, –3) meets the *yz* plane.
5. Find the equation of the plane passing through the points (1, 2, 3) and (0, –1, 0) and parallel to the line

$$\frac{x-1}{2} = \frac{y+2}{3} = \frac{2}{-3}.$$

ANSWERS

1. $4\sqrt{3}$ units; $\vec{r} = -\hat{i} - \hat{j} - \hat{k} + t(4\hat{i} + 4\hat{j} + 4\hat{k})$.
2. $\vec{r} \cdot (17\hat{i} + 2\hat{j} - 7\hat{k}) - 2b = 0$
3. $4x - 6y + 12z + 7 = 0$
4. $\left(0, -\frac{5}{2}, \frac{9}{2}\right)$
5. $6x - 3y + z = 3$.

UNSOLVED QUESTIONS

SECTION-I

1. Show that the area of parallelogram having diagonals $(3\hat{i} + \hat{j} - 2\hat{k})$ and $(\hat{i} - 3\hat{j} + 4\hat{k})$ is $5\sqrt{3}$ units.
2. Find the angles between the lines $\frac{x+4}{3} = \frac{y-1}{5} = \frac{z+3}{4}$ and $\frac{x+1}{1} = \frac{y-4}{1} = \frac{z+5}{2}$.
3. Find the distance of the point (1, –2, +3) from the plane $x - y + z - 5 = 0$ measured along a line parallel to the line $\frac{x}{2} = \frac{y}{3} = \frac{z}{-6}$.
4. Find the angle between the line $\frac{x+1}{2} = \frac{y}{3} = \frac{z-3}{6}$ and the plane $10x + 2y - 11z = 3$.
5. Find the foot of the perpendicular from the point (3, –1, 11) on the line

$$\frac{x}{2} = \frac{y-2}{3} = \frac{z-3}{4}.$$

Also find the length of perpendicular segment.

6. Find the coordinates of the point where the line through the points (5, 1, 6) and (3, 4, 1) crosses the *yz* plane.
7. Find the angle between lines

$$\vec{r} = 2\hat{i} - 5\hat{j} + \hat{k} + \lambda(3\hat{i} + 2\hat{j} + 6\hat{k})$$

and $$\vec{r} = 7\hat{i} - 6\hat{k} + \mu(\hat{i} + 2\hat{j} + 2\hat{k}).$$

8. Find the image of point $(-1, -1, 3)$ in the plane $2x + 3y - 4z - 10 = 0$.
9. Write the vector equation of the plane whose cartesian equation is $2x + 4y - 5z = 3$.
10. Find the vector equation of plane passing through intersection of the planes

$$\vec{r} = (\hat{i} + \hat{j} + \hat{k}) = 6$$

and $\vec{r} = (2\hat{i} + 3\hat{j} + 4\hat{k}) = -5$ and the point $(1, 1, 1)$.

ANSWERS

2. $\cos^{-1}\left(\frac{8\sqrt{3}}{15}\right)$ 3. 1 unit 4. $^{-1}\left(\frac{8}{21}\right)$

5. $(2, 5, 7); 5\sqrt{3}$ units 6. $\left(0, \frac{17}{2}, \frac{-12}{2}\right)$ 7. $\cos^{-1}\left(\frac{19}{21}\right)$

8. $\left(\frac{79}{29}, \frac{133}{29}, -\frac{129}{29}\right)$ 9. $\vec{r}\,.(2\hat{i} + 4\hat{j} - 5\hat{k}) = 3$

10. $\vec{r}\,.(20\hat{i} + 23\hat{j} + 26\hat{k}) = 69$

SECTION-II

1. Find the shortest distance between the lines l_1 and l_2 whose vector equation are $\vec{r} = \hat{i} + \hat{j} + \lambda(2\hat{i} - \hat{j} + \hat{k})$ and $\vec{r} = 2\hat{i} + \hat{j} - \hat{k} + \mu(3\hat{i} - 5\hat{j} + 2\hat{k})$.
2. Find the vector equation of a line passing through the point with position vector $(2\hat{i} - 3\hat{j} - 5\hat{k})$ and perpendicular to the plane $\vec{r}\,.(6\hat{i} - 3\hat{j} + 5\hat{k}) + 2 = 0$. Also, find the point of intersection of this line and plane.
3. Find the equation of the plane which contains the two parallel planes

$$\frac{x-3}{3} = \frac{y+4}{2} = \frac{z-1}{1} \quad \text{and} \quad \frac{x+1}{3} = \frac{y-2}{2} = \frac{z}{1}.$$

4. Find the distance of the point $(2, 2, -1)$ from the plane $x + 2y - z = 1$ measured parallel to the line

$$\frac{x+1}{2} = \frac{y+1}{2} = \frac{z}{3}.$$

5. Find the equation of the plane through the points $(1, 0, -1)$, $(3, 2, 2)$ and parallel to the line

$$\frac{x-1}{1} = \frac{y-1}{-2} = \frac{z-2}{3}.$$

6. Find the equation of the plane through intersection of planes

$$3x - 4y + 5z = 10$$
$$2x + 2y - 3z = 4$$

and parallel to the line $x = 2y = 3z$.

7. Find the shortest lines between $\vec{r} = (2\hat{i} + 3\hat{k}) + \lambda(2\hat{i} - \hat{j})$ and $\vec{r} = (4\hat{i} + 3\hat{k}) + \mu(3\hat{i} + \hat{j} + \hat{k})$.
8. Find the equation of the line through the points $(-1, 2, 3)$ which is perpendicular to lines

$$\frac{x}{2} = \frac{y-1}{-3} = \frac{z+2}{-2} \quad \text{and} \quad \frac{x+3}{-1} = \frac{y+2}{2} = \frac{z-1}{3}.$$

ANSWERS

1. $\dfrac{10}{\sqrt{59}}$ 2. $\vec{r} = (2\hat{i} - 3\hat{j} - 5\hat{k}) + \lambda(6\hat{i} - 3\hat{j} + 5\hat{k})$ and $\left(\dfrac{76}{35}, \dfrac{-108}{35}, \dfrac{-34}{7}\right)$

3. $8x + y - 26z + 6 = 0$ 4. $2\sqrt{17}$ units 5. $4x - y - 2z - 6 = 0$

6. $x - 20y + 27z = 14$ 7. $\sqrt{30}$ 8. $\dfrac{x+1}{5} = \dfrac{y-2}{4} = \dfrac{z-3}{-1}$

HOTS

1. If a line makes angles α, β, γ, δ with diagonals of a cube, prove that

$$\cos 2\alpha + \cos 2\beta + \cos 2\gamma + \cos 2\delta = -\frac{4}{3}.$$

2. Find the coordinates of those points one the line $\dfrac{x-1}{2} = \dfrac{y+2}{3} = \dfrac{z-3}{6}$ which is at distance of 3 units from point (1, –2, 3)
3. The vertices of triangle are $A(5, 4, 6)$, $B(1, -1, 3)$ and $C(4, 3, 2)$. The internal bisector of $\angle BAC$ meets BC in D. Find AD.
4. Find the foot of perpendicular drawn from the point $2\hat{i} - \hat{j} + 5\hat{k}$ to the line $\vec{r} = (11\hat{i} - 2\hat{j} - 8\hat{k}) + \lambda(10\hat{i} - 4\hat{j} - 11\hat{k})$. Also find the length of perpendicular.

ANSWERS

2. $\left[\dfrac{-1}{7}, \dfrac{-5}{7}, \dfrac{39}{7}\right]$ or $\left[\dfrac{-13}{7}, \dfrac{-23}{7}, \dfrac{3}{7}\right]$ 3. $\dfrac{\sqrt{1530}}{8}$ units 4. $\sqrt{14}$ units.

❑❑❑

CHAPTER 12

LINEAR PROGRAMMING

Linear Constraints→In business, we want to make the best use of our limited resources like money, labour, time, materials, etc.

The limitations on the resources can often be expressed in the form of linear inequations known as linear constraints.

Formulation of a Linear Programming Problem:

Step 1. Identitify the unknown in this given LPP. Denote by x and y.

Step 2. Formulate the objective function in terms of x and y. Be sure whether it is to be maximized or minimized.

Step 3. Translate all the constraints in the form of linear inequations.

Step 4. Solve these inequations simultaneously. Mark the common area by a shaded region. This the feasible region.

Step 5. Find the coordinates of all the vertices of the feasible region.

Step 6. Find the value of the objective function at each vertex of this feasible region.

Step 7. Find the values of x and y for which the objective function $z = ax + by$ has maximum or minimum value.

Types of Linear Programming Problems:

1. Manufacturing Problems
2. Diet Problems
3. Transporation Problems.

L.P.P. PROBLEM FORMULATION

Min/Max $Z = CX$

Subject to constraints:

$$AX \geq B$$
$$X \geq 0$$

Here $X \geq 0$ is called Non-negative restriction and Z is called the objective function.

SOLVED QUESTIONS

SECTION-III

1. *A manufacturer makes two types of cups A and B. Three machines are required to manufacture the cups and time in minutes required by each is as given below:*

Types of Cup	*Machine*		
	I	*II*	*III*
A	12	18	6
B	6	0	9

Each machine is available for a maximum period of 6 hours per day. If profit on each cup A is Rs. 3 and on B is Rs. 2. Show that 15 cups of type A and 30 cups of type B should be manufactured per day to get the maximum profit.

Solution: Let manufacturer make x and y number of cups of type A and type B respectively

$$x \geq 0 \qquad y \geq 0$$

Total project $\quad z = 3x + 2y$

$$12x + 6y \leq 360 \qquad \text{[For } I \text{ machine]}$$

$$18x \leq 360 \qquad [II \text{ machine}]$$

$$x \leq 20$$

$$6x + 9y \leq 360 \qquad [III \text{ machine}]$$

Maximise $\quad z = 3x + 2y$

Subject to constraints

$$12x + 6y \leq 360$$

$$x \leq 20$$

$$6x + 9y \leq 360$$

$$x \geq 0 \quad y \geq 0.$$

We draw lines

$12x + 6y = 360$

x	30	0
y	0	60

$6x + 9y = 360$

x	60	0
y	0	40

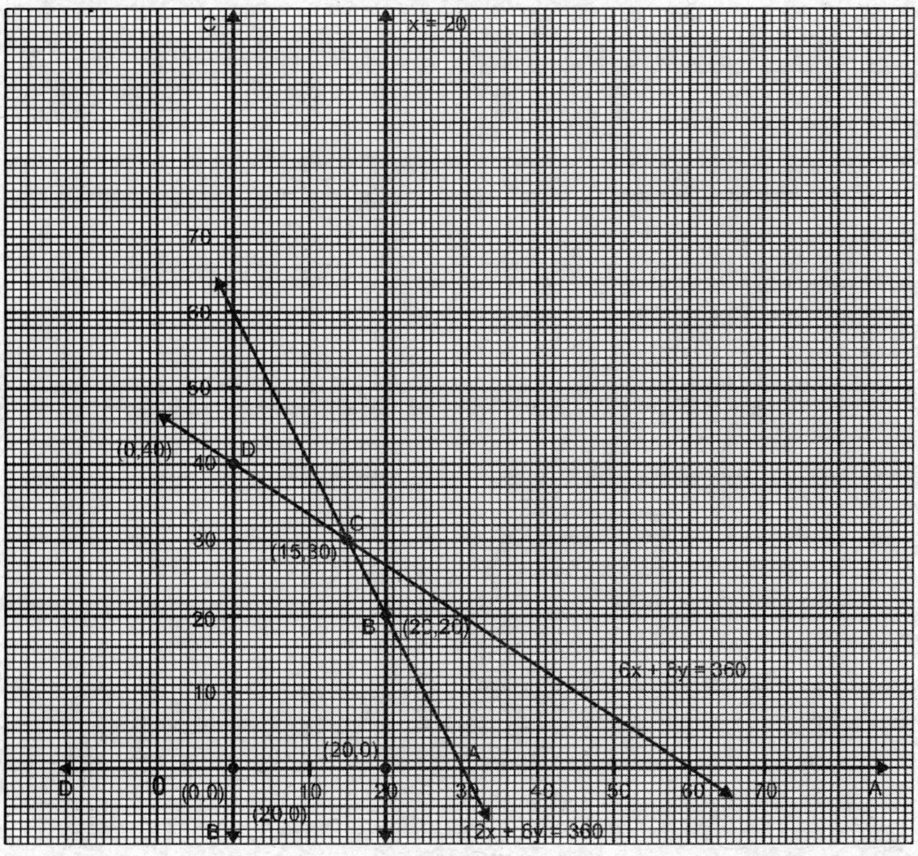

Fig. 12.1

OABCD is the convex plane.

CORNER POINT METHOD

Convexplane	Corner Point	$z = 3x + 2y$	
O	(0, 0)	0	
A	(20, 0)	60	
B	(20, 20)	100	
C	(15, 30)	105	← Maximum profit
D	(0, 40)	80	

Maximum profit is at (15, 30)

15 cups of type A and 30 cups of type B.

2. *A company sells two different products A and B. The two products produced have a total capacity of* 500 *man-hours. It takes* 5 *hours to produce a unit of B. The demand in the market shows that the maximum number of units of A that can be sold is* 70 *and that of B is* 125. *Profit on each unit of A is Rs.* 20 *and B is Rs.* 15. *How many units of A and B should be produced to maximise profit. Form a L.P.P and solve it graphically.*

Solution: Total profit z = Rs. $(20x + 15y)$

Total profit need to be maximised

Subject to the below constraints

x = Number of units of A $\qquad$ y = Number of units of B

$5x + 3y \leq 500$ $\qquad$ $x \leq 70$ and $y \leq 125$

$x \geq 0$ and $y \geq 0$

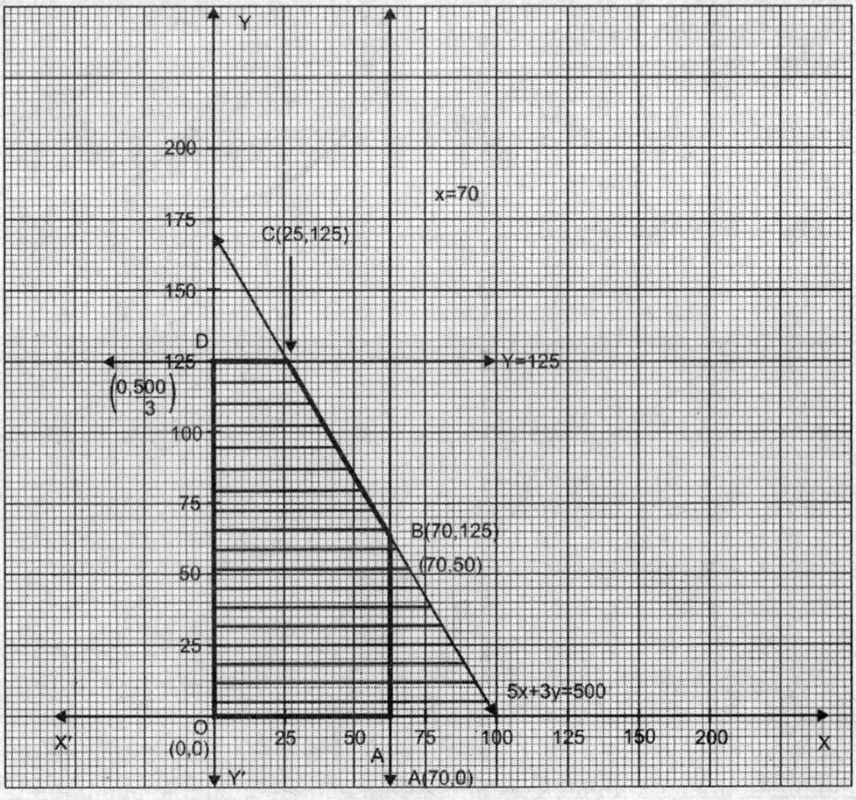

Fig. 12.2

OABCD is the convex plane.

Convex plane	Corner Point Method	$z=20x+15y$
0	$(0,0)$	$20(0)+15\times(0)=0$
A	$(70,0)$	$20\times 70+15\times(0)=14$
B	$(70,50)$	$20\times 70+15\times 50=215$
C	$(25,125)$	$20\times 25+15\times 125=2375$
D	$(0,125)$	$20\times 0+15\times 125=1875$

Maximum volume of Z is 2375 at point (25, 125).
Thus, $x = 25$, $y = 125$ is optimal solution of the given L.P.P.
25 units of product A and 125 units of product B.
Maximum profit = Rs. 2375.

3. *Find the minimum value of* $3x + 5y$ subject to constraints

$$\begin{aligned} -2x+y &\leq 4 \\ x+y &\geq 3 \\ x-2y &\leq 2 \\ x \geq 0, \quad & y \leq 0. \end{aligned}$$

Solution: We have to minimise

$$P = 3x+5y$$

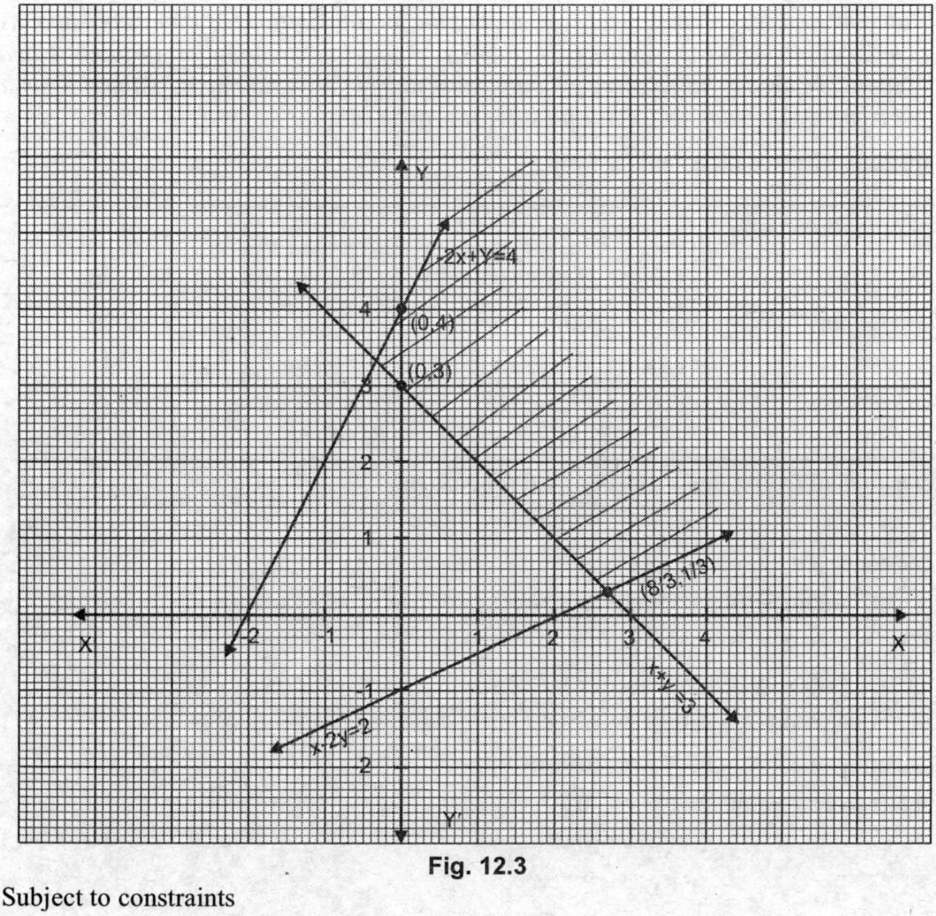

Fig. 12.3

Subject to constraints

$$\begin{aligned} -2x+y &\leq 4 \\ x+y &\geq 3 \end{aligned}$$

$$x - 2y \le 2$$

$$x \ge 0, \quad y \ge 0.$$

The corner points of feasible region are $A\left(\frac{8}{3}, \frac{1}{3}\right)$, $B(0, 3)$ and $C(0, 4)$

At A $\qquad P = 3x + 5y = 8 + \frac{5}{3} = \frac{29}{3}$

At B $\qquad P = 3.0 + 5.3 = 15$

At C $\qquad P = 3.0 + 5.4 = 20$

$\therefore$ Value of P is minimum at A

$\therefore \qquad x = \frac{8}{3}, \quad y = \frac{1}{3}$

Minimum value $= \frac{29}{3}$.

4. *A diet for a sick person must contain at least* 4000 *units of vitamins,* 50 *units of minerals and* 1400 *units of calories. Two foods A and B are available at a cost of Rs.* 5 *and Rs.* 4 *per unit respectively. One unit of food A contains* 200 *units of vitamins,* 1 *unit of minerals and* 40 *units of calories, while one unit of the food B contains* 100 *units of vitamins,* 2 *units of minerals and* 40 *units of calories. Find what combination of foods A and B should be used to have least cost, but it must satisfy the requirements of the sick person. Frame the question as L.P.P. and solve it graphically.*

Solution: Given data in tabular form.

Contents of food	*Food*		*Requirements*
	A	*B*	
Vitamins	200	100	4000
Minerals	1	2	50
Calories	40	40	1400
Cost	Rs. 5	Rs. 4	

Let x units of food A and y units of food B be taken

$$\text{cost } z = 5x + 4y$$

and constants are

$$200x + 100y \ge 4000 \quad \text{or} \quad 2x + y \ge 40$$

$$x + 2y \ge 50$$

$$40(x + y) \ge 1400 \quad \text{or} \quad x + y \ge 35$$

$$x \ge 0, \qquad y \ge 0$$

To minimise cost $\qquad z = 5x + 4y$

Subject to constraint $\quad 2x + y \ge 40$

$$x + 2y \ge 50$$

$$x + y \ge 35$$

$$x \ge 0 \qquad y \ge 0$$

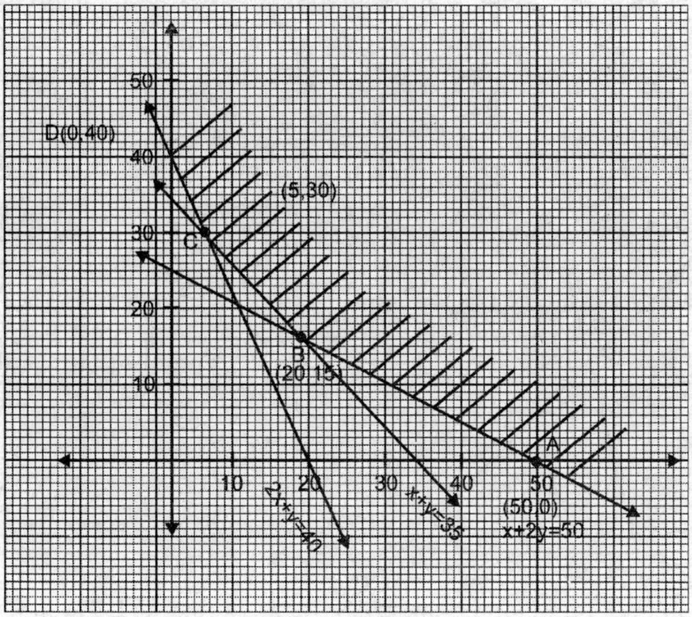

Fig. 12.4

Corner points of feasible region are

$$A(50,0),\quad B(20,15),\quad C(5,30) \text{ and } D(0,40)$$

$$\begin{aligned} \text{Value of } z &= 5x+4y \\ \text{at } A\,(50,0) &= 5\times 40 = 250 \\ \text{at } B\,(20,15) &= 5\times 20 + 4\times 15 = 160 \\ C\,(5,30) &= 145 \\ D(0,40) &= 160 \end{aligned}$$

Cost is least at $C(5, 30)$ $\quad x = 5,\ y = 30$

5 units of Food A and 30 units of Food B be mixed for minimum cost and meeting the requirements.

5. *An aeroplane can carry a maximum of* 200 *passengers. A profit of Rs.* 400 *is made on each first class ticket and a profit of Rs.* 300 *is made an each second class ticket. The airlines reserves atleast* 20 *seats for first class. However, atleast four times as many passengers prefer to travel by second class than first class. Determine how many tickets of each type must be sold to maximise profit for the airline. Form an L.P.P. and solve it graphically.*

Solution: Let x and y be the number of first class and second class passengers respectively.

From the problem we have

$$x + y \leq 200$$

$$x \geq 20 \quad \text{and} \quad y \geq 4x$$

$$x \geq 0 \quad \text{and} \quad y \geq 0$$

Maximise $\quad z = 400x + 300y$

Subject to contraint $\quad x + y \leq 200$

$$x \geq 20, \quad y \geq 4x$$

$$x \geq 0, \quad y \geq 0$$

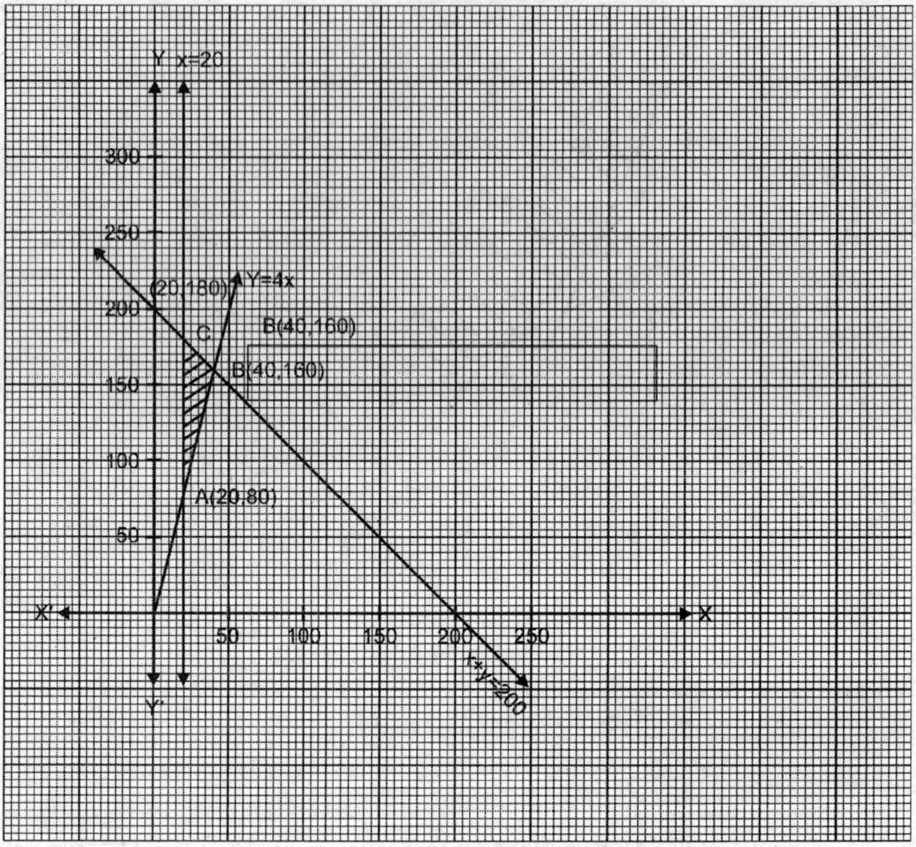

Fig. 12.5

Value of $Z = 400x + 300y$

at $A(20, 80) = 400 \times 20 + 300 \times 80 = 32000$

at $B(40, 160) = 400 \times 40 + 300 \times 160 = 64000$

at $C(20, 180) = 400 \times 20 + 300 \times 180$

$= 62000$

Profit is maximum at B (40, 160)

40 = Number of first class passengers

160 = Number of second class passengers.

6. *There are two factories located at P and Q. From these points a certain commodity is to be delivered to each of three depots A, B and C. The weekly requirements of the depots are 5, 5 and 4 units whereas the productions of the factories are 8 and 6 units. The cost of transportation per unit is given below:*

From/To	*Cost in Rs.*		
	A	*B*	*C*
P	160	100	150
Q	100	120	100

How many units should be transported from each factory to each depot in order that the transportation cost in minimum. What is the transportation cost?

Solution. Let x and y units of commodity be transported from the factory at P to the depots at A and B respectively.

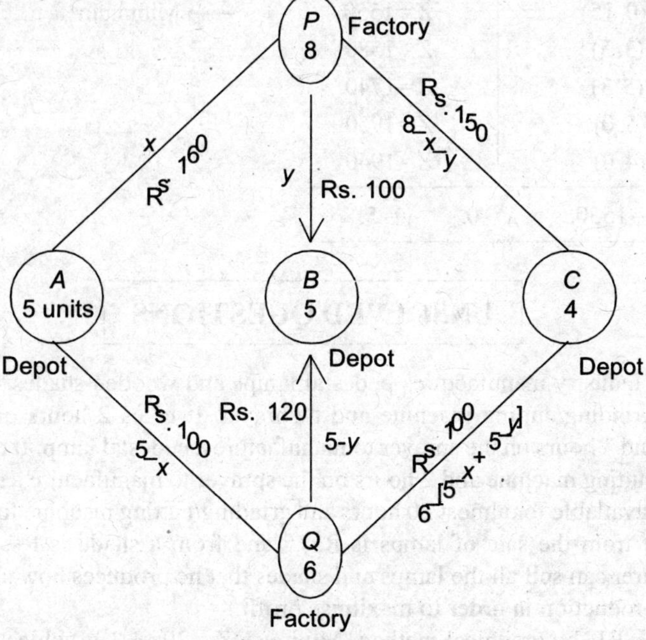

Fig. 12.5

Since the goods transported should be greater than or equal to zero, hence $x, y \geq 0$.

Transportation cost z.

$$= 160x + 100y + 100\,(5 - x) + 120\,(5 - y) + 100(x + y - 4) + 150(8 - x - y)$$

$$= 10(x - 7y + 190).$$

Hence, Minimum $Z = 10x - 70y + 1900$

Subject to constraints;

$$x + y \leq 8$$
$$x \leq 5$$
$$y \leq 5$$
$$x + y \geq 4$$
$$x \geq 0; \quad y \geq 0$$

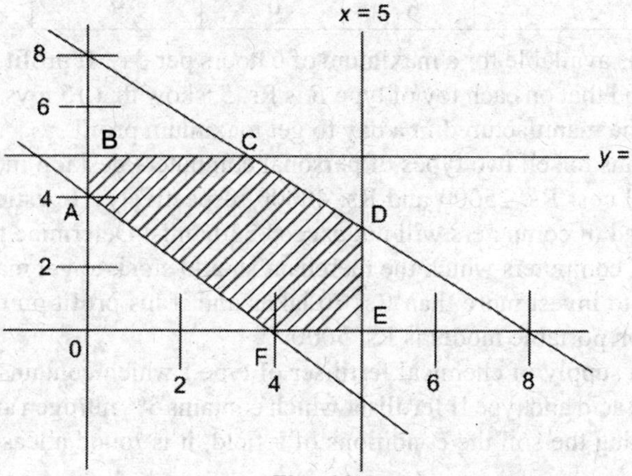

Fig. 12.6

$ABCDEF$ is a feasible region. Hence, by corner point:

$A(0, 4)$	$Z = 1620$
$B(0, 15)$	$Z = 1550$ $\longrightarrow$ Minimum
$C(3, 5)$	$Z = 1580$
$D(5, 3)$	$Z = 1740$
$E(5, 0)$	$Z = 1950$
$F(4, 0)$	$Z = 1940$

Hence $Z = 1550$, $x = 0$, $y = 5$.

UNSOLVED QUESTIONS

1. A cottage industry manufactures pedestal lamps and wooden shades. Each requires the use of a grinding/cutting machine and a sprayer. It takes 2 hours on grinding/cutting machine and 3 hours on the sprayer to manufacture a pedestal lamp. It takes 1 hour on the grinding/cutting machine and 2 hours on the sprayer to manufacture a shade. On one day sprayer is available for almost 20 hours and grinding/cutting machine for almost 12 hours. The profit from the sale of lamps is Rs. 5 and from a shade is Rs. 3. Assuming that manufacturer can sell all the lamps and shades that he produces how should he schedule his daily production in order to maximise profit.
2. Solve the L.P.P. by graphical method. Minimise $Z = 20x + 10y$ subject to constraints

$$\begin{aligned} x + 2y &\leq 40 \\ 3x + y &\geq 0 \\ 4x + 3y &\geq 60 \\ x &\geq 0 \\ y &\geq 0. \end{aligned}$$

3. A manufacturer makes two types of toys A and B. Three machines are needed for this purpose. The time required for each toy on the machine is given below:

Type of Toys	*Machines*		
	I	*II*	*III*
A	12	18	6
B	6	0	9

Each machine is available for a maximum of 6 hours per day. If profit on each toy of type A is Rs. 7.50 and that on each toy of type B is Rs. 5, show that 15 toys of type A and 30 of type B should be manufactured in a day to get maximum profit.

4. A merchant plans to sell two types of personal computers desktop model and a portable model that will cost Rs. 25000 and Rs. 40000 respectively. He estimates that the total monthly demand of computers will not exceed 250 units. Determine the number of units of each type of computers which the merchant should stock to get maximum profit if he does not want to invest more than Rs. 70 lakhs and if his profit on the desktop models Rs. 4500 and on portable model is Rs. 5000.
5. A farmer has a supply of chemical fertiliser of type I which contains 10% nitrogen and 6% phosphoric acid and type II fertiliser which contains 5% nitrogen and 10% phosphoric acid. After testing the soil the conditions of a field, it is found atleast 14 kg of nitrogen

and 14 kg of phosphoric acid is required for a good crop. The fertilizer type I costs Rs. 2 per kg and type II cost Rs. 3 per Kg. How many kilograms of each fertilizer should be used to meet the requirement and the cost should be minimum.

ANSWERS

1. 4 pedestal lamps and 4 wooden shade
   Maximum profit = Rs. 32
2. Minimum at (6, 12)
   Minimum value of Z = 240
4. Desktop model = 200 units
   50 units of portable models
   Maximum profit = Rs. 11,50,000
5. Type I = 100 kg
   Type II = 80 kg

❑❑❑

CHAPTER 13

PROBABILITY

INDEPENDENT EVENTS

If E_1 and E_2 are independent events then

$$P(E_1 \text{ and } E_2) = P(E_1 \cap E_2) = P(E_1) \times P(E_2)$$

CONDITIONAL PROBABILITY

Let A and B are two events, then the probability of occurrence of A under the condition that B has already occurred, is called conditional probability, denoted by $P(A/B)$

$$P(A/B) = \frac{P(A \cap B)}{P(B)}$$

$$P(B/A) = \frac{P(A \cap B)}{P(A)}$$

Baye's Theorem. If $E_1, E_2, \ldots. E_n$ are n non-empty events which constitute a partition of sample space S, *i.e.*, $E_1, E_2, \ldots. E_n$ are pairwise disjoint and $E_1 \cup E_2 \cup \ldots \cup E_n = S$ and A is any event of non-zero probability, then

$$P(E_i/A) = \frac{P(E_i).P(A/E_i)}{\sum_{i=1}^{n} P(E_i)P(A/E_i)} \quad \forall\ i = 1, 2, 3, \ldots, n$$

PROBABILITY DISTRIBUTION

Probability distribution of a random variable→If a random variable x takes the values $x_1, x_2, \ldots. x_n$ with respective probabilities $p_1, p_2, \ldots p_n$, then the probability distribution of x is given by:

X	x_1	x_2	x_3	...	...	x_n
$P(x)$	p_1	p_2	p_3	...	...	p_n

The above probability distribution of x is defined only when $p_i > 0$ and $\sum_{i=1}^{n} p_i = 1$.

Mean→(Expected value of x, denoted by $E(x)$)

$$\mu = E(x) = \sum_{i=1}^{n} x_i\, p_i = np$$

Variance→ $$\sigma^2 = \sum_{i=1}^{n} x_i^2\, p_i - \mu^2 = npq$$

Standard Deviation→ $$\sigma = \sqrt{\text{variance}} = \sqrt{npq}$$

Binomial Distribution→A random variable x taking values 0, 1, 2, ... n is said to have a binomial distribution with parameters n and p, its probability distribution is given by

$$P(x = r) = {}^nC_r\, p^r\, q^{n-r}$$

q be probability of non-success and n is the number of trials.

$$p + q = 1$$

SOLVED QUESTIONS

SECTION-II

1. *A problem in mathematics is given to three candidates whose chances of solving it are $\frac{1}{3}, \frac{2}{7}$ and $\frac{3}{8}$ respectively. If all three try to solve the problem simultaneously, find the probability that exactly one of them can solve it.*

Solution: Let A, B, C be the events of solving the problem by 3 students.

Then $P(A) = \frac{1}{3}, P(B) = \frac{2}{7}$ and $P(C) = \frac{3}{8} \Rightarrow P(\overline{A}) = 1 - \frac{1}{3} = \frac{2}{3}$ and $P(C) = 1 - \frac{3}{8} = \frac{5}{8}$

$$P(\overline{B}) = 1 - \frac{2}{7} = \frac{5}{7}$$

Required Probability

= $P(A$ solves, B fails, C *fails)* + $P(A$ fails, B solves, C fails) + $P(A$ fails, B fails, C solves)

$= P(A \cap \overline{B} \cap \overline{C}) + P(\overline{A} \cap B \cap \overline{C}) + P(\overline{A} \cap \overline{B} \cap C)$

$= \frac{1}{3}\left(1 - \frac{2}{7}\right)\left(1 - \frac{3}{8}\right) + \frac{2}{3} \times \frac{2}{7} \times \frac{5}{8} + \frac{2}{3} \times \frac{5}{7} \times \frac{3}{8}$

$= \frac{25}{168} + \frac{20}{168} + \frac{30}{168}$

$= \frac{75}{168} = \frac{25}{56}$.

2. *A and B toss a coin alternately till one of them tosses a head and wins the game. If A starts the game, find their respective probabilities of winning.*

Solution: P (Head) $= \frac{1}{2}$; P(Not Tail) $= \frac{1}{2}$

In A's Ist throw, his probability of winning $= \frac{1}{2}$

A gets his second chance if A and B both fail in the first round.

∴ A's probability of winning in 2nd round $= \frac{1}{2} \cdot \frac{1}{2} \cdot \frac{1}{2} = \frac{1}{2^3}$.

Similarly

A's probability of winning 3rd round $= \frac{1}{2^5}$.

$$\text{Probability of A's winning} = \frac{1}{2} + \frac{1}{2^3} + \frac{1}{2^5} \cdots\cdots = \frac{\frac{1}{2}}{1 - \frac{1}{2^2}} = \frac{2}{3}.$$

$$\left[S_\infty = \frac{a}{1-r} \text{ in G.P.}\right]$$

Probability of B's winning $= 1 - \frac{2}{3} = \frac{1}{3}$.

3. *If A and B are two independent events, show that the probability of occurrence of atleast one of A and B is given by* $1 - P(A')\,P(B')$.

Solution: P(atleast one of A and B)

$$\begin{aligned}
&= P(A \cup B)\\
&= P(A) + P(B) - P(A \cap B)\\
&= P(A) + P(B) - P(A)\,P(B)\\
&= P(A) + P(B)\,[1 - P(A)]\\
&= P(A) + P(B) \times P(A')\\
&= 1 - P(A') + P(B) \times P(A')\\
&= 1 - P(A')\,[1 - P(B)]\\
&= 1 - P(A')\,P(B').
\end{aligned}$$

4. *If x follows binomial distribution with mean 3 and variance* $\frac{3}{2}$, *find* $P(x \le 5)$.

Solution: Here $\quad np = 3 \quad$ and $\quad npq = \frac{3}{2}$

$$\therefore \quad q = \frac{1}{2} = \frac{npq}{np} \qquad [\text{ Mean} = np, \text{ Variance} = npq]$$

$$p = 1 - q = 1 - \frac{1}{2} = \frac{1}{2}$$

$$np = 3 \quad \text{gives} \quad \frac{1}{2}n = 3$$

$$P(X = r) = {}^{n}C_r\, p^r\, q^{n-r} = {}^{6}C_r \left(\frac{1}{2}\right) r$$

$$\begin{aligned}
P(X \le 5) &= 1 - P(x = 6)\\
&= 1 - {}^{6}C_6 \left(\frac{1}{2}\right)^6\\
&= 1 - \frac{1}{64} = \frac{63}{64}.
\end{aligned}$$

5. *A bag contains 50 tickets numbered 1, 2, 3 ... 50 of which five are drawn at random and arranged in ascending order of numbers appearing on tickets* $(x_1 < x_2 < x_3 < x_4 < x_5)$. *Find the probability that* $x_3 = 30$.

Solution: Total no. of possible outcomes $= n(S) = {}^{50}C_5$.

Number of favourable cases for drawing 2 tickets having number less than 30 $= {}^{29}C_2$.

Then third ticket bearing number 30 can be drawn in ${}^{1}C_1$ way of the remaining 20 tickets.

Number of ways of drawing 2 tickets $= {}^{20}C_2$.

No. of favourable cases $= P(E) = {}^{29}C_2 \times {}^{1}C_1 \times {}^{20}C_2$.

$$\text{Required probability} = \frac{{}^{29}C_2 \times {}^{1}C_1 \times {}^{20}C_2}{{}^{50}C_5}$$

$$= \frac{\frac{29 \times 28}{2 \times 1} \times 1 \times \frac{20 \times 19}{2 \times 1}}{\frac{50 \times 49 \times 48 \times 47 \times 46}{5 \times 4 \times 3 \times 2 \times 1}} = \frac{551}{15134}.$$

6. *A man is known to speak truth 3 out of 4 times. He throws a die and reports that it is a six. Find the probability that it is actually a six.*

Solution: E = Event that man reports that six occurs

S_1 = Event that six occurs

S_2 = Event that six does not occur.

$P(S_1) = \frac{1}{6} \qquad P(S_2) = \frac{5}{6}$

$P\left(\frac{E}{S_1}\right)$ = Probability that man reports that six occurs given that six has occurred = $\frac{3}{4}$

$P\left(\frac{E}{S_2}\right)$ = Probability that man reports that six occurs that six has not occurred

= Probability that man does not speak truth = $\frac{1}{4}$.

$$P\left(\frac{S_1}{E}\right) = \frac{P(S_1)\,P\left(\frac{E}{S_1}\right)}{P(S_1)\,P\left(\frac{E}{S_1}\right) + P(S_2)\,P\left(\frac{E}{S_2}\right)} \quad \text{[Baye's Theorem]}$$

$$= \frac{\frac{1}{6}\cdot\frac{3}{4}}{\frac{1}{6}\cdot\frac{3}{4}+\frac{5}{6}\cdot\frac{1}{4}} = \frac{3}{3+5} = \frac{3}{8}.$$

7. *A coin is biased so that head is 3 times as likely to occur as tail. If a coin is tossed twice, find the probability distribution of number of tails.*

Solution: Let Probability that a biased coin will show tail be p Probability that it shows head would be $3p$.

$$\text{Sum of probability} = 1$$

$$p + 3p = 1$$

$$p = \frac{1}{4}$$

$$P(H) = \frac{3}{4} \quad P(T) = \frac{1}{4}$$

X denotes the number of tails in two tosses of coin, then X is a random variable which can take values 0, 1, 2.

$P(X=0)$ = Probability of getting both heads

$= P(H \cap H)$

$= P(H)\,.\,P(H) = \frac{3}{4}\cdot\frac{3}{4} = \frac{9}{16}$

$P(X=1)$ = Probability of getting 1 tail and 1 head

$= P(H \cap T) + P(T \cap H)$

$= P(H) \times P(T) + P(T) \times P(H)$

$= \frac{3}{4} \times \frac{1}{4} + \frac{1}{4} \times \frac{3}{4} = \frac{6}{16}$

$$P(X=2) = \text{Probability of getting both tails}$$
$$= P(T \cap T)$$
$$= P(T)\,P(T) = \frac{1}{4}\cdot\frac{1}{4} = \frac{1}{16}$$

Probability distribution of x.

X	0	1	2
$P(X)$	$\frac{9}{16}$	$\frac{6}{16}$	$\frac{1}{16}$

8. *A and B throw a pair of die turn by turn. The first to throw 9 is awarded a prize. If A starts the game, show that probability of A getting the prize is* $\frac{9}{17}$.

Solution: No of favourable cases of 9(63, 54, 45, 36) = 4

$$P(E) = P(9) = \frac{4}{36} = \frac{1}{9}$$

Let F is event be getting a number other than 9

$$P(F) = 1 - \frac{1}{9} = \frac{8}{9}$$

$$P(A \text{ getting 9 before } B) = P(A \text{ getting 9 in first throw})$$
$$+ P(A \text{ getting 9 in 3rd throw when } B \text{ fails in 2nd throw})$$
$$= \frac{1}{9} + \frac{8}{9}\cdot\frac{8}{9}\cdot\frac{1}{9} + \left(\frac{8}{9}\right)^4 \frac{1}{9}.$$

$$P(A \text{ getting 9 before } B) = \frac{\frac{1}{9}}{1-\left(\frac{8}{9}\right)^2}$$

$$= \frac{\frac{1}{9}}{\frac{17}{81}} = \frac{9}{17}$$

Probability of A getting the prize is $\frac{9}{17}$.

9. 12 *cards, numbered* 1 *to* 12, *are placed in a box mixed up thoroughly and then a card is drawn at random from the box. If it is known that the number drawn on the card is more than* 3, *find the probability that it is an even number.*

Solution: Let A be the event that the card taken out has on even number and B be the event that the card taken out act bears a number greater than 3.

Now
$$S = \{1, 2, 3, 4, 5, 6, 7, 8, 9, 10, 11, 12\}$$
$$A = \{2, 4, 6, 8, 10, 12\}$$
$$B = \{4, 5, 6, 7, 8, 9, 10, 11, 12\}$$
$$A \cap B = \{4, 6, 8, 10, 12\}$$
$$P(A) = \frac{6}{12} = \frac{1}{2} \qquad P(B) = \frac{9}{12}$$
$$P(A \cap B) = \frac{5}{12}$$

$$P\left(\frac{A}{B}\right) = \frac{P(A\cap B)}{P(B)} = \frac{\frac{5}{12}}{\frac{9}{12}} = \frac{5}{9}.$$ [Conditional Probabitily]

10. *A fair die is rolled. If* 1 *turns up, a ball is picked up at random from bag A. If* 2 *or* 3 *turn up, a ball is picked up from bag B. If* 4, 5, 6 *turn up, a ball is picked up from bag C. Bag A contains* 3 *red and* 2 *white balls; bag B contains* 3 *red and* 4 *white balls, bag C contains* 4 *red and* 5 *white balls. The die is rolled, a bag is picked and a ball is drawn.*

(*i*) *What are the chances of drawing a red ball.*

(*ii*) *If the ball drawn is red, what are the chances that it was picked up from bag B.*

Solution: Let A_1 = Event that bag A is picked so

$$\Rightarrow \quad P(A_1) = \frac{1}{6}$$

A_2 = Event that bag B is picked

$$\Rightarrow \quad P(A_2) = \frac{2}{6}$$

A_3 = Event that bag C is picked

$$\Rightarrow \quad P(A_3) = \frac{3}{6}$$

R = Event that red ball is drawn.

(*i*)
$$P(R) = P(A_1)\,P(R/A_1) + P(A_2)\,P(R/A_2) + P(A_3)\,P(R/A_3)$$

$$= \frac{1}{6}\times\frac{3}{5}+\frac{2}{6}\times\frac{3}{7}+\frac{3}{6}\times\frac{4}{9}=\frac{293}{630}.$$

(*ii*) Using Bayes theorem

$$P(A_2/R) = \frac{P(A_2)\,P(R/A_2)}{P(A_1)\,P(R/A_1) + P(A_2)\,P(R/A_2) + PA_3[R/A_3]}$$ [Using Baye's Theorem]

$$= \frac{\frac{2}{6}\cdot\frac{3}{7}}{\frac{293}{630}} = \frac{90}{293}.$$

SECTION-III

1. 3 *bad eggs are mixed with* 7 *good ones,* 3 *eggs are taken at random from the lot. Find the probability distribution of number of bad eggs drawn. Find also the mean and variance of probability distribution.*

Solution: Let x be the number of bad eggs, x can taken value 0, 1, 2 and 3.

Now $$P(x=0) = P(3\text{ good eggs}) = \frac{{}^{7}C_3}{{}^{10}C_3} = \frac{7.6.5}{10.9.8} = \frac{7}{24}$$

$$P(x=1) = P(1\text{ bad, }2\text{ good eggs}) = \frac{{}^{3}C_1\,.\,{}^{7}C_2}{{}^{10}C_3} = \frac{3\times\frac{7\times 6}{2}}{\frac{10.9.8}{3.2.1}} = \frac{2}{40}$$

$$P(x=2) = P(2 \text{ bad, } 1 \text{ good eggs}) = \frac{{}^3C_2 \cdot {}^7C_1}{{}^{10}C_3} = \frac{3 \times 7}{\frac{10 \times 9 \times 8}{3 \times 2 \times 1}} = \frac{7}{40}$$

$$P(x=3) = \frac{{}^3C_3}{{}^{10}C_3} = \frac{1}{120}$$

Required probability distribution

x	0	1	2	3
$P(x)$	$\frac{7}{24}$	$\frac{21}{40}$	$\frac{7}{40}$	$\frac{1}{120}$

Mean and Variance

x	$P(x) = pi$	$pi\ x_i$	$P_i x_i^2$
0	$\frac{7}{24}$	0	0
1	$\frac{21}{40}$	$\frac{21}{40}$	$\frac{21}{40}$
2	$\frac{7}{40}$	$\frac{7}{20}$	$\frac{7}{10}$
3	$\frac{1}{120}$	$\frac{1}{40}$	$\frac{3}{40}$
		$\Sigma p_i x_i = \frac{36}{40}$	$\Sigma P_i x_i^2 = \frac{52}{40}$

Mean $\qquad N = \Sigma P_i x_i = \frac{36}{40} = 0.9$

Variance $\qquad = \Sigma p_i x_i^2 - (\mu)^2$

$$= \frac{52}{40} - (0.9)^2$$

$$= 1.3 - 0.81 = 0.49.$$

2. *Suppose that a pair of fair dice are tossed and let the random variable x denote the sum of points*

(*a*) *Obtain probability distribution for x.*

(*b*) *Construct a graph for this probability distribution.*

(*c*) *Find mean of x.*

(*d*) *Find variance and standard deviation of x.*

Solution: Sample space S has 36 points

S = {(1, 1) (1, 2) (1, 3) (1, 4) (1, 5) (1, 6) (2, 1) (2, 2) (2, 3) (2, 4) (2, 5) (2, 6) (3, 1) (3, 2) (3, 3) (3, 4) (3, 5) (3, 6) (4, 1) (4, 2) (4, 3) (4, 4) (4, 5) (4, 6) (5, 1) (5, 2) (5, 3) (5, 4) (5, 5) (5, 6) (6, 1) (6, 2) (6, 3) (6, 4) (6, 5) (6, 6)} (*a*) Probability distribution is

x	$P(x)$
2	$\frac{1}{36}$
3	$\frac{2}{36}$
4	$\frac{3}{36}$
5	$\frac{4}{36}$
6	$\frac{5}{36}$
7	$\frac{6}{36}$
8	$\frac{5}{36}$
9	$\frac{4}{36}$
10	$\frac{3}{36}$
11	$\frac{2}{36}$
12	$\frac{1}{36}$

(*b*) Bar graph

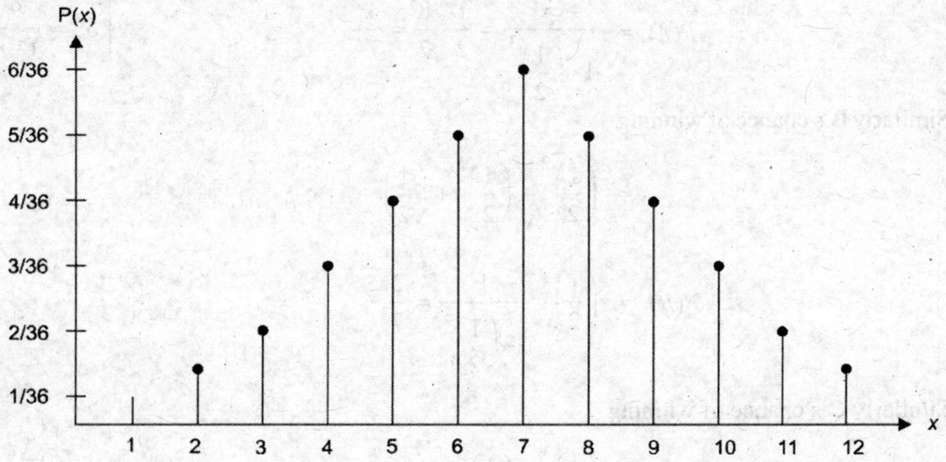

Fig. 13.1

(*c*) Mean, $\mu = \Sigma p_i x_i = \frac{1}{36}(2.1 + 3.2 + 4.3 .... + 12.1)$

$$= \frac{252}{36} = 7$$

(*d*) $\Sigma p_i x_1^2 = \frac{1}{36}$ (14 + 2.9 + 3.16 + 4.25 + 5.36 + 6. 49 + 5.67 + 4.81 +3.100 + 2.121 + 1.144]

$$= \frac{1}{36} \times 1974 = \frac{329}{6}$$

$$\sigma^2 = \Sigma p_i x_1^2 - \mu^2 = \frac{329}{6} - 49 = \frac{35}{6}$$

$$\sigma = \sqrt{5.83} = 2.41.$$

3. *A, B and C in order toss a coin. First one to throw a head wins. What are their respective chances of winning? Assume that the game may continue indefinitely.*

Solution: Chance of throwing a head = $\frac{1}{2}$

In his first throw, A's chance of winning = $\frac{1}{2}$

A get his second throw only if *A, B, C* all fail in first round.
So A's chance of winning in 2nd round (4th turn)

$$= \frac{1}{2} \cdot \frac{1}{2} \cdot \frac{1}{2} \cdot \frac{1}{2} = \left(\frac{1}{2}\right)^4.$$

Similarly A's chance of winning in 3rd round = $\left(\frac{1}{2}\right)^7$.

A's chance of winning = $\frac{1}{2} + \left(\frac{1}{2}\right)^4 + \left(\frac{1}{2}\right)^7 + ... \infty$

$$P(A) = \frac{\frac{1}{2}}{1-\left(\frac{1}{2}\right)^3} = \frac{1}{2} \cdot \frac{8}{7} = \frac{4}{7}. \qquad \left[S_\infty = \frac{9}{1-r}\right]$$

Similarly B's chance of winning

$$= \left(\frac{1}{2}\right)^2 + \left(\frac{1}{2}\right)^5 + \left(\frac{1}{2}\right)^8 + ... \infty$$

$$P(B) = \left(\frac{1}{2}\right)^2 \frac{1}{1-\left(\frac{1}{2}\right)^3} = \frac{2}{7}.$$

Similarly C's chance of winning

$$= \left(\frac{1}{2}\right)^3 + \left(\frac{1}{2}\right)^6 + \left(\frac{1}{2}\right)^9 + ... \infty$$

$$= \frac{\left(\frac{1}{2}\right)^3}{\left[1-\left(\frac{1}{2}\right)^3\right]} = \frac{1}{8} \cdot \frac{8}{7}$$

$$P(C) = \frac{1}{7}.$$

We can check our calculation $P(A) + P(B) + P(C) = \frac{4}{7} + \frac{2}{7} + \frac{1}{7} = 1.$

4. *Suppose that 5% of men and 0.25% of women have grey hair. A grey haired person is selected at random. What is probability of this person being male? Assume that there are equal number of males and females.*

Solution: Let the Event

M : male is chosen

F : female is chosen

G : grey haired person is chosen.

$$P(M) = \frac{1}{2} \qquad P(E) = \frac{1}{2}$$

$P(G/M)$ = Probability that grey haired person is chosen, when it is known that a person is male

$$= 5\% = \frac{5}{100} = 0.05$$

$$P(G/F) = 0.25\% = 0.0025$$

By Baye's Theorem

$P(M/G)$ = Probability that the person is male when it is known that the person chosen is a grey haird

$$= \frac{P(M \cap G)}{P(G)}$$

$$= \frac{P(M \cap G)}{P(G \cap M) + P(G \cap F)}$$

$$= \frac{P(M) \,.\, P(G/M)}{P(M).P(G/M) + P(F).P(G/F)} \qquad \text{[Baye's Theorem]}$$

$$= \frac{\frac{1}{2} \times 0.05}{\frac{1}{2} \times 0.05 + \frac{1}{2} \times 0.0025}$$

$$= \frac{0.05}{0.0525} = \frac{20}{21}.$$

5. *In a bulb factory, machines A, B and C manufacture 60%, 30% and 10% bulbs respectively. 1%, 2% and 3% of bulbs produced respectively by A, B, C are found to be defective. A bulb is picked up at random from total production and found to be defective. Find the probability that this bulb was produced by the machine A.*

Solution: Let E_1, E_2, E_3 be the events that the bulb has been manufactured on machines *A*, *B* and *C* respectively.

Let A be event that bulb is defective

$$P(E_1) = \frac{60}{100} = \frac{6}{10}, \quad P(E_2) = \frac{30}{100} = \frac{3}{10}$$

and $$P(E_3) = \frac{10}{100} = \frac{1}{10}$$

$$P(A/E_1) = \frac{1}{100}, \quad P(A/E_2) = \frac{2}{100} \quad \text{and} \quad P(A/E_3) = \frac{3}{100}$$

$$P(E_1/A) = \frac{P(E_1).P(A/E_1)}{P(E_1).P(A/E_1)+P(E_2).P(A/E_2)+P(E_3).P(A/E_3)}$$

[Baye's Theorem]

$$= \frac{\frac{6}{10} \times \frac{1}{1000}}{\frac{6}{10} \times \frac{1}{100} + \frac{3}{10} \times \frac{2}{100} + \frac{1}{10} \times \frac{3}{100}}$$

$$= \frac{6}{6+6+3} = \frac{\cancel{6}^2}{\cancel{15}_5} = \frac{2}{5}.$$

6. *Find the probability distribution of number of white balls drawn in a random draw of 3 balls, without replacement from a bag containing 4 white and 6 red balls. Also find mean and variance of the distribution.*

Solution: Number of white balls = 4.

Number of red balls = 6.

Total = 10.

We shall find the probability distribution of x where x is the number of white balls drawn in a random draw of 3 balls without replacement.

$$P(x=0) = \frac{^6C_3}{^{10}C_3} = \frac{6 \times 5 \times 7}{10 \times 9 \times 8} = \frac{1}{6}$$

$$P(x=1) = \frac{^4C_1 \times {}^6C_2}{^{10}C_3} = \frac{1}{2}$$

$$P(x=2) = \frac{^4C_2 \times {}^6C_1}{^{10}C_3} = \frac{36}{120} = \frac{3}{10}$$

$$P(x=3) = \frac{^4C_3}{^{10}C_3} = \frac{4}{120} = \frac{1}{30}$$

Required Probability distribution

X_i	0	1	2	3
$P_{(Xi)}$	$\frac{1}{6}$	$\frac{1}{2}$	$\frac{3}{10}$	$\frac{1}{30}$

To calculate Mean and Variance

X	p_i	$p_i x_i$	$p_i x_i^2$
0	$\frac{1}{6}$	0	0
1	$\frac{1}{2}$	$\frac{1}{2}$	$\frac{1}{2}$
2	$\frac{3}{10}$	$\frac{3}{5}$	$\frac{6}{5}$
3	$\frac{1}{30}$	$\frac{1}{10}$	$\frac{3}{10}$
		$\Sigma P_i X_i = 1.2$	$\Sigma P_i X_i^2 = 2$

$$\begin{aligned} \text{Mean} &= \Sigma p_i x_i = 1.2 \\ \text{Variance} &= \Sigma (p_i x_i^2) - (\text{mean})^2 \\ &= 2 - 1.44 \\ &= 0.56. \end{aligned}$$

7. *A person buys a lottery ticket in 50 lotteries, in each of which his chance of winning a prize is $\frac{1}{100}$. What is probability that he will win a prize (i) atleast once, (ii) exactly once, (iii) atleast twice?*

Solution: p denotes a chance of winning a prize *i.e.* $p = \frac{1}{100}$ and $q = 1 - p = \frac{99}{100}$.

Let x denote the number of prizes in 50 lotteries tickets, then x is a binomial distribution with parameters $n = 50$ $p = \frac{1}{100}$ such that

$$\begin{aligned} P(x = r) &= {}^nC_r\, p^r q^{n-r} \\ &= {}^{50}C_r \left(\frac{1}{100}\right)^r \left(\frac{99}{100}\right)^{50-r} \\ r &= 0, 1, 2, \ldots, 50. \end{aligned}$$

(*i*) Probability of winning atleast one prize

$$\begin{aligned} &= P(x \geq 1) \\ &= 1 - P(x = 0) \\ &= 1 - {}^{50}C_0 \left(\frac{1}{100}\right)^0 \left(\frac{99}{100}\right)^{50-0} \\ &= 1 - {}^{50}C_0 \left(\frac{99}{100}\right)^{50}. \end{aligned}$$

(*ii*) Probability of winning exactly one prize

$$\begin{aligned} &= P(x = 1) \\ &= {}^{50}C_1 \left(\frac{1}{100}\right)^1 \left(\frac{99}{100}\right)^{49} \\ &= \frac{1}{2} \times \left(\frac{99}{100}\right)^{49}. \end{aligned}$$

(*iii*) Probability of winning a at least two prizes

$$= P(x \geq 2)$$

$$= 1 - [P(x = 0) + P(x = 1)]$$

$$= 1 - \left[{}^{50}C_0 \left(\frac{1}{100}\right)^0 \left(\frac{99}{100}\right)^{50-0} + {}^{50}C_1 \left(\frac{1}{100}\right)^1 \left(\frac{99}{100}\right)^{49} \right]$$

$$= 1 - \left[\left(\frac{99}{100}\right)^{50} + \frac{1}{2}\left(\frac{99}{100}\right)^{49} \right]$$

$$= 1 - \left(\frac{99}{100}\right)^{49} \left[\frac{99}{100} + \frac{1}{2}\right]$$

$$= 1 - \frac{149}{100}\left(\frac{99}{100}\right)^{49}.$$

8. *There are three coins. One is a two headed coin (having head on both faces) another is a biased coin that comes up with tail 25% of the times and third is an unbiased coin. One of the three coins is chosen at random and tossed and it shows head. What is the probability that it was the two headed coin.*

Solution: Let us define the following events

A_1 : Two headed coin is chosen

A_2 : Biased coin is chosen

A_3 : Unbiased coin is chosen

H : Getting head on the coin

$P(A_1) = \frac{1}{3}$ = Probability that a two headed coin is chosen

$P(A_2) = \frac{1}{3}$ = Probability that a biased coin is chosen

$P(A_3) = \frac{1}{3}$ = Probability that unbiased coin is chosen

$P\left(\frac{H}{A_1}\right) = 1$ = Probability of getting head given that a two headed coin is chosen

$P\left(\frac{H}{A_2}\right) = \frac{3}{4}$ = Probability of getting a head given that a biased coin is chosen

$P\left(\frac{H}{A_3}\right) = \frac{1}{2}$ = Probability of getting head given that on unbiased coin is chosen

Hence by BAYE'S THEOREM

$$P\left(\frac{A_1}{H}\right) = \frac{P(A_1)P\left(\frac{H}{A_1}\right)}{P(A_1)P\left(\frac{H}{A_1}\right) + P(A_2)P\left(\frac{H}{A_2}\right) + P(A_3)P\left(\frac{H}{A_3}\right)}$$

$$= \frac{\frac{1}{3} \cdot 1}{\frac{1}{3} \cdot 1 + \frac{1}{3} \cdot \frac{3}{4} + \frac{1}{3} \cdot \frac{1}{2}}$$

$$= \frac{\frac{1}{3} \cdot 1}{\frac{1}{3} \times \left[1 + \frac{3}{4} + \frac{1}{2}\right]}$$

$$= \frac{1}{\left[1 + \frac{3}{4} + \frac{1}{2}\right]}$$

$$= \frac{4}{4+3+2}$$

$$= \frac{4}{9}$$

UNSOLVED QUESTIONS

SECTION-II

1. If four throws with a pair of a dice what is the chance of throwing doublet alteast twice.
2. *A, B* and *C* throw a die turn by turn. Whoever throws '5' first wins. If *A* starts, find their respective chances of winning.
3. Suppose that 8% people are left handed what is the probability that 4 or more of a random sample of 50 people are left handed.
4. An urn contains 100 white and 3 black balls. Another urn contains 3 white and 5 black balls. Two balls are drawn from the first urn and put into the second urn and then a ball is drawn from the second urn. Find the probability that it is a white ball.
5. x speaks truth 4 out of 5 times. A die is tossed. He reports that there is six. What is the probability that actually there was six?
6. In a school 8% of the boys and 2% of the girls have an I.Q. of more than 120. In the school 60% of the students are boys. A student with I.Q. more than 120 is selected. Find the probability that the student selected is a boy.
7. Three urns, *A, B* and *C* contains 6 blue, 4 black; 4 blue, 6 black and 5 blue, 5 black balls respectively. One urn is selected at random and a ball is drawn from it. If the ball is blue, find the probability that it was drawn from urn *A*.
8. In a hurdle race, a player had to cross 10 hurdles. The probability that he will clear each hurdle is $\frac{5}{6}$ What is the probability that he will knock down in fewer than 2 hurdles?

ANSWERS

1. $\frac{19}{144}$ 2. $A : \frac{36}{91},\ B : \frac{30}{91},\ C : \frac{25}{91}$ 3. 0.574

4. $\frac{59}{130}$ 5. $\frac{4}{9}$ 6. $\frac{6}{7}$

7. $\frac{1}{2}$ 8. $\frac{5}{2}\left(\frac{5}{6}\right)^9$

SECTION-III

1. Three groups of children contain 3 girls and 1 boy; 2 girls and 2 boys; 1 girl and 3 boys respectively. One child is selected at random from each group. Find the chance that the three selected comprise one girl and two boys.
2. A Random variable x has following probability distribution

X	0	1	2	3	4	5	6	7
$P(x)$	0	K	$2K$	$2K$	$3K$	K^2	$2K^2$	$7K^2 + K$

Determine

(*i*) K (*ii*) $P(x < 3)$ (*iii*) $P(x > 6)$ (*iv*) $P[o < x < 3]$

3. A letter is known to have come from either TATANAGAR or CALCUTTA. On the envelope just two consecutive letters TA are visible. What is the probability that letter has come from
   (*i*) Tatanager (*ii*) Calcutta?
4. Two bags A and B contain 4 white and 3 Black Balls and 2 white and 3 black balls respectively. From bag A two balls are transferred to bag B. Find the probability of drawing.
   (*a*) 2 white balls from bag B.
   (*b*) 2 black balls from bag B.
   (*c*) 1 white and 1 black ball from bag B.
5. A and B throw alternatively a pair of dice. A wins if he throws 6 before B throws 7 and B wins if he throws 7 before A throws 6. Find their respective chance of winning if A begins.
6. Given three identical boxes I, II and III, each containing two coins. In box I, both are gold coins, in box II, both are silver coins and in box III, there is one gold and one silver coin. A person chooses a box at random and takes out a coin. If the coin is gold, what is the probability that the other coin in the box is also of gold.

ANSWERS

1. $\frac{13}{32}$ 2. (*i*) $\frac{1}{10}$ (*ii*) $\frac{3}{10}$ (*iii*) $\frac{17}{100}$ (*iv*) $\frac{3}{10}$

3. (*i*) $\frac{7}{11}$ (*ii*) $\frac{4}{11}$ 4. (*a*) $\frac{5}{21}$ (*b*) $\frac{4}{21}$ (*c*) $\frac{4}{7}$

5. $P(A \text{ wins}) = \frac{30}{61}$, $P(B \text{ wins}) = \frac{31}{61}$ 6. $\frac{2}{3}$

HOTS

1. A bag contains $n + 1$ coins. It is known that one of these coins show head on both sides where as other coins are fair. One coin is selected at random and tossed. If the probability that toss results in heads is $\frac{7}{12}$. Find the value of n.
2. Cards are dealt one by one from a well shuff red pack until on ace appears. Find the probability that exactly n cards are dealt before the first appears.
3. There are two bags one of which contains 3 Black and 4 White balls while Second one contains 4 Black and 3 White Balls. A die is cast. If the face 1 or 3 turns up, a ball is chosen from the first bag, otherwise the ball is chosen from second bag. Find the probability that a black ball is chosen.

4. **The chance of one event happening is the square of chance of another event happening. The odds against the first are cubes of the odds against the second. Find the chance of each.**

ANSWERS

1. 5   2. $\dfrac{4.(49-n)(50-n)(51-n)}{49.50.51.52}$ 3. $\dfrac{11}{21}$

4. First Event = $\dfrac{1}{9}$, Second Event = $\dfrac{1}{3}$

❑❑❑

Value Based Question for CBSE Class XII

1. Consider the functions f and g, f: {1, 2, 3} {a, b, c} and g : {a, b, c} {punctuality, honesty, sincerity} defined as $f(1) = a, f(2) = b, f(3) = c$, $g(a)$ = punctuality, $g(b)$ = honesty, $g(c)$ = sincerity. Show that f, g and gof are invertible. If a, b, c are three students who are awarded prizes for the three values given in the function g, which value would you prefer to be rewarded and why?

   Expected answers : Any of the three values– Punctuality, Honesty and Sincerity or all of the above values will help a student to get award.

2. Let R be a relation defined as R = {(x,y) : x and y study in the same class}. Show that R is an equivalence relation.

   If x is a brilliant student and y is a slow learner and x helps y in his studies, what quality does x possess?

   Expected answers : (a) Concern about fellow students (b) Co-operation
   (c) Knowledge sharing (d) Empathy

3. Prove that f: R → R is a bijection given by $f(x)$ = +3. Find f– 1(x). Can truthfulness and honesty have any relation?

   Expected answer : Yes, truthfulness and honesty are bijective relation. Generally a person who is honest will follow truthfulness and vice versa.

4. Let A be the set of all students of class XII in a school and R be the relation, having the same sex on A, then prove that R is an equivalence relation. Do you think, co-education may be helpful in child development and why?

   Expected answer : Co-education helps in balanced development of mind resulting in shaping a better citizen of a country.

5. Show that the function f: defined by $f(x) = 3x + 4$ is an invertible function.

   If x represents the number of systematic hours of study that a student puts in and $f(x)$ represents the marks scored by him, from the graph of the above function, which value will be rewarded?

   Expected answer : (a) Time Management (b) Improvised study habit
   (c) Better performance

6. Set A = {a, b, c} and B = {1, 2, 3}. Define a relation from a set A to set B by x R y iff y is a true friend of x. If R = {(a, 1), (b, 2), (c, 3)}

   Is R *a* bijective function? Do you think true friendship important in life? How?

   Expected answer : It is well said that – A friend in need is a friend indeed. That's why friendship is important as it does hardly looks at caste, money or social status of people.

7. Let L be the set of all the lines in a plane and R be the relation in L defined by R = {(l, m) : l // m}. Show that R is an equivalence relation. Let l represent the ideologies of Gandhiji and m represent the ideologies

of Netaji Subhash Chandra Bose. Even though their ideologies ran on parallel tracks, both had the common goal to achieve independence of India. Which common value did they both exhibit?

Expected answer : (a) Patriotism (b) Sacrifice

(c) Concern for the independence (d) Pride

8. If h denotes the number of honest people and p denotes the number of punctual people and a relation between honest people and punctual people is given as $h = p + 5$. If P denotes the number of people who progress in life and a relation between number of people who progress and honest people is given as $P = (h/8) + 5$. Find the relation between number of people who progress in life and punctual people. How does the punctuality important in the progress of life?

Answer : Punctuality brings discipline in life and for progress in life this discipline is a must.

9. Let * be a binary operation defined by A * B = A U B. Prove that * is commutative and associateive. If X is the number of people in a locality, A is a set of children and B is a set of citizens aged above 75 years living in the same locality then is * a binary opertion for these sets as defined here. What qualities should A exhibit towards B?

Answer : (a) Respect for Elders (b) Helping the elders

(c) Kindness (d) Sympathy and Empathy

Matrices and Determinants

10. There are three families. First family consists of 2 male members, 4 female members and 3 children. Second family consists of 3 male members, 3 female members and 2 children. Third family consists of 2 male members, 2 female members and 5 children. Male member earns Rs. 500 per day and spends Rs. 300 per day. Female member earns Rs. 400 per day and spends Rs. 250 per day and child member spends Rs. 40 per day. Find the money each family saves per day using matrices? What is the necessity of saving in the family?

Answer : Saving is necessary as it helps in adverse situation.

11. There are 2 families A & B. There are 4 men, 6 women and 2 children in family A, 2 men, 2 women and 4 children in family B. The recommended daily allowance for calories is 2400 for men, 1900 for women, 1800 for children and 45 gms of proteins for men, 55 gms for women and 33 gms for children. Represent the above information using matrices. Using matrix multiplication, calculate the total requirement of calories and proteins for each of the 2 families. What awareness can you create among people about the balanced diet?

Answer :

(a) Proper amount of calories and proteins are vital for the growth.

(b) Avoid fast food and beverages

(c) Vegetarian food helps us to control many ailments.

(d) Take early breakfast as long hour of fast in harmful for the body.

12. The cost of 4 chocolates, 3 samosas and 2 apples is Rs. 60 and that of 2 chocolates, 4 samosas, and 6 apples is Rs. 90. The cost of 6 chocolates, 2 samosas, 3 apples is Rs. 70. Find the cost of each item by matrix method. What do you think is the healthiest diet? Suggest an item that could replace chocolates and samosas to make the diet healthier?

Answer : (a) Fruits (b) Salads (b) Juices (d) Sprouts

13. An amount of Rs. 600 crores is spent by the government in three schemes. Scheme A is for saving girl child from the cruel parents who don't want girl child and get the abortion before her birth. Scheme B is for saving of newlywed girls from death due to dowry. Scheme C is planning for good health for senior citizen. Now twice the amount spent on Scheme C together with amount spent on Scheme A is Rs. 700 crores. And three times the amount spent on Scheme A together with amount spent on Scheme B and Scheme C is Rs. 1200 crores. Find the amount spent on each Scheme using matrices? What is the importance of saving girl child?

Answer : (a) The population of girls comparative to boys is less creating gender gaps which is harmful in long run.

(b) We have no right to kill the girl child.

14. Using matrix method solve the following system of equations

$x + 2y + z = 7$

$x - y + z = 4$

$x + 3y + 2z = 10$

If X represents the number of persons who take food at home, Y represents the number of persons who take junk food in market and z represent the number of persons who take food at hotel, which way of taking food you prefer and why?

Answer : Obviously, taking food at home. Junk food causes obesity and other ailments in long run. It is also not a healthy diet. The qualities of food served at hotel may be tasty but there is no guarantee that the food served is fit for health.

Continuity and Differentiability

15. A car driver is driving a car on a dangerous path given by

$$f(x) = 2x - 1 \text{ if } x < 0$$
$$= 2x + 1 \text{ if } x \geq 0$$

Find the dangerous point (point of discontinuity) on the path. Whether the driver should pass that point or not? Justify your answers.

Answer : No, life is precious and it should be saved. Speeding thrills but it kills.

16. An enemy jet is flying along the curve $y = x^2 + 7$. A soldier is placed at the point (3, 7). Find the nearest distance between the soldier and the jet. The soldier refuses to fire the jet when it is nearest to him? Is this act of the solider justifiable? Discusss.

Answer : No, the soldier should discharge his duty without any prejudice.

17. The bottom of a rectangular fish tank is 30 cm X 15 cm. Water is pumped into the tank either by man-made pump at the rate of 50 cubic cm/minute or by motor pump at the rate of 75 cubic cm/minute. Find the rate at which the level of the water in the tank is rising when water is pumped by motor pump. Which pump would you prefer and why?

Answer : The motor pump as it saves the labour and works faster than the man-made pump.

18. A car parking company has 500 subscribers and collects fixed charges of Rs. 300 per subscriber per month. The company proposes to increase the monthly subscription and it is believed that for every increase of Re. 1, one subscriber will discontinue the service. What increase will bring maximum income to the company? What values are driven by this problem?

Answer : (a) Sharing car or car pool service (b) Pollution Control

(c) Less density of car on road (d) Saving energy

19. A farmer wants to construct a circular well and a square garden in his field. He wants to keep sum of their perimeters fixed. Then prove that the sum of their areas is least when the side of square garden is double the radius of the circular well.

Do you think good planning can save energy, time and money?

Answer : Yes, Good planning is necessary to execute any work. This not only saves energy but it also saves time and money.

20. An expensive square piece of golden color board of side 24 cm is to be made into a box without top by cutting a square from each corner and folding the flaps to form a box. What should be the side of the square piece to be cut from each corner of the board to hold maximum volume and minimize the wastage? What is the importance of minimizing the wastage in utilizing the resources?

Answer : India is a developing country so we should utilize our resources in proper way. The government is also taking various initiatives to reduce wastage. Proper utilization will save the things for the future generation.

Integration and Application of Integrals

21. Integrity is an integral part of a student's life. Elucidate. Similarly find the value of the integral

$\int dx / x^2 - 6x + 7$

Answer : Honesty, goodness, discipline

22. Write the importance of integration in our life.

Answer : Integration (Unity) is important in life. It is said – United we stand and divided we fall or unity is strength.

23. A circular Olympic gold medal has a radius 2 cm. Taking the centre at the origin, find its area by method of integration. What is the importance of Olympic Games for a sportsman and why?

Answer : Olympic games are a supreme platform for a sportsman. In Olympic games all countries of the world participate and try their best to make their country proud.

24. Using integration find the area of the bounded region $y = 1 + |x + 1|$; $x = -3$, $x = 3$ and $y = 0$. The required area is divided into two regions and the students are asked to put a posters on "Child Labour" and "Education for all" in those two. Which theme according to you deserves a bigger space? Justify.

Answer : Education for all. The government has made it compulsory for every child in the age group 6 to 14 years to have access to free and compulsory education. This will in turn help in reducing the child labour.

25. Evaluate as the limit of a sum : $\int_1^4 (x+2)\,dx$.

In a public function what limit should be mentioned while addressing the audience.

Answer : Dignity and decorum, self – control, decency and humility.

Differential Equation

26. Solve the differential equation: $dy/dx + y/x = 0$, where x denotes the percentage population living in a city & y denotes the area for living a healthy life by population. Find the particular solution when $x = 100$ and $y = 1$.

Is higher density of population harmful? Justify your answer.

Answer : Yes, a higher density of population is harmful. Higher population decreases the living area and cutting the jungles results in causing climate change.

27. Solve the differential equation

$x\,(x^2 - 1)\,dy/dx = 1$; $y = 0$ when $x = 2$

If 'y' is distance and x is the time. dy/dx is velocity.

Ravi rides a vehicle beyond the limit on a highway. What suggestions would you give him to help him understand the risks of over speeding.

Answer : Speed thrills but it kills. Over speeding is dangerous for life.

Vector and Three Dimensions Geometry

28. Two groups of students representing 'SAVE MOTHER EARTH' and 'GO GREEN' are standing on two planes represented by the equations $\vec{r}.\left(\hat{i}+\hat{j}+2\hat{k}\right)=5$ and $\vec{r}.\left(2\hat{i}-\hat{j}+\hat{k}\right)=8$. What is the angle between the 2 planes? Name few activities which should be taken up to save mother earth.

Answer : (a) Avoid over use of natural resources (b) Save environment by planting more trees

(c) Ban on plastics (d) Control pollution

29. Find the image of the point (1, 2, 3) in the plane $x+2y+4z=38$. Represent the image of the point with one life skill.

Answer : (a) Honesty (b) Truthfulness (c) Punctuality

30. Consider the earth as a plane having equation $5x+9y-10z+138=0$. A monument is standing vertically such that it is at the point (1, 2, –3). Find the height of the monument. How can we save our monuments?

Answer : (a) We should not write on the walls

(b) We should not throw garbage nearby the monuments

31. Three hoardings are displayed at the points A, B and C displaying A (Do not litter), B (Keep your place clean) and C (Go green). If these 3 points form a triangle ABC, find the area of the triangle ABC using method of vectors if points A, B and C are (0, 2, 1), (4, 8, 2) and (8, 4, 3) respectively. Give your views in two lines about "GO GREEN".

Answer : (a) Plant more trees (b) Stop Deforestation

Linear Programming Problem

32. If a class XII student aged 17 years, rides his motor cycle at 40 km/hr, the petrol cost is Rs. 2 per km. If he rides at a speed of 70 km/hr, the petrol cost increases Rs. 7 per km. He has Rs. 100 to spend on petrol and wishes to cover the maximum distance within one hour. Solve this by LPP.

1. What is benefit of driving at an economical speed?
2. Should a child below 18 years be allowed to drive a motorcycle? Give reasons.

Answer : 1. Driving at an economical speed consumes less petrol and thus saves money.

2. No, it is against the traffic rule to drive before attaining 18 years of age.

33. An NGO is helping the poor people of earthquake hit village by providing medicines. In order to do this they set up a plant to prepare two medicines A and B. There is sufficient raw material available to make 20000 bottles of medicine A and 40000 bottles of medicine B but there are 45000 bottles into which either of the medicine can be put. Further it takes 3 hours to prepare enough material to fill 1000 bottles of medicine A and takes 1 hour to prepare enough material to fill 1000 bottles of medicine B and there are 66 hours available for the operation. If the bottle of medicine A is used for 8 patients and bottle of medicine B is used for 7 patients, how the NGO should plan the production to cover maximum patients? How can you help others in case of natural disaster?

Answer : The NGO should have the unique Emergency toll free number where the people can contact easily. Moreover, in situation like earthquake we should not get panic over the loss as it is out of human control to stop such calamity.

34. A manufacturer makes cycles and scooters. Processing of these products is done on two machines A and B. The cycle parts need 2 hours on machine A and 6 hours on machine B. Parts of a scooter needs 4 hours on machine A and 2 hours on machine B. Machine A is available for 16 hours per day and Machine B is available for 30 hours per day. Profit gained by the manufacturers from a cycle and scooter is Rs. 1000 and Rs. 3000 respectively. Find with the help of a graph what should be the daily production of each of the two products to maximize the profit? Which of the above modes of transport is a better option and why?

Answer : (a) Cycling is the best way of exercising. (b) It reduces the pollution.

Probability

35. An insurance company insured 2000 scooter drivers, 4000 car drivers and 6000 truck drivers. The probability of an accident involving a scooter driver, car driver and a truck is 0.01, 0.03 and 0.15 respectively. One of the insured persons meets with an accident. What is the probability that he is a scooter driver?

Write down any two practices that would enhance road safety.

Answer : (a) Don't use mobile phones while driving.

(b) Rash driving should be avoided.

(c) Obey traffic rule.

(d) Use Helmet while driving scooter and tie seat belt while driving car or truck.

36. In a group consisting of equal number of men and women, 10% men and 45% women are unemployed. What is the probability that a person selected at random is employed?

Suggest 2 steps to enhance employability of youth.

Answer : (a) Opening up new industrial units

(b) Vocational Training should be simultaneously given to students for better employment

37. A man is known to speak truth 5 out of 6 times. He draws a ball from the bag containing 4 white and 6 black balls and reports that it is white. Find the probability that it is actually white? Do you think that speaking truth is always good?

Answer : Yes, speaking truth is always good. There might be some situation when speaking truth may save some one's life.

38. In a school, 30% of the students have 100% attendance. Previous year result report tells that 70% of all students having 100% attendance attained A grade and 10% of remaining students attained A grade in their annual examination. At the end of the year, one student is chosen at random and he has an A grade. What is the probability that the student has 100% attendance? Also state the factors which affect the result of a student in the examination.

Answer : (a) Regular study (b) Punctuality (c) Hard work (d) Proper practice (e) Time management

39. A company has two plants of scooter manufacturing. Plant I manufacture 70% Scooter and plant-II manufactures 30%. At plant-I, 80 % of the scooters are maintaining pollution norms and in plant-II 90% of the scooters are maintaining pollution norms. A Scooter is chosen at random and is found to be fit on pollution norms. What is the probability that it has come from plant II. What is importance of pollution norms for a vehicle?

Answer : Pollution is hazardous for health. It causes skin disease, cancer and some other ailments. Pollution norms help in reducing the pollution level and maintaining clean environment.

40. Group A contains the students who try to solve the problem by knowledge, Group B contains the students who guess to solve the problem, Group C contains the students who give answer by cheating. If n (A) = 20, n (B) = 15, n (C) = 10, and if 2 students are selected at random, find the probability that they are from group C. Do you think that cheating habit spoils the career?

Answer : Yes, cheating habit spoils the career in long run. One can get good marks by cheating in exam but can't boast of sound knowledge.

IMPORTANT SUPPLEMENTARY QUESTIONS

Chapter-1

1. If $f(x) = \log \frac{1+x}{1-x}$ Show $f\left(\frac{2x}{1+x^2}\right) = 2f(x)$ **1 Mark**

Ans. $$f\left(\frac{2x}{1+x^2}\right) = \log\frac{1+\frac{2x}{1+x^2}}{1-\frac{2x}{1+x^2}} = \log\frac{\frac{1+x^2+2x}{\cancel{1+x^2}}}{\frac{1+x^2-2x}{\cancel{1+x^2}}} = \log\frac{(1+x)^2}{(1-x)^2} = 2\log\frac{1+x}{1-x} = 2f(x)$$

2. Let * be a binery operation on set Q difined by $a * b = \frac{ab}{4}$

Show that

(i) 4 is the identity element of * on Q

(ii) $a^{-1} = \frac{16}{a}$ **4 Marks**

Ans. Let e be the identity element

According to question

$$a * e = \frac{ae}{4} = a$$

$\Rightarrow \quad \cancel{a}e = 4\cancel{a}$

$\Rightarrow \quad e = 4$

Hence, 4 is the identity element

Again, let a^{-1} be the inverse of a

$$a * a^{-1} = e$$

$\Rightarrow \quad \frac{aa^{-1}}{4} = 4 \qquad (e = 4 \text{ shown above})$

$\Rightarrow \quad a^{-1} = \frac{16}{a}$

Chapter-2

Inverse Trigonometry Function

1. Express $\text{Sin}^{-1}\left\{x\sqrt{1-x} - \sqrt{x}\sqrt{1-x^2}\right\}$ in simplest form **4 Marks**

Ans. We know, $\text{Sin}^{-1}\text{A} - \text{Sin}^{-1}\text{B} = \text{Sin}^{-1}\left\{\text{A}\sqrt{1-\text{B}^2} - \text{B}\sqrt{1-\text{A}^2}\right\}$

Hence, $\text{Sin}^{-1}\left\{x\sqrt{1-x}-\sqrt{x}\sqrt{1-x^2}\right\}$

$= \text{Sin}^{-1}x - \text{Sin}^{-1}\sqrt{x}$

2. If $\text{Cos}^{-1}x + \text{Cos}^{-1}y + \text{Cos}^{-1}z = \pi$ Prove $x^2 + y^2 + z^2 + 2xyz = 1$

Ans. $\text{Cos}^{-1}x + \text{Cos}^{-1}y + \text{Cos}^{-1}z = \pi$

$\Rightarrow \text{Cos}^{-1}x + \text{Cos}^{-1}y = \pi - \text{Cos}^{-1}z$

$\Rightarrow \text{Cos}^{-1}\left\{xy-\sqrt{1-x^2}-\sqrt{1-y^2}\right\} = \pi - \text{Cos}^{-1}z$

$\Rightarrow xy-\sqrt{1-x^2}\sqrt{1-y^2} = \text{Cos}(\pi - \text{Cos}^{-1}z) = -z$

$\Rightarrow xy + z = \sqrt{1-x^2}\sqrt{1-y^2}$

Squiring both sides

$x^2y^2 + z^2 + 2xyz = (1 - x^2)(1 - y^2)$

$\Rightarrow \cancel{x^2y^2} + z^2 + 2xyz = 1 - x^2 - y^2 + \cancel{x^2y^2}$

$\Rightarrow x^2 + y^2 + z^2 + 2xyz = 1$

3. Prove $\tan^{-1}\left\{\dfrac{a\cos x - b\sin x}{b\cos x + a\sin x}\right\} = \tan^{-1}\dfrac{a}{b} - x$

Divide N^r | D^r by $b \cos x$

$= \tan^{-1}\dfrac{a}{b} - \tan^{-1}(\tan x)$ $\left[\text{using } \tan^{-1}A - \tan^{-1}B = \tan^{-1}\dfrac{A-B}{1+AB}\right]$

$= \tan^{-1}\dfrac{a}{b} - x$

Chapter-3

1. Find the area of triangle with verticis (0, 0) (6, 0) and (4, 3) **1 Mark**

Ans. Area of Triangle $= \dfrac{1}{2}\begin{vmatrix} 0 & 0 & 1 \\ 6 & 0 & 1 \\ 4 & 3 & 1 \end{vmatrix}$

$= \dfrac{1}{2}(18 - 0) = 9$ sq. unit

Chapter-4

1. If $A = \begin{bmatrix} 2 & -1 \\ 3 & 4 \end{bmatrix}$ find $(A^{-1})^{-1}$ **1 Mark**

Ans. We know $(A^{-1})^{-1} = A$

Hence $(A^{-1})^{-1} = \begin{bmatrix} 2 & -1 \\ 3 & 4 \end{bmatrix}$

2. Express the matrix $\begin{bmatrix} 3 & 3 & -1 \\ -2 & -2 & 1 \\ -4 & -5 & 2 \end{bmatrix}$ as the sum of Symmetric and Skew-symmetric matrix. **4 Mraks**

Ans. $A = \begin{bmatrix} 3 & 3 & -1 \\ -2 & -2 & 1 \\ -4 & -5 & 2 \end{bmatrix}$

We have $A = \dfrac{A+A'}{2} + \dfrac{A-A'}{2}$

$$A' = \begin{bmatrix} 3 & -2 & -4 \\ 3 & -2 & -5 \\ -1 & 1 & 2 \end{bmatrix}$$

$$\Rightarrow \quad A+A' = \begin{bmatrix} 3 & -2 & -4 \\ 3 & -2 & -5 \\ -1 & 1 & 2 \end{bmatrix} + \begin{bmatrix} 3 & 3 & -1 \\ -2 & -2 & 1 \\ -4 & -5 & 2 \end{bmatrix} = \begin{bmatrix} 6 & 1 & -5 \\ 1 & -4 & -4 \\ -5 & -4 & 4 \end{bmatrix}$$

$$= \begin{bmatrix} 6 & 1 & -5 \\ 1 & -4 & -4 \\ -5 & -4 & 4 \end{bmatrix}$$

Hence $\dfrac{A+A'}{2} = \begin{bmatrix} 3 & 1/2 & -5/2 \\ 1/2 & -2 & -2 \\ -5/2 & -2 & 2 \end{bmatrix} = P$

$$P' = \begin{bmatrix} 3 & 1/2 & -5/2 \\ 1/2 & -2 & -2 \\ -5/2 & -2 & 2 \end{bmatrix} = P$$

Hence P is symmetric

Find $\dfrac{A-A'}{2} = Q$ (say)

Show $Q' = -Q$ is skew-symmetric

Remember every square matrix can be express as the sum of symmetric and skew-symmetric matrix

3. Prove that the product of matrics

$\begin{bmatrix} \cos^2\theta & \cos\theta\sin\theta \\ \cos\theta\sin\theta & \sin^2\theta \end{bmatrix}$ and $\begin{bmatrix} \cos^2\phi & \cos\phi\sin\phi \\ \cos\phi\sin\phi & \sin^2\phi \end{bmatrix}$ is a null matrix when θ and ϕ differ by an odd multiple of $\frac{\pi}{2}$ **4 Marks**

Ans. $$AB = \begin{bmatrix} \cos^2\theta & \cos\theta\sin\theta \\ \cos\theta\sin\theta & \sin^2\theta \end{bmatrix}\begin{bmatrix} \cos^2\phi & \cos\phi\sin\phi \\ \cos\phi\sin\phi & \sin^2\phi \end{bmatrix}$$

$$= \begin{bmatrix} \cos^2\theta & \cos\theta\sin\theta \\ \cos\theta\sin\theta & \sin^2\theta \end{bmatrix}\begin{bmatrix} \cos^2\phi & \cos\phi\sin\phi \\ \cos\phi\sin\phi & \sin^2\phi \end{bmatrix}$$

$$= \begin{bmatrix} \cos^2\theta\cos^2\phi + \cos\theta\sin\theta\cos\phi\sin\phi & \cos^2\theta\cos\phi\sin\phi + \cos\theta\sin\theta\sin^2\phi \\ \cos\theta\sin\theta\cos^2\phi + \sin^2\theta\cos\phi\sin\phi & \cos\theta\sin\theta.\cos\phi\sin\phi + \sin^2\theta.\sin^2\phi \end{bmatrix}$$

$$= \begin{bmatrix} \cos\theta\cos\phi(\cos\theta\cos\phi + \sin\theta\sin\phi) & \cos\theta\sin\phi(\cos\theta\cos\phi + \sin\theta\sin\phi) \\ \sin\theta\cos\phi(\cos\theta\cos\phi + \sin\theta\sin\phi) & \sin\theta.\sin\phi(\cos\theta.\cos\phi + \sin\theta\sin\phi) \end{bmatrix}$$

$$= \begin{bmatrix} \cos\theta\cos\phi[\cos(\theta-\phi)] & \cos\theta\sin\phi[\cos(\theta-\phi)] \\ \sin\theta\cos\phi[\cos(\theta-\phi)] & \sin\theta\sin\phi[\cos(\theta-\phi)] \end{bmatrix}$$

$$= \begin{bmatrix} 0 & 0 \\ 0 & 0 \end{bmatrix} \qquad \therefore \cos(\theta-\phi) = \cos\frac{\pi}{2} = 0$$

Chapter-5

1. $y = \frac{1}{2}\left[\tan^{-1}\frac{2x}{1-x^2} + 2\tan^{-1}\frac{1}{x}\right]$ $0 < x < 1$. Find dy/dx **1 Mark**

Ans. Put $x = \tan\theta$

$$y = \frac{1}{2}\left[\tan^{-1}(\tan 2\theta) + 2\tan^{-1}\left(\frac{1}{\tan\theta}\right)\right]$$

$$= \frac{1}{2}\left[2\theta + 2\tan^{-1}(\cot\theta)\right]$$

$$= \left[\theta + \tan^{-1}\left(\tan\left(\frac{\pi}{2} - \theta\right)\right)\right]$$

$$= \theta + \frac{\pi}{2} - \theta$$

$$= \frac{\pi}{2}$$

$$\frac{dy}{d\theta} = 0$$

$$\frac{dx}{d\theta} = \sec^2\theta$$

Hence $\frac{dy}{dx} = 0$

2. If $y = e^{a\cos^{-1}x}$, $-1 \le x \le 1$ show

$$\left(1-x^2\right)\frac{d^2y}{dx^2} - x\frac{dy}{dx} - x^2y = 0$$

Ans. $y = e^{a\cos^{-1}x}$

$$\Rightarrow y_1 = e^{a\cos^{-1}x} \times \frac{a\times -1}{\sqrt{1-x^2}}$$

$$\Rightarrow \sqrt{1-x^2}\,y_1 = -a\,e^{a\cos^{-1}x} = -ay$$

Squiring both sides

$$(1-x^2)\,y_1^2 = a^2y^2$$

Differentaling w.r.t x

$$\left(1-x^2\right).2y_1y_2 + y_1^2x - 2x = a^2 \times 2y\,y_1$$

$$\Rightarrow \left(1-x^2\right)y_2 - xy_1 - a^2y = 0$$

Chapter-6

3. Show that $\frac{x}{a}+\frac{y}{b}=1$ touches the curve $y = be^{-x/a}$ at the print where the curve crosses y-axis

Ans. The curve crosses y-axis when $x = 0$

$$y = b\,e^{-x/a} = b\,e^0 = b$$

Hence the curve crosses y-axis at $(0, b)$

$$y = b\,e^{-x/a}$$

$$y_1 = b\,e^{-x/a}\;\frac{-1}{a}$$

$$y_{1(0,b)} = \frac{-b}{a}$$

Equation of tangent

$$y - b = \frac{-b}{a}(x-0)$$

$$ya - ab = -bx$$

$$ya + xb = ab$$

$$\frac{y\cancel{a}}{\cancel{a}b}+\frac{x\cancel{b}}{a\cancel{b}}=\frac{ab}{ab} \qquad \text{(Divide by } ab)$$

$$\Rightarrow \quad \frac{x}{a}+\frac{y}{b}=1$$

4. Show that $f(x) = \tan^{-1}(\sin x + \cos x)$ is strictly increasing in $[0, \pi/4]$

Ans. $f(x) = \tan^{-1}(\sin x + \cos x)$

$$f'(x)=\frac{1}{1+(\sin x+\cos x)^2}(\cos x-\sin x)$$

$f(x)$ is increasing function if $f'(x) > 0$

$$\Rightarrow \quad \frac{\cos x-\sin x}{1+(\sin x+\cos x)^2}>0$$

Since, $1 + (\sin x + \cos x)^2 > 0$

Hence, $\cos x - \sin x > 0$

$1 > \tan x$

$\Rightarrow \quad \tan x < 1$

$\Rightarrow \quad x \in (0, \pi/4)$

Chapter-7

1. $\int_0^{\pi/2} \log\left(\frac{4+3\sin x}{4+3\cos x}\right)dx$ **1 Mark**

Ans. $I = \int_0^{\pi/2} \log\left(\frac{4+3\sin x}{4+3\cos x}\right)dx$

$$I = \int_0^{\pi/2} \log\left(\frac{4+3\sin\left(\frac{\pi}{2}-x\right)}{4+3\cos\left(\frac{\pi}{2}-x\right)}\right)dx \quad \text{...(i)}$$

$$= \int_0^{\pi/2} \log\left(\frac{4+3\cos x}{4+3\sin x}\right)dx \quad \text{...(ii)}$$

Add (i) and (ii)

$$I+I = \int_0^{\pi/2} \log\left(\frac{\cancel{4+3\cos x}}{\cancel{4+3\sin x}}\cdot\frac{\cancel{4+3\sin x}}{\cancel{4+3\cos x}}\right)dx$$

$$= \int_0^{\pi/2} \log 1\, dx$$

$$= 0$$

2. $\int \frac{\sin x+\cos x}{\sqrt{\sin 2x}}dx$ **4 Marks**

$$= \int \frac{\sin x + \cos x}{\sqrt{1-1+\sin 2x}} dx$$

$$= \int \frac{\sin x + \cos x}{\sqrt{1-(1-\sin 2x)}} dx$$

$$= \int \frac{\sin x + \cos x}{\sqrt{1-(\sin x - \cos x)^2}} dx$$

Put $\sin x - \cos x = u$

$\Rightarrow$ $(\cos x + \sin x)\, dx = du$

$$\int \frac{du}{\sqrt{1-u^2}} = \sin^{-1} u + c$$

$= \sin^{-1}(\sin x - \cos x) + c$

3. $$\int \left[\log(\log x) + \frac{1}{(\log x)^2} \right] dx$$

Put $\log x = u$

$\Rightarrow$ $x = e^u$

$\Rightarrow$ $dx = e^u \text{du}$

$$= \int \left(\log u + \frac{1}{u^2} \right) e^u\, du$$

$$= \int \left(\log u + \frac{1}{u} - \frac{1}{u} + \frac{1}{u^2} \right) e^u\, du$$

$$= \int e^u \left(\log u + \frac{1}{u} \right) du - \int e^u \left(\frac{1}{u} - \frac{1}{u^2} \right) du$$

$$= e^u \log u - e^u \quad \frac{1}{u} \; + \left[\int [f(x) + f'(x)] e^x dx = e^x f(x) \right]$$

$$= x \log(\log x) - x \quad \frac{1}{\log x} \; + \text{c}$$

Chapter-10

1. Find the volume of parallelpiped whose edge are $\vec{a} = 2\hat{i} + 3\hat{j} + 4\hat{k}, \vec{b} = \hat{i} + 2\hat{j} - k$ and $\vec{c} = 3\hat{i} - \hat{j} + 2k$

Ans. Volume of parallelpiped = $\left[\vec{a} \quad \vec{b} \quad \vec{c} \right]$

$$= \begin{vmatrix} 2 & 3 & 4 \\ 1 & 2 & -1 \\ 3 & -1 & 2 \end{vmatrix} = |\, 2\,(4-1) - 3\,(2+3) + 4\,(-1-6)\,|$$

$= |6 - 15 - 28|$

$= 37$ cubic unit

2. Find the value of λ such that $\vec{a} = \hat{i} - \hat{j} + \hat{k}$, $\vec{b} = 2\hat{i} + \hat{j} - \hat{k}$ and $\vec{c} = ?\hat{i} - \hat{j} + \lambda\hat{k}$ are coplanar

Ans. $\vec{a}, \vec{b}$ and $\vec{c}$ will be coplanar if $\left[\vec{a}\ \vec{b}\ \vec{c}\right] = 0$

$$= \begin{vmatrix} 1 & -1 & 1 \\ 2 & 1 & -1 \\ \lambda & -1 & \lambda \end{vmatrix} = 0$$

$= 1\ (\lambda - 1) + 1\ (xl + 1) + 1\ (-2 - 1) = 0$

$\Rightarrow \cancel{\chi} - 1 + 3\lambda - 2 - y = 0$

$\Rightarrow 3\lambda = 3$

$\lambda = 1$

3. Show that the four points (–1, 4, –3), (3, 2, –5), (–3, 8, –5) and (–3, 2, 1) are coplanar

Ans. Four points A, B, C and D will be coplanar if $\left[\overrightarrow{AB}\,\overrightarrow{AC}\,\overrightarrow{AD}\right] = 0$

$$\overrightarrow{AB} = \left(3\hat{i} + 2\hat{j} - 5\hat{k}\right) - \left(-\hat{i} + 4\hat{j} - 3\hat{k}\right)$$

$$= 4\hat{i} - 2\hat{j} - 2\hat{k}$$

$$\overrightarrow{AC} = \left(-3\hat{i} + 8\hat{j} - 5\hat{k}\right) - \left(-\hat{i} + 4\hat{j} - 3\hat{k}\right)$$

$$= -2\hat{i} + 4\hat{j} - 2\hat{k}$$

$$\overrightarrow{AD} = \left(-3\hat{i} + 2\hat{j} + \hat{k}\right) - \left(-\hat{i} + 4\hat{j} - 3\hat{k}\right)$$

$$= -2\hat{i} - 2\hat{j} + 4\hat{k}$$

$$\text{Now} \quad \left[\overrightarrow{AB}\,\overrightarrow{AC}\,\overrightarrow{AD}\right] = \begin{vmatrix} 4 & -2 & -2 \\ -2 & 4 & -2 \\ -2 & -2 & 4 \end{vmatrix}$$

$= 4\ (16 - 4) + 2\ (-8 - 4) - 2\ (4 + 8)$

$= 48 - 24 - 24$

$= 0$

Hence points are collinear

4. For any three vectors $\vec{a}$, $\vec{b}$ and $\vec{c}$ prove that

$$\left[\vec{a}+\vec{b}\quad \vec{b}+\vec{c}\quad \vec{c}+\vec{a}\right] = 2\left[\vec{a}\ \vec{b}\ \vec{c}\right]$$

Ans. We know, $\left[\vec{a}\ \vec{b}\ \vec{c}\right]=\vec{a}.\left(\vec{b}\times\vec{c}\right)$

Hence, $\left[\vec{a}+\vec{b}\quad \vec{b}+\vec{c}\quad \vec{c}+\vec{a}\right]=\left(\vec{a}+\vec{b}\right)\left[\left(\vec{b}+\vec{c}\right)\times\left(\vec{c}+\vec{a}\right)\right]$

$$= \left(\vec{a}+\vec{b}\right)\left[\vec{b}\times\vec{c}+\vec{b}\times\vec{a}+\vec{c}\times\vec{c}+\vec{c}\times\vec{a}\right]$$

$$= \vec{a}.\left(\vec{b}\times\vec{c}\right)+\vec{a}.\left(\vec{b}\times\vec{a}\right)+\vec{a}.\left(\vec{c}\times\vec{c}\right)+\vec{a}.\left(\vec{c}\times\vec{a}\right)$$

$$= \vec{b}.\left(\vec{b}\times\vec{c}\right)+\vec{b}\ \left(\vec{b}\times\vec{a}\right)+\vec{b}.\left(\vec{c}\times\vec{c}\right)+\vec{b}.\left(\vec{c}\times\vec{a}\right)$$

$$= \left[\vec{a}\ \vec{b}\ \vec{c}\right]+\left[\vec{a}\ \vec{b}\ \vec{a}\right]+\left[\vec{a}\ \vec{c}\ \vec{c}\right]+\left[\vec{a}\ \vec{c}\ \vec{a}\right]+\left[\vec{b}\ \vec{b}\ \vec{c}\right]+\left[\vec{b}\ \vec{b}\ \vec{a}\right]+\left[\vec{b}\ \vec{c}\ \vec{c}\right]+\left[\vec{b}\ \vec{c}\ \vec{a}\right]$$

$$= \left[\vec{a}\ \vec{b}\ \vec{c}\right]+0+0+0+0+0+0+\left[\vec{a}\ \vec{b}\ \vec{c}\right]$$

$$= 2\left[\vec{a}\ \vec{b}\ \vec{c}\right] \qquad \left[\because \left[\vec{a}\ \vec{b}\ \vec{a}\right]=0=\left[\vec{a}\ \vec{c}\ \vec{c}\right]....\right]$$

QUESTION PAPER-1

CLASS-XII

Time allowed : 3 hours *Maximum Marks : 100*

SECTION-A

Questions numbers **1** to **10** carry **1** mark each.

1. What is the range of the fucntion $f(x) = \frac{|x-1|}{(x-1)}$?

2. What is the principal value of $\sin^{-1}\left(-\frac{\sqrt{3}}{2}\right)$?

3. If $A = \begin{pmatrix} \cos\alpha & -\sin\alpha \\ \sin\alpha & \cos\alpha \end{pmatrix}$, then for what value of α is A an identity matrix?

4. What is the value of the determinant $\begin{vmatrix} 0 & 2 & 0 \\ 2 & 3 & 4 \\ 4 & 5 & 6 \end{vmatrix}$?

5. Evaluate : $\int \frac{\log x}{x} dx$

6. What is the degree of the following differential equation?

$$5x\left(\frac{dy}{dx}\right)^2 - \frac{d^2y}{dx^2} - 6y = \log x$$

7. Write a vector of magnitude 15 units in the direction of vector where the position vector of y and z axis is double of x-axis.

8. Write the vector equation of the following line : $\frac{x-5}{3} = \frac{y+4}{7} = \frac{6-z}{2}$

9. If $\begin{pmatrix} 1 & 2 \\ 3 & 4 \end{pmatrix}\begin{pmatrix} 3 & 1 \\ 2 & 5 \end{pmatrix} = \begin{pmatrix} 7 & 11 \\ k & 23 \end{pmatrix}$, then write the value of k.

10. What is the cosine of the angle which the vector $\sqrt{2}\hat{i} + \hat{j} + \hat{k}$ makes with y-axis?

SECTION-B

Questions numbers **11** to **22** carry **4** mark each.

11. On a multiple choice examination with three possible answers (out of which only one is correct) for each of the five questions, what is the probability that a candidate would get four or more correct answers just by guessing?

12. Find the position vector of a point R which divides tha line joining two points P and Q whose position vectors are $(2\vec{a} + \vec{b})$ and $(\vec{a} - 3\vec{b})$ respectively, externally in the ratio 1 : 2. Also, show that P is the mid point of the line segment RQ.

13. Find the Cartesian equation of the plane passing through the points A (0, 0, 0) and B (3, –1, 2) and parallel to the line $\frac{x-4}{1}=\frac{y+3}{-4}=\frac{z+1}{7}$

14. Using elementary row operations, find the inverse of the following matrix : $\begin{pmatrix} 2 & 5 \\ 1 & 3 \end{pmatrix}$.

15. Let Z be the set of all integers and R be the relation on Z defined as R = $\{(a,b) : a, b \in Z$, and $(a-b)$ is divisible by 5$\}$. Prove that R is an equivalence relation.

16. Prove the following : $\tan^{-1}\sqrt{x}=\frac{1}{2}\cos^{-1}\left(\frac{1-x}{1+x}\right)$, $x \in (0, 1)$

OR

Prove the following : $\cos^{-1}\left(\frac{12}{13}\right)+\sin^{-1}\left(\frac{3}{5}\right)=\sin^{-1}\left(\frac{56}{65}\right)$

17. Show that the function f defined as follows, is continuous at $x = 2$, but not differentiable there at :

$$f(x)=\begin{cases} 3x-2, & 0<x\le 1 \\ 2x^2-x, & 1<x\le 2 \\ 5x-4 & x>2 \end{cases}$$

OR

Find $\frac{dy}{dx}$, if $y=\sin^{-1}\left[x\sqrt{1-x}-\sqrt{x}\sqrt{1-x^2}\right]$

18. Evaluate: $\int e^x\left(\frac{\sin 4x-4}{1-\cos 4x}\right)dx$

OR

Evaluate : $\int \frac{1-x^2}{x(1-2x)}dx$

19. Evaluate : $\int_{\pi/6}^{\pi/3} \frac{\sin x+\cos x}{\sqrt{\sin 2x}}dx$

20. Find the points on the curve $y = x^3$ at which the slope of the tangent is equal to the y-coordinate of the point.

21. Find the general solution of the differential equation $x\log x.\frac{dy}{dx}+y=\frac{2}{x}.\log x$

OR

Find the particular solution of the differential equation satisfying the given conditions :

$\frac{dy}{dx}=y\tan x$, given that $y = 1$ when $x = 0$.

22. Find the particular solution of the differential equation satisfying the given conditions :
$x^2dy + (xy + y^2)\, dx = 0$; $y = 1$ when $x = 1$.

SECTION-C

Questions numbers **23** to **29** carry **6** mark each.

23. A small firm manufactures gold rings and chains. The total number of rings and chains manufactured per day is atmost 24. It takes 1 hour to make a ring and 30 minutes to make a chain. The maximum number of hours available per day is 16. If the profit on a ring is Rs. 300 and that on a chain is Rs. 190, find the number of rings and chains that should be manufactured per day, so as to earn the maximum profit. Make it as an L.P.P. and solve it graphically.

24. A card from of 52 cards is lost. From the remaining cards of the pack, two cards are drawn at random and are found to be both clubs. Find the probability of the lost card being of clubs.

OR

From a lot of 10 bulbs, which includes 3 defectives, a sample of 2 bulbs is drawn at random. Find the probability distribution of the number of defective bulbs.

25. The points A (4, 5, 10), B (2, 3, 4) and C (1, 2, –1) are three vertices of a parallelogram ABCD. Find the vector equations of the sides AB and BC and also find the coordinates of point D.

26. Using integration, find the area of the region bounded by the curve $x^2 = 4y$ and the line $x = 4y - 2$.

OR

Evaluate : $\displaystyle\int_0^{\pi} \frac{x \tan x}{\sec x + \tan x}\, dx$

27. Show that the right circular cylinder, open at the top, and of given surface area and maximum volume is such that its height is equal to the radius of the base.

28. Find the values of x for which $f(x) = [x\,(x-2)]^2$ is an increasing function. Also, find the points on the curve, where the tangent is parallel to x-axis.

29. Using properties of determinants, show the following:

$$\begin{vmatrix} (b+c)^2 & ab & ca \\ ab & (a+c)^2 & bc \\ ac & bc & (a+b)^2 \end{vmatrix} = 2abc(a+b+c)^3.$$

SOLVED QUESTION PAPER-1
WITH MARKING SCHEME
SECTION-A

1. Range : {–1, 1} **2.** $\frac{-\pi}{3}$ **3.** $\alpha = 0°$ 1×10 m

4. 8 **5.** $\frac{1}{2}(\log x)^2 + c$ **6.** 1

7. $5\hat{i} - 10\hat{j} + 10\hat{k}$ **8.** $\vec{r} = 5\hat{i} - 4\hat{j} + 6\hat{k} + \lambda\left(3\hat{i} + 7\hat{j} - 2\hat{k}\right)$ **9.** $k = 17$ **10.** $\frac{1}{2}$

SECTION-B

11. Probability of selecting corect choice $= \frac{1}{3}$ 1 m

Probability of selecting wrong choice $= \frac{2}{3}$ ½ m

Probability distribution is given by $\left(\frac{2}{3} + \frac{1}{3}\right)^5$ 1 m

we want to compute, P (4 correct answers) + P (5 correct answers) ½ m

$$= \left(\frac{1}{3}\right)^5 + 5C_4\left(\frac{1}{3}\right)^4\left(\frac{2}{3}\right) = \frac{11}{243}$$ 1 m

12. 

Position vector of R is $\frac{(\vec{a} - 3\vec{b}) \times 1 - (2\vec{a} + \vec{b})(2)}{1 - 2}$ 1 m

$= 3\vec{a} + 5\vec{b}$ 1 m

Mid-point of RQ is $\frac{3\vec{a} + 5\vec{b} + \vec{a} - 3\vec{b}}{2}$ 1 m

$= 2\vec{a} + \vec{b}$ ½ m

Which is position vector of P ½ m

13. Equation of plane passing through (0, 0, 0) is

$a(x - 0) + b(y - 0) + c(z - 0) = 0 \Rightarrow ax + by + cz = 0$ ...(i) 1 m

It passes through (3, –1, 2)

$\therefore$ $3a - b + 2c = 0$ ...(ii) ½ m

line $\frac{x-4}{1} = \frac{y+3}{-4} = \frac{z+1}{7}$ is | | to the plane (i)

$\Rightarrow \quad a - 4b + 7c = 0$ ...(iii) 1 m

From (ii) and (iii), $a = 1$, $b = -19$ and $c = -11$ (using cross product) 1 m

Equation of plane is $x - 19y - 11z = 0$ ½ m

14. Here $A = \begin{bmatrix} 2 & 5 \\ 1 & 3 \end{bmatrix}$

Writing $A = IA \Rightarrow \begin{bmatrix} 2 & 5 \\ 1 & 3 \end{bmatrix} = \begin{bmatrix} 1 & 0 \\ 0 & 1 \end{bmatrix} A$ ½ m

Applying $R_1 \to R_1 - R_2$, we get $\begin{bmatrix} 1 & 2 \\ 1 & 3 \end{bmatrix} = \begin{bmatrix} 1 & -1 \\ 0 & 1 \end{bmatrix} A$ 1 m

Applying $R_2 \to R_2 - R_1$, we get $\begin{bmatrix} 1 & 2 \\ 0 & 1 \end{bmatrix} = \begin{bmatrix} 1 & -1 \\ -1 & 2 \end{bmatrix} A$ 1 m

Applying $R_1 \to R_1 - 2R_2$, we get $\begin{bmatrix} 1 & 0 \\ 0 & 1 \end{bmatrix} = \begin{bmatrix} 3 & -5 \\ -1 & 2 \end{bmatrix} A$ 1 m

$\Rightarrow A^{-1} = \begin{bmatrix} 3 & -5 \\ -1 & 2 \end{bmatrix}$ ½ m

15. $R = \{(a, b) : a, b \in Z$ and $(a - b)$ is divisible by 5$\}$

(i) $a - a = 0$ which is divisible by 5 1 m

$\therefore$ R is reflexive

(ii) $a - b$ is divisible by 5 and so is $b - a$ 1 m

$\therefore$ R is symmetric 1 m

(iii) $a - c = (a - b) + (b - c)$

Let $a - b = 5m$ and $b - c = 5n$ 1½ m

$\therefore \quad a - c = 5(m + n) \Rightarrow a - c$ is divisible by 5

$\therefore$ R is transitive ½ m

$\therefore$ R is an equivalence – relation

16. Let $x = \tan^2\theta \Rightarrow \sqrt{x} = \tan\theta$ 1 m

LHS $= \tan^{-1}(\sqrt{x}) = \tan^{-1}(\tan\theta) = \theta$ 1 m

RHS $= \frac{1}{2}\cos^{-1}\left(\frac{1-\tan^2 ?}{1+\tan^2\theta}\right) = \frac{1}{2}\cos^{-1}(\cos 2\theta)$ 1 m

$= \frac{1}{2}\, 2\theta = \theta$ 1 m

$\Rightarrow$ LHS = RHS 1 m

OR

$\cos^{-1}\frac{12}{13} = \tan^{-1}\frac{5}{12}$ ½ m

$\sin^{-1}\frac{3}{5} = \tan^{-1}\frac{3}{4}$ ½ m

$\sin^{-1}\frac{56}{65} = \tan^{-1}\frac{56}{33}$ 1 m

LHS = $\tan^{-1}\frac{5}{12} + \tan^{-1}\frac{3}{4}$

$= \tan^{-1}\left[\frac{\frac{5+9}{12}}{1-\frac{5}{16}}\right] = \tan^{-1}\left(\frac{14}{\cancel{12}3}\times\frac{\cancel{16}4}{11}\right)$ 2 m

$= \tan^{-1}\frac{56}{33} = \text{RHS}$

17. LHL = $\lim_{h\to 0} f(2-h) = \lim_{h\to 0}\left[2(2-h)^2 - (2-h)\right] = 6$ ...(i) ½ m

RHL = $\lim_{h\to 0} f(2+h) = \lim_{h\to 0}[5(2+h)-4] = 6$ ...(ii) ½ m

$f(2) = 8 - 2 = 6$ ...(iii) 1 m

From (i), (ii), and (iii), $f(x)$ is continuous at x = 2

RHD = $\lim_{h\to 0}\left[\frac{\{5(2+h)-4\}-(6)}{h}\right] \neq$ LHD = $\lim_{h\to 0}\left[\frac{\{(2h-3)(h-2)-6\}}{h}\right]$ as $5 \neq 7$ ½ + ½ m

$\therefore$ $f(x)$ is not differentiable there at 1 m

OR

$y = \sin^{-1}\left[x\sqrt{1-x} - \sqrt{x}\sqrt{1-x^2}\right]$ ...(i)

Let $x = \sin\alpha$ and $\sqrt{x} = \sin\theta$ 1 m

$\therefore$ (i) becomes $y = \sin^{-1}[\sin\alpha\cos\theta - \cos\alpha\sin\theta]$ ½ m

$= \sin^{-1}[\sin(\alpha-\theta)] = \alpha - \theta$ ½ m

$= \sin^{-1}x - \sin^{-1}\sqrt{x}$ 1 m

$\therefore$ $\frac{dy}{dx} = \frac{1}{\sqrt{1-x^2}} - \frac{1}{2\sqrt{x}\sqrt{1-x}}$ 1 m

18. $I = \int e^x\left(\frac{\sin 4x - 4}{1-\cos 4x}\right)dx$

$$= \int e^x \left[\frac{\sin 4x}{1-\cos 4x} - \frac{4}{1-\cos 4x} \right] dx$$ 1 m

$$= \int e^x \left[\frac{2\sin 2x \cos 2x}{2.\sin^2 2x} - \frac{4}{2\sin^2 2x} \right] dx$$ 1 m

$$= \int e^x \left[\cot 2x - 2\operatorname{cosec}^2 2x \right] dx$$ ½ m

This is of the form = $\int e^x [f(x) + f'(x)]\, dx$ ½ m

$\therefore$ I $= e^x \cot 2x + c$ 1 m

OR

$$I = \int \frac{1-x^2}{x(1-2x)} dx = \frac{1}{2} \int \frac{2-2x^2}{x-2x^2} dx$$

$$= \frac{1}{2} \int \left[1 + \frac{2-x}{x(1-2x)} \right] dx$$ 1 m

$$= \frac{x}{2} + \frac{1}{2} \int \frac{2-x}{x(1-2x)} dx$$ ½ m

Let $\frac{2-x}{x(1-2x)} = \frac{A}{x} + \frac{B}{1-2x}$. Therefore, we get A = 2, B = 3 1 m

$$\therefore\ I = \frac{x}{2} + \frac{1}{2} \int \left(\frac{2}{x} + \frac{3}{1-2x} \right) dx$$ ½ m

$$= \frac{x}{2} + \log|x| - \frac{3}{4} \log|1-2x| + c$$ 1 m

19. Let $\sin x - \cos x = t \Rightarrow (\cos x + \sin x)\, dx = dt$, Also, $\sin 2x = 1 - t^2$

When $x = \frac{\pi}{3}$, $t = \frac{\sqrt{3}-1}{2}$, when $x = \frac{\pi}{6}$, $t = \frac{1-\sqrt{3}}{2}$ 1 m

$\therefore$ Given integral becomes $I = \int_{\frac{1-\sqrt{3}}{2}}^{\frac{\sqrt{3}-1}{2}} \frac{dt}{\sqrt{1-t^2}}$ 1 m

$$= \left[\sin^{-1} t \right]_{\frac{1-\sqrt{3}}{2}}^{\frac{\sqrt{3}-1}{2}} = \sin^{-1}\left(\frac{\sqrt{3}-1}{2} \right) - \sin^{-1}\left(\frac{1-\sqrt{3}}{2} \right)$$ 2 m

or $$2\sin^{-1}\left(\frac{\sqrt{3}-1}{2}\right)$$

20. Equation of curve is $y = x^3 \Rightarrow \frac{dy}{dx} = 3x^2$ ...(i) 1 m

(i) = y – coordinate of the point $\Rightarrow 3x^2 = y = x^3 \Rightarrow x^2 (x - 3) = 0$

$\Rightarrow x = 0, x = 3$ 1 m

When $x = 0, y = 0$ when $x = 3, y = 27$ 1 m

The points are (0, 0), (3, 27) ½ + ½ m

21. The given differential equation can be written as

$$\frac{dy}{dx} + \frac{1}{x\log x} y = \frac{2}{x^2}$$ ½ m

I.F. = $e^{\int \frac{1}{x\log x}dx} = e^{\log(\log x)} = \log x$ 1 m

The solution is $y \log x = \int \frac{2}{x^2} . \log x \, dx + c$ ½ m

or $y . \log x = 2\left[\log x\left(\frac{-1}{x}\right) + \int \frac{dx}{x^2}\right] + c = 2\left[\frac{-\log x}{x} - \frac{1}{x}\right] + c$ 1½ m

$\Rightarrow y . \log x = -\frac{2}{x}[1 + \log x] + c$ ½ m

OR

Given differential equation can be written as

$$\int \frac{dy}{y} = \int \tan x dx$$ 1 m

or $\log y = \log \sec x + c$ 1 m

when, $x = 0, y = 1 \Rightarrow c = 0$

[Note : $c = 1$, if constant is taken as $\log c$] 1 m

$\therefore$ $\log y = \log \sec x$

or $y = \sec x$ 1 m

22. The given differential equation can be written as

$\frac{dy}{dx} + \frac{xy + y^2}{x^2} = 0$. Let $y = vx \Rightarrow \frac{dy}{dx} = v + x\frac{dv}{dx}$ 1 m

$\Rightarrow v + x\frac{dv}{dx} + (v + v^2) = 0$

$\Rightarrow x\frac{dv}{dx} = -v(2 + v)$ 1 + ½ m

or $\dfrac{dv}{v(2+v)} = -\dfrac{dx}{x}$

or $\int\left(\dfrac{1}{v} - \dfrac{1}{2+v}\right)dv = -2\int\dfrac{dx}{x}$ ½ m

$\Rightarrow$ $\log\dfrac{v}{v+2} = \log\dfrac{c}{x^2}$

or $\dfrac{y}{y+2x} = \dfrac{c}{x^2}$ ½ m

when $x = 1, y = 1 \Rightarrow c = \dfrac{1}{3}$

$\therefore$ The solution becomes

$y + 2x = 3x^2 y$ ½ m

SECTION-C

23. Let x be the number of gold rings and y, the number of chains

The objective function is Z = 300 x + 190 y 1 m

Constraints are : $x + y \leq 24$

$x + \dfrac{y}{2} \leq 16$ or $2x + y \leq 32$

$x \geq 0, y \geq 0$ 2 m

Getting corners of feasible region as

A (0, 24), B (8, 16), C (16, 0), O (0, 0)

Z (0, 0) = 0, Z_A = 4560, Z_C = 4800

Z_B = 300 × 8 + 190 × 16 = 2400 + 3040 = 5440

$\therefore$ Z is maximum at B (8, 16)

$\therefore$ For maximum profit, Rings = 8, chains = 16 1 m

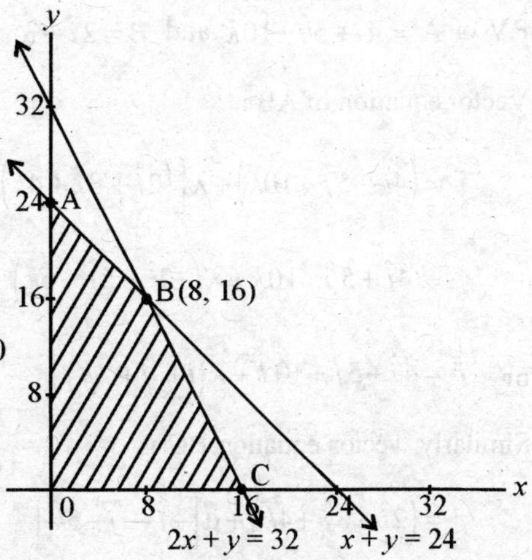

Correct graph 2 m

24. Let E_1 be the event that lost card is that of clubs

E_2 be event that lost card is not of clubs

A : Two cards of clubs are drawn from remaining cards 1 m

P (E1) = $\dfrac{1}{4}$, P (E2) = $\dfrac{3}{4}$ ½ m

$P\left(A/E_1\right) = {}^{12}c_2/{}^{51}c_2 = \dfrac{\cancel{12}^2 \times 11}{\cancel{51}_{17} \times \cancel{50}_{25}} = \dfrac{22}{425}$ 1 m

$P\left(A/E_2\right) = {}^{13}c_2/{}^{51}c_2 = \dfrac{13 \times \cancel{12}^2}{\cancel{51}_{17} \times \cancel{50}_{25}} = \dfrac{26}{425}$ 1 m

$$P\left(\frac{E_1}{A}\right) = \frac{P\left(\frac{A}{E_1}\right).P(E_1)}{\sum P(E_1).P\left(\frac{A}{E_1}\right)}$$ 1 m

$$= \frac{\frac{22}{425}\times\frac{1}{4}}{\frac{22}{425}\times\frac{1}{4}+\frac{26}{425}\times\frac{3}{4}} = \frac{11}{50}$$ 1 + ½ m

OR

Let x be the random variate giving number of defective bulbs, X can take values 0, 1, 2 1 m

$$P(X = 0) = \frac{7c_2}{10c_2} = \frac{7}{15},\ P(x=1) = \frac{7c_1 \times 3c_1}{10c_2} = \frac{7}{15},\ P(X=2) = \frac{3c_2}{10c_2} = \frac{1}{15}$$ 3 m

∴ Probability distribution of X is 2 m

X	0	1	2
P(X)	$7/15$	$7/15$	$1/15$

25. P.V. of $A = 4\hat{i}+5\hat{j}+10\hat{k}$ and $B = 2\hat{i}+3\hat{j}+4\hat{k}$

Vector equation of AB is

$$\vec{r} = \left(4\hat{i}+5\hat{j}+10\hat{k}\right)+\lambda\left[\left(2\hat{i}+3\hat{j}+4\hat{k}\right)-\left(4\hat{i}+5\hat{j}+10\hat{k}\right)\right]$$

$$= 4\hat{i}+5\hat{j}+10\hat{k}+\lambda\left(-2\hat{i}-2\hat{j}-6\hat{k}\right)$$ 1 + 1 m

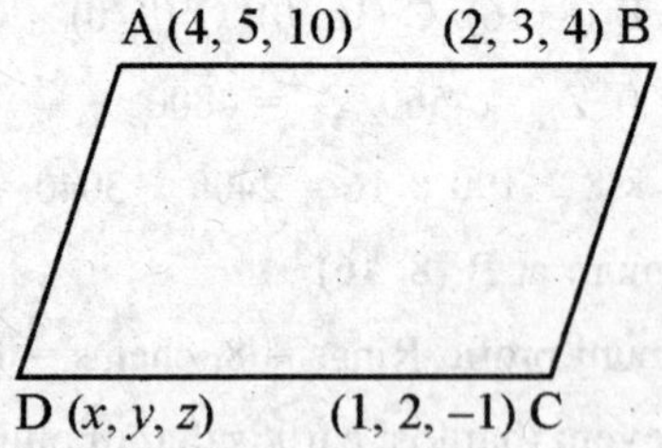

or $\vec{r} = 4\hat{i}+5\hat{j}+10\hat{k}+\lambda\left(\hat{i}+\hat{j}+3\hat{k}\right)$

Similarly, vector equation BC is 1½ m

$$\vec{r} = \left(2\hat{i}+3\hat{j}+4\hat{k}\right)+\mu\left[-\hat{i}-\hat{j}-5\hat{k}\right]$$

or $\vec{r} = 2\hat{i}+3\hat{j}+4\hat{k}+\mu\left(\hat{i}+\hat{j}+5\hat{k}\right)$

Mid-point of AC is $\frac{5}{2}\hat{i}+\frac{7}{2}\hat{j}+\frac{9}{2}\hat{k}$ 1 m

Mid-point of BD is $\frac{x+2}{2}\hat{i}+\frac{3+y}{2}\hat{j}+\frac{4+z}{2}\hat{k}$ 1 m

Coordinates of D are (3, 4, 5) ½ m

26. Point of intersection of curve and line has x corrdinates x = 2, x = –1 1 m

Required area $= \int_{-1}^{2} \frac{x+2}{4} dx - \int_{-1}^{2} \frac{x^2}{4} dx$ 1 + 1 m

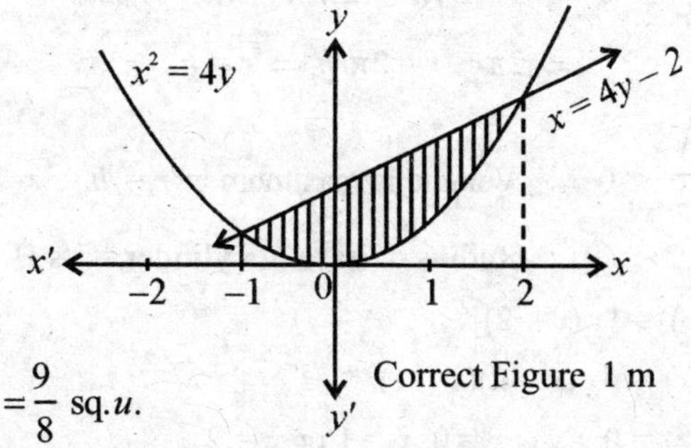

Correct Figure 1 m

$= \frac{1}{4}\left[\frac{x^2}{2} + 2x - \frac{x^3}{3}\right]_{-1}^{2}$ 1 m

$= \frac{1}{4}\left[\left(2+4-\frac{8}{3}\right) - \left(\frac{1}{2} - 2 + \frac{1}{3}\right)\right] = \frac{9}{8}$ sq.*u.* 1 m

OR

$I = \int_0^{\pi} \frac{x \tan x dx}{\sec x + \tan x} \Rightarrow I = \int_0^{\pi} \frac{(\pi - x) \tan x}{\sec x + \tan x} dx$ 1 m

$2I = \int_0^{\pi} \frac{\pi \tan x}{\sec x + \tan x} = \pi \int_0^{\pi} \frac{\sin x}{1 + \sin x} dx$ ½ m

$= \pi \int_0^{\pi} \left(1 - \frac{1}{1 + \sin x}\right) dx = \pi \int_0^{\pi} \left(1 - \frac{1 - \sin x}{\cos^2 x}\right) dx$ 2 m

$= \pi \int_0^{\pi} \left(1 - \sec^2 x + \sec x \tan x\right) dx$ 1 m

$= \pi \left[x - \tan x + \sec x\right]_0^{\pi} = \pi\,[\pi - 1 - 1]$ 1 m

$\therefore\ I = \frac{\pi^2}{2} - \pi = \frac{\pi}{2}[\pi - 2]$ ½ m

27. Let *r* be the radius of base of cylinder and *h*, be its height which is open at the top 1 m

s = Surface area $= 2\pi r h + \pi r^2$ or $\frac{s - \pi r^2}{2\pi r} = h$ 1 m

V = Volume of cylinder $= \pi r^2 h$

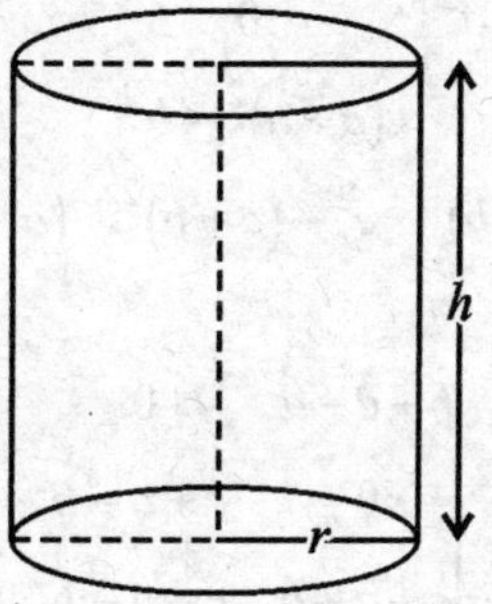

$= \pi r^2 \left(\frac{s - \pi r^2}{2\pi r}\right) = \frac{r}{2}\left(s - \pi r^2\right)$

$= \frac{rs}{2} - \frac{\pi}{2}.r^3$ 1½ m

$\frac{dv}{dr} = \frac{s}{2} - \frac{\pi}{2}.3r^2$

$\frac{dv}{dr} = 0 \Rightarrow s = 3\pi r^2 = 2\pi rh + \pi r^2$

$\Rightarrow 2\pi r \cdot r = 2\pi rh \Rightarrow r = h$ 1½ m

$\frac{d^2v}{dr^2} < 0 \Rightarrow$ Volume is maximum at $r = h$

$\therefore$ Radius of base of cylinder = its Height ½ + ½ m

28. $f(x) = [x(x-2)]^2$

$f'(x) = 4x(x-2)(x-1)$

$f'(x) = 0$ gives $x = 0, x = 1$ or $x = 2$ 1½ m

$\therefore$ Intervals are $(-\infty, 0), (0, 1), (1, 2), (2, \infty)$ 2 m

Increasing in $[0, 1]$ and $[2, \infty]$

$\Rightarrow$ or $0 \geq x \geq 1$ and $x \leq 2$ 1½ m

The point where tangents are parallel to x axis are (0, 0), (1, 1), (2, 0) 1 m

29. $\Delta = \begin{vmatrix} (b+c)^2 & ba & ca \\ ab & (c+a)^2 & bc \\ ac & bc & (a+b)^2 \end{vmatrix}$; Applying $R_1 \to a R_1, R_2 \to b R_2, R_3 \to c R_3$ we get

$= \frac{1}{abc}\begin{vmatrix} a(b+c)^2 & ba^2 & ca^2 \\ ab^2 & b(c+a)^2 & cb^2 \\ ac^2 & bc^2 & c(a+b)^2 \end{vmatrix}$ 1 m

$= \begin{vmatrix} (b+c)^2 & a^2 & a^2 \\ b^2 & (c+a)^2 & b^2 \\ c^2 & c^2 & (a+b)^2 \end{vmatrix}$ (After removing a, b, c from columns) ½ m

Applying $C_1 \to C_1 - C_3, C_2 \to C_2 - C_3$, we get

$\Delta = \begin{vmatrix} (b+c)^2 - a^2 & 0 & a^2 \\ 0 & (c+a)^2 - b^2 & b^2 \\ c^2 - (a-b) & c^2 - (a+b)^2 & (a+b)^2 \end{vmatrix}$

$= (a+b+c)^2 \begin{vmatrix} b+c-a & 0 & a^2 \\ 0 & c+a-b & b^2 \\ c-a-b & c-a-b & (a+b)^2 \end{vmatrix}$ ½ m

Applying $R_3 \to R_3 - (R_1 + R_2)$, we get

$$\Delta = (a+b+c)^2 \begin{vmatrix} b+c-a & 0 & a^2 \\ 0 & c+a-b & b^2 \\ -2b & -2a & 2ab \end{vmatrix}$$ 1 m

Applying $C_1 \to aC_1$ and $C_2 \to bC_2$ we get

$$\Delta = \frac{(a+b+c)^2}{ab} \begin{vmatrix} ab+ac-a^2 & 0 & a^2 \\ 0 & b(c+a-b) & b^2 \\ -2ba & -2ab & 2ab \end{vmatrix}$$ ½ m

Applying $C_1 \to C_1 + C_3$, $C_2 \to C_2 + C_3$ we get

$$\Delta = \frac{(a+b+c)^2}{ab} \begin{vmatrix} a(b+c) & a^2 & a^2 \\ b^2 & b(a+c) & b^2 \\ 0 & 0 & 2ab \end{vmatrix}$$ ½ m

$$= \frac{(a+b+c)^2}{ab} \times ab \times 2ab \begin{vmatrix} b+c & a & a \\ b & c+a & b \\ 0 & 0 & 1 \end{vmatrix}$$ ½ m

$= 2\,ab\,(a+b+c)^2\,[(b+c)(c+a) - ab]$

$= 2\,ab\,(a+b+c)^2\,[bc + c^2 + ab + ac - ab]$

$= 2\,abc\,(a+b+c)^3$ ½ m

QUESTION PAPER-2

CLASS-XII

SECTION-A

Questions numbers **1** to **10** carry **1** mark each.

1. If $f: R \to R$ be defind by $f(x) = (3 - x^3)^{1/3}$, then find $fof(x)$.
2. Write the principal value of $\sec^{-1}(-2)$.
3. What positive value of x makes the following pair of determinants equal?

$$\begin{vmatrix} 2x & 3 \\ 5 & x \end{vmatrix}, \begin{vmatrix} 16 & 3 \\ 5 & 2 \end{vmatrix}$$

4. Evaluate : $\int \sec^2(7-4x)\,dx$
5. Write the adjoint of the following matrix : $\begin{pmatrix} 2 & -1 \\ 4 & 3 \end{pmatrix}$
6. Write the value of the following integral : $\int_{-p/2}^{p/2} \sin^5 x dx$
7. A is a square matrix of order 3 and | A | = 7. Write the value of | adj.A |.
8. Write the distance of the following plane from the origin.

   $2x - y + 2z + 1 = 0$
9. Write a vector of magnitude 9 units in the direction of vector $-2\hat{i} + \hat{j} + 2\hat{k}$
10. Find λ if $\left(2\hat{i} + 6\hat{j} + 14\hat{k}\right) \times \left(\hat{i} - \lambda\hat{j} + 7\hat{k}\right) = \vec{0}$

SECTION-B

Questions numbers **11** to **12** carry **4** mark each.

11. A family has 2 children. Find the probability that both are boys, if it is known that
    (i) at least one of the children is a boy,
    (ii) the elder child is a boy.
12. Show that the relation S in the set $A = \{x \in Z : 0 \le x \le 12\}$ given by $S = \{(a, b) : a, b \in Z, |a - b|$ is divisible by 4$\}$ is an equivalence relation. Find the set of all elements related to 1.
13. Prove the following : $\tan^{-1} x + \tan^{-1}\left(\frac{2x}{1-x^2}\right) = \tan^{-1}\left(\frac{3x-x^2}{1-3x^2}\right)$

OR

Prove the following : $\cos[\tan^{-1}\{\sin(\cot^{-1} x)\}] = \sqrt{\frac{1+x^2}{2+x^2}}$

14. Express the following matrix as the sum of a symmetric and a skew symmetric matrix, and verify your result :

$$\begin{pmatrix} 3 & -2 & -4 \\ 3 & -2 & -5 \\ -1 & 1 & 2 \end{pmatrix}$$

15. If $\vec{a} = \hat{i} + \hat{j} + \hat{k}$, $\vec{b} = 4\hat{i} - 2\hat{j} + 3\hat{k}$ and $\vec{c} = \hat{i} - 2\hat{j} + \hat{k}$, find a vector of magnitude 6 units which is parallel to the vector $2\vec{a} - \vec{b} + 3\vec{c}$.

OR

Let $\vec{a} = \hat{i} + 4\hat{j} + 2\hat{k}$, $\vec{b} = 3\hat{i} - 2\hat{j} + 7\hat{k}$ and $\vec{c} = 2\hat{i} - \hat{j} + 4\hat{k}$. Find a vector $\vec{d}$ which is perpendicular to both $\vec{a}$ and $\vec{b}$ and $\vec{c} \cdot \vec{d} = 18$.

16. Find the points on the line $\frac{x+2}{3} = \frac{y+1}{2} = \frac{z-3}{2}$ at a distance of 5 units from the point P (1, 3, 3).

OR

Find the distance of the point P (6, 5, 9) from the plane determined by the points A (3, –1, 2), B (5, 2, 4) and C (–1, –1, 6).

17. Solve the following differential equation :

$$\left(x^2 - 1\right)\frac{dy}{dx} + 2xy = \frac{1}{x^2 - 1}; |x| \neq 1$$

OR

Solve the following differential equation:

$$\sqrt{1 + x^2 + y^2 + x^2y^2} + xy\frac{dy}{dx} = 0$$

18. Show that the differential equation $(x - y)\frac{dy}{dx} = x + 2y$, is homogeneous and solve it.

19. Evaluate the following : $\int \frac{x+2}{\sqrt{(x-2)(x-3)}}\, dx$

20. Evaluate the following : $\int_1^2 \frac{5x^2}{x^2 + 4x + 3}\, dx$

21. If $y = e^{a \sin^{-1} x}$, $-1 \leq x \leq 1$, then show that $\left(1 - x^2\right)\frac{d^2y}{dx^2} - x\frac{dy}{dx} - a^2y = 0$.

22. If $y = \cos^{-1}\left(\frac{3x + 4\sqrt{1 - x^2}}{5}\right)$, find $\frac{dy}{dx}$.

SECTION-C

Questions numbers **23** to **29** carry **4** mark each.

23. Using properties of determinants, prove the following :

$$\begin{vmatrix} x & x^2 & 1+px^3 \\ y & y^2 & 1+py^3 \\ z & z^2 & 1+pz^3 \end{vmatrix} = (1+pxyz)(x-y)(y-z)(z-x)$$

OR

Find the inverse of the following matrix using elementary operations :

$$A = \begin{pmatrix} 1 & 2 & -2 \\ -1 & 3 & 0 \\ 0 & -2 & 1 \end{pmatrix}$$

24. A bag contains 4 balls. Two balls are drawn at random, and are found to be white. What is the probability that all balls are white?

25. One kind of cake requires 300 g of flour and 15 g of fat, another kind of cake requires 150 g of flour and 30 g of fat. Find the maximum number of cakes which can be made from 7.5 kg of flour and 600 g of fat, assuming that there is no shortage of the other ingradients used in making the cakes. Make it as an L.P.P. and solve it graphically.

26. Find the coordinates of the foot of the perpendicular and the perpendiular distance of the point P(3,2,1) from the plane $2x - y + z + 1 = 0$. Find also, the image of the point in the plane.

27. Find the area of the circle $4x^2 + 4y^2 = 9$ which is interior to the parabola $x^2 = 4y$.

OR

Using integration, find the area of the triangle ABC, coordinates of whose vertices are A (4, 1), B (6, 6) and C (8, 4).

28. If the length of three sides of a trapezium other than the base is 10 cm each, find the area of the trapezium, when it is maximum.

29. Find the intervals in which f(x) = sin 3x is increasing or decreasing in [0, $\pi/2$].

SOLVED QUESTION PAPER-2
WITH MARKING SCHEME

SECTION-A

$1 \times 10 = 10$ m

1. x 2. $\frac{2\pi}{3}$ 3. $x = 4$ 4. $-\frac{1}{4}\tan(7-4x)+c$ 5. $\begin{pmatrix} 3 & 1 \\ -4 & 2 \end{pmatrix}$

6. zero 7. 49 8. $\frac{1}{3}$ 9. $-6\hat{i}+3\hat{j}+6\hat{k}$ 10. -3

SECTION-B

11. Let event A is that the family has two boys

(i) event B : At least one is a boy

P (both boys, given that at least one is a boy) = P (A/B) ½ m

$$= \frac{P(A \cap B)}{P(B)} = \frac{P\{(B,B)\}}{P\{(B,G),(G,B),(B,B),\}}$$ ½ + ½ m

$$= \frac{1/4}{3/4} = \frac{1}{3}$$ ½ m

(ii) $$= \frac{P(A \cap C)}{P(C)} = \frac{P\{(B,B)\}}{P\{(B,G),(B,B)\}}$$ 1 m

$$= \frac{1/4}{2/4} = \frac{1}{2}$$ 1 m

12. (i) For all $a \in$ A, $(a, a) \in$ S ($\because$ $a - a = 0$ is divisible by 4)

$\therefore$ S is reflexive in A 1 m

(ii) For all $a, b \in$ A, if $(a, b) \in$ S then $|a - b|$ is divisible by 4.

Hence $|b - a|$ is also divisible by 4 $\Rightarrow$ S is symmetric in A 1 m

(iii) $a, b, c \in$ A, Let $(a, b) \in$ S and $(b, c) \in$ S

i.e., $|a - b|$ is divisible by 4 and $|b - c|$ is divisible by 4

$\Rightarrow$ $(a - b) = \pm 4p$, $(b - c) = \pm 4q$, adding to get $a - c = 4m \Rightarrow (a, c) \in$ S 1½ m

$\Rightarrow$ S is transitive in A

Hence S is an equivalence relation

Elements related to 1 are {1, 5, 9} ½ m

13. LHS $= \tan^{-1}\left[\dfrac{x+\dfrac{2x}{1-x^2}}{1-x\dfrac{2x}{1-x^2}}\right]$ 2 m

$= \tan^{-1}\left[\dfrac{x\left(1-x^2\right)+2x}{1-x^2-2x^2}\right]$ 1 m

$= \tan^{-1}\left[\dfrac{3x-x^3}{1-3x^2}\right] = \text{RHS}$ 1 m

OR

LHS $= \cos\left[\tan^{-1}\left\{\sin\left(\cot^{-1}x\right)\right\}\right]$

$= \cos\left[\tan^{-1}\left\{\sin\left(\sin^{-1}\dfrac{1}{\sqrt{1+x^2}}\right)\right\}\right]$ 1 m

$= \cos\left[\tan^{-1}\left(\dfrac{1}{\sqrt{1+x^2}}\right)\right] = \cos\left[\cos^{-1}\dfrac{\sqrt{1+x^2}}{\sqrt{2+x^2}}\right]$ 1 + 1 m

$= \dfrac{\sqrt{1+x^2}}{\sqrt{2+x^2}} = \text{RHS}$ 1 m

14. $A = \begin{pmatrix} 3 & -2 & -4 \\ 3 & -2 & -5 \\ -1 & 1 & 2 \end{pmatrix}$, then $A' = \begin{pmatrix} 3 & 3 & -1 \\ -2 & -2 & 1 \\ -4 & -5 & 2 \end{pmatrix}$ 1 m

Writing $A = \dfrac{1}{2}(A + A') + \dfrac{1}{2}(A - A')$ ½ m

$\dfrac{1}{2}(A + A') = \begin{pmatrix} 3 & 1/2 & -5/2 \\ 1/2 & -2 & -2 \\ -5/2 & -2 & 2 \end{pmatrix}$ ½ m

$\dfrac{1}{2}(A - \mathbf{A}') = \begin{pmatrix} 0 & -5/2 & -3/2 \\ 5/2 & 0 & -3 \\ 3/2 & 3 & 0 \end{pmatrix}$ ½ m

and $\begin{pmatrix} 3 & -2 & -4 \\ 3 & -2 & -5 \\ -1 & 1 & 2 \end{pmatrix} = \begin{pmatrix} 3 & 1/2 & -5/2 \\ 1/2 & -2 & -2 \\ -5/2 & -2 & 2 \end{pmatrix} + \begin{pmatrix} 0 & -5/2 & -3/2 \\ 5/2 & 0 & -3 \\ 3/2 & 3 & 0 \end{pmatrix}$ 1 m

Thus A = B + C

Where B is Symmetric matrix and C is skew symmetric matrix ½ m

15. $2\vec{a}-\vec{b}+3\vec{c}=\left(2\hat{i}+2\hat{j}+2\hat{k}\right)-\left(4\hat{i}-2\hat{j}+3\hat{k}\right)+\left(3\hat{i}-6\hat{j}+3\hat{k}\right)=\hat{i}-2\hat{j}+2\hat{k}$ 2 m

$\left|2\vec{a}-\vec{b}+3\vec{c}\right|=3$ 1 m

$\therefore$ Required vector $=2\hat{i}-4\hat{j}+4\hat{k}$ 1 m

OR

A vector perpendicular to $\vec{a}$ and $\vec{b}=\vec{a}\times\vec{b}=32\hat{i}-\hat{j}-14\hat{k}$ ½ + 1 m

Let $\vec{d}=\lambda\left(32\hat{i}-\hat{j}-14\hat{k}\right)$ ½ m

$\therefore$ $\vec{c}.\vec{d}=18 \Rightarrow \lambda(64+1-56)=18 \Rightarrow \lambda=2$ 1½ m

$\therefore$ $\vec{d}=64\hat{i}-2\hat{j}-28\hat{k}$ ½ m

16. Any point Q on the given line is Q $(3\lambda-2, 2\lambda-1, 2\lambda+3)$ 1 m

$PQ^2=(3\lambda-3)^2+(2\lambda-4)^2+(2\lambda)^2=17\lambda^2-18\lambda-16\lambda+25$ 1 m

$PQ^2=(5)^2 \Rightarrow 17\lambda(\lambda-2)=0 \Rightarrow \lambda=0$ or $\lambda=2$ 1 m

$\therefore$ The points are Q (–2, –1, 3) and R (4, 3, 7) ½ + ½ m

OR

Normal to the plane passing through A, B and C is

$$\overrightarrow{AB}\times\overrightarrow{BC}=\begin{vmatrix}\hat{i} & \hat{j} & \hat{k}\\ 2 & 3 & 2\\ -6 & -3 & 2\end{vmatrix}=12\hat{i}-16\hat{j}+12\hat{k} \text{ or } 3\hat{i}-4\hat{j}+3\hat{k}$$ 1½ m

$\therefore$ Equation of plane is $\vec{r}\left(3\hat{i}-4\hat{j}+3\hat{k}\right)=19$ or $3x-4y+3z-19=0$ 1½ m

Distance of P (6, 5, 9) from the plane $=\dfrac{|18-20+27-19|}{\sqrt{(3)^2+(-4)^2+(3)^2}}=\dfrac{6}{\sqrt{34}}$ 1 m

17. Given differential equation can be written as

$$\frac{dy}{dx}+\frac{2x}{x^2-1}y=\frac{1}{(x^2-1)^2}$$ 1 m

Which is of the form $\dfrac{dy}{dx}+P(x).y=Q(x)$

$$\int P(x)\,dx=\int\frac{2x}{x^2-1}dx=\log\left|x^2-1\right|$$ ½ m

$\therefore$ Intergrating factor $=e^{\int P(x)dx}=(x^2-1)$ 1 m

$\therefore$ The solution is $(x^2-1)\cdot y = \int \frac{1}{(x^2-1)^2}(x^2-1)\,dx$ 1 m

$$(x^2-1)\cdot y = \frac{1}{2}\log\left|\frac{x-1}{x+1}\right| + c$$ ½ m

OR

Given differential equation can be written as

$$\sqrt{(1+x^2)}\cdot\sqrt{(1+y^2)} + xy\frac{dy}{dx} = 0$$ ½ m

$$\Rightarrow \frac{y}{\sqrt{1+y^2}}dy = -\frac{\sqrt{1+x^2}}{x}dx$$ ½ m

Integrating both sides, we get

$$\sqrt{1+y^2} = -\int\frac{\sqrt{1+x^2}}{x^2}\cdot x\,dx = -\int\frac{t^2\,dt}{t^2-1} \text{ where } (1+x^2) = t^2$$ 1 m

$$\sqrt{1+y^2} = -\int\left(1+\frac{1}{t^2-1}\right)dt = -t - \frac{1}{2}\log\frac{t-1}{t+1} + c$$ 1 + 1 m

$$\Rightarrow -\sqrt{1+x^2} - \frac{1}{2}\log\left|\frac{\sqrt{1+x^2}-1}{\sqrt{1+x^2}+1}\right| = c$$

or $$\sqrt{1+y^2} + \sqrt{1+x^2} + \frac{1}{2}\log\left|\frac{\sqrt{1+x^2}-1}{\sqrt{1+x^2}+1}\right| = c$$

18. Given differential equation can be written as

$$\frac{dy}{dx} = \frac{x+2y}{x-y} = \frac{1+2\,y/x}{1-y/x} = f\left(\frac{y}{x}\right)$$

hence, the differential equation is homogeneous. 1 m

Taking $\frac{y}{x} = v$ or $y = vx \Rightarrow \frac{dy}{dx} = v + x\frac{dy}{dx}$ ½ m

$$\therefore \quad v + x\frac{dv}{dx} = \frac{1+2v}{1-v} \text{ or } x\frac{dv}{dx} = \frac{1+2v}{1-v} - v = \frac{1+v+v^2}{1-v}$$

$$\Rightarrow \int\frac{v-1}{v^2+v+1}dv = \int -\frac{dx}{x}$$ 1 m

$$\Rightarrow \frac{1}{2}\int\frac{2v+1-3}{v^2+v+1}dv = -\log|x| + c$$

or $\frac{1}{2}\log\left|v^2+v+1\right|-\frac{3}{2}\int\frac{dv}{\left(v+\frac{1}{2}\right)^2+\left(\frac{\sqrt{3}}{2}\right)^2}=-\log|x|+c$

$\Rightarrow \log|v^2+v+1|+\log x^2 = 2\sqrt{3}\tan^{-1}\left(\frac{2v+1}{\sqrt{3}}\right)+c$ 1 m

$\Rightarrow \log|y^2+xy+x^2| = 2\sqrt{3}\tan^{-1}\left(\frac{2y+x}{\sqrt{3}x}\right)+c$ ½ m

19. Here $I = \int\frac{x+2}{\sqrt{x^2-5x+6}}dx = \frac{1}{2}\int\frac{2x-5+9}{\sqrt{x^2-5x+6}}dx$ 1 m

$= \frac{1}{2}\int\frac{2x-5}{\sqrt{x^2-5x+6}}dx+\frac{9}{2}\int\frac{1}{\sqrt{\left(x-\frac{5}{2}\right)^2-\left(\frac{1}{2}\right)^2}}dx$ 1 m

$= \sqrt{x^2-5x+6}+\frac{9}{2}\log\left|\left(x-\frac{5}{2}\right)+\sqrt{x^2-5x+6}\right|+c$ 1 + 1 m

20. $I = \int_1^2\frac{5x^2}{x^2+4x+3}dx = 5\int_1^2 1-\frac{4x+3}{x^2+4x+3}dx$ 1 m

$= 5\,[x]_1^2-10\int_1^2\frac{2x+4-\frac{5}{2}}{x^2+4x+3}dx$ ½ m

$= 5-10\left[\log\left|x^2+4x+3\right|\right]_1^2+25\int_1^2\frac{1}{(x+2)^2-(1)^2}dx$ 1 m

$= 5-10\log\frac{15}{8}+25.\frac{1}{2}\left[\log\left|\frac{x+2-1}{x+2+1}\right|\right]_1^2$ 1 m

$= 5-10\log\frac{15}{8}+\frac{25}{2}\log\frac{6}{5}$ ½ m

Note : If solved using partial fractions, the answer be of the

$5+\frac{5}{2}\log\frac{3}{2}-\frac{45}{2}\log\left(\frac{5}{4}\right)$

21. $\frac{dy}{dx}=e^{a\sin^{-1}x}\frac{a}{\sqrt{1-x^2}}=\frac{ay}{\sqrt{1-x^2}}$ 1 m

$\Rightarrow \sqrt{1-x^2}.\frac{dy}{dx}=ay \quad ...(i)$ ½ m

$\Rightarrow \sqrt{1-x^2}.\frac{d^2y}{dx^2}-\frac{x}{\sqrt{1-x^2}}.\frac{dy}{dx}=a\frac{dy}{dx}$ 1 m

$$\Rightarrow \quad (1-x^2)\frac{d^2y}{dx^2} - x\frac{dy}{dx} - a\sqrt{1-x^2}\ \frac{dy}{dx} = 0$$ ½ m

$$\Rightarrow \quad (1-x^2)\frac{d^2y}{dx^2} - x\frac{dy}{dx} - a^2 y = 0 \text{ [Using (i)]}$$ 1 m

22. $y = \cos^{-1}\left[\frac{3}{5}x + \frac{4}{5}\sqrt{1-x^2}\right]$

$= \cos^{-1}\left[\frac{3}{5}.\cos ? + \frac{4}{5}\sin ?\right]$ where $x = \cos\theta$ 1 m

$= \cos^{-1}[\cos\alpha . \cos\theta + \sin\alpha . \sin\theta]$, $\because$ *if* $\frac{3}{5} = \cos\alpha$, then $\frac{4}{5} = \sin\alpha$ 1 m

$= \cos^{-1}[\cos(\alpha - \theta)] = \alpha - \theta = \cos^{-1}\left(\frac{3}{5}\right) - \cos^{-1} x$ 1 m

$\Rightarrow \frac{dy}{dx} = \frac{1}{\sqrt{1-x^2}}$ $\left[\text{Note:Answercanalsobe} - \frac{1}{\sqrt{1-x^2}}\right]$ 1 m

SECTION-C

23. LHS $= \begin{vmatrix} x & x^2 & 1+px^3 \\ y & y^2 & 1+py^3 \\ z & z^2 & 1+pz^3 \end{vmatrix} = \begin{vmatrix} x & x^2 & 1 \\ y & y^2 & 1 \\ z & z^2 & 1 \end{vmatrix} + p\begin{vmatrix} x & x^2 & x^3 \\ y & y^2 & y^3 \\ z & z^2 & z^3 \end{vmatrix}$ 1 m

$= \begin{vmatrix} 1 & x & x^2 \\ 1 & y & y^2 \\ 1 & z & z^2 \end{vmatrix} + pxyz\begin{vmatrix} 1 & x & x^2 \\ 1 & y & y^2 \\ 1 & z & z^2 \end{vmatrix}$ ½ m

$= (1 + pxyz)\begin{vmatrix} 1 & x & x^2 \\ 1 & y & y^2 \\ 1 & z & z^2 \end{vmatrix}$ ½ m

$= (1 + pxyz)\begin{vmatrix} 1 & x & x^2 \\ 0 & y-x & y^2-x^2 \\ 0 & z-x & z^2-x^2 \end{vmatrix}$ $\begin{matrix} R_2 \to R_2 - R_1 \\ R_3 \to R_3 - R_1 \end{matrix}$ 1 m

$= (1 + pxyz)(x - y)(z - x)\begin{vmatrix} 1 & x & x^2 \\ 0 & -1 & -(x+y) \\ 0 & 1 & z+x \end{vmatrix}$ ½ m

$$= (1 + pxyz)(x - y)(z - x)\begin{vmatrix} 1 & x & x^2 \\ 0 & 0 & z-y \\ 0 & 1 & z+x \end{vmatrix} \quad R_2 \to R_2 + R_3$$ 1 m

$$= (1 + pxyz)(x - y)(y - z)(z - x)\begin{vmatrix} 1 & x & x^2 \\ 0 & 0 & -1 \\ 0 & 1 & z+x \end{vmatrix}$$ ½ m

$$= (1 + pxyz)(x - y)(y - z)(z - x) \cdot 1 = \text{RHS}$$ 1 m

OR

Writing $\begin{pmatrix} 1 & 2 & -2 \\ -1 & 3 & 0 \\ 0 & -2 & 1 \end{pmatrix} = \begin{pmatrix} 1 & 0 & 0 \\ 0 & 1 & 0 \\ 0 & 0 & 1 \end{pmatrix} A$ 1 m

$R_2 \to R_2 + R_1 \Rightarrow \begin{pmatrix} 1 & 2 & -2 \\ 0 & 5 & -2 \\ 0 & -2 & 1 \end{pmatrix} = \begin{pmatrix} 1 & 0 & 0 \\ 1 & 1 & 0 \\ 0 & 0 & 1 \end{pmatrix} A$ 1 m

$R_2 \to R_2 + 2R_3 \Rightarrow \begin{pmatrix} 1 & 2 & -2 \\ 0 & 1 & 0 \\ 0 & -2 & 1 \end{pmatrix} = \begin{pmatrix} 1 & 0 & 0 \\ 1 & 1 & 2 \\ 0 & 0 & 1 \end{pmatrix} A$ 1 m

$R_3 \to R_3 + 2R_2 \Rightarrow \begin{pmatrix} 1 & 2 & -2 \\ 0 & 1 & 0 \\ 0 & 0 & 1 \end{pmatrix} = \begin{pmatrix} 1 & 0 & 0 \\ 1 & 1 & 2 \\ 2 & 2 & 5 \end{pmatrix} A$ 1 m

$R_1 \to R_1 + 2R_3 \Rightarrow \begin{pmatrix} 1 & 2 & 0 \\ 0 & 1 & 0 \\ 0 & 0 & 1 \end{pmatrix} = \begin{pmatrix} 5 & 4 & 10 \\ 1 & 1 & 2 \\ 2 & 2 & 5 \end{pmatrix} A$ ½ m

$R_1 \to R_1 - 2R_2 \Rightarrow \begin{pmatrix} 1 & 0 & 0 \\ 0 & 1 & 0 \\ 0 & 0 & 1 \end{pmatrix} = \begin{pmatrix} 3 & 2 & 6 \\ 1 & 1 & 2 \\ 2 & 2 & 5 \end{pmatrix} A$ ½ m

Hence $A^{-1} = \begin{pmatrix} 3 & 2 & 6 \\ 1 & 1 & 2 \\ 2 & 2 & 5 \end{pmatrix}$ 1 m

24. E_1 : Bag contains 2 white balls and 2 non whites

E_2 : Bag contains 3 white balls and 1 non whites 1 m

E_3 : Bag contains 4 white balls

A : Getting two white balls

$$P(E_1) = \frac{1}{3}, P(E_2) = \frac{1}{3}, P(E_3) = \frac{1}{3}$$ ½ m

$$P(A/E_1) = \frac{2c_2}{4c_2} = \frac{1}{6}, \; P(A/E_2) = \frac{3c_2}{4c_2} = \frac{1}{2}, \; P(A/E_3) = 1$$ 1½ m

$$P(E_3/A) = \frac{P(E_3).P(A/E_3)}{P(E_1)P(A/E_1) + P(E_2)P(A/E_2) + P(E_3)P(A/E_3)}$$ 1 m

$$= \frac{\frac{1}{3}.1}{\frac{1}{3}.\frac{1}{6} + \frac{1}{3}.\frac{1}{2} + \frac{1}{3}.1}$$ 1 m

$$= \frac{6}{10} = \frac{3}{5}$$ 1 m

25. Let x cakes of first type and y cakes of second type are made

Maximise $S = x + y$ 1 m

subject to $300x + 150y \leq 7500$ or $2x + y \leq 50$

$15x + 30y \leq 600$ or $x + 2y \leq 40$ 2 m

$x \geq 0, y \geq 0$

Vertices of feasible region are A (0, 20), B (20, 10) C (25, 0)

Maximum cakes = 20 + 10 = 30 1 m

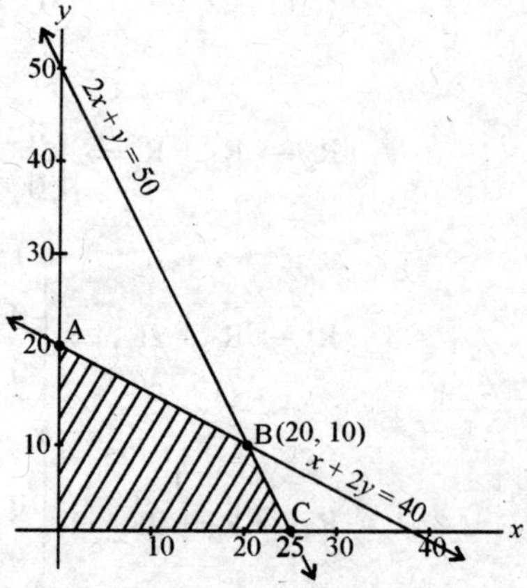

Correct graph 2 m

26. Let Q be the foot of perpendicular from P to the plane

∴ Equation of PQ is $\frac{x-3}{2} = \frac{y-2}{-1} = \frac{z-1}{1}$ 1 m

Any point on this line is $(2\lambda + 3, -\lambda + 2, \lambda + 1)$ ½ m

If this point is Q, then it must satisfy the equation of plane

∴ $2(2\lambda + 3) - (-\lambda + 2) + (\lambda + 1) + 1 = 0$ 1 m

⇒ $\lambda = -1$ ½ m

∴ coordinates of foot of perpendicular are Q (1, 3, 0) 1 m

Perpendicular distance = PQ = $\sqrt{4+1+1} = \sqrt{6}$ units 1 m

Let P′ (x, y, z) be the image, then $\frac{x+3}{2} = 1, \; \frac{y+2}{2} = 3, \; \frac{z+1}{2} = 0$

∴ P′ is (–1, 4, –1) 1 m

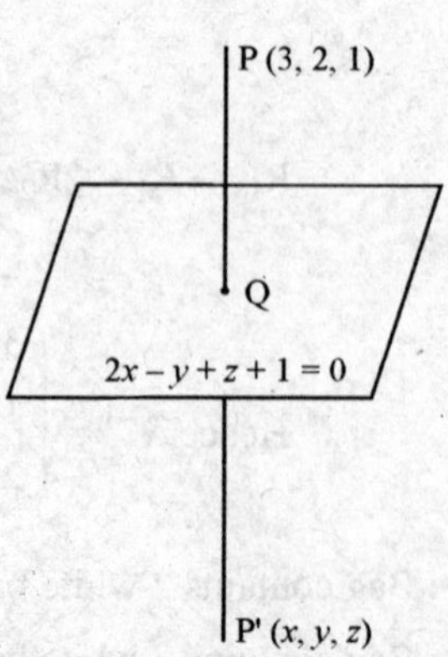

Correct Figure 1 m

27. Solving $4x^2 + 4y^2 = 9$ and $x^2 = 4y$

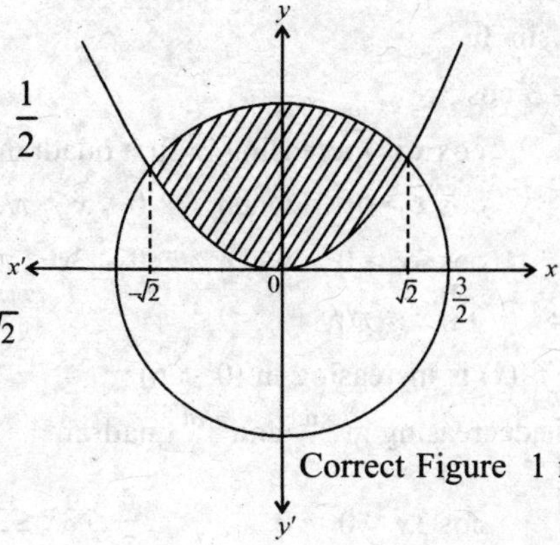

We get $x = \pm\sqrt{2}$ (as points of intersection) or $y = \frac{1}{2}$ ½ m

Required are $= 2\left[\int_0^{\sqrt{2}} \sqrt{\frac{9}{4} - x^2}\, dx - \int_0^{\sqrt{2}} \frac{1}{4}x^2 dx\right]$ 2 m

$= 2\left[\frac{x}{2}\sqrt{\frac{9}{4} - x^2} + \frac{9}{8}\sin^{-1}\frac{2x}{3} - \frac{x^3}{12}\right]_0^{\sqrt{2}}$ 1½ m

Correct Figure 1 m

$= 2\left(\frac{\sqrt{2}}{2}.\frac{1}{2} + \frac{9}{8}\sin^{-1}\frac{2\sqrt{2}}{3} - \frac{2\sqrt{2}}{12}\right)$ ½ m

$= \left(\frac{\sqrt{2}}{6} + \frac{9}{4}\sin^{-1}\frac{2\sqrt{2}}{3}\right)$ sq. units ½ m

OR

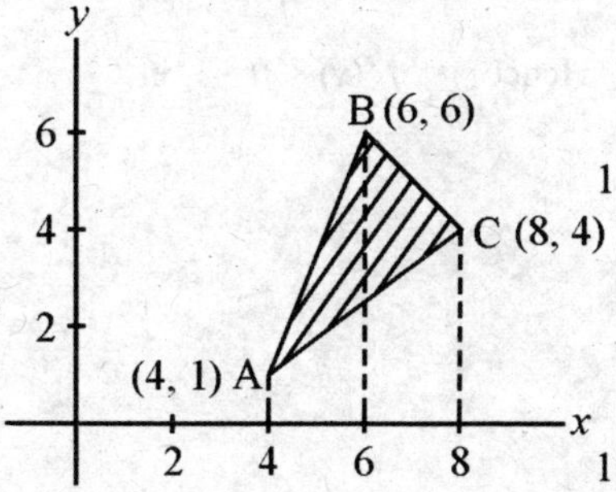

Equations of AB, BC and AC respectively are

$y = \frac{5}{2}x - 9,\ y = 12 - x,\ y = \frac{3}{4}x - 2$ 1½ m

Required area $= \int_4^6 \left(\frac{5}{2}x - 9\right) dx + \int_6^8 (12 - x)\, dx - \int_4^8 \left(\frac{3}{4}x - 2\right) dx$ 2 m

$= \left[\frac{5x^2}{4} - 9x\right]_4^6 + \left[12x - \frac{x^2}{2}\right]_6^8 - \left[\frac{3x^2}{8} - 2x\right]_4^8$ 1½ m

$= (7 + 10 - 10)$ sq units $= 7$ sq units 1 m

28. Let ABCD be the given trapezium with AD = DC = BC = 10 cm.

Draw DP ⊥ AB and CQ ⊥ AB and let AP = x cm => QB = x cm 1 m

Area of trapezium, $A = \frac{1}{2}[10 + (10 + 2x)]\sqrt{100 - x^2}$ 1 m

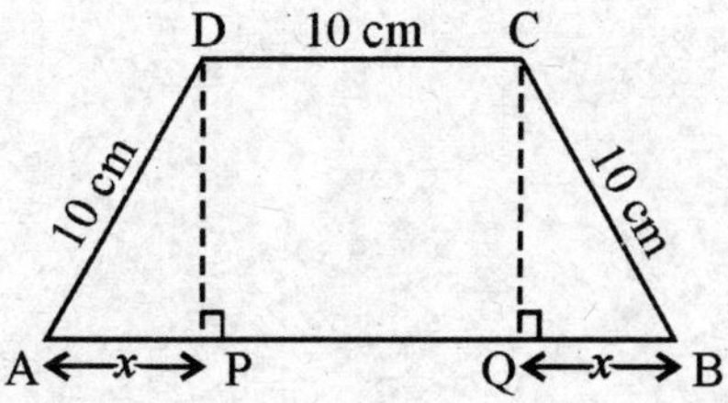

$A = (x + 10)\sqrt{100 - x^2}$

Let $S = (x + 10)^2 \quad (100 - x^2)$

$\Rightarrow \frac{ds}{dx} = -2x(x + 10)^2 + 2(x + 10)(100 - x^2)$

$= 2(x + 10)^2\ (-x + 10 - x)$

$= 2(x + 10)^2\ (10 - 2x)$ 1 m

$\frac{ds}{dx} = 0 \Rightarrow x = 5$ [rejecting $x = -10$] 1 m

$\frac{d^2s}{dx^2} = -4(x + 10)^2 + 4(x + 10)(10 - 2x) = -900$ (– ve) 1 m

∴ Maximum Area $A = 15\sqrt{75}$ cm^2 or $75\sqrt{3}$ cm^2 1 m

29. $f(x) = \sin 3x$ 6 m

$f'(x) = 3 \cos 3x$

Since $\cos x$ is increasing in first quadrant

$\cos x > 0$ when $0 < x < \pi/2$

$\cos 3x > 0$ when $0 < 3x < \pi/2$

$\Rightarrow$ $0 < x < \pi/6$

Hence $f'(x)$ is increasing in $(0, \pi/6)$

$\cos x$ is decreasing in 2nd and 3rd quadrant

$\cos 3x < 0$ if $\frac{\pi}{2} \le 3x \le 3\frac{\pi}{2}$

$\Rightarrow$ $\frac{\pi}{6} \le x \le \frac{\pi}{2}$

Hence, $f'(x) < 0$ in $\left[\frac{\pi}{6}, \frac{\pi}{2}\right]$

QUESTION PAPER-3

CLASS-XII

Time allowed : 3 hours *Maximum Marks : 100*

SECTION A

1. Give an example to show that the relation R in the set of natural numbers, defined by $R = \{(x, y), x, y \in N, x \leq y^2\}$ is not transitive.

2. Write the principal value of $\cos^{-1}\left(\cos \frac{5\pi}{3}\right)$.

3. Find x, if $\begin{pmatrix} 5 & 3x \\ 2y & z \end{pmatrix} = \begin{pmatrix} 5 \\ 12 \end{pmatrix} \begin{matrix} 4 & 1 \\ 6 \end{matrix}$

4. For what value of a, $\begin{pmatrix} 2a & -1 \\ -8 & 3 \end{pmatrix}$ is a singular matrix?

5. A square matrix A, of order 3, has $|A| = 5$, find $|A \text{ adj. } A|$.

6. Evaluate: $\int 5^x\, dx$

7. Write the value of $\int_{\pi/2}^{\pi/2} \sin^5 x dx$.

8. Find the position vector of the midpoint of the line segment joining the points $A(5\hat{i} + 3\hat{j})$ and $B(3\hat{k} + \hat{i})$.

9. If $\vec{a} = 2\hat{i} - \hat{j} + 3\hat{k}$ and $\vec{b} = (6\hat{i} + \lambda\hat{j} + 9\hat{k})$ and $\vec{a} \parallel \vec{b}$, find the value of λ.

10. Find the distance of the point (a, b, c) from x-axis.

SECTION B

11. Let N be the set of all natural numbers and R be the relation in $N \times N$ defined by (a, b) $R(c, d)$ if $ad = bc$. Show that R is an equivalence relation.

12. Prove that $\tan^{-1}\left(\frac{1}{4}\right) + \tan^{-1}\left(\frac{2}{9}\right) = \frac{1}{2}\cos^{-1}\left(\frac{3}{5}\right)$.

OR

Solve for x : $\sin^{-1}(1-x) - 2\sin^{-1} x = \frac{\pi}{2}$.

13. Using properties determinants, prove that: $\begin{vmatrix} a^2+1 & ab & ac \\ ab & b^2+1 & bc \\ ca & cb & c^2+1 \end{vmatrix} = (1 + a^2 + b^2 + c^2)$.

14. For what values of a and b, the function f defind as:

$$f(x) = \begin{cases} 3ax + b, & \text{if } x < 1 \\ 11, & \text{if } x = 1 \\ 5ax - 2b, & \text{if } x > 1 \end{cases}$$ is continuous at $x = 1$.

15. If $x^y + y^x = a^b$, find $\frac{dy}{dx}$

OR

If $x = a(\cos t + 1\, t \sin t)$ and $y = b(\sin - t\cos t)$, find $\frac{d^2y}{dx^2}$.

16. Find the intervals in which the following function is strictly increasing or strictly decreasing $f(x) = 20 - 9x + 6x^2 - x^3$.

OR

For the curve $y = 4x^4 - 2x^5$, find all points at which the tangent passes through origin.

17. Evaluate: $\int \frac{\sin x + \cos x}{\sqrt{\sin x - \cos x}}\, dx$

OR

Evaluate: $\int e^x \left(\frac{x^2+1}{(x+1)^2}\right) dx$

18. Form th differential equation of the family of circles having radii 3.

19. Solve the following differential equation: $\sqrt{1+x^2+y^2+x^2y^2} + xy\frac{dy}{dx} = 0.$

20. If the sum of two unit vectors is a unit vector, show that the magnitude of their difference is $\sqrt{3}$.

21. Find whether the lines $\vec{r} = (\hat{i} - \hat{j} - \hat{k}) + \lambda(2\hat{i} + \hat{j})$ and $\vec{r} = (2\hat{i} - \hat{j}) + \mu(\hat{i} + \hat{j} - \hat{k})$ intersect or not. If intersecting, find their point intersection.

22. Three balls are drawn one by one without replacement from a bag containing 5 white and 4 green balls. Find the probability distribution of number of green balls drawn.

SECTION C

23. If $A = \begin{pmatrix} 2 & 1 & 3 \\ 4 & -1 & 0 \\ -7 & 2 & 1 \end{pmatrix}$, find A^{-1} and hence solve the following system of equations.

$2x + y + 3z = 3,\ 4x - y = 3$
$-7x + 2y + z = 2$

OR

Using elementary transformations, final the inverse of the matrix: $\begin{pmatrix} 1 & -1 & 2 \\ 0 & 2 & -3 \\ 3 & -2 & 4 \end{pmatrix}$

24. If the length of three sides of a trapezium, other than the base are equal to 10 cm each, then find the area of trapezium when it is maximum.

25. Draw a rough sketch of the region enclosed between the circles $x^2 + y^2 = 4$ and $(x-2)^2 + y^2 = 1$. Using integration, find the area of the enclosed region.

26. Evaluate $\int_1^2 (x^2 + x + 2)\, dx$ as a limit of sums.

OR

Evaluate $\int_0^1 \sin^{-1}\left(x\sqrt{1-x} - \sqrt{x}\sqrt{1-x^2}\right) dx,\ 0 \le x \le 1.$

27. Find the coordinates of the foot of the perpendicular and the perpendicular distance of the point (1, 3, 4) from the plane $2x - y + z + 3 = 0$. Find also, the image of the point in the plane.

28. An aeroplane can carry a maximum of 200 passengers. A profit of Rs. 1000 is made on each executive class ticket and a profit of Rs. 600 is made on each economy class ticket. The airlines reserves at least 20 seats for the executive class. However, at least 4 times as many passengers prefer to travel by economy class, than by the executive class. Determine how many tickets of each type must be sold, in order to maximise profit for the airline. What is the maximum profit? Make an L.P.P. and solve it graphically.

29. A fair die is rolled. If 1 turns up, a ball is picked up at random from bag *A*, 2 or 3 turns up, a ball is picked up at random from bag *B*, otherwise a ball is picked up from bag *C*. Bag *A* contains 3 red and 2 white balls, bag *B* contains 3 red and 4 white balls and bag *C* contains 4 red and 5 white balls. The die is rolled, a bag is picked up and a ball is drawn from it. If the ball drawn is red, what is the probability that bag *B* was picketed up?

SOLVED QUESTION PAPER-3
WITH MARKING SCHEME

SECTION A

(1 mark for correct answer for Qs. 1 to 10)

1. $(8, 3) \in R, (3, 2) \in R$ but $(8, 2) \notin R$. **2.** $\frac{\pi}{3}$ **3.** $x = 4$ **4.** $a = \frac{4}{3}$

5. 125 **6.** $\frac{5^x}{\log 5} + c$ **7.** Zero **8.** $4\hat{i} + \hat{j}$ **9.** $\lambda = -3$ **10.** $\sqrt{b^2 + c^2}$

SECTION B

11. For any $(a, b) \in N \times N$, $ab = ba$

$\Rightarrow$ $(a, b)\ R\ (a, b)$. Thus R is reflexive. 1

Let $(a, b)R\ (c, d)$ for any $a, b, c, d \in N$

$\therefore$ $ad = bc$

$\Rightarrow$ $cb = da \Rightarrow (c, d)R\ (a, b)$

$\therefore$ R is symmetric 1

Let $(a, b)R\ (c, d)$ and $(c, d)R\ (e, f)$ for $a, b, c, d, e, f \in N$

then $ad = bc$ and $ef = de$

$\Rightarrow$ $adef = bcde$ or $af = be \Rightarrow (a, b)R\ (e, f)$

$\therefore$ R is transitive 1½

Since, R is reflexive, symmetric and transitive, hence R is an equivalence relation. ½

12. L.H.S. $= \tan^{-1}\left(\frac{\frac{1}{4}+\frac{2}{9}}{1-\frac{1}{4}\cdot\frac{2}{9}}\right) = \tan^{-1}\left(\frac{17}{34}\right) = \tan^{-1}\left(\frac{1}{2}\right)$ 1½

$= \frac{1}{2}\left(2\tan^{-1}\left(\frac{1}{2}\right)\right) = \frac{1}{2}\cos^{-1}\left[\frac{1-\left(\frac{1}{2}\right)^2}{1+\left(\frac{1}{2}\right)^2}\right]$ 1¼

$= \frac{1}{2}\cos^{-1}\left(\frac{1-\frac{1}{4}}{1+\frac{1}{4}}\right) = \frac{1}{2}\cos^{-1}\frac{3}{5} = \text{RHS}$ 1

OR

$\sin^{-1}(1-x)\ 2\sin^{-1}x = \frac{\pi}{2} \Rightarrow \sin^{-1}(1-x) = \frac{\pi}{2} + 2\sin^{-1}x$ ½

$\Rightarrow$ $(1-x) = \sin\left(\frac{\pi}{2} + 2\sin^{-1}x\right) = \cos(2\sin^{-1}x)$ ½

$\Rightarrow$ $(1-x) = \cos(2\alpha)$ where $\sin^{-1}x = \alpha$ or $x = \sin\alpha$ ½

$\Rightarrow$ $(1-x) = 1 - 2\sin^2\alpha = 1 - 2x^2, \quad \therefore \quad 2x^2 - x = 0$ 1

$\Rightarrow$ $x(2x-1) = 0$ ½

$\therefore$ $x = 0, \frac{1}{2}$

Since $x=\frac{1}{2}$ does not satisfy the given equation $\therefore \quad x=0$

13. LHS $=\frac{1}{abc}\begin{vmatrix} a(a^2+1) & a^2b & a^2c \\ ab^2 & b(b^2+1) & b^2c \\ ac^2 & bc^2 & c(c^2+1)\end{vmatrix}=\frac{abc}{abc}\begin{vmatrix} a^2+1 & a^2 & a^2 \\ b^2 & b^2+1 & b^2 \\ c^2 & c^2 & c^2+1\end{vmatrix}$ 1

$R_1 \to R_1+R_2+R_3=\begin{vmatrix} 1+a^2+b^2+c^2 & 1+a^2+b^2+c^2 & 1+a^2+b^2+c^2 \\ b^2 & b^2+1 & b^2 \\ c^2 & c^2 & c^2+1\end{vmatrix}$ 1

$=(1+a^2+b^2+c^2)\begin{vmatrix} 1 & 1 & 1 \\ b^2 & b^2+1 & b^2 \\ c^2 & c^2 & c^2+1\end{vmatrix}=(1+a^2+b^2+c^2)\begin{vmatrix} 1 & 0 & 0 \\ b^2 & 1 & 0 \\ c^2 & 0 & 1\end{vmatrix}$ 1

$=(1+a^2+b^2+c^2).1=(1+a^2+b^2+c^2)$ 1

14. $\lim\limits_{x\to 1} - f(x)=3a+b$, RHL $=\lim\limits_{x\to 1} + f(x)=5a-2a$, $f(1)=11$ 2

$\therefore \quad 3a+b=11, \quad 5a-2b=11$ 1

Solving to get $a=3, b=2$ 1

15. Put $x^y=u$ and $y^x=v \quad \therefore \quad u+v=a^b \quad \Rightarrow \quad \frac{du}{dx}+\frac{dv}{dx}=0$ ½

$\log u=y\log x \quad \Rightarrow \quad \frac{1}{u}\frac{du}{dx}=\frac{y}{x}=\log x.\frac{dy}{dx} \quad \therefore \quad \frac{du}{dx}=y.x^{y-1}+x^y.\log x.\frac{dy}{dx}$ 1

$\log v=x\log y \quad \Rightarrow \quad \frac{1}{v}.\frac{dv}{dx}=\frac{x}{y}\frac{dy}{dx}+\log y \quad \therefore \quad \frac{dv}{dx}=xy^{x-1}.\frac{dy}{dx}+y^2.\log y$ 1

$\therefore \quad y.x^{y-1}+x^y\log x\frac{dy}{dx}+xy^{x-1}+y^x\log y=0$ 1

OR

$\frac{dx}{dt}=a\,(-\sin t+t\cos t+\sin t)=$ at $\cos t$ 1

$\frac{dy}{dt}=b\,(\cos t+t\sin t-\cos t)=$ at $\cos t$ 1

$\therefore \quad \frac{dy}{dx}=\frac{b}{a}.\tan t \Rightarrow \frac{d^2y}{dx^2}=\frac{b}{a}\sec^2 t.\frac{dt}{dx}$ 1

$\therefore \quad \frac{d^2y}{dx^2}=\frac{b}{a}\sec^2 t.\frac{1}{\text{atcos}1}=\frac{b\sec^2 t}{a^2t}$ 1

16. $f^1(x)=0 \quad \Rightarrow \quad -9+12x-3x^2=0 \quad \Rightarrow \quad -(3)(x-1)(x-3)=0$ 1

$\therefore \quad x=1, x=3$

$\therefore$ the intervals are $(-\infty, 1), (1, 3), (3, \infty)$ 1

Getting $f(x)$ to be strickly decreasing in $(-\infty, 1)\cup(3, \infty)$ 1

and strickly increasing in $(1, 3)$ 1

OR

Let (x_1, y_1) be a point on the given curve, the tangent at which passs through origin.

$\therefore$ Slope of tangent $= \dfrac{y_1}{x_1}$ ...(*i*) ½

also, $\dfrac{dy}{dx} = 12x^2 - 10x^4 \Rightarrow$ slope of tangent $= 12{x_1}^2 - 10{x_1}^4$ ...(*ii*) ½

$\Rightarrow \dfrac{y_1}{x_1} = 12x_1^2 - 10x_1^4$ or $y_1 = 12x_1^3 - 10x_1^4 \Rightarrow 4x_1^3 - 2x_1^5 = 12x_1^3 - 10x_1^5$ 1

solving to get $x_1 = 0$ or $1 - {x_1}^2 = 0$ *i.e.* $x_1 = \pm 1$ 1

Hence the required points are (0, 0), (1, 2) and (–1, –2) 1

17. Putting $(\sin x - \cos x) = t$ to get $(\cos x + \sin x)\, dx = dt$ 1

and $\sin^2 x + \cos^2 x - 2 \sin x \cos x = t^2$ or $\sin x \cos x = \dfrac{1}{2}(1 - t^2)$ ½

$\therefore$ Given integral $= \sqrt{2} \displaystyle\int \frac{dt}{\sqrt{1-t^2}} = \sqrt{2} \,.\, \sin^{-1} t + c$ 1½

$= \sqrt{2} \sin^{-1} (\sin x - \cos x) + c$ 1

OR

$\displaystyle\int e^x . \frac{x^2+1}{(x+1)^2} dx = \int e^x . \frac{\left[(x^2+1)^2 - 2x\right]}{(x+1)^2} dx$ 1

$\displaystyle = \int e^x\, dx - 2 \int e^x . \frac{(x+1-1)}{(x+1)^2} dx$ 1

$\displaystyle = e^x - 2 \int \left[\frac{1}{x+1} - \frac{1}{(x+1)^2}\right] e^x\, dx$ 1

$\displaystyle = e^x - 2 . \frac{e^x}{x+1} + c \quad \left[\text{using } \int e^x \left(f(x) + f^1(x)\right) dx = e^x f(x) + c\right]$ 1

18. The equation of the family of circles is $(x - a)^2 + (y - b)^2 = 0$ ...(*i*) ½

$\Rightarrow 2(x - a) + 2(y - b)\dfrac{dy}{dx} = 0$ or $(x - a) = -(y - b)\dfrac{dy}{dx}$ ...(*ii*) 1

$\Rightarrow 1 + (y - b)\dfrac{d^2y}{dx^2} + \left(\dfrac{dy}{dx}\right)^2 = 0 \Rightarrow (y - b) = -\dfrac{\left[1 + \left(\dfrac{dy}{dx}\right)^2\right]}{\dfrac{d^2y}{dx^2}}$ ...(*ii*) 1

from (*ii*), $(x - a) = + \dfrac{\left[1 + \left(\dfrac{dy}{dx}\right)^2\right]}{\dfrac{d^2y}{dx^2}} \cdot \dfrac{dy}{dx}$ ½

putting in (*i*) to get $\left[\dfrac{1 + \left(\dfrac{dy}{dx}\right)^2}{\dfrac{d^2y}{dx}}\right]^2 \left(\dfrac{dy}{dx}\right)^2 + \left[\dfrac{1 + \left(\dfrac{dy}{dx}\right)^2}{\dfrac{d^2y}{dx^2}}\right]^2 = 9$ ½ or $\left[\dfrac{1+\left(\dfrac{dy}{dx}\right)^2}{\dfrac{d^2y}{dx}}\right]^2\left[\left(\dfrac{dy}{dx}\right)^2+1\right]=9 \Rightarrow \left[1+\left(\dfrac{dy}{dx}\right)^2\right]^2=9\left(\dfrac{d^2y}{dx}\right)^2$ ½

19. Given differential equation can be written as

$\sqrt{(1+x^2)\,(1+y^2)}\ +xy\dfrac{dy}{dx}=0$ ½

$\Rightarrow \quad \dfrac{\sqrt{1+x^2}}{x}dx+\dfrac{y}{\sqrt{1+y^2}}dy=0$ ½

$\therefore \quad \displaystyle\int\frac{y}{\sqrt{1+y^2}}dy=-\int\frac{\sqrt{1+x^2}}{x^2}\,xdx$ ½

Putting $1+y^2=u^2$ and $1+x^2=v^2$ to get $ydy=udu$ and $xdx=vdv$ ½

$\therefore \quad \displaystyle\int\frac{udu}{u}=-\int\frac{v.vdv}{v^2-1}=-\int\frac{v^2-1+1}{v^2-1}dv=\int\left(1+\frac{1}{v^2+1}\right)dv$ 1

$u=-v-\dfrac{1}{2}\log\left|\dfrac{v-1}{v+1}\right|+c \ or\ \sqrt{1+y^2}=-\sqrt{1+x^2}-\dfrac{1}{2}\log\left|\dfrac{\sqrt{1+x^2}-1}{\sqrt{1+x^2}+1}\right|+c$ 1

20. Let $\hat{a}$, $\hat{b}$ and $\hat{c}$ be unit vector such that $\hat{a}+\hat{b}=\hat{c}$ 1

$\therefore \quad |\hat{a}+\hat{b}|=1 \quad \Rightarrow \quad 1=|\hat{a}+\hat{b}|^2=\hat{a}^2+\hat{b}^2+2\hat{a}+b=2+2\hat{a}\,.\,b$ 1

$\Rightarrow \quad (2\hat{a}\,.\,\hat{b})=1-2=-1$ ...(*i*) ½

Now $\quad |\hat{a}-\hat{b}|^2=\hat{a}^2+\hat{b}^2-2\hat{a}\,.\,\hat{b}=1+1-(-1)=3$ 1½

$\Rightarrow \quad |\hat{a}-\hat{b}|=\sqrt{3}$ ½

21. Given lines are $\vec{r}=(1+2\lambda)\,\hat{i}+(-1+\lambda)\,\hat{j}-\hat{k}$ and

$\vec{r}=(2+\mu)\,\hat{i}+(-1+\mu)\,\hat{j}-\mu\hat{k}$ 1

Solving (*ii*) and (*iii*) to get $\lambda=1$, $\mu=1$, which satisfy (*i*) hence the line are intersecting and point intersection is $(3, 0, -1)$ 1

22. Let X denotes the random variable, 'number of green balls,

X:	0	1	2	3	1
$P(X)$:	$\dfrac{5c_3}{9c_3}$	$\dfrac{5c_2\,.4c_1}{9c_3}$	$\dfrac{5c_1\,.4c_1}{9c_3}$	$\dfrac{4c_3}{9c_3}$	1
	$=\dfrac{5}{42}$	$\dfrac{10}{21}$	$\dfrac{5}{14}$	$\dfrac{1}{21}$	2

SECTION C

23. $|A|=2(-1)-1(4)+3(1)=-3\neq 0 \ A^{-1}=\dfrac{1}{|A|}$ adj A 1

Th cofactors are $\quad A_{11}=-1,\ A_{12}=-4,\ A_{13}=1$

$A_{21}=5,\ A_{22}=23,\ A_{23}=-11$ 2

$A_{31}=3,\ A_{32}=12,\ A_{33}=-6$

$$\therefore \qquad A^{-1} = -\frac{1}{3}\begin{pmatrix} -1 & 5 & 3 \\ -4 & 23 & 12 \\ 1 & -11 & -6 \end{pmatrix}$$ ½

Given equations can be written as

$$\begin{pmatrix} 2 & 1 & 3 \\ 4 & -1 & 0 \\ -7 & 2 & 1 \end{pmatrix}\begin{pmatrix} x \\ y \\ z \end{pmatrix} = \begin{pmatrix} 3 \\ 3 \\ 2 \end{pmatrix} \text{ or } A \,.\, X = B$$ 1

$$\therefore \qquad X = A^{-1} \,.\, B$$

$$\therefore \qquad \begin{pmatrix} x \\ y \\ z \end{pmatrix} = -\frac{1}{3}\begin{pmatrix} -1 & 5 & 3 \\ -4 & 23 & 12 \\ 1 & -11 & -6 \end{pmatrix}\begin{pmatrix} 3 \\ 3 \\ 2 \end{pmatrix} = \begin{pmatrix} -6 \\ -27 \\ 14 \end{pmatrix}$$

$$\therefore \qquad x = -6, \quad y = -27, \quad z = 14$$ ½

OR

$$\text{Let } A = \begin{pmatrix} 1 & -1 & 2 \\ 0 & 2 & -3 \\ 3 & -2 & 4 \end{pmatrix} \text{ then } \begin{pmatrix} 1 & -1 & 2 \\ 0 & 2 & -3 \\ 3 & -2 & 4 \end{pmatrix} = \begin{pmatrix} 1 & 0 & 0 \\ 0 & 1 & 0 \\ 0 & 0 & 1 \end{pmatrix} A$$ ½

$$R_3 \to R_3 - 3R_1 \;\Rightarrow\; \begin{pmatrix} 1 & -1 & 2 \\ 0 & 2 & -3 \\ 0 & +1 & -2 \end{pmatrix} = \begin{pmatrix} 1 & 0 & 0 \\ 0 & 1 & 0 \\ -3 & 0 & 1 \end{pmatrix} A$$ 1

$$R_3 \leftrightarrow R_3 \;\Rightarrow\; \begin{pmatrix} 1 & -1 & 2 \\ 0 & 1 & -2 \\ 0 & 2 & -3 \end{pmatrix} = \begin{pmatrix} 1 & 0 & 0 \\ -3 & 0 & 1 \\ 0 & 1 & 0 \end{pmatrix} A$$ 1

$$R_3 \to R_3 - 2R_2 \;\Rightarrow\; \begin{pmatrix} 1 & -1 & 2 \\ 0 & 1 & -2 \\ 0 & 0 & 1 \end{pmatrix} = \begin{pmatrix} 1 & 0 & 0 \\ -3 & 0 & 1 \\ 6 & 1 & -2 \end{pmatrix} A$$ 1

$$R_1 \to R_1 + R_2 \;\Rightarrow\; \begin{pmatrix} 1 & 0 & 0 \\ 0 & 1 & -2 \\ 0 & 0 & 1 \end{pmatrix} = \begin{pmatrix} -2 & 0 & 1 \\ -3 & 0 & 1 \\ 6 & 1 & -2 \end{pmatrix} A$$ 1

$$R_2 \to R_2 + 2R_3 \;\Rightarrow\; \begin{pmatrix} 1 & 0 & 0 \\ 0 & 1 & 0 \\ 0 & 0 & 1 \end{pmatrix} = \begin{pmatrix} -2 & 0 & 1 \\ 9 & 2 & -3 \\ 6 & 1 & -2 \end{pmatrix} A$$ 1

$$\text{Hence} \qquad A^{-1} = \begin{pmatrix} -2 & 0 & 1 \\ 9 & 2 & -3 \\ 6 & 1 & -2 \end{pmatrix}$$ ½

24. $AD = DC = BC = 10$ cm.

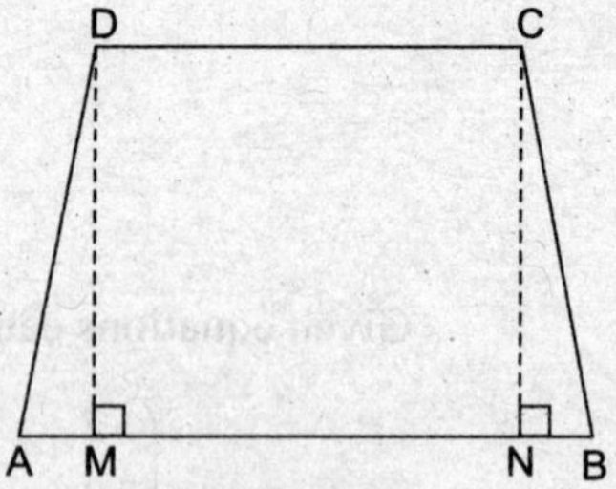

$\Delta ADM \cong \Delta BCN \quad \therefore \quad AM = BN = x(\text{say})$

$\therefore \qquad DM = \sqrt{10^2 - x^2}$ 1

Area $(A) = \frac{1}{2}\,(10 + 10 + 2x)$

$\sqrt{100 - x^2} = \frac{1}{2}\,(10 + x)\sqrt{100 - x^2}$ 1

Let $\qquad S = A^2 = (10 + x)^2\,(100 - x^2)$

$\frac{ds}{dx} = 0 \;\Rightarrow\; (10 + x)^2\,(-2x) + (100 - x^2)\,2(10 + x) = 0$ ½

$(10 + x)^2\,(-2x + 20 - 2x) = 0 \;\Rightarrow\; x = 5$ 1

$\frac{d^2s}{dx^2} = (10 + x)^2\,(-4) + (20 - 4x)\;2(10 + x) < 0$ at $x = 5$ 1

$\therefore$ for Maximum area, $x = 5$ ½

Maximum area $= 15\sqrt{75} = 75\sqrt{3}$ cm^2 1

25. Correct figure

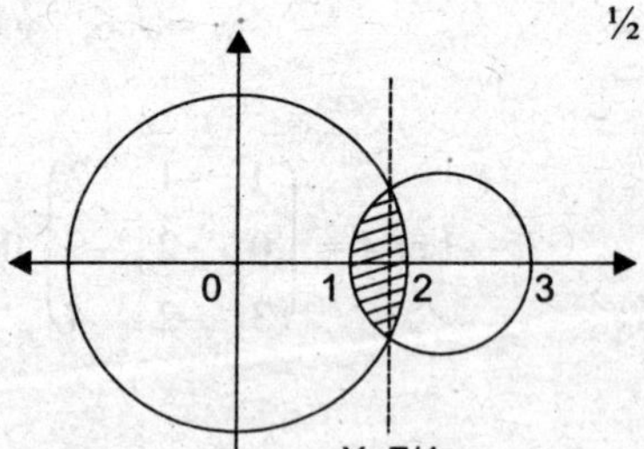

Solving $x^2 + y^2 = 4$ and $(x - 2)^2 + y^2 = 1$

we get $x = \frac{7}{4}$ 1

$\therefore \qquad$ Required area $= 2\left[\int_{7/4}^{2} \int \sqrt{4 - x^2}\,dx + \int_{1}^{7/4} \sqrt{1 - (x-2)^2}\,dx\right]$ 1

$= 2\left[\left[\frac{x}{2}\sqrt{4 - x^2} + 2\sin^{-1}\frac{x}{2}\right]_{\frac{7}{4}}^{2} + \left[\frac{x-2}{2}\sqrt{1 - (x-2)^2} + \frac{1}{2}\sin^{-1}(x-2)\right]_{1}^{\frac{7}{4}}\right]$ 1

$= 2\left[\pi - \frac{7}{8}\frac{\sqrt{15}}{4} - 2\sin^{-1}\frac{7}{8} + \left(-\frac{1}{8}.\frac{\sqrt{15}}{4} + \frac{1}{2}\sin^{-1}\left(-\frac{1}{4}\right) + \frac{1}{2}\cdot\frac{\pi}{2}\right)\right]$ 1

$= \frac{5\pi}{2} - \frac{\sqrt{15}}{2} - \sin^{-1} - 4\sin^{-1}\left(\frac{7}{8}\right)$ sq. u 1

26. Here $\qquad f(x) = (x^2 + x + 2),\; h = \frac{b - a}{n} = \frac{1}{n}$ ½

$\int_{1}^{2} f(x)\,dx = \lim_{n\to\infty} \frac{1}{n}.\,[f(1) + f(1+h) + f(1+2h) + \ldots\ldots\ldots + 1[1 + (n-1)h]]$ 1

$= \lim_{n\to\infty} \frac{1}{n}\,.\,[4 + (4 + 3h + h^2) + (4 + 6h + 4h^2)$

$+ \ldots\ldots\ldots + (4 + (n - 1)\,3h + (n - 1)^2\,h^2]$ 2

$= \lim_{n\to\infty} \frac{1}{n}\left[4n + \frac{3}{4}\cdot\frac{1}{n^2}\,\frac{n(n-1)(2n-1)}{6}\right]$ ½

$$= \lim_{n\to\infty}\left[4+\frac{3}{2}\left(1-\frac{1}{n}\right)+\frac{1}{6}\left(1-\frac{1}{n}\right)\left(2-\frac{1}{n}\right)\right]$$ ½

$$= 4+\frac{3}{2}+\frac{1}{3} = \frac{24+9+2}{6} = \frac{35}{6}$$ ½

OR

put $x = \sin\alpha$ and $\sqrt{x} = \sin\beta$ ½

$\therefore$ $$\sin^{-1}\left[x\sqrt{1-x}-\sqrt{x}\sqrt{1-x^2} = \sin^{-1}\right][\sin\alpha\cos\beta-\cos\alpha\sin\beta]$$

$$= \sin^{-1}[\sin(\alpha-\beta)] = \alpha-\beta = \sin^{-1}x-\sin^{-1}\sqrt{x}$$ ½

$\therefore$ Given integral $$= \int_0^1(\sin^{-1}x-\sin^{-1}\sqrt{x})dx = \int_0^1\sin^{-1}x\,dx-\int_0^1\sin^{-1}\sqrt{x}\,dx$$ 1

$$= \left[x\cdot\sin^{-1}x\right]_0^1-\frac{1}{2}\int_0^1\frac{2x}{\sqrt{1-x^2}}dx-\left[x.\sin^{-1}\sqrt{x}\right]_0^1+\int_0^1\frac{1}{\sqrt{1-x}}\,\frac{1}{2\sqrt{x}}.\,x\,dx$$ 1

$$= \frac{\pi}{2}+\left[\sqrt{1-x^2}\right]_0^1-\frac{\pi}{2}+\frac{1}{2}\int_0^1\frac{\sqrt{x}}{\sqrt{1-x}}dx$$ 1

$$= -1+\frac{1}{2}\int_1^0\frac{-\sqrt{1-t^2}.2t\,dt}{t}\quad\{1-x=t^2,\ dx=-2t\,dt\}$$ 1

$$= -1+\int_1^0\sqrt{1-t^2}\,dt = 1+\left[\frac{t}{2}\sqrt{1-t^2}+\frac{1}{2}\sin^{-1}t\right]_0^1 = \left(-1+\frac{\pi}{4}\right)$$ 1

27. Let Q be the foot of perpendicular from P to the plane and $P'(x, y, z)$ be the image of P in the plane.

$\therefore$ The equations of line through P and Q is

$$\frac{x-1}{2} = \frac{y-3}{-1} = \frac{z-4}{1}$$ 1

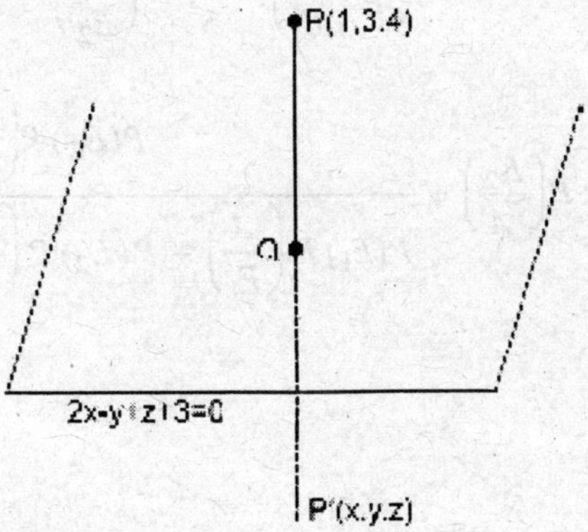

The coordinates of Q (for some value of λ) are

$(2\lambda+1, -\lambda+3, \lambda+4)$ ½

Since Q lies on the plane,

$\therefore$ $2(2\lambda+1)-1(\lambda+3)+(\lambda+4)+3 = 0$ 1

Solving to get $\lambda = -1$ ½

$\therefore$ coordinates of foot of perpendicular (Q) are $(-1, 4, 3)$ ½

Perpendicular distance (PQ) $= \sqrt{(2)^2+(-1)^2+(1)^2} = \sqrt{6}$ units ½

Since Q is mid point of PP'

$\therefore \quad \frac{x+1}{2} = -1, \frac{y+3}{2} = 4, \frac{z+4}{2} = 3 \Rightarrow x = -3, y = 5, z = 2$ 1

$\therefore$ Image of P is $(-3, 5, 2)$ 1

28. Let, number of excutive class tickets to be sold, be x and that of economy class b y.

$\therefore$ LPP becomes : Maximise Profit $(P) = 1000x + 600y$ 1

Subject to: $x \geq 0, \; y \geq 0$

$x + y \leq 200$ 1½

$y \geq 4x$ or $4x - y \leq 0$

$x \geq 20$

For correct graph

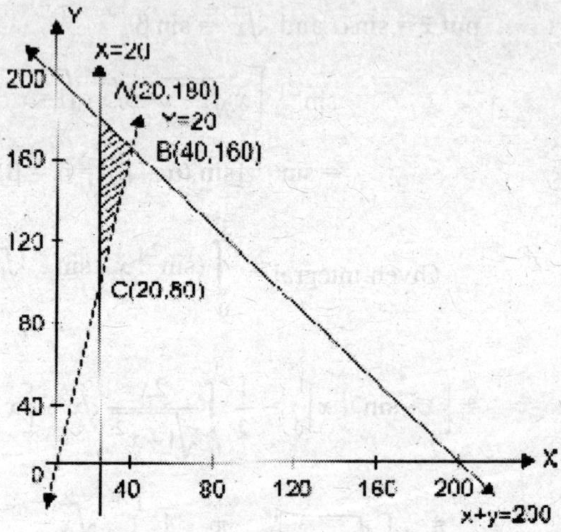

Getting vertices of feasible region as $A(20, 180)$, $B(40, 160)$, $C(20, 80)$ ½

Profit at A = Rs. 128000

Profit at B = Rs. 136000

Profit at C = Rs. 68000

$\therefore$ Max profit = Rs. 136000 for 40 executive and 160 economy tickets.

29. Let the events be defined as:

E_1 : Bag A is selected

E_2 : Bag B is selected

E_3 : Bag C is selected

A : A red ball is selected

$\therefore \quad P(E_1) = \frac{1}{2}, P(E_2) = \frac{2}{6} = \frac{1}{3}$ and $P(E_3) = \frac{3}{6} = \frac{1}{2}$ 1

$P\left(\frac{A}{E_1}\right) = \frac{3}{5}, P\left(\frac{A}{E_2}\right) = \frac{3}{7}$ and $P\left(\frac{A}{E_3}\right) = \frac{4}{9}$ 1

$$P\left(\frac{E_2}{A}\right) = \frac{P(E_2)P\left(\frac{P}{E_2}\right)}{P(E_1)P\left(\frac{A}{E_1}\right) + P(E_2)P\left(\frac{A}{E_2}\right) + P(E_2)P\left(\frac{A}{E_2}\right)} = \frac{\frac{1}{3}\cdot\frac{3}{7}}{\frac{1}{6}\cdot\frac{3}{5} + \frac{1}{3}\cdot\frac{3}{7} + \frac{1}{2}\cdot\frac{4}{9}}$$ 2

❑❑❑

QUESTION PAPER-4

CLASS-XII

Time allowed : 3 hours *Maximum Marks : 100*

SECTION A

1. Write the number of all one-one functions from the set $A = \{a, b, c\}$ to itself.

2. Find x if $\tan^{-1} 4 + \cot^{-1} x = \frac{\pi}{2}$.

3. What is the value of $|3\ I_3|$, where I_3 is the identity matrix of order 3?

4. For what value of k, the matrix $\begin{bmatrix} 2-k & 3 \\ -5 & 1 \end{bmatrix}$ is not invertible?

5. If A is a matrix of order 2×3 and B is a matrix of order 3×5, what is the order of matrix $(AB)'$ or T?

6. Write a value of $\int \frac{dx}{\sqrt{4-x^2}}$

7. Find $f(x)$ satisfying the following: $\int e^x (\sec^2 x + \tan x)\, dx = e^x f(x) + c$.

8. In a triangle ABC, the sides AB and BC are represented by vectors $2\hat{i} - \hat{j} + 2\hat{k}$; $\hat{i} + 3\hat{j} + 5\hat{k}$ respectively. Find the vector representing CA.

9. Find the value λ for which the vector $\vec{a} = 3\hat{i} + \hat{j} - 2\hat{k}$ and $\vec{b} = \hat{i} + \lambda\hat{j} - 3\hat{k}$ are perpendicular to each other.

10. Find the value of λ such that the line $\frac{x-2}{9} = \frac{y-1}{\lambda} = \frac{z+3}{-6}$ is perpendicular to the plane $3x - y - 2x = 7$.

SECTION B

11. Show that the function $f : R \to R$ defined by $f(x) = 2x^3 - 7$, for $x \in R$ is bijective.

OR

Let $f, g : R \to R$ be defined as $f(x) = |x|$ and $g(x) = [x]$ where $[x]$ denotes the greatest integer less than or equal to x. Find $fog\left(\frac{5}{2}\right)$ and $gof\left(-\sqrt{2}\right)$.

12. Prove that $\tan^{-1} 1 + \tan^{-1} 2 + \tan^{-1} 3 = \pi$.

13. If $A = \begin{bmatrix} 3 & -5 \\ -4 & 2 \end{bmatrix}$ show that $A^2 - 5A - 14I = 0$. Hence find A^{-1}.

14. Show that $f(x) = |x - 3|,\ \forall\, x \in R$, is continuous but not differentiable at $x = 3$.

OR

If $\tan\left(\frac{x^2 - y^2}{x^2 + y^2}\right) = a$, then prove that $\frac{dy}{dx} = \frac{y}{x}$.

15. Verify Rolle's Theorem for the function f, given by $f(x) = e^x (\sin x - \cos x)$ on $\left[\frac{\pi}{4}, \frac{5\pi}{4}\right]$.

16. Using differentials, find the approximate value of $\sqrt{25.2}$.

OR

Two equal sides of an isocles triangle with fixed base 'a' are decreasing at the rat of 9 cm/ scond. How fast is the area of the triangle decreasing when the two sides are equal 'a'.

17. Evaluate $\int_{-1}^{\frac{1}{2}} [x\cos(\pi x)]\, dx$.

18. Solve the following differential equation: $ye^{x/y}\, dx = (xe^{x/y} + y)dy$.

19. Solve the following differential equation:

$$(1 + y + x^2y)\, dx + (x + x^3)dx = 0, \text{ where } y = 0 \text{ when } x = 1.$$

20. If $\vec{a}$, $\vec{b}$ and $\vec{c}$ are three unit vectors such that $\vec{a} \cdot \vec{b} = \vec{a} \cdot \vec{c} = 0$ and angle between $\vec{b}$ and $\vec{c}$ is $\frac{\pi}{6}$, prove that $\vec{a} = \pm 2\, (\vec{b} \times \vec{c})$.

21. Show that the four points (0, –1, –1), (4, 5, 1), (3, 9, 4) and (–4, 4, 4) are coplanar. Also find the equation of the plane containing them.

22. A coin is biased so that the head is 3 times as likely to occur as tail. If the coin is tossed three times, find the probability distribution of number of tails.

OR

How many times must a man loss a fair coin, so that the probability of having at least one bead is more than 80%?

SECTION C

23. Using properties of determinants, show that

$$\Delta = \begin{vmatrix} (b+c)^2 & ab & ca \\ ab & (a+b)^2 & bc \\ ac & be & (a+b)^2 \end{vmatrix} = 2abe\,(a + b + c)^3.$$

24. The sum of the perimeter of a circle and a square is k, where k is some constant. Prove that the sum of their areas is least when the side of square is double the radius of the circle.

OR

A helicopter is flying along the curve $y = x^2 + 2$. A solider is placed at the point (3, 2). Find the nearest distance between the soldier

25. Evaluate: $\int \frac{1}{\sin x(5 - 4\cos x)} dx$

OR

Evaluate: $\int \sqrt{\frac{1-\sqrt{x}}{1+\sqrt{x}}}\, dx$

26. Using integration, find the area of the region $\left\{(x, y) : |x-1| \le y \le \sqrt{5-x^2}\right\}$

27. Show that the lines $\frac{x+3}{-3} = \frac{y-1}{1} = \frac{z-5}{5}$ and $\frac{x+1}{-1} = \frac{y-2}{2} = \frac{z-5}{5}$ are coplanar. Also find the equation of the plane.

28. From a pack of 52 cards, a card is lost. From the remaining 51 cards, two cards are drawn at random (without replacement) and are found to be both diamonds. What is the probability that the lost card was a card of heart?

29. A diet for a sick person must contain at leas 4000 units of vitamins, 50 units of minerals and 1400 calories. Two foods X and Y are available at a cost of Rs. 4 and Rs. 3 per unit respectively. One unit of food X contains 200 units of vitamins, 1 unit of minerals and 40 calories, whereas 1 unit of food Y contains 100 units of vitamins, 2 units of minerals and 40 calories. Find what combination of foods X and Y should be used to have least cost, satisfying the requirements. Make it an LPP and solve it graphically.

SOLVED QUESTION PAPER-4
WITH MARKING SCHEME

SECTION A

(1 mark for correct answer for Qs. 1 to 10)

1. 6 **2.** 4 **3.** 27 **4.** 17 **5.** 5×2

6. $\sin^{-1}\left(\frac{x}{2}\right)$ **7.** $\tan x$ **8.** $-(3\hat{i}+2\hat{j}+7\hat{k})$ **9.** $\lambda = -9$ **10.** $\lambda = -3$

SECTION B

11. Let x, y be any two elements of R (domain)

then $f(x) = f(x) \Rightarrow 2x^3 - 7 = 2y^3 - 7$

$\Rightarrow \quad x^3 = y^3 \quad \Rightarrow \quad x = y$ 1

so, f is an injective function

Let y be any element of R (co-domain)

$\therefore \quad f(x) = y \quad \Rightarrow \quad 2x^3 - 7 = y$

$\Rightarrow \quad x^3 = \frac{y+7}{2} \Rightarrow x = \left(\frac{y+7}{2}\right)^{\frac{1}{3}}$

Now for all $y \in R$ (co-domain), there exists $x = \left(\frac{y+7}{2}\right)^{\frac{1}{3}} \in R$ (domain 1

such that $f(x) = f\left\{\left(\frac{y+7}{2}\right)^{1/3}\right\} = 2\left\{\left(\frac{y+7}{2}\right)^{1/3}\right\}^3 - 7 = 2.\frac{y+7}{2} - 7 = y$ 1

so, f is surjective

Hence, f is a bijective function

OR

$fog\left(\frac{5}{2}\right) = f\left[g\left(\frac{5}{2}\right)\right] = f(2) = |2| = 2$ 2

$gof\left(-\sqrt{2}\right) = g\left[f\left(-\sqrt{2}\right)\right] = g\left[\left|-\sqrt{2}\right|\right] = g\left[\sqrt{2}\right] = 1$ 2

12. L.H.S. $= \tan^{-1} 1 + \tan^{-2} 2 + \tan^{-1} 3$ ½

$= \frac{\pi}{4} + \frac{\pi}{2} - \cot^{-1} + \frac{\pi}{2} - \cot^{-1} 3$ ½

$= \frac{5\pi}{4} - \tan^{-1}\left(\frac{1}{2}\right) - \tan^{-1}\left(\frac{1}{3}\right)$ ½

$= \frac{5\pi}{4} - \left(\tan^{-1}\frac{1}{2} + \tan^{-1}\frac{1}{3}\right)$ ½

$= \frac{5\pi}{4} - \tan^{-1}\left(\frac{\frac{1}{2}+\frac{1}{3}}{1-\frac{1}{2}\cdot\frac{1}{3}}\right)$ 1

$= \frac{5\pi}{4} - \frac{\pi}{4}$ ½

$= \pi = $ RHS.

13. $A = \begin{bmatrix} 3 & -5 \\ -4 & 2 \end{bmatrix} \Rightarrow A^2 = \begin{bmatrix} 3 & -5 \\ -4 & 2 \end{bmatrix}\begin{bmatrix} 3 & -5 \\ -4 & 2 \end{bmatrix} = \begin{bmatrix} 29 & -25 \\ -20 & 24 \end{bmatrix}$ ½

$A^2 - 5A - 141 = \begin{bmatrix} 29 & -25 \\ -20 & 24 \end{bmatrix} - 5\begin{bmatrix} 3 & -5 \\ -4 & 2 \end{bmatrix} - 14\begin{bmatrix} 1 & 0 \\ 0 & 1 \end{bmatrix}$ ½

$= \begin{bmatrix} 29 & -25 \\ -20 & 24 \end{bmatrix} + \begin{bmatrix} -15 & 25 \\ 20 & -10 \end{bmatrix} + \begin{bmatrix} -14 & 0 \\ 0 & -14 \end{bmatrix}$

$\begin{bmatrix} 29-15-14 & -25+25-0 \\ -20+20+0 & 24-10-14 \end{bmatrix} = \begin{bmatrix} 0 & 0 \\ 0 & 0 \end{bmatrix} = 0$ 1

Premultiplying $A^2 - 5A - 14I = 0$ by A^{-1}, we get

$A^{-1}, A^2 - 5A^{-1} A - 14A^{-1} I = 0$

or, $A - 15 - 14A^{-1} = 0$ ½

or $A^{-1} = \frac{1}{14}(A - 5I) = \frac{1}{14}\left\{\begin{bmatrix} 3 & -5 \\ -4 & 2 \end{bmatrix} + \begin{bmatrix} -5 & 0 \\ 0 & -5 \end{bmatrix}\right\} = \frac{1}{14}\begin{bmatrix} -2 & -5 \\ -4 & -3 \end{bmatrix}$ 1

14. $f(x) = |(x-3)| \Rightarrow f(x) = \begin{cases} x-3 & \text{if } x \geq 3 \\ -(x-3) & \text{if } x < 3 \end{cases}$ ½

$\lim\limits_{x \to 3'} f(x) = \lim\limits_{x \to 3'} -(x-3) = 0$ ½

$\lim\limits_{x \to 3^+} f(x) = \lim\limits_{x \to 3^+} (x-3) = 0$ ½

and $f(3) = 3 - 3 = 0$

$\therefore \lim\limits_{x \to 3^-} f(x) = \lim\limits_{x \to 3^-} f(3) = f(3)$

$\therefore$ $f(x)$ is continuous at $x = 3$ ½

For differentiability

$Lf(3) = \lim\limits_{x \to 3^-} \frac{f(x) - f(3)}{x-3} = \lim\limits_{x \to 3^-} \frac{-(x-3) - 0}{x-3} = -1$ ½

$Rf(3) = \lim\limits_{x \to 3^+} \frac{f(x) - f(3)}{x-3} = \lim\limits_{x \to 3^+} \frac{(x-3) - 0}{x-3} = 1$ ½

$\therefore Lf'(3) \neq Rf'(3)$

so, $f(x)$ is not differentiable at $x = 3$ 1

OR

$\tan\left(\frac{x^2 - y^2}{x^2 + y^2}\right) = a$

$\Rightarrow \frac{x^2 - y^2}{x^2 + y^2} = \tan^{-1} a$ ...(1) ½

Differentiating (1) w.r.t. x, we get

$$\frac{(x^2 + y^2)\left(2x - 2y\frac{dy}{dx}\right) - (x^2 - y^2)\left(2x + 2y\frac{dy}{dx}\right)}{(x^2 + y^2)} = 0$$

or, $2x(x^2+y^2)-2y(x^2+y^2)\dfrac{dy}{dx} - 2x(x^2-y^2)-2y(x^2-y^2)\dfrac{dy}{dx}=0$ 2

or, $\dfrac{dy}{dx}\left[-2x^2y-\cancel{2y^3}-2x^2y+\cancel{2y^3}\right]=\cancel{2x^3}-2xy^2+\cancel{2x^3}-2xy^2$ 1

$\Rightarrow \dfrac{dy}{dx}[-4x^2y]=-4xy^2$

$\Rightarrow \dfrac{dy}{dx}=\dfrac{-4xy^2}{-4x^2y}=\dfrac{y}{x}$ ½

15. We know that e^x, $\sin x$ and $\cos x$ functions are continuous and differentiable everywhere. Product, sum and difference of two continuous functions is again a continuous function, so

f is also continuous in $\left[\dfrac{\pi}{4},\dfrac{5\pi}{4}\right]$ 1

Now, $f\left(\dfrac{\pi}{4}\right)=e^{\frac{\pi}{4}}\left(\sin\dfrac{\pi}{4}-\cos\dfrac{\pi}{4}\right)=0$

$f\left(\dfrac{5\pi}{4}\right)=e^{\frac{5\pi}{4}}\left(\sin\dfrac{5\pi}{4}-\cos\dfrac{5\pi}{4}\right)=0$

$\Rightarrow f\left(\dfrac{\pi}{4}\right)=f\left(\dfrac{5\pi}{4}\right)$ 1

$\therefore$ Rolle's theorem is applicable

$f'(x)=e^x(\sin x-\cos x)+e^x(\cos x+\sin x)=2e^x\sin x$

$\therefore$ $f'(x)=0$ gives $2e^x\sin x=0$

or $\sin x=0 \Rightarrow x=0,\pi$ 1

Now $\pi\in\left(\dfrac{\pi}{4},\dfrac{5\pi}{4}\right)$

$\therefore$ Th theorem is verified with $x=\pi$ 1

16. Let $x=25,\ x+\Delta x=25.2$ so $\Delta x=0.2$ 1

Let $y=\sqrt{x}\Rightarrow\dfrac{dy}{dx}=\dfrac{1}{2\sqrt{x}}=\dfrac{1}{2\sqrt{25}}=\dfrac{1}{10}$ at $x=25$ 1

$dy=\dfrac{dy}{dx}\cdot\Delta x$

or $\Delta y=\dfrac{dy}{dx}\cdot\Delta x=\dfrac{1}{10}\times 0.2=0.02$ 1

$\therefore$ $\sqrt{25.2}=y+\Delta y=5+0.02=5.02$ 1

OR

Let A be the area of ΔABC in which $AB=AC=x$ and $BC=a$

$\therefore$ $A=\dfrac{1}{2}BC\times AD=\dfrac{1}{2}a\sqrt{x^2-\dfrac{a^2}{4}}=\dfrac{a}{4}\sqrt{4x^2-a^2}$

$\dfrac{dA}{dt}=\dfrac{a}{4}\cdot\dfrac{1}{2\sqrt{4x^2-a^2}}\cdot 8x-\dfrac{dx}{dt}=\dfrac{ax\times 9}{\sqrt{4x^2-a^2}}$

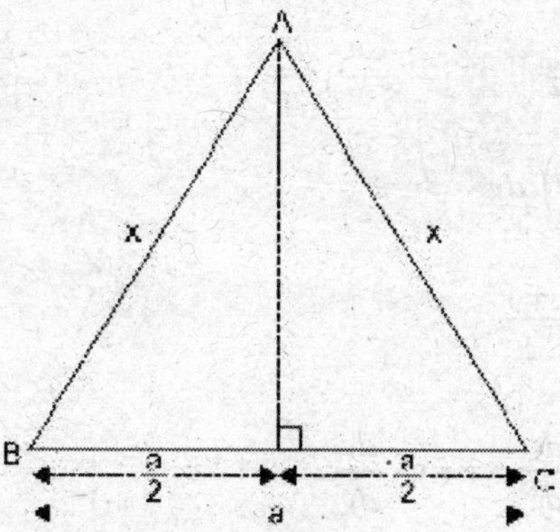

$\therefore \quad \left(\frac{dA}{dt}\right)_{at\,x=a} = \frac{9a.a}{\sqrt{3a^2}} = 3\sqrt{3}\ \text{cm}^2/\text{second}$ 1

17. $I = \int_{-1}^{1/2} |x\cos(\pi x)|\,dx$

Three cases arise:

Case I: $-1 < x < \frac{-1}{2}$

$\Rightarrow \quad -\pi < \pi x < -\frac{\pi}{2}$

$\Rightarrow \quad \cos \pi x < 0 \Rightarrow x \cos \pi x > 0$ ½

Case II: $-\frac{1}{2} < x < 0$

$-\frac{\pi}{2} < \pi x < 0$

$\Rightarrow \quad \cos(\pi x) > 0$

$\Rightarrow \quad x\cos(\pi x) < 0$ ½

Case III: $0 < x < \frac{1}{2}$

$\Rightarrow \quad 0 < \pi x < \frac{\pi}{2}$

$\Rightarrow \quad \cos \pi x > 0$

$\Rightarrow \quad x\cos \pi x > 0$ ½

$\therefore \quad I = \int_{-1}^{-1/2} x\cos\pi x\,dx + \int_{-1/2}^{0} -x\cos\pi x\,dx + \int_{0}^{1/2} x\cos\pi x\,dx$ 1

$= \left[\frac{x\sin\pi x}{\pi} + \frac{\cos\pi x}{\pi^2}\right]_{1-}^{\frac{-1}{2}} - \left[\frac{x\sin\pi x}{\pi} + \frac{\cos\pi x}{\pi^2}\right]_{\frac{-1}{2}}^{0} + \left[\frac{x\sin\pi x}{\pi} = \frac{\cos\pi x}{\pi^2}\right]_{0}^{\frac{1}{2}}$ 1

$\left[\left(\frac{1}{2\pi}+0\right)-\left(0-\frac{1}{\pi^2}\right)\right]-\left[-\left(\frac{1}{2\pi}+0\right)+\left(0+\frac{1}{\pi^2}\right)\right]+\left[-\left(0-\frac{1}{\pi^2}\right)\right]+\left(\frac{1}{2\pi}+0\right)$

$\frac{1}{2\pi} + \cancel{\frac{1}{\pi^2}} + \frac{1}{2\pi} - \cancel{\frac{1}{\pi^2}} + \frac{1}{2\pi} - \frac{1}{\pi^2}$

$$= \frac{3}{2\pi} - \frac{1}{\pi^2}$$ ½

18. $y e^{\frac{x}{y}}\, dx = \left(x e^{x/y} + y\right) dy$

$\Rightarrow \quad \frac{dy}{dx} = \frac{x e^{\frac{x}{y}} + y}{y - e^{\frac{x}{y}}}$ ½

Let $\quad x = vy \Rightarrow \frac{dx}{dy} = v + y \cdot \frac{dv}{dy}$ ½

$\therefore \quad v + y\frac{dv}{dy} = \frac{vy.e^v + y}{y - e^v}$ 1

$\Rightarrow \quad y\frac{dv}{dy} = \frac{vye^v + y}{y.e^v} - v = \frac{\cancel{vye^v} + y - \cancel{vye^v}}{y.e^v} = \frac{1}{e^v}$ ½

$\Rightarrow \quad e^v\, dv = \frac{dy}{y}$ 1

Integrating we get $e^v = \log y + \log c = \log cy$ 1

Substituting $v = \frac{x}{y}$, we get ½

$e^{x/y} = \log cy$

19. $(1 + y + x^2 y)\, dx + (x + x^3)\, dy = 0$

$\Rightarrow \quad x(1 + x^2)\, dy = -[1 + (x + x^3)\, dy = 0$

$\Rightarrow \quad \frac{dy}{dx} = \frac{-1 - y(1-x)^2}{x(1-x^2)} = \frac{-1}{x} \cdot y - \frac{1}{x(1+x^2)}$ 1

or $\quad \frac{dy}{dx} + \frac{1}{x} \cdot y = -\frac{1}{x(1+x^2)}$

$\therefore \quad \text{I.F.} = \int e^{\frac{1}{x}dx} = e^{\log x} = x$ 1

$\therefore$ The solution is

$$y \,.\, x = -\int \frac{1}{x(1+x^2)}.\, xdx = -\int \frac{dx}{1+x^2} = \tan^{-1} x + c$$ 1

when $\quad x = 1,\ y = 0$

$\therefore \quad 0 = -\tan^{-1}(1) + c \ \Rightarrow \ e = \frac{\pi}{4}$ ½

$\therefore \quad xy = -\tan^{-1} x + \frac{\pi}{4}$ ½

20. $\vec{a}\,,\ \vec{b} = 0$ and $\vec{a}\,.\,\vec{c} = 0$ ½

$\Rightarrow \quad \vec{a} \perp \vec{b}$ and $\vec{a} \perp \vec{c}$

$\therefore \quad \vec{a}$ is $\perp$ to the plane of $\vec{b}$ and $\vec{c}$

$\Rightarrow \quad \vec{a}$ is parallel to $\vec{b} \times \vec{c}$ 1

Let $\quad \vec{a} = k(\vec{b} \times \vec{c})$, where k is a scalar

$\therefore \quad |\vec{a}| = |k||\vec{b} \times \vec{c}|$

$\Rightarrow \quad |\vec{a}| = |k||\vec{b}||\vec{c}| \sin \dfrac{\pi}{6}$ 1

$\therefore \quad 1 = |k| \cdot \dfrac{1}{2} \Rightarrow |k| = 2$ 1½

$\therefore \quad k = \pm 2$ ½

$\therefore \quad \vec{a} = \pm 2(\vec{b} \times \vec{c})$

21. Equation of plane passing through (0, –1, –1) is

$a(x - 0) + b(y + 1) + c(z + 1) = 0$ ...(*i*) ½

(*i*) pass through (4, 5, 1) and (3, 9, 4)

$\Rightarrow \quad 4a + 6b + 2c - 0$ or $2a + 3b + c = 0$ ...(*ii*) 1

and $\quad 3a + 10b + 5c = 0$ ....(*iii*)

from (*ii*) and (*iii*), we get

$$\frac{a}{15-10} = \frac{-b}{10-3} = \frac{c}{20-0} \Rightarrow \frac{a}{5} = \frac{-b}{7} = \frac{c}{11} = k \text{ (say)}$$ 1

$\therefore \quad a - 5k, b = -7k, c = 11k$ ...(*iv*)

Putting these values of *a, b, c* in (*i*), we get

$5kx - 7k(y + 1) + 11k(z + 1) = 0$

or $\quad 5x - 7y + 11z + 4 = 0$ ...(*v*) ½

Putting the point (–4, 4, 4) in (*v*), we get

$-20 - 28 + 44 + 4 = 0$ which is satisfied ½

$\therefore$ The given points are co-planar and equation of plane is $5x - 7z + 4 = 0$ ½

22. According to the given question

$P(H) = \dfrac{3}{4}, P(T) = \dfrac{1}{4}$ ½

Let *X* be the random variate, which can take values 0, 1, 2, 3.

$P(X = 0) = P(\text{No Tails}) = P(HHH) = \dfrac{3}{4} \times \dfrac{3}{4} \times \dfrac{3}{4} = \dfrac{27}{64}$ ½

$P(X = 1) = P(1 \text{ Tail}) = P(HHT) + P(HTH) + P(THH)$

$= \dfrac{3}{4} \times \dfrac{3}{4} \times \dfrac{1}{4} + \dfrac{3}{4} \times \dfrac{1}{4} \times \dfrac{3}{4} + \dfrac{1}{4} \times \dfrac{3}{4} \times \dfrac{3}{4} = \dfrac{27}{64}$ 1

$P(X = 2) = P(2 \text{ Tail}) = P(HTT) + P(THT) + P(TTH)$

$= \dfrac{3}{4} \times \dfrac{1}{4} \times \dfrac{1}{4} + \dfrac{1}{4} \times \dfrac{3}{4} \times \dfrac{1}{4} + \dfrac{1}{4} \times \dfrac{1}{4} \times \dfrac{3}{4} = \dfrac{9}{64}$ 1

$P(X = 3) = P(3 \text{ Tail}) = P(TTT)$

$\dfrac{1}{4} \times \dfrac{1}{4} \times \dfrac{1}{4} = \dfrac{1}{64}$ ½

Reqd. Probability Distribution is

X	0	1	2	3
P(*X*)	27/64	27/64	9/64	1/64

OR

For a fair coin, $p(H) = \dfrac{1}{2}$ and $P(T) = \dfrac{1}{2}$ where *H* and *T* denote Head and Tail respectively. ½

Let the coin be tossed n times

$\therefore$ Required probability $= 1 - p$ (all Tails)

$$= 1 - \frac{1}{2^n} \quad ...(i) \quad 1\frac{1}{2}$$

It has to be > 80% 1

Total probability = 1

$\therefore$ (i) has to be $> \frac{4}{5}$

$\therefore$ $1 - \frac{1}{2^n} > \frac{4}{5} \Rightarrow n = 3$

$\therefore$ The fair coin has to be tossed 3 times for the desired situation. 1

SECTION C

23. $\Delta = \begin{vmatrix} (b+c)^2 & ab & ca \\ ab & (a+c)^2 & bc \\ ac & bc & (a+b)^2 \end{vmatrix}$

Operating $R_1 \to a R_1, R_1 \to b R_2,\ R_3 \to c R_3,$ to get

$$\Delta = \frac{1}{abc} \begin{vmatrix} a(b+c)^2 & a^2b & a^2c \\ ab^2 & b(a+c)^2 & b^2c \\ ac^2 & b^2c & c(a+b)^2 \end{vmatrix} = \frac{abc}{abc} \begin{vmatrix} (b+c)^2 & a^2 & a^2 \\ b^2 & (a+c)^2 & b^2 \\ c^2 & c^2 & (a+b)^2 \end{vmatrix} \quad 1\frac{1}{2}$$

Operating $c_2 \to c_2 - c_1, c_3 - c_1$, to get

$$\Delta = \begin{vmatrix} (b+c)^2 & a^2-(b+c)^2 & a^2-(b+c)^2 \\ b^2 & (a+c)^2-b^2 & 0 \\ c^2 & 0 & (a+b)^2-c^2 \end{vmatrix} = (a+b+c)^2 \begin{vmatrix} (b+c)^2 & a-b-c & a-b-c \\ b^2 & a+b-c & 0 \\ c^2 & 0 & a+b-c \end{vmatrix}$$

1½

Operating $R_1 \to R_1 - (R_2 + R_3)$ to get

$$\Delta = (a+b+c)^2 \begin{vmatrix} 2bc & -2c & -2b \\ b^2 & a+c+b & 0 \\ c^2 & 0 & a+b+c \end{vmatrix} \quad c_2 \to c_2 + \frac{1}{b} c_1, c_3 \to c_3 - \frac{1}{c} c_1$$

$$= (a+b+c)^2 \begin{vmatrix} 2bc & 0 & 0 \\ b^2 & a+c & \frac{b^2}{c} \\ c^2 & \frac{c^2}{c} & a+b \end{vmatrix} \quad 1+1$$

$(a+b+c)^2\ [2bc(a^2 + ac + ab + bc + bc)] = (a+b+c)^2\ (2bc)\ a(a+b+c)$

$= (a+b+c)^3\ 2abc$ 1

24. Let the radius of circle be r and side of square be x

$\therefore \quad 2\pi r + 4x = k$ ...(A) 1

Let A be the sum of the areas of circle and square

$\therefore \quad A = \pi r^2 + x^2$

$$= \pi\left[\frac{k-4x}{2\pi}\right]^2 + x^2$$ [using (A)] 1

$$= \pi\left[\frac{k^2+16x^2-8kx}{4\pi^2}\right]^2 + x^2$$

$$= \frac{k^2+16x^2+8kx}{4\pi} + x^2$$ ½

$$\therefore \quad \frac{dA}{dx} = \frac{1}{4\pi}[0 + 32x - 8k] + 2x$$

$$= \frac{1}{4\pi}[32x - 8k + 8\pi x]$$ ½

For optimisation $\frac{dA}{dx} = 0 \Rightarrow (32 + 8\pi x) = 8k$

$$\Rightarrow \quad x = \frac{k}{4+\pi}$$ ...(i) 1

$$\therefore \quad \frac{d^2A}{dx^2} - \frac{1}{4\pi}[32 + 8\pi] > 0 \Rightarrow \text{Minima}$$ ½

Putting the value of x in (A) to get

$$2\pi r + 4 \,.\, \frac{k}{4+\pi} = k$$

$$\Rightarrow \quad 2\pi r = k - \frac{4k}{4+\pi} + \frac{\pi k}{4+\pi}$$ 1

$$2r = \frac{k}{4+\pi}$$ ...(ii)

From (i) and (ii), $x = 2r$ ½

OR

Let $P(x, y)$ be the position of the Helicopter and the position of soldier at $A(3, 2)$

$$\therefore \quad AP = \sqrt{(x-3)^2 + (y-2)^2} = \sqrt{(x-3)^2 + (x^2)^2}$$ $\left[\begin{array}{c}\therefore\ y - x^2 + 2\text{isthe}\\ =n\text{ofcurve}\end{array}\right]$ 2

Let $\quad AP^2 = z = (x-3)^2 + x^4$

$$\Rightarrow \quad \frac{dz}{dx} = 2(x-3) + 4x^3$$ 1

For opetimisation $\frac{dz}{dx} = 0 \Rightarrow 2x^3 + x - 3 = 0$

or $\quad (x-1)(2x + 2x + 3) = 0 \Rightarrow x = 1$ $\left[\begin{array}{l}\text{otherfactor}\\ \text{givsnorealvalues}\end{array}\right]$ 1

$$\frac{d^2z}{dx^2} = 6x^2 + 1 > 0 \quad \Rightarrow \quad \text{Minima}$$

when $x = 1,\ y = x^2 + 2 = 3$

$\therefore$ The required point is (1, 3) 1

And distance $AP = \sqrt{(1-3)^2 + (3-2)^2} = \sqrt{5}$ 1

25. $\int \frac{1}{\sin x(5 - 4\cos x)} dx = \int \frac{\sin x}{\sin^2 \times (5 - 4\cos x)} dx$ ½

$$= \int \frac{\sin x}{(1 - \cos^2 x)(5 - 4\cos x)} dx$$

$$= -\int \frac{dt}{(1 - t^2)(5 - 4t)}, \text{ where } \cos x - t, dt = -\sin x\, dx$$

$$= -\int \frac{dt}{(1 - t)(1 + t)(5 - 4t)}$$ 1

Let Let $\frac{1}{(1-t)(1+t)(5-4t)} = \frac{A}{1-t} + \frac{B}{1+1} + \frac{C}{5-4t}$ ½

$\Rightarrow$ $1 = A(1 + 1)(5 - 4t) + B(1 - 1)(5 - 4t) + c(1 - t^2)$ ...(*i*)

Putting $t = 1$ in (*i*) to get $A = \frac{1}{2}$

Putting $t = -1$ in (*i*) to get $B = \frac{1}{18}$

Putting $t = \frac{5}{4}$ in (*i*) to get $C = -\frac{16}{9}$ 1½

$\therefore$ $1 = -\left[\frac{1}{2}\int \frac{dt}{1-t} + \frac{1}{18}\int \frac{dt}{1-t} - \frac{16}{9}\int \frac{dt}{5-4t}\right]$

$$-\left[-\frac{1}{2}\log|1-t| + \frac{1}{18}\log|1+t| - \frac{16}{9\times4}\log|5-4t|\right] + c$$ 1½

$$= \frac{1}{2}\log|1 - \cos x| - \frac{1}{18}\log|1 + \cos x| - \frac{4}{9}\log|5 - 4\cos x| + c$$ 1

OR

$$1 = \int\sqrt{\frac{1-\sqrt{x}}{1+\sqrt{x}}}\,dx = \int \frac{\sqrt{1-\sqrt{x}}\,.\sqrt{1-\sqrt{x}}}{\sqrt{1+\sqrt{x}}\ \sqrt{1-\sqrt{x}}}\,dx = \int \frac{1-\sqrt{x}}{\sqrt{1-x}}\,dx$$ 1½

$$= \int \frac{dx}{\sqrt{1-x}} - \int \frac{\sqrt{x}}{\sqrt{1-x}}\,dx = I_1 - I_2$$ ½

$$I_1 = \int (1-x)^{1/2}\,dx = -2(1-x)^{1/2} + c_1 \text{ or } -2\sqrt{1-x} + c_1$$ 1

$I_2 = \int \frac{\sqrt{x}}{\sqrt{1-x}}\,dx$: Let $x = \sin^2\theta$, $dx = 2\sin\theta\cos\theta\, d\theta$ ½

$$= \int \frac{\sin\theta . 2\sin\theta\cos\theta\, d\theta}{\cos\theta} = 2\int \sin^2\theta\, d\theta$$ 1

$$= \int (1-\cos 2\theta)\, d\theta = \theta - \frac{\sin 2\theta}{2} = \theta - \sin\theta\cos\theta + c_2$$ 1

$$= \sin^{-1}\sqrt{x} - \sqrt{x}\sqrt{1-x} + c_2$$

$$\therefore \quad I = -2\sqrt{(1-x)} - \sin^{-1}\sqrt{x} + \sqrt{x}\sqrt{1-x} + C$$ ½

$$= \sqrt{1-x}\left[\sqrt{x} - 2\right] - \sin^{-1}\sqrt{x} + C$$

26. Equations of curves are

$$x^2 + y^2 = 5 \text{ and } y = \begin{Bmatrix} 1-x, & x<1 \\ x-1, & x>1 \end{Bmatrix}$$

correct figure 1

Points of intersection are $c(2, 1)$ ½

$D(-1, 2)$

Required Area = Area of $(ABCDE)$ – Area of $(ADEA)$ – Area of $(ABCA)$ ½

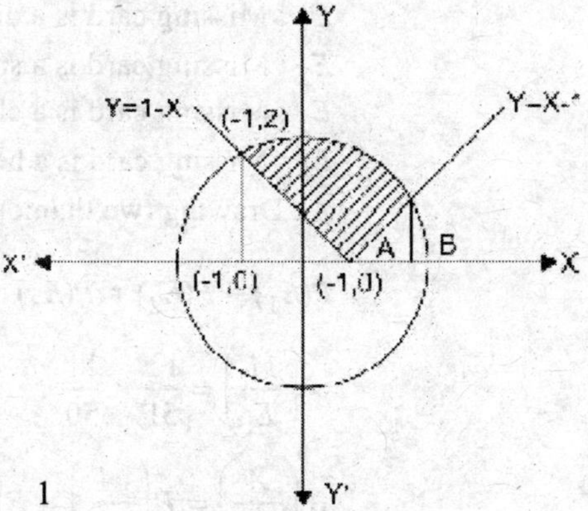

$$= \int_{-1}^{2} \sqrt{5-x^2}\, dx - \int_{1}^{4} (1-x)\, dx - \int_{-1}^{2} (x-1)\, dx$$ 1

$$= \left[\frac{x}{2}\sqrt{5-x^2} + \frac{5}{2}\sin^{-1}\frac{x}{\sqrt{5}}\right]_{-1}^{2} - \left[x - \frac{x^2}{2}\right]_{-1}^{1} - \left[\frac{x^2}{2} - x\right]_{1}^{2}$$ 1

$$= \left[\left\{1 + \frac{5}{2}\sin^{-1}\frac{2}{\sqrt{5}}\right\} - \left\{-\frac{1}{2}\times 2 + \frac{5}{2}\sin^{-1}\left(\frac{-1}{\sqrt{5}}\right)\right\}\right] - \left[\left(1-\frac{1}{2}\right) - \left(-1-\frac{1}{2}\right)\right]$$

$$- \left[(2-2) - \left(\frac{1}{2} - 1\right)\right]$$

$$= 1 + \frac{5}{2}\sin^{-1}\frac{2}{\sqrt{5}} + 1 - \frac{5}{2}\sin^{-1}\left(\frac{-1}{\sqrt{5}}\right) - 2 - \frac{1}{2}$$

$$= -\frac{1}{2} + \frac{5}{2}\left[\sin^{-1}\frac{2}{\sqrt{5}} - \sin^{-1}\left(\frac{-1}{\sqrt{5}}\right)\right]$$ ½

27. Lines $\frac{x-x_1}{l_1} = \frac{y-y_1}{m_1} = \frac{z-z_1}{n_1}$ and $\frac{x-x_2}{l_2} = \frac{y-y_2}{m_2} = \frac{z-z_2}{n_2}$ are 1½

coplanar if $\begin{vmatrix} x_2-x_1 & y_2-y_1 & z_2-z_1 \\ I_1 & m_1 & n_2 \\ I_2 & m_2 & n_2 \end{vmatrix} = 0$

In this case $\begin{vmatrix} -2 & -1 & 0 \\ -3 & 1 & 5 \\ -1 & 2 & 5 \end{vmatrix} = -2(5-10) + 1(-15+5) + 0 = 10 - 10 = 0$ 1½

$\therefore$ Lines are coplanar

Equation of plane containing this is

$$\begin{vmatrix} x+3 & y-1 & z-5 \\ -3 & 1 & 5 \\ -1 & 2 & 5 \end{vmatrix} = 0$$

$\Rightarrow$ $5x - 10y + 5z = 0$

or $x - 2y + z = 0$ 1½

28. Let events E_1, E_2, E_3, E_4 and A be defined as follows:

E_1 : Missing card is a diamond

E_2 : Missing card is a spade

E_3 : Missing card is a club 1

E_4 : Missing card is a heart

A : Drawing two diamond cards

$P(E_1) = P(E_2) = P(E_3) = P(E_4) = \frac{1}{4}$ ½

$P\left(\frac{A}{E_1}\right) = \frac{12}{51} \times \frac{11}{50}$ ½

$P\left(\frac{A}{E_2}\right) = P\left(\frac{A}{E_3}\right) = P\left(\frac{A}{E_4}\right) = \frac{13}{51} \times \frac{12}{50}$ 1

$$P\left(\frac{E_4}{A}\right) = \sum_{i=1}^{4} \frac{P(E_4).P\left(\frac{A}{E_4}\right)}{P(E_i).P\left(\frac{A}{E_i}\right)}$$ 1

$$\frac{\frac{1}{4} \cdot \frac{13}{51} \times \frac{12}{50}}{\frac{1}{4}\left[\frac{12\times11 + 13\times12 + 13\times12 + 13\times12}{51 \cdot 50}\right]}$$ 1

$$= \frac{13\times\cancel{12}}{3\times13\times\cancel{12} + \cancel{12}\times11} = \frac{13}{39+11} = \frac{13}{50}$$ 1

29. Let x and y be the units taken of Food A and Food B respectively then LPP is, ½

Minimise $z = 4x + 3y$

Subject to constraints

$200x + 100y \geq 4000$ or $2x + y \geq 40$

$x + 2y \geq 50$

$40x + 40y \geq 1400$ or $x + y \geq 35$

$x \geq 0,\ y \geq 0$ 1½

Correct Graph 2

The corness of feasible region are

$A(50, 0),\ B(20, 15),\ C(5, 30),\ D(0, 40)$ 1

$Z_A = 200,\ Z_B = 125,\ Z_C = 110,\ Z_D = 120$

$\therefore$ Z is minimum at C

$\therefore$ 5 units of Food A and 30 units of Food B

will give the minimum cost (which is Rs. 110) 1

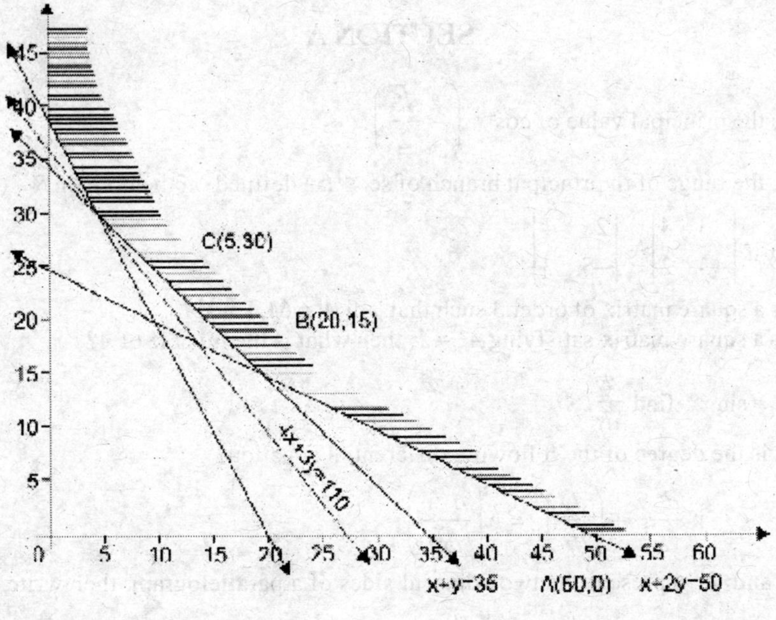

❑❑❑

QUESTION PAPER-5

CLASS-XII

Time allowed : 3 hours *Maximum Marks : 100*

SECTION A

1. Write the principal value of $\cos^{-1}\left(-\frac{\sqrt{3}}{2}\right)$.

2. Write the range of th principal branch of $\sec^{-1}(x)$ defined on the domain $R-(-1, 1)$.

3. Find x if $\begin{vmatrix} 3 & 4 \\ -5 & 2 \end{vmatrix} = \begin{vmatrix} 2x & 4 \\ -5 & 3 \end{vmatrix}$.

4. If A is a square matrix of order 3 such that $|\text{adj } A| = 64$. Find $|A'|$.

5. If A is a square matrix satisfying $A^2 = 1$, then what is the inverse of A?

6. If $f(x) = \sin x°$, find $\frac{dy}{dx}$

7. What is the degree of the following differential equation?

$$y\frac{d^2y}{dx^2} + \left(\frac{dy}{dx}\right)^2 = x\left(\frac{d^2y}{dx^3}\right)^2$$

8. If $\vec{a}$ and $\vec{b}$ represent the two adjacent sides of a parallelogram, then write the area of parallelogram in terms of $\vec{a}$ and $\vec{b}$.

9. Find th angle between two vectors $\vec{a}$ and $\vec{b}$ if $|\vec{a}|=3, |\vec{b}|=4$ and $|\vec{a}\times\vec{b}|=6$.

10. Find the direction cosins of a line, passing through origin and lying and lying in the first octant, making qual angles with the three coordinate axes.

SECTION B

11. Show that the relation R in the set $A = \{x; x \in Z, 0 \leq x \leq 12\}$ given by $R = \{(a, b) : |a-b|$ is divisible by 4$\}$ is an equivalence relation. Find the set of all elements related to 1.

12. Solve for x : $2\tan^{-1}(\sin x) = \tan^{-1}(2\sec x), 0 < x \frac{\pi}{2}$

OR

Show that : $\tan\frac{1}{2}\left[\sin^{-1}\frac{2x}{1+x^2} + \cos^{-1}\frac{1-y^2}{1+y^2}\right] = \frac{x+y}{1-xy}, |x|<1, y>0\, xy<1$

13. If none of a, b and c is zero, using properties of determinants prove that:

$$\begin{vmatrix} -bc & b^2+bc & c^2-bc \\ a^2+ac & -ac & c^2+ac \\ a^2+ab & b^2+ab & -ab \end{vmatrix} = (bc+ca+ab)^3$$

14. If $\sqrt{1-x^2}+\sqrt{1-y^2} = a(x-y)$, prove that $\frac{dy}{dx} = \sqrt{\frac{1-y^2}{1-x^2}}$

15. If $y = \left(x+\sqrt{x^2-1}\right)^m$, then show that $(x^2+1)\frac{d^2y}{dx^2} + x\frac{dy}{dx} = m^2y = 0$

16. Find all the points of dicontinuity of the function $f(x)=(x^2)$ on $[1, 2)$, where [.] denotes the greatest integer function.

OR

Differentiate $\sin^{-1}\left(2x\sqrt{1-x^2}\right)$ w.r.t. $\cos^{-1}\left(\frac{1-x^2}{1+x^2}\right)$

17. Evaluate: $\int \frac{1}{\cos(x-a)\cos(x-b)}dx$

OR

Evaluate: $\int x(\log x)^2 .dx$

18. Evaluate : $\int \frac{x}{x^2-1}dx$

19. Using properties of definite integrals, evaluate: $\int_0^{\pi} \frac{xdx}{4-\cos^2 x}$

20. The dot products of a vector with the vectors $\hat{i}-3\hat{k}$, $\hat{i}-2\hat{k}$ and $\hat{i}+\hat{j}+4\hat{k}$ are 0, 5 and 8 respectively. Find the vector.

21. Find the equation of plane passing through the point (1, 2, 1) and perpendicular to the line joining the points (1, 4, 2) and (2, 3, 5). Also, find the perpendicular distance of the plane from the origin.

OR

Find the equation of the perpendicular drawn from the point $P(2, 4, -1)$ to the line $\frac{x+5}{1}=\frac{y+3}{4}=\frac{z-6}{-9}$.

22. A biased die is twice as likely to show an even number as an odd number. The di is rolled three times. If occurrence of an even number is considered a success, then write th probability distribution of number of succsses. Also find th mean number of success.

SECTION C

23. Using matrics, solve the following system of equations:

$$\frac{1}{x}-\frac{1}{y}+\frac{1}{z}=4;\ \frac{2}{x}+\frac{1}{y}+\frac{3}{z}=0;\ \frac{1}{x}-\frac{1}{y}+\frac{1}{z}=2x\neq 0, y\neq 0, z\neq 0$$

24. Show that the volume of the greatest cylinder which can be inscribed in a cone of height h and semivertical angle α, is $\frac{4}{27}\pi h^3 \tan^2 \alpha$.

OR

Show that the normal at any point θ to the curve $x=a\cos\theta+a\theta\sin\theta$ and $y=a\sin\theta-a\theta\cos\theta$ is at a constant distance from the origin.

25. Find the area of the region : $\{(x, y): 0\le y\le x^2, 0\le x+2; 0\le x\le 3\}$

26. Find the particular solution of the differential equation

$$(xdy-ydx)y.\sin\left(\frac{y}{x}\right)=(ydx+xdy)x\cos\frac{y}{x},\ \text{given that } y=\pi \text{ when } x=3$$

27. Find the equation of the plan passing through the point (1, 1, 1) and containing the line $\vec{r}=(+3\hat{i}+\hat{j}+5\hat{k})+\lambda(3\hat{i}-\hat{j}+5\hat{k})$. Also, show that the plan contains th line $\vec{r}=(-2\hat{i}+2\hat{j}+5\hat{k})+\lambda(\hat{i}-2\hat{j}-5\hat{k})$

28. A company sells two different products A and B. The two products are produced in a common production process which has a total capacity of 500 man hours. It takes 5 hours to produce a unit of A and 3 hours to produce a unit of B. The demand in the market shows that the maximum number of units of A that can be sold is 70 and that of B is 125. Profit on each unit of A is Rs. 20 and on B is Rs. 15. How many units of A and B should be produced to maximise the profit. Form an L.P.P. and solve it graphically.

29. Two bags A and B contain 4 white and 3 black balls and 2 white and 2 black balls respectively. From bag A, two balls are drawn at random and then transferred to bag B.A ball is then drawn from bag B and is found to be a black ball. What is the probability that the transferred balls were *I* white and 1 black?

OR

In an examination 10 equations of true-false type are asked. A student tosses a fair coin to determine his answer to each question. If the coin falls heads, he answers 'true' and if it falls tails, h answers 'false'. Show that the probability that he answers at most 7 questions correctly is $\frac{121}{128}$.

SOLVED QUESTION PAPER-5
WITH MARKING SCHEME
SECTION A

(1 mark for correct answer for Qs. 1 to 10)

1. $\frac{5\pi}{6}$ **2.** $\left[0, \frac{\pi}{2}\right) \cup \left(\frac{\pi}{2}, \pi\right]$ **3.** $x = 1$ **4.** $|A'| = \pm 8$ **5.** $A^{-1} = A$

6. $\frac{\pi}{180} \cos x°$ **7.** 2 **8.** $|\vec{a} \times \vec{b}|$ **9.** $\frac{\pi}{6}$ **10.** $< \frac{1}{\sqrt{3}}, \frac{1}{\sqrt{3}}, \frac{1}{\sqrt{3}} >$

SECTION B

11. (*i*) $\forall a \in A,\ |a - a| = 0$ is divisible by 4. $\therefore$ R is reflexive ...(*i*) ½

(*ii*) $a, b \in A, (a, b) \in R \Rightarrow |a - b|$ is divisible by 4.

$\Rightarrow |b - a|$ is divisible by 4 $\therefore$ R is symmetric ...(*ii*) ½

(*iii*) $a, b, c \in A, (a, b) \in R$ and $(b, c) \in R$

$\Rightarrow |a - b|$ is divisible by 4 and $|b - c|$ is divisible by 4

$\therefore$ $(a - b)$ and $(b - c)$ are divisible by 4 and so

$(a - b) + (b - c) = (a - c)$ is divisible by 4. Hence 1

$|a - c|$ is divisible by 4 $\Rightarrow$ $(a, c) \in R$. Hence R is transitive

Hence R is an equivalence relation from (*i*), (*ii*) and (*iii*). ½

Set of all elements of A, related to 1 is $\{1, 5, 9\}$

12. Given equation can be written as

$$\tan^{-1}\left(\frac{2\sin x}{1-\sin^2 x}\right) = \tan^{-1}\left(\frac{2}{\cos x}\right),\ 0 < x < \frac{\pi}{2} \qquad 1½$$

$$\Rightarrow \frac{2\sin x}{\cos^2 x} = \frac{2}{\cos x} \Rightarrow \tan x = 1 \qquad 1½$$

$$\Rightarrow x = \frac{\pi}{4}$$

OR

$$\text{LHS} = \tan \frac{1}{2}\ (2\tan^{-1} x + 2\tan^{-1} y) \qquad 1½$$

$$= \tan(\tan^{-1} x + \tan^{-1} y) = \tan \tan^{-1}\left(\frac{x+y}{1-xy}\right) \qquad 1½$$

$$= \frac{x+y}{1-xy} \qquad 1$$

13. Given determinant can be written as

$$\Delta = \frac{1}{abc}\begin{vmatrix} -abc & ab(b+c) & ac(b+c) \\ ab(a+c) & -abc & bc(a+c) \\ ac(a+b) & bc(b+a) & -abc \end{vmatrix}$$

$$\Delta = \frac{abc}{abc}\begin{vmatrix} -bc & ab+ac & ab+ac \\ ab+bc & -ac & ab+bc \\ ac+bc & bc+ac & -ab \end{vmatrix} \begin{matrix} R_1 \to R_1 + R_2 + R_3 \\ = (ab+bc+ac) \end{matrix} \begin{vmatrix} 1 & 1 & 1 \\ ab+bc & -ac & ab+bc \\ ac+bc & bc+ac & -ab \end{vmatrix} \qquad 1$$

$$C_2 \to C_2 - C_1,\quad C_3 \to C_3 - C_1 \qquad \Delta = (ab+bc+ac)\begin{vmatrix} 1 & 0 & 0 \\ ab+bc & -(ab+bc+ac) & ab+bc \\ ac+bc & 0 & -(ab+bc+ac) \end{vmatrix} \qquad 1$$

$= (ab + bc + ac)^3$ 1

14. Putting $x = \cos\alpha$ and $y = \cos\beta$ to get

$$\sin\alpha + \sin\beta = a(\cos\alpha - \cos\beta) \Rightarrow \frac{2\sin\frac{\alpha+\beta}{2}\cos\left(\frac{\alpha-\beta}{2}\right)}{-2\sin\frac{\alpha+\beta}{2}\sin\frac{\alpha-\beta}{2}} = a \qquad 1$$

$$\Rightarrow \cot\left(\frac{\alpha-\beta}{2}\right) = -a, \Rightarrow \alpha - \beta = 2\cot^{-1}(-a) \text{ or } \cos^{-1}x - \cos^{-1}y = 2\cot^{-1}(-a) \qquad 1$$

Differentiating to get $-\dfrac{1}{\sqrt{1-x^2}} + \dfrac{1}{\sqrt{1-y^2}}\dfrac{dy}{dx} = 0$ 1

$$\Rightarrow \qquad \frac{dy}{dx} = \sqrt{\frac{1-y^2}{1-x}} \qquad 1$$

15. Getting $\dfrac{dy}{dx} = m.\left(x+\sqrt{x^2+1}\right)^{m-1}\left(1+\dfrac{x}{\sqrt{x^2+1}}\right) = \dfrac{m\left(x+\sqrt{x^2+1}\right)^m}{\sqrt{x^2+1}} = \dfrac{m}{\sqrt{x^2+1}}y$ 1

$$\Rightarrow \qquad \sqrt{x^2+1}\,\frac{dy}{dx} = my \qquad ...(i) \quad ½$$

$$\Rightarrow \qquad (x^2+1)\frac{d^2y}{dx^2} + x\cdot\frac{dy}{dx} = m\sqrt{x^2+1}\,\frac{dy}{dx} = m\,.\,my = m^2y \text{ (using } i) \qquad 1$$

$$\text{or} \qquad (x^2+1)\frac{d^2y}{dx^2} + x\frac{dy}{dx} - m^2y = 0 \qquad ½$$

16. $f(x) = [x^2],\ 1 \le x < 2 \Rightarrow f(x) = \begin{cases} 1, & 1 \le x < \sqrt{2} \\ 2, & \sqrt{2} \le x < \sqrt{3} \\ 3, & \sqrt{3} \le x < 2 \end{cases}$ 1

At $x = \sqrt{2}$ LHL = 1, RHL = 2 $\therefore$ $x = \sqrt{2}$ is a discontinuity of $f(x)$ 1½

At $x = \sqrt{3}$ LHL = 2, RHL = 3 $\therefore$ $x = \sqrt{3}$ is also a discontinuity of $f(x)$ 1

i.e. $\sqrt{2}$, $\sqrt{3}$ are two discontinuities in [1, 2) ½

OR

Let $y = \sin^{-1}\left(2x\sqrt{1-x^2}\right)$ and $z = \cos^{-1}\left(\dfrac{1-x^2}{1+x^2}\right)$ ½

Put $x = \sin\theta$ to get

$y = \sin^{-1}(\sin 2\theta) = 2\theta = 2\sin^{-1}x$ and $z = 2\tan^{-1}x$ 1½

$$\frac{dy}{dx} = \frac{2}{\sqrt{1-x^2}} \text{ and } \frac{dz}{dx} = \frac{2}{1+x^2} \qquad 1$$

$$\Rightarrow \qquad \frac{dy}{dx} = \frac{11x^2}{\sqrt{1-x^2}} \qquad 1$$

17. $I = \int \frac{1}{\cos(x-a)\cos(x-b)}\,dx = \frac{1}{\sin(b-a)}\int \frac{\sin[(x-a)-(x-b)]}{\cos(x-a)\cos(x-b)}\,dx$ 1

$= \frac{1}{\sin(b-a)}\int \left[\frac{\sin(x-a)\cos(x-b)}{\cos(x-a)\cos(x-b)} - \frac{\cos(x-a)\sin(x-b)}{\cos(x-a)\cos(x-b)}\right] dx$ 1

$= \frac{1}{\sin(b-a)}\int [\tan(x-a) - \tan(x-b)]\,dx$ 1

$= \frac{1}{\sin(b-a)}\,[\log|\sec(x-a)| - \log|\sec(x-b)|] + c$ 1

OR

$I = \int (\log x)^2\, x\,dx = (\log x)^2\,\frac{x^2}{2} \cdot \int 2.\frac{\log x}{x}.\frac{x^2}{2}\,dx$ 1½

$= \frac{x^2}{2}.(\log x)^2 - \log x\,.\,\frac{x^2}{2} + \int \frac{1}{x}.\frac{x^2}{2}\,dx$ 1½

$= \frac{x^2}{2}\,(\log x)^2 - \frac{x^2}{2}\,\log x = \frac{x^2}{4} + c$ or $\frac{x^2}{2}\left[(\log x)^2 - \log x + \frac{1}{2}\right] + c$ 1

18. $\frac{x}{x^3-1} = \frac{x}{(x-1)(x^2+x+1)} = \frac{A}{x-1} + \frac{Bx+C}{x^2+x+1} \Rightarrow x = A(x^2+x+1) + (Bx+C)(x-1)$ 1

Δ $\quad A + B = 0,\ A - B + C = 1$ and $A - C = 0 \Rightarrow \mathrm{A} = \frac{1}{3},\ b = \frac{1}{3},\ c = \frac{1}{3}$ 1

$\therefore \quad I = \int \frac{x}{x^3-1}\,dx = \frac{1}{3}\int \frac{1}{x-1}\,dx - \frac{1}{3}\int \frac{x-1}{x^2+x+1}\,dx$ 1

$= \frac{1}{3}\log|x-1| - \frac{1}{6}\int \frac{2x+1}{x^2+x+1}\,dx\,\frac{1}{2}\int \frac{1}{x^2+x+1}\,dx$ 1

$= \frac{1}{3}\log|x-1| - \frac{1}{6}\log|x^2+x+1| + \frac{1}{2}\int \frac{1}{\left(x+\frac{1}{2}\right)^2 + \left(\sqrt{\frac{3}{2}}\right)^2}\,dx$

$= \frac{1}{3}\log|x-1| - \frac{1}{6}\log|x^2+x+1| + \frac{1}{\sqrt{3}}\tan^{-1}\frac{2x+1}{\sqrt{3}} + c$ ½

19. $\quad I = \int_0^{\pi} \frac{x\,dx}{4-\cos^2 x} = \int_0^{\pi} \frac{(\pi-x)\,dx}{4-\cos^2(\pi-x)} = \int_0^{\pi} \frac{(\pi-x)\,dx}{4-\cos^2 x}$ 1

$\therefore \quad 2I = \pi\int_0^{\pi} \frac{1}{4-\cos^2}\,dx = 2\pi\int_0^{\pi/2} \frac{\sec^2 x}{4-\tan^2 x+3}$ 1

$I = \frac{\pi}{4}\int_0^{\infty} \frac{dt}{t^2+3/4},\ \tan x = t \Rightarrow I = \frac{\pi}{2}\cdot\frac{2}{\sqrt{3}}\tan^{-1}\frac{2t}{\sqrt{3}}\tan^{-1}\frac{2t}{\sqrt{3}}\Bigg]_0^{\infty}$ 1

$I = \frac{\pi}{2\sqrt{3}}\cdot\frac{\pi}{2} = \frac{\pi^2}{4\sqrt{3}}$ 1

20. Let the required vector be . $\vec{a} = x\hat{i} + y\hat{j} + z\hat{k}$

$\therefore \qquad \vec{a}\,.(\hat{i}-3\hat{k})=0 \;\Rightarrow\; x-3z=0$ ...(*i*) 1

$\vec{a}\,.(\hat{i}-2\hat{k})=0 \;\Rightarrow\; x-2z=5$ ...(*ii*) ½

$\vec{a}\,.(\hat{i}+\hat{j}+4\hat{k})=8 \;\Rightarrow\; x+y+4z=8$ ...(*iii*) ½

solving (*i*) and (*ii*) to get $x = 15, z = 5$ 1

Putting in (*iii*) to get $y = -27$ ½

$\vec{a} = 15\hat{i} - 27\hat{j} + 5\hat{k}$ ½

21. Here $\vec{a} = \hat{i} + 2\hat{j} + \hat{k}$ and $\vec{n} = (2-1)\hat{i} + (3–4)\hat{j} + (5–2)\hat{k} = \hat{i} - \hat{j} + 3\hat{k}$ 1

$\therefore$ equation of plane is $\vec{r}\,.(\hat{i}-\hat{j}+3\hat{k}) = (\hat{i}+2\hat{j}+\hat{k}).(\hat{i}-\hat{j}+3\hat{k}) = 2$ 1 + 1

or $\qquad x - y + 3x - 2 = 0$

Distance from origin $= \dfrac{2}{\sqrt{1+1+9}} = \dfrac{2}{\sqrt{11}}$ or $\dfrac{2\sqrt{11}}{11}$ units 1

OR

Any point on the given line is, $(\lambda - 5,\ 4\lambda - 3,\ -9\lambda + 6)$ for some value of λ, this point is Q, such that PQ is $\perp$ to the line 1

$\Rightarrow \qquad (\lambda - 7)\,1 + (4\lambda - 7)4 + (-9\lambda + 7)(-9) = 0 \Rightarrow \lambda = 1$ 1½

$\therefore \qquad Q$ is $(-4, 1, -3)$ and equation of line PQ is

$$\frac{x-2}{6} = \frac{y-4}{3} = \frac{z+1}{2}$$ 1

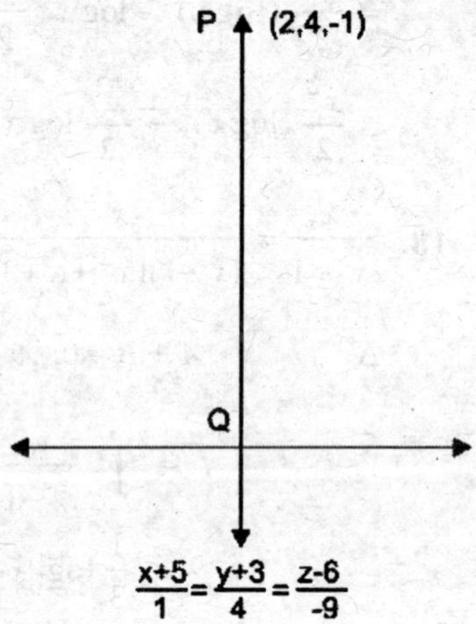

22. Getting $P(\text{odd number}) = \dfrac{1}{3}$, $P(\text{even number}) = \dfrac{2}{3}$ ½

Let X be the random variable "getting an even number"

$\therefore$

X	0	1	2	3
$P(X)$	$\frac{1}{27}$	$\frac{6}{27}$	$\frac{12}{27}$	$\frac{8}{27}$
$X.P(X)$	0	$\frac{6}{27}$	$\frac{24}{27}$	$\frac{24}{27}$

Mean $= \sum XP(X) = \dfrac{54}{27} = 2$ 1

SECTION C

23. Given equation can be written as $\begin{pmatrix} 1 & -1 & 1 \\ 2 & 1 & -3 \\ 1 & 1 & 1 \end{pmatrix} \begin{pmatrix} \frac{1}{x} \\ \frac{1}{y} \\ \frac{1}{z} \end{pmatrix} = \begin{pmatrix} 4 \\ 0 \\ 2 \end{pmatrix}$ or $A\,.\,X = B$ ½

$|A| = 1(4) + 1(5) + 1(1) = 10 \neq 0 \quad \therefore \quad X = A^{-1} . B$ 1

cofactors are:

$A_{11} = 4, \; A_{12} = -5, \; A_{13} = 1$

$A_{21} = 4, \; A_{22} = 0, \quad A_{23} = -3$ 2

$A_{31} = 4, \; A_{32} = 5, \quad A_{33} = 3$

$$\therefore \quad A^{-1} = \frac{1}{10}\begin{pmatrix} 4 & 2 & 2 \\ -5 & 0 & 5 \\ 1 & 2 & 3 \end{pmatrix}$$

$$\begin{pmatrix} \frac{1}{x} \\ \frac{1}{y} \\ \frac{1}{z} \end{pmatrix} = \frac{1}{10}\begin{pmatrix} 4 & 2 & 2 \\ -5 & 0 & 5 \\ 1 & -2 & 3 \end{pmatrix}\begin{pmatrix} 4 \\ 0 \\ 2 \end{pmatrix} = \begin{pmatrix} 2 \\ -1 \\ 1 \end{pmatrix}$$ 1

$\Rightarrow \quad x = \frac{1}{2}, \; y = -1, \; z = 1$ ½

24. Let the radius of inscribed cylinder be x and its height be y

$\therefore$ Volume $(v) = \pi x^2 y$ ½

$= \pi(h - y)^2 \tan^2 \alpha . y$

$= \pi \tan^2 \alpha \, [h^2 y - 2hy^2 + y^3]$ 1

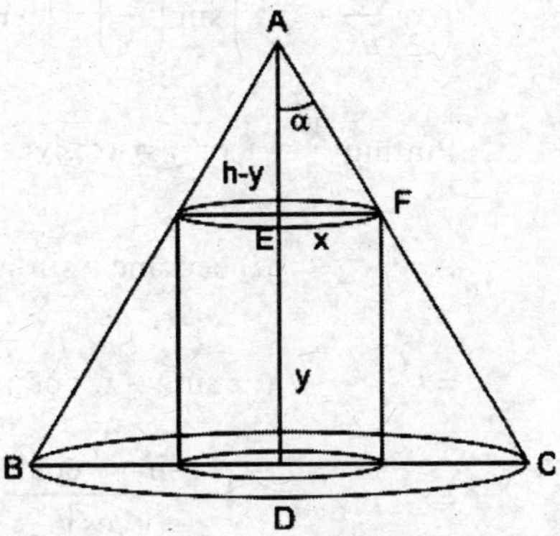

$\frac{dv}{dy} = \pi \tan^2 \alpha [h^2 - 4hy + 3y^2]$ 1

$\frac{dv}{dy} = 0 \Rightarrow 3y^2 - 4hy + h^2 = 0$

or $3(y - h)(3y - h) = 0$

$\Rightarrow \quad y = h, \; y = \frac{4}{3}$ 1½

since $y = h$ is not possible $\therefore \; y = \frac{4}{3}$ is the only point

$\frac{d^2v}{dy^2} = 6y - 4h = 6\left(\frac{h}{3}\right) - 4h = -2h < 0 \quad \therefore \; y = \frac{h}{3}$ is a maximum 1

$= \frac{4}{27} \pi h^2 \tan^2 \alpha$

OR

$\frac{dx}{d\theta} = -a \sin \theta + a \sin \theta + a \theta \cos \theta = a \theta \cos \theta$ 1

$\frac{dy}{d\theta} = -a \cos \theta - a \cos \theta + a \theta \sin \theta = a \theta \sin \theta$ 1

$\Rightarrow \quad \frac{dy}{dx} = \tan \theta \quad \therefore$ slope of normal $= -\cot \theta$ 1

$\therefore$ Equation of normal is

$$y - a(\sin\theta - \theta\cos\theta) = \frac{\cos\theta}{\sin\theta} - [x - a(\cos\theta + \theta\sin\theta)] \qquad 1$$

Simplifying to get $x\cos\theta + y\sin\theta - a = 0$

Length of perpendicular from orgin $= \dfrac{|a|}{\sqrt{\sin^2\theta + \cos^2\theta}} = |a|$ (constant) 1

25. For correct figure getting points of intersection as $x = -1$, $x = 2$ ½

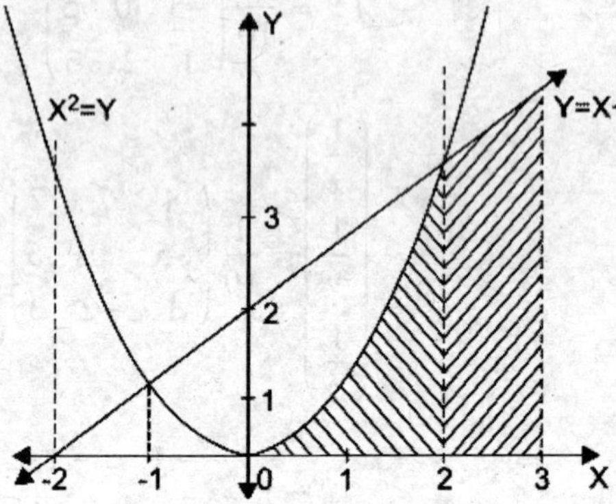

Required area

$= \int_0^2 x^2\,dx + \int_2^3 (x+2)\,dx$ 2

$\left[\dfrac{x^3}{3}\right]_0^2 + \left[\dfrac{(x+2)^2}{2}\right]_2^3$ 1½

$\dfrac{8}{3} + \dfrac{25}{2} - 8 = \dfrac{43}{6}$ sq. U 1

26. Given differential equation can be written as

$\left(xy\dfrac{dy}{dx} - y^2\right)\sin\left(\dfrac{y}{x}\right) = \left(xy + x^2\dfrac{dy}{dx}\right)\cos\left(\dfrac{y}{x}\right)$ ½

Putting $\dfrac{y}{x} = v$ or $y = vx$ gives $\dfrac{dy}{dx} = v + x\dfrac{dv}{dx}$ 1

$\therefore$ (*i*) become $v\sin v\left(v + x\dfrac{dv}{dx}\right) - v^2\sin v = v\cos v + \left(v + x\dfrac{dv}{dx}\right)\cos v$ 1

$\Rightarrow$ $(vx\sin v - x\cos v)\dfrac{dv}{dx} = 2v\cos v$

$\Rightarrow$ $-\displaystyle\int \frac{v\sin v - \cos v}{v\cos v}\,dv = -\int \frac{2}{x}\,dx \Rightarrow \log|v\cos v| = -2\log x + \log c$ 1+1

$\Rightarrow$ $x^2 . v . \cos v = c \Rightarrow xy\cos\dfrac{y}{x} = c$ 1½

$x = 3,\ y = \pi$ gives $c = \dfrac{3\pi}{2}$ ½

$\Rightarrow$ solution is $2xy\cos\dfrac{y}{x} = 3\pi$ ½

27. Let the given point be $A(1, 1, 2)$ and the point on the line is $P(-3, 1, 5)$

$\therefore$ $\overline{AP} = -4\hat{i} + 4\hat{k}$ 1

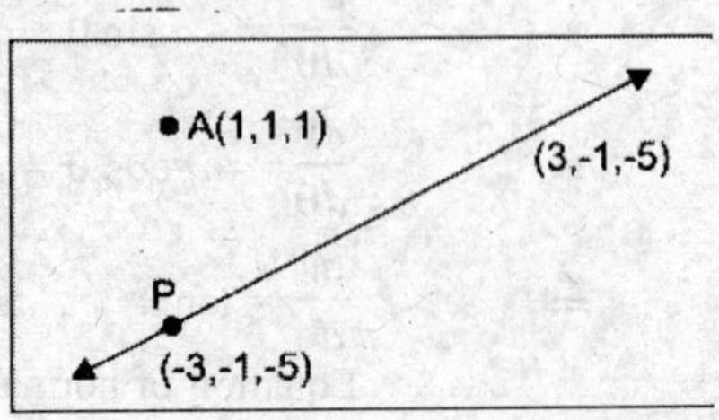

$\therefore$ The vector $\perp$ to the plane is

$(-4\hat{i} + 4\hat{k}) \times (3\hat{i} - \hat{j} - 5\hat{k})$

$= 4\hat{i} + 8\hat{j} + 4\hat{k}$ or $\hat{i} - 2\hat{j} + \hat{k}$ 1½

$\therefore$ Equation of plane is

$$\vec{r} \cdot (\hat{i} - 2\hat{j} + \hat{k}) = (\hat{i} + \hat{j} + \hat{k}) \cdot (\hat{i} - 2\hat{j} + \hat{k}) = 0 \qquad ...(i)$$ 1½

or $\quad x - 2y + z = 0$

Now, $\quad$ since $(\hat{i} - 2\hat{j} - 5\hat{k}) \cdot (\hat{i} - 2\hat{j} + \hat{k}) = 1 + 4 - 5 = 0$

$\therefore$ $\quad$ The line $\vec{r} = (-\hat{i} + 2\hat{j} + 5\hat{k}) + \lambda(\hat{i} - 2\hat{j} - 5\hat{k})$ is parallel to the plane 1

Also $(-1 - 4 + 5) = 0 \quad \Rightarrow \quad$ point lines on plane

hence the plane contains the line.

28. Let x be the number of units of A and y of B, which are produced

$\therefore$ LPP is Maximise $z = 20x + 15y$ 1

Subject to $\quad 15x + 3y \le 500$

$x \le 70$ 1½

$y \le 125$

$x \ge 0, \ y \ge 0$ 2

Getting vertices of feasible region is: 2

$A(0, 125)$, $B(25, 125)$, $C(70, 50)$, $D(70, 0)$ ½

Maximum Profit = Rs. 2375 at B

$\therefore$ Number of Units of $A = 25$ 1

Number of Units of $B = 125$

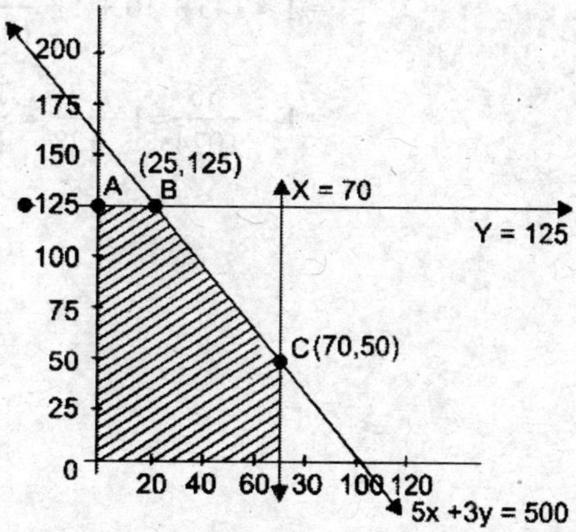

29. Let the events are defined as:

E_1 : 2 white balls are transferred from A to B

E_2 : 2 black balls are transferred

E_3 : 1 white and 1 black ball is transferred

A : 1 black ball is drawn from B

$$P(E_1) = \frac{4c_2}{7c_2} = \frac{4.3}{7.6} = \frac{2}{7},\ P(E_2) = \frac{3c_2}{7c_2} = \frac{3.2}{7.6},\ P(E_3) = \frac{4c_1}{7c_2} = \frac{4}{7}$$ 1½

$$P\left(\frac{A}{E_1}\right) = \frac{2}{6} = \frac{1}{3},\ P\left(\frac{A}{E_2}\right) = \frac{4}{6} = \frac{2}{3},\ P\left(\frac{A}{E_3}\right) = \frac{3}{6} = \frac{1}{2}$$ 1½

$$P\left(\frac{E_3}{A}\right) = \frac{P(E_3).P\left(\frac{A}{E_3}\right)}{P(E_1)P\left(\frac{A}{E_1}\right) + P(E_2)P\left(\frac{A}{E_2}\right) + P(E_3)P\left(\frac{A}{E_3}\right)}$$ ½

$$= \frac{\frac{4}{7} \times \frac{1}{2}}{\frac{2}{7} \cdot \frac{1}{2} + \frac{1}{7} \cdot \frac{2}{3} + \frac{4}{7} \cdot \frac{1}{2}}$$ ½

$$= \frac{3}{5}$$ 1

OR

$$P(\text{answer is true}) = \frac{1}{2}$$

$$P(\text{answer is false}) = \frac{1}{2}$$ 1

$P(\text{at most 7 correct}) = 1 - \{P(8) + P(9) + P(10)$ 2

(where $P(8)$ etc means probability of 8 correct answers)

$$= 1 - \left\{ {}^{10}C_8 \left(\frac{1}{2}\right)^8 \cdot \left(\frac{1}{2}\right)^2 + {}^{10}C_9 \left(\frac{1}{2}\right)^9 \left(\frac{1}{2}\right) + {}^{10}C_{10} \left(\frac{1}{2}\right)^{10} \right\}$$ 1

$$= 1 - \left\{ {}^{10}C_2 + {}^{10}C_1 + {}^{10}C_0 \right\} \left(\frac{1}{2}\right)^{10}$$ 1

$$= 1 - \{45 + 10 + 1\} \frac{1}{1024}$$

$$= 1 - \frac{56}{1024} = 1 - \frac{7}{128} = \frac{121}{128}$$ 1

❑❑❑

CBSE QUESTION PAPER

Time allowed: 3 hours **[*Maximum marks: 100*]**

SECTION-A

Question numbers **1** to **10** carry **1** mark each.

1. If $2\begin{bmatrix}3 & 4\\5 & x\end{bmatrix}+\begin{bmatrix}1 & y\\0 & 1\end{bmatrix}=\begin{bmatrix}7 & 0\\10 & 5\end{bmatrix}$, find $(x - y)$.

2. Solve the following matrix equation for x :, $[x \quad 1]\begin{bmatrix}1 & 0\\-2 & 0\end{bmatrix}=0$.

3. If $\begin{vmatrix}2x & 5\\8 & x\end{vmatrix}=\begin{vmatrix}6 & -2\\7 & 3\end{vmatrix}$, write the value of x.

4. Write the antiderivative of $3\sqrt{x}+\dfrac{1}{\sqrt{x}}$

5. If $\sin\left(\sin^{-1}\dfrac{1}{5}+\cos^{-1}x\right)=1$, then find the value of x.

6. Let * be a binary operation, on the set of all non-zero real numbers, given by a * b = $\dfrac{ab}{5}$ for all $a, b \in R - \{10\}$. Find the value of x, given that $2 * (x * 5) = 10$.

7. Find the projection of the vector $\hat{i}+3\hat{j}+7\hat{k}$ on the vector $2\hat{i}-3\hat{j}+6\hat{k}$.

8. Write the vector equation of the plane, passing through the point (a, b, c) and parallel to the plane $\vec{r}.\left(\hat{i}+\hat{j}+\hat{k}\right)=2$.

9. Evaluate : $\displaystyle\int_0^{\pi/2} e^x(\sin x-\cos x)\,dx$.

10. Write a unit vector in the direction of the sum of the vectors $\vec{a}=2\hat{i}+2\hat{j}-5\hat{k}$ and $\vec{b}=2\hat{i}+\hat{j}-7\hat{k}$.

SECTION-B

Question numbers **11** to **22** carry **4** marks each.

11. Prove that, for any three vectors $\vec{a},\vec{b},\vec{c}$

$$\left[\vec{a}+\vec{b},\ \vec{b}+\vec{c},\ \vec{c}+\vec{a}\right]=2\left[\vec{a},\vec{b},\vec{c}\right]$$

OR

Vectors $\vec{a}$, $\vec{b}$ and $\vec{c}$ are such that $\vec{a}+\vec{b}+\vec{c}=\vec{0}$ and $|\vec{a}|=3$, $|\vec{b}|=5$ and $|\vec{c}|=7$. Find the angle between $\vec{a}$ and $\vec{b}$.

12. Solve the following differential equation :

$$(x^2-1)\frac{dy}{dx}+2xy=\frac{2}{x^2-1}.$$

13. Evaluate : $\int \frac{\sin^6 x+\cos^6 x}{\sin^2 x.\cos^2 x}dx$

OR

$$\int (x-3)\sqrt{x^2+3x-18}\,dx$$

14. Find the intervals in which the function $f(x) = 3x^4 - 4x^3 - 12x^2 + 5$ is

(a) strictly increasing (b) strictly decreasing

OR

Find the equations of the tangent and normal to the curve $x = a \sin^3 \theta$ and $y = a \cos^3 \theta$ at $\theta = \frac{\pi}{4}$.

15. Let A = {1, 2, 3, ..., 9} and R be the relation in A × A defined by (a, b), (c, d) if a + d = b + c for (a, b), (c, d) in A × A. Prove that R is equivalence relation. Also obtain the equivalence class [(2, 5)].

16. Prove that $\cot^{-1}\left(\frac{\sqrt{1+\sin x}+\sqrt{1-\sin x}}{\sqrt{1+\sin x}-\sqrt{1-\sin x}}\right)=\frac{x}{2}; x\in\left(0,\frac{\pi}{4}\right)$.

OR

Prove that $2\tan^{-1}\left(\frac{1}{5}\right)+\sec^{-1}\left(\frac{5\sqrt{2}}{7}\right)+2\tan^{-1}\left(\frac{1}{8}\right)=\frac{\pi}{4}$.

17. If $y = x^x$, prove that $\frac{d^2y}{dx^2}-\frac{1}{y}\left(\frac{dy}{dx}\right)^2-\frac{y}{x}=0$.

18. Assume that each born child is equally likely to be a boy or a girl. If a family has two children, what is the conditional probability that both are girls ? Given that

(i) the youngest is a girl. (ii) atleast one is a girl.

19. Using properties of determinants, prove the following :

$$\begin{vmatrix} x^2+1 & xy & xz \\ xy & y^2+1 & yz \\ xz & yz & z^2+1 \end{vmatrix} = 1+x^2+y^2+z^2$$

20. Differentiate $\tan^{-1}\left(\frac{\sqrt{1+x^2}-1}{x}\right)$ with respect to $\sin^{-1}\left(\frac{2x}{1+x^2}\right)$, when $x \neq 0$.

21. Find the particular solution of the differential equation $\frac{dy}{dx}=\frac{x(2\log x+1)}{\sin y+y\cos y}$, given that $y=\frac{\pi}{2}$ when $x = 1$.

22. Show that lines $\vec{r} = (\hat{i} + \hat{j} - \hat{k}) + \lambda(3\hat{i} - \hat{j})$ and $\vec{r} = (4\hat{i} - \hat{k}) + \mu(2\hat{i} + 3\hat{k})$ intersect. Also find their point of intersection.

SECTION-C

Question numbers **23** to **29** carry **6** marks each.

23. A dealer in rural area wishes to purchase a number of sewing machines. He has only ₹ 5,760 to invest and has space for at most 20 items for storage. An electronic wewing machine cost him ₹ 360 and a manuall operated sewing machine ₹ 240. He can sell an electronic sewing machine at profit of ₹ 22 and a manually operated wewing machine at a profit of ₹ 18. Assuming that he can sell all the items that he can buy, how should he invest his money in order to maximize his profit? Make it as a LPP and solve it graphically.

24. A card from a pack of 52 playing cards is lost. From the remaining cards of the pack three cards are drawn at random (without replacement) and are found to be all spades. Find the probability of the lost card being a spade.

OR

From a lot of 15 bulbs which include 5 defectives, a sample of 4 bulbs is drawn one by one with replacement. Find the probability distribution of number of defective bulbs. Hence find the mean of the distribution.

25. Find the area of the region in the first quadrant enclosed by the *x*-axis, the line y = x and the circle $x^2 + y^2 = 32$.

26. Find the distance between the point (7, 2, 4) and the plane determined by the points A (2, 5, –3), B (–2, –3, 5) and C (5, 3, –3).

OR

Find the distance of the point (–1, –5, –10) from the point of intersection of the line $\vec{r} = 2\hat{i} - \hat{j} + 2\hat{k} + \lambda(3\hat{i} + 4\hat{j} + 2\hat{k})$ and the plane $\vec{r} \cdot (\hat{i} - \hat{j} + \hat{k}) = 5$.

27. Two schools P and Q want to award their selected students on the values of Discipline, Politeness and Punctuality. The school P wants to award ₹ *x* each, ₹ *y* each and ₹ *z* each for the three respective values to its 3, 2 and 1 students with a total award money of ₹ 1,000. School Q wants to spend ₹ 1,500 to award its 4, 1 and 3 students on the respective values (by giving the same award money for the three values as before). If the total amount of awards for one prize on each value is ₹ 600, using matrices, find the award money for each value.

A part from the above three values, suggest one more value for awards.

28. Evaluate : $\displaystyle\int_0^{\pi/2} \frac{x \sin x \cos x}{\sin^4 x + \cos^4 x} dx$

29. Of all the closed right circular cylindrical cans of volume 128 π cm^3, find the dimensions of the can which has minimum surface area.

SOLUTIONS

SECTION-A

1. $\begin{bmatrix} 6 & 8 \\ 10 & 2x \end{bmatrix} + \begin{bmatrix} 1 & y \\ 0 & 1 \end{bmatrix} = \begin{bmatrix} 7 & 0 \\ 10 & 5 \end{bmatrix}$

$\begin{bmatrix} 7 & 8+y \\ 10 & 2x+1 \end{bmatrix} = \begin{bmatrix} 7 & 0 \\ 10 & 5 \end{bmatrix}$

Equality of Matrix

$8 + y = 0 \quad \Rightarrow \quad y = -8$

$2x + 1 = 5 \quad \Rightarrow \quad x = 2$

2. $[x-2 \quad 0] = [0 \quad 0]$

$x = 2$

3. $2x^2 - 40 = 18 + 14$

$2x^2 = 32 + 40 = 72 \ \Rightarrow \ x^2 = 36$

$x = \pm 6$

4. $\int \left(3\sqrt{x} + \frac{1}{\sqrt{x}}\right) dx$

$= 3\int \sqrt{x}dx + \int (x)^{-1/2} dx \quad = 3\frac{x^{3/2}}{\frac{3}{2}} + \frac{x^{1/2}}{\frac{1}{2}} + C \ = \frac{\not{3} \times 2}{\not{3}} x^{3/2} + 2x^{1/2} + C \ = 2 \times x^{3/2} + 2x^{1/2} + C$

5. $\text{Sin}^{-1} 1 = \text{Sin}^{-1} \frac{1}{5} + \text{Cos}^{-1} x$

$\frac{\pi}{2} = \text{Sin}^{-1} \frac{1}{5} + \text{Cos}^{-1} x$

$\text{Sin}^{-1} x + \text{Cos}^{-1} x = \text{Sin}^{-1} \frac{1}{5} + \text{Cos}^{-1} x \qquad$ Hence, $x = \frac{1}{5}$

6. $a * b = \frac{ab}{5}$

$x * 5 = \frac{\not{5} x}{\not{5}} = x$

$2 * x = \frac{2x}{5}$

By question, $\quad \frac{2x}{5} = 10 \quad \Rightarrow \quad x = 25$

7. $\vec{a} = \hat{i} + 3\hat{j} + 7\hat{k}$ and $2\hat{i} - 3\hat{j} + 6\hat{k}$

Projection of $\vec{a}$ on $\vec{b} = \frac{\vec{a}.\vec{b}}{|\vec{b}|}$

$\vec{a}.\vec{b} = 2 - 9 + 42 = 35$

$\left|\vec{b}\right| = \sqrt{4+9+36} = 7$

Hence projection of $\vec{a}$ on $\vec{b} = \frac{35}{7} = 5$

8. $\vec{r} = \left(a\hat{i} + b\hat{j} + c\hat{k}\right) + \lambda\left(\hat{i} + \hat{j} + \hat{k}\right)$

9. $\int_0^{\pi/2} e^x \left(\text{Sin}\, x - \text{Cos}\, x\right) dx$

$= \int_0^{\pi/2} e^x \,\text{Sin}\, x\, dx - \int_0^{\pi/2} e^x \,\text{Cos}\, x\, dx$

$\quad I_1 - I_2$

$= \int_0^{\pi/2} e^x \sin x\, dx - \left[\cos x . e^x + \int \sin x\, e^x\, dx\right]^{\pi/2}$

$= \left[-\cos x .\, e^x\right]_0^{\pi/2} = 0$

10. $\vec{a} + \vec{b}$

$= 4\hat{i} + 3\hat{j} - 12\hat{k}$

Unit vector $= \frac{\vec{a}+\vec{b}}{\left|\vec{a}+\vec{b}\right|} = \frac{4\hat{i} + 3\hat{j} - 12\hat{k}}{13}$

SECTION-B

11. $\left(\vec{a} + \vec{b}\right) . \left[\left(\vec{b} + \vec{c}\right) \times \left(\vec{c} + \vec{a}\right)\right]$

$= \left(\vec{a} + \vec{b}\right) . \left[\vec{b} \times \vec{c} + \vec{b} \times \vec{a} + \vec{c} \times \vec{c} + \vec{c} \times \vec{a}\right]$

$= \left[\vec{a}\,\vec{b}\,\vec{c}\right] + \left[\vec{a}\,\vec{b}\,\vec{a}\right] + \left[\vec{a}\,\vec{c}\,\vec{c}\right] + \left[\vec{a}\,\vec{c}\,\vec{a}\right] + \left[\vec{b}\,\vec{b}\,\vec{c}\right] + \left[\vec{b}\,\vec{b}\,\vec{a}\right] + \left[\vec{b}\,\vec{c}\,\vec{c}\right] + \left[\vec{b}\,\vec{c}\,\vec{a}\right]$

$= \left[\vec{a}\,\vec{b}\,\vec{c}\right] + \left[\vec{a}\,\vec{b}\,\vec{c}\right] = 2\left[\vec{a}\,\vec{b}\,\vec{c}\right]$

12. $\frac{dy}{dx} + \frac{2x}{x^2-1} y = \frac{2}{\left(x^2-1\right)^2}$ ...(i)

Here, $P = \frac{2x}{x^2-1}$ and $Q = \frac{2}{\left(x^2-1\right)^2}$

$\text{I.F.} = e^{\int \frac{2x}{x^2-1} dx} = e^{\log\left(x^2-1\right)} = x^2 - 1$

Multiply (i) by IF and integrate

$y . (x^2 - 1) = 2\int \frac{1}{\left(x^2-1\right)^2} . \left(x^2 - 1\right) dx$

$$= 2\int \frac{dx}{x^2 - 1^2} = \cancel{2} \times \frac{1}{\cancel{2}} \log \frac{x-1}{x+1} + C$$

13. $\text{Sin}^6 x + \text{Cos}^6 x = (\text{Sin}^2 x + \text{Cos}^2 x)^3 - 3\sin^2 x \cos^2 x$

$= 1 - 3\sin^2 x \,.\, \cos^2 x$

$$\int \frac{\text{Sin}^6 x + \text{Cos}^6 x}{\text{Sin}^2 x . \text{Cos}^2 x} dx$$

$$= \int \frac{\text{Sin}^2 x + \text{Cos}^2 x}{\text{Sin}^2 x . \text{Cos}^2 x} dx - 3\int \frac{\text{Sin}^2 x . \text{Cos}^2 x}{\text{Sin}^2 x . \text{Cos}^2 x} dx$$

$$= \int \text{Sec}^2 x \, dx + \int \text{Cosec}^2 x \, dx - 3\int dx$$

$$= \tan x - \cot x - 3x + c$$

OR

$$\text{I} = \int (x-3)\sqrt{x^2 + 3x - 18}\, dx$$

Put $x^2 + 3x - 18 = t$

$(2x + 3)dx = dt$

Let $x - 3 = \text{A}(2x + 3) + \text{B}$

Compare coefficients :

We get $\text{A} = \frac{1}{2}$ and $\text{B} = \frac{-9}{2}$

$$\text{I} = \frac{1}{2}\int (2x+3)\sqrt{x^2 + 3x - 18}\, dx - \frac{9}{2}\int \sqrt{x^2 + 3x - 18}\, dx$$

$$= \frac{1}{2}\int \sqrt{t}\, dt - \frac{9}{2}\int \sqrt{x^2 + 3x + \left(\frac{3}{2}\right)^2 - 18 - \frac{9}{4}}\, dx$$

$$= \frac{1}{2}\left[\frac{2t^{\frac{3}{2}}}{3}\right] - \frac{9}{2}\int \sqrt{\left(x + \frac{3}{2}\right)^2 - 18 - \frac{9}{4}}\, dx$$

$$= \frac{1}{3}\left(x^2 + 3x - 18\right)^{\frac{3}{2}} - \frac{9}{8}(2x+3)\sqrt{x^2 + 3x - 18} + \frac{729}{16}\log\left|\left(x + \frac{3}{2}\right) + \sqrt{x^2 + 3x - 18}\right| + c$$

14. $f(x) = 3x^4 - 4x^3 - 12x^2 + 5$

$f'(x) = 12x^2 - 12x^2 - 24x = 12x\,(x^2 - x - 2)$

$f'(x) = 12x\,(x - 2)(x + 1)$

Put $f'(x) = 0 \Rightarrow x = 0, -1, 2$

Intervals are

$(-\infty, -1), (-1, 0), (0, 2), (2, \infty)$

Intervals	Sign of $f'(x)$	Nature of $f(x)$
$(-\infty, -1)$	– ve	Strictly Dec.
$(-1, 0)$	+ ve	Strictly Inc.
$(0, 2)$	– ve	Strictly Dec.
$(2, \infty)$	+ ve	Strictly Inc.

$f(x)$ is strictly increasing in $(-1, 0)$ & $(2, \infty)$, and
$f(x)$ is strictly decreasing in $(-\infty, -1)$ & $(0, 2)$

OR

$x = a\sin^3\theta \quad y = a\cos^3\theta$

$$\frac{dx}{d\theta} = 3a\sin^2\theta\cos\theta \quad \Rightarrow \quad \frac{dy}{d\theta} = -3a\cos^2\theta\sin\theta$$

$$\frac{dy}{dx} = \frac{-3a\cos^2\theta\sin\theta}{3a\sin^2\theta\cos\theta} = -\cot\theta \quad \Rightarrow \quad \left.\frac{dy}{dx}\right]_{\theta=\frac{\pi}{4}} = -1$$

Equation of tangent at $\theta = \frac{\pi}{4}$

$$y - a\cos^3\frac{\pi}{4} = -1\left(x - a\sin^3\frac{\pi}{4}\right) \quad \Rightarrow \quad y + x = \frac{2a}{2\sqrt{2}} \quad \Rightarrow \quad y + x = \frac{a}{\sqrt{2}}$$

equation of normal at $\theta = \frac{\pi}{4}$

$$y - \frac{a}{2\sqrt{2}} = 1\left(x - \frac{1}{1\sqrt{2}}\right) \quad \Rightarrow \quad y - x = 0$$

15. First Let us prove that the relation is

(i) Reflexive (ii) Symmetric (iii) Transitive

(i) **Reflexive :** (a, b) R (a, b)

$\Rightarrow a + b = b + a$ which is true ($\because$ addition is commutative)

$\therefore$ Given relation is reflexive.

(ii) **Symmetric :** If (a, b) R (c, d)

$\Rightarrow a + d = b + c$

then (c, d) R (a, b)

$\Rightarrow c + b = d + a \quad \Rightarrow b + c = a + d$ ($\because$ addition is commutative)

$\therefore$ Given relation is symmetric

(iii) **Transitive :** (a, b) R (c, d)

$\Rightarrow a + d = b + c$ ...(i)

and (c, d) R (e, f)

$\Rightarrow c + f = d + e$ ...(ii)

Adding (i) and (ii) we get $a + f = b + e$ $\therefore (a, b)$ R (e, f)

$\Rightarrow$ Given relation is transitive $\Rightarrow$ Given relation is equivalance relation.

The equivalence class for [(2, 5)] is [(2, 5)], [(5, 2)].

16. $\cot^{-1}\left(\dfrac{\sqrt{1+\sin x}+\sqrt{1-\sin x}}{\sqrt{1+\sin x}-\sqrt{1-\sin x}}\right)$

$$\cot^{-1}\left(\frac{\cos\frac{x}{2}+\sin\frac{x}{2}+\cos\frac{x}{2}-\sin\frac{x}{2}}{\cos\frac{x}{2}+\sin\frac{x}{2}-\cos\frac{x}{2}+\sin\frac{x}{2}}\right)$$

$$\cot^{-1}\left(\cot\frac{x}{2}\right)=\frac{x}{2}$$

OR

$$2\tan^{-1}\left(\frac{1}{5}\right)+\sec^{-1}\left(\frac{5\sqrt{2}}{7}\right)+2\tan^{-1}\left(\frac{1}{8}\right)$$

$$\Rightarrow\ 2\left[\tan^{-1}\left(\frac{\frac{1}{5}+\frac{1}{8}}{1-\frac{1}{40}}\right)\right]+\sec^{-1}\left(\frac{5\sqrt{2}}{7}\right)\ \Rightarrow\ 2\left[\tan^{-1}\left(\frac{1}{3}\right)\right]+\sec^{-1}\left(\frac{5\sqrt{2}}{7}\right)$$

$$\Rightarrow\ \tan^{-1}\frac{3}{4}+\sec^{-1}\left(\frac{5\sqrt{2}}{7}\right)\ \Rightarrow\ \tan^{-1}\left(\frac{3}{4}\right)+\tan^{-1}\left(\frac{1}{7}\right)=\tan^{-1}(1)=\frac{\pi}{4}$$

17. Take log on both sides

$y=x^x$

$\log y=x\log x$

$\dfrac{1}{y}\dfrac{dy}{dx}=x.\dfrac{1}{x}+\log x$

$\dfrac{dy}{dx}=y(1+\log x)=x^x(1+\log x)$

Now proceed

18. $S=\{B_1B_2,\ B_1G_2,\ G_1G_2,\ G_1B_2\}$

(i) both are girls $A=\{G_1G_2\}$

$P(A)=\dfrac{1}{4}$

(ii) yongest is a girl $B=\{B_1G_2,\ G_1G_2\}$

$\Rightarrow\ P(B)=\dfrac{2}{4}=\dfrac{1}{2}$

$A\cap B=\{G_1G_2\}$

$\Rightarrow\ P(A\cap B)=\dfrac{1}{4}$

(i) $P\left(\dfrac{A}{B}\right)=\dfrac{P(A\cap B)}{P(B)}=\dfrac{\frac{1}{4}}{\frac{2}{4}}=\dfrac{1}{2}$

C = at least one is a girl

$\{B_1G_2,\ G_1G_2,\ G_1B_2\}$

$$P(C) = \frac{3}{4}$$

$$A \cap C \{G_1 G_2\} \Rightarrow P(A \cap C) = \frac{1}{4}$$

(ii) $P\left(\frac{A}{C}\right) = \frac{P(A \cap C)}{P(C)} = \frac{1/4}{3/4} = \frac{1}{3}$

19. Multiply R_1 by x, R_2 by y and R_3 by z

$$\frac{1}{xyz}\begin{vmatrix} x^3+x & x^2y & x^2z \\ xy^2 & y^3y & y^2z \\ xz^2 & yz^2 & z^3+z \end{vmatrix}$$

Now take x, y, z common from c_1, c_2 and c_3

$$\frac{1.\cancel{xyz}}{\cancel{xyz}}\begin{vmatrix} x^2+1 & x^2 & x^2 \\ y^2 & y^2+1 & y^2 \\ z^2 & z^2 & z^2+1 \end{vmatrix}$$

$= R_1 \to R_1 + R_2 + R_3$

$$\begin{vmatrix} 1+x^2+y^2+z^2 & 1+x^2+y^2+z^2 & 1+x^2+y^2+z^2 \\ y^2 & y^2+1 & y^2 \\ z^2 & z^2 & 1+z^2 \end{vmatrix}$$

Now take $1 + x^2 + y^2 + z^2$ common from R_1

$$= 1 + x^2 + y^2 + z^2 \begin{vmatrix} 1 & 1 & 1 \\ y^2 & y^2+1 & y^2 \\ z^2 & z^2 & 1+z^2 \end{vmatrix}$$

$R_2 \to R_2 - R_1$ and $R_3 \to R_3 - R_2$

$$= (1 + x^2 + y^2 + z^2)\begin{vmatrix} 1 & 0 & 0 \\ y^2 & 1 & -1 \\ z^2 & 0 & 1 \end{vmatrix}$$

Expanding along R_1

$(1 + x^2 + y^2 + z^2)[1 + 0] = 1 + x^2 + y^2 + z^2$

20. $y = \frac{\tan^{-1}\sqrt{1+x^2}-1}{x}$ $\qquad z = \text{Sin}^{-1}\frac{2x}{1+x^2}$

Put $x = \tan\theta$

Now, find $dy/dz = \frac{\frac{dy/d\theta}{dx/d\theta}}{\frac{dz/d\theta}{dx/d\theta}}$

21. $\int(\text{Sin}\, y + y\,\text{Cos}\, y)\,dy = \int(2x\log x + x)\,dx$

$\Rightarrow\; -\cos y + \int y\cos y\,dy = \int 2x\log x\,dx + \dfrac{x^2}{2} + c$

$-\cos y + y\sin y + \cos y = 2\log x \cdot \left(\dfrac{x^2}{2}\right) - \dfrac{x^2}{2} + \dfrac{x^2}{2} + c$

$y\sin y = x^2\log x + c$

When $y = \dfrac{\pi}{2}; x = 1 \Rightarrow c = \dfrac{\pi}{2}$ $\qquad\therefore\; y\sin y = x^2\log x + \dfrac{\pi}{2}$

22. Equation of plane passing through the inter section of

$\vec{r}.\vec{n}_1 = q_1$ and $\vec{r}.\vec{n}_2 = q_2$

$= \quad \vec{r}\left[\vec{n}_1 + \lambda\vec{n}_2\right] = q_1 + \lambda q_2$

Place the value and solve.

23. Let the person buy x electronic sewing machine and y manually operated sewing machine

$\Rightarrow\; x, y \geq 0$

Also $x + y \leq 20$ [storage constraints]

$360\,x + 240\,y \leq 5760$

i.e., $3x + 2y \leq 48$

objective function is $z = 22\,x + 18\,y$

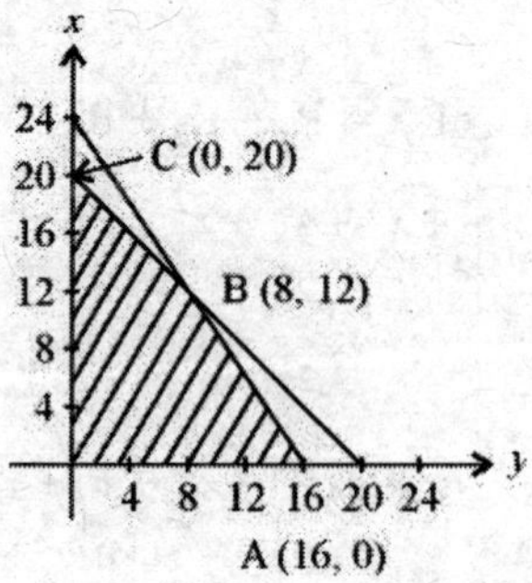

Point	$z = 22\,x + 18\,y$
A (16, 0)	352
B (8, 12)	392 (maxima)
C (0, 20)	360

The dealer should buy 8 electronic and 12 manual sewing machines. He will make a maximum profit of ₹ 392.

24. Let A : getting three spade cards

E_1 : lost card is a spade $\Rightarrow$ P $(E_1) = \dfrac{^{13}C_1}{^{52}C_1}$ $\qquad$ E_2 : lost card is a diamond $\Rightarrow$ P$(E_2) = \dfrac{^{13}C_1}{^{52}C_1}$

E_3 : lost card is a club $\Rightarrow$ P $(E_3) = \dfrac{^{13}C_1}{^{52}C_1}$ $\qquad$ E_4 : lost card is a heart $\Rightarrow$ P$(E_4) = \dfrac{^{13}C_1}{^{52}C_1}$

$$\text{P(A)} = \sum_{i=1}^{4}\text{P}(\text{E}_i).\text{P}(\text{A}\,|\,\text{E}_i) \quad = \frac{^{13}C_1}{^{52}C_1}\times\frac{^{12}C_3}{^{51}C_3} + 3\times\frac{^{13}C_1}{^{52}C_1}\times\frac{^{13}C_3}{^{51}C_3}$$

Required probability = P $(E_1\,|\,A)$

$$= \frac{\text{P}(\text{E}_1).\text{P}(\text{A}\,|\,\text{E}_1)}{\text{P}(\text{A})} = \frac{\dfrac{^{13}C_1}{^{52}C_1}\times\dfrac{^{12}C_3}{^{51}C_3}}{\dfrac{^{13}C_1}{^{52}C_1}\times\dfrac{^{12}C_3}{^{51}C_3} + 3\times\dfrac{^{13}C_1}{^{52}C_1}\times\dfrac{^{13}C_3}{^{51}C_3}} = \frac{10}{49}$$

OR

Let success be defined as getting a defective bulb. If x indicates success then $x = \{0, 1. 2, 3, 4\}$

Probability of success, $P = \frac{5}{15} = \frac{1}{3}$ and $q = 1 - \frac{1}{3} = \frac{2}{3}$

We use $P(x) = {}^nC_x\, p^x q^{n-x}$, where n is the number of trials.

x	0	1	2	3	4
P(x)	$\frac{16}{81}$	$\frac{32}{81}$	$\frac{24}{81}$	$\frac{8}{81}$	$\frac{1}{81}$

Mean, $\mu = \sum_{i=1}^{5} x_i\, P(x_i) = \frac{4}{3}$

25. Solving $y = x$ and $x^2 + y^2 = 32$

we get $x = \pm 4$

Required area = Area of region OCABO

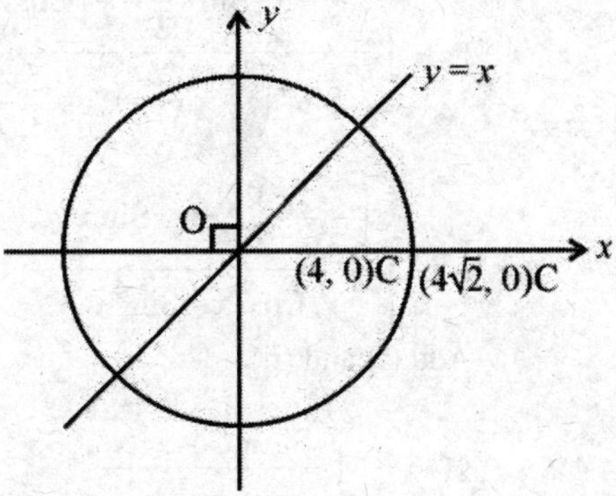

$$= \int_0^4 x\,dx + \int_0^{4\sqrt{2}} \sqrt{32 - x^2}\,dx$$

$$= \frac{x^2}{2}\Big|_0^4 + \left[\frac{x}{2}\sqrt{32 - x^2} + \frac{32}{2}\sin^{-1}\frac{x}{4\sqrt{2}}\right]_4^{4\sqrt{2}}$$

$$= \left[\frac{(4)^2}{2} - \frac{(0)^2}{2}\right] + \left[16\sin^{-1}1 - \left(\frac{4}{2}\sqrt{16}\sin^{-1}\frac{1}{\sqrt{2}}\right)\right]$$

$$= 8 + \left[16 \times \frac{\pi}{2} - \left(8 + 16\frac{\pi}{4}\right)\right] = 4\pi \text{ sq. units}$$

26. Equation of plane $\begin{vmatrix} x-2 & y-5 & z+3 \\ -4 & -8 & 8 \\ 3 & -2 & 0 \end{vmatrix} = 0$

or $2x + 3y + 4z = 7$

Distance from $(7, 2, 4) = \frac{29}{\sqrt{29}} = \sqrt{29}$

OR

See Book Qs. No. 4, Pg. 158

27. $3x + 2y = 1000$

$4x + y + 3z = 1500$

$x + y + z = 600$

The corresponding system of matrix equations is

$$AX = B \text{ where } A = \begin{bmatrix} 3 & 2 & 1 \\ 4 & 1 & 3 \\ 1 & 1 & 1 \end{bmatrix}, \quad X = \begin{bmatrix} x \\ y \\ z \end{bmatrix} \text{ and } B = \begin{bmatrix} 1000 \\ 1500 \\ 600 \end{bmatrix}$$

$$\Rightarrow \quad |A| = \begin{vmatrix} 3 & 2 & 1 \\ 4 & 1 & 3 \\ 1 & 1 & 1 \end{vmatrix} = -5 \qquad A^{-1} = \frac{1}{|A|} adj A = \frac{1}{-5}\begin{bmatrix} -2 & -1 & 5 \\ -1 & 2 & -5 \\ 3 & -1 & -5 \end{bmatrix}$$

$$\Rightarrow \quad X = A^{-1} B = \begin{bmatrix} 100 \\ 200 \\ 300 \end{bmatrix}$$

$x = ₹100,\ y = ₹200,\ z = ₹300$

28. $$I = \int_0^{\pi/2} \frac{x \operatorname{Sin} x \operatorname{Cos} x\, dx}{\operatorname{Sin}^4 x + \operatorname{Cos}^4 x}$$

$$I = \int_0^{\pi/2} \frac{\left(\frac{\pi}{2} - x\right) \operatorname{Sin}\left(\frac{\pi}{2} - x\right) \operatorname{Cos}\left(\frac{\pi}{2} - x\right)}{\operatorname{Sin}^4\left(\frac{\pi}{2} - x\right) + \operatorname{Cos}^4\left(\frac{\pi}{2} - x\right)} dx \qquad \text{...(i)}$$

$$I = \int_0^{\pi/2} \frac{\left(\frac{\pi}{2} - x\right) \operatorname{Cos} x \operatorname{Sin} x\, dx}{\operatorname{Cos}^4 x + \operatorname{Sin}^4 x} \qquad \text{...(ii)}$$

Add (i) and (ii)

$$2I = \frac{\pi}{2} \int_0^{\pi/2} \frac{\operatorname{Sin} x \operatorname{Cos} x\, dx}{\operatorname{Sin}^4 x + \operatorname{Cos}^4 x}$$

Divide by $\operatorname{Cos}^4 x$

$$= \frac{\pi}{2} \int_0^{\pi/2} \frac{\tan x \sec^2 x\, dx}{1 + \tan^4 x}$$

Put $\tan x = \mu$ and proceed

29. Given, $V = 128\pi = \pi r^2 h$

Minimize : $S = 2\pi r h + 2\pi r^2$

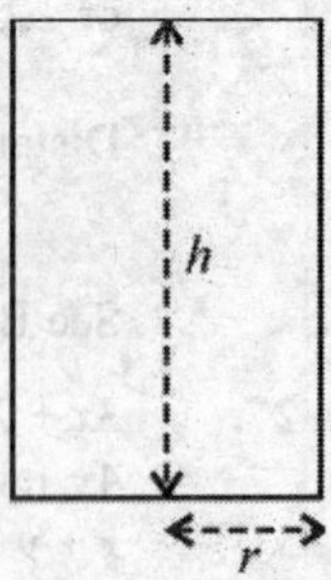

Put $\quad h = \dfrac{128}{r^2}$

$\therefore \quad S(r) = \dfrac{256\pi}{r} + 2\pi r^2 \Rightarrow S'(r) = \dfrac{256\pi}{r^2} + 4\pi r$

For $\quad$ CPs : $S'(r) = 0 \Rightarrow \dfrac{256\pi}{r^2} + 4\pi r = 0 \Rightarrow r = 4$ cm

Now $\quad S''(4) > 0$ at $r = 4$ is point of minima

$\Rightarrow \quad h = \dfrac{128\pi}{\pi \times 4 \times 4} = 8\text{cm}$

$\therefore \quad$ For minimum surface area the can should have a radius of 4 cm and a height of 8 cm.